TRANSLATION RIGHT OR WRONG

TRANSLATION RIGHT OR WRONG

Susana Bayó Belenguer, Eiléan Ní Chuilleanáin & Cormac Ó Cuilleanáin
EDITORS
assisted by Giulia Zuodar

FOUR COURTS PRESS

Set in 10.5pt on 13.5pt Bembo for
FOUR COURTS PRESS LTD
7 Malpas Street, Dublin 8, Ireland
www.fourcourtspress.ie
and in North America for
FOUR COURTS PRESS
c/o ISBS, 920 N.E. 58th Avenue, Suite 300, Portland, OR 97213.

A catalogue record for this title
is available from the British Library.

ISBN 978-1-84682-372-5

Printed in England
by Antony Rowe Ltd, Chippenham, Wilts.

Contents

PART 2: HISTORY AND POLITICS OF TRANSLATION

PART 3: TRANSLATION NOW

Acknowledgments

Many people have contributed to the publication of this book, and to the success of the conference which led up to it. Special thanks are due to Valentina Salis, Antonella Trombatore and their helpers, to Ken Baker for bringing a display of St Jerome publications to the conference, to Lawrence Venuti and Jo Balmer for giving the keynote lectures, to Eoin O'Dell and Peter Sirr for launching two books at the conference: *Translation and censorship* (edited by Eiléan Ní Chuilleanáin, Cormac Ó Cuilleanáin and David Parris) and *Mallarmé Sonnets*, a bilingual edition in French and English by David Scott and Mark Raftery-Skehan. We would also like to thank the many fine speakers at the conference whose contributions we were unable to include, for reasons of thematic coherence, in the present volume.

For valuable funding we are grateful to ILE – Ireland Literature Exchange, who provided sponsorship for the conference, and to Trinity Association and Trust, the Department of Italian and the School of English, Trinity College Dublin, who have contributed to the publication costs of the book.

For peer reviewing and editorial advice we are extremely grateful for the time and expertise of Peter Arnds, Anna Chahoud, Ciaran Cosgrove, Katherine Farmar, Phyllis Gaffney, Mary Gallagher, Johnnie Gratton, John Kearns, Corinna Salvadori Lonergan, Liam Mac Cóil, Laura Incalcaterra McLoughlin, Lindsay Myers, Máirín Ní Dhonnchadha, David Parris, Amanda Piesse, Ian Ross, David Singleton, George Talbot, Mary Shine Thompson, Carl Vogel and James Whiston.

Two openings from *The Young Inferno*, by John Agard and Satoshi Kitamura, appear in the essay by Virginia Jewiss, 'Hell for kids', by kind permission of Frances Lincoln Publishers, London. The illustrations by Aline Cantono di Ceva, in the same essay, are reproduced by gracious permission of Mandragora Publishing, Florence. The Department of Manuscripts and Rare Books at the Royal Library, Copenhagen, generously granted permission to print, from their marvellous Guaman Poma Website, the images from the *Nueva corónica y buen gobierno* which appear in the essay by Sabine Dedenbach-Salazar Sáenz.

We thank Four Courts Press for publishing both this volume and its predecessor, *Translation and censorship* (Dublin, 2009). Achim Bednorz supplied a wonderfully pensive photographic image for the jacket design; it comes from the Cappella Colleoni, Bergamo.

The editors wish to express particular thanks to Giulia Zuodar, whose patience, erudition, good judgment, good humour and excellent organizational skills kept the project moving forward.

Acknowledgements

Introduction

Susana Bayó Belenguer, Eiléan Ní Chuilleanáin & Cormac Ó Cuilleanáin

> The truth is that there are no universally accepted principles of translation, because the only people who are qualified to formulate them have never agreed amongst themselves, but have so often and for so long contradicted each other that they have bequeathed to us a volume of confused thought which must be hard to parallel in other fields of literature.
>
> T.H. Savory, *The art of translation*

> Welcome to the world of translation – a compromised world of half-rights and half-wrongs.
>
> Douglas Robinson, *Becoming a translator*

Translation right or wrong brings new perspectives to bear on a long-lived and sometimes controversial issue. The essays collected here revisit some of the most obvious questions asked about translations, and situate them in the context of actual translation practice and in relation to the cultural systems that frame our expectations and our responses to translated texts. The authors have chosen a variety of starting-points, from classical poems to commercial advertising, and have taken account of the various motivations for translation and the constraints and the new opportunities that affect the process, including those of developing technologies.

The question of 'right' or 'wrong' translation continues to crop up, especially in cultural and educational settings where there is room for opinion and debate. If the question is posed in too simple a manner, however, it can seem inappropriate. Until the second half of the twentieth century, the discussion of good or bad, better or worse translations lacked clear definition, partly because indistinct terminology ('faithfulness', 'spirit', 'truth') revolved around a perennial debate over literal versus free translation dating back to classical times. The essays in this volume illustrate the multitude of ways in which the question can be asked, and their implications for the nature of the translator's task, and the translator's relationship with text, author, reader and the various other players involved in transferring ideas through the encounters of language. From the classical period onwards the process has been fraught, and some of the faultlines have been revisited over two millennia.

CLASSICAL AND TRADITIONAL CRITIQUES

Artistic translation in the Latin world involved imitating and challenging the Greek model. The Roman ideal reader was bilingual, and so Catullus replaced Sappho's beloved with his own Lesbia.[1] The quarrel about 'sense for sense' versus 'word for word', the disputed point when 'fidelity in transcription' degenerates into 'pestilent minuteness', to quote St Jerome's spirited defence of his own practice, are closely related to the encounter with the foreign to which the translator exposes the reader.[2] Defence of domestication comes often in the context of religious ideology. Eugene Nida, an expert on Bible translation into non-Western languages, who regarded the goal of Bible translation as the diffusion of the Christian ideology, defined a translation as 'right' when it achieved 'dynamic equivalence', when it improved readability by substituting the elements of the source culture with elements of the target culture (provided that they convey the same thought). However the opposition between the readable and the unfamiliar may not be absolute: in 1530 Martin Luther boasted that his translation had cleared away the 'boulders' that might have made the reader's experience less 'smooth'; the motive of his translation however led him to emphasize the unfamiliar doctrine of salvation by faith and thus to foreground the unexpected element. His opponents (he says) concede that his translation is correct: 'They will admit that it is right but they brand the telling of it as wrong, though nothing can be simultaneously right and wrong'.[3]

Doctrinal soundness is just one of the criteria to be invoked in the essays that follow. Like the welfare of children, or the fascist version of political correctness, or the legal question of whether the translator's fee has been honestly earned, these issues have implications which may go well beyond the aesthetic. Still, readers and critics invoke such criteria as fluency, fidelity, naturalness, 'flavour' – and many translators set out to provide versions that satisfy some or all of them. In the twentieth century the criteria used by critics, reviewers and scholars in evaluating the success of a translation were often arbitrary, or excessively dependent on individual taste. Translations tended to be measured in terms of their accurate correspondence to an original text, or the eloquence of their phrasing in a new language, but these two criteria were rarely combined in a broader theoretical framework. Deviations from the chosen ideal were stigmatized; if one translation was preferred, this often involved disparaging other

1 Ellen Greene, 'Re-figuring the feminine voice: Catullus translating Sappho', *Arethusa* 32:1 (Winter 1999), 1–18. **2** Jerome's Letter to Pammachius, in Latin with a facing English translation, can be consulted at www.bible-researcher.com/jerome.pammachius.html, accessed 17 July 2012. **3** Martin Luther, 'Ein Sendbrief D.M. Luthers. Von Dolmetschen und Fürbit der Heiligenn' in *Dr Martin Luthers Werke* (Weimar, 1909), Band 30, Teil II, pp 632–46.

versions, often on the basis of small details, sometimes in pursuit of the elusive and hazy ideal of a definitive translation (which many scholars would now classify as an oxymoron).

Translation criticism tended to be all the more lively as the absence of a generally accepted theoretical framework left individual writers and scholars free to adopt widely divergent criteria of evaluation. The novelist Milan Kundera complains that the translator, wishing to 'invest the text with his own creativity', chooses synonyms and varied vocabulary wherever possible, thereby failing to repeat exactly the words of his author, whose personal style should be the translator's 'supreme authority'. Kundera appeals: 'O ye translators, do not sodonymize us!'[4] Opting for a diametrically opposite criterion of translation quality, Donald Carne-Ross condemns an eminent academic who has aimed at 'scrupulous, self-effacing fidelity', thereby failing to be sufficiently free and fluent when translating Homer's *Odyssey*: 'Lattimore's translation is not very idiomatic [...] Lattimore, who seldom seems very interested in the story [...] contrives to obscure the action with unnecessary or ill-placed words and sentences set back to front [...] Lattimore makes us force our way through the tongue-tripping clutter'. And Lattimore's admirers are also to blame; his 'mistaken ambition of exactness' is partly the fault of those defective critics who 'might have helped him to resist his dangerously simple-minded approach to the art of translation [...] But instead of criticism he has received praise [...] The critics, at all events, have done their job and Professor Lattimore is now probably beyond the reach of help'.[5]

NEW PERSPECTIVES REQUIRE A DIFFERENT FOCUS

Trenchant views like those just quoted can be cogent, stylish and eminently readable, but in the early twenty-first century the question of 'right or wrong' needs to be asked and answered more systematically, with an awareness of all the factors in play. The ideal of a 'definitive translation', against which other versions could be judged, also implied the existence of a universal canon according to which a text could be judged as 'right' or 'wrong'. These prescriptive certainties gradually lost ground before the descriptive approach that made a strong appearance towards the end of the century: James Holmes in 1972 had sketched a preliminary map of translation studies as a natural science focused on theoretical and

4 Milan Kundera, *Testaments betrayed*, translated by Linda Asher (London, 1995), pp 108–10. Interestingly, the paperback edition (London, 1996) deletes the most memorable parts of this protest. See Michelle Woods, *Translating Milan Kundera* (Clevedon, 2006), for the complexities of Kundera's interactions with translation. 5 Donald Carne-Ross, 'A mistaken ambition of exactness', *Delos*, 2 (1968), 171–97.

descriptive branches, and the development of his project was later carried forward by Gideon Toury.[6] Toury's categories of 'adequate' translations (which adhere to the norms of the source language) versus 'acceptable' translations (which acclimatize the original to its new surroundings by subscribing to the norms of the target culture) seemed much more productive than a simple 'right or wrong' choice.[7] Peter Newmark offered a similar distinction between semantic translation ('faithful' to the source, with a literal bias) and communicative translation ('idiomatic', with a bias towards freedom).[8] Once the possibility of different underlying approaches had been granted, any analysis of the results needed to become more self-aware in grounding and methods.

Besides which, we have become less comfortable with telling people just how wrong they are. For a long time, according to the linguist Anna Wierzbicka, 'the concepts "right" and "wrong" were perceived by speakers of English as symmetrical, and the two words were often juxtaposed, analogously to *right* and *left*'. But during the twentieth century (if not earlier),

> The use of *wrong* appears to have declined, in comparison with *right* [...] One might venture to suggest that the decline of *wrong* (in relation to *right*) paralleled (and perhaps was related to) the spread of the pejorative word judgmental: it is bad to be judgmental [...].[9]

Also, we live in a time when philosophical certainty has been challenged, especially in the realms of meaning and value. Returning to our own field, quite apart from the philosophical and social changes just noted, a growing academic interest in studying translations within their host cultures, and as a distinctive form of writing and communication linked to larger cultural systems, brought further complications to the 'right or wrong' question, which for a time could be relegated to the background. There was a new awareness of the multiplicity of factors involved in translation, and an increased recognition that the audiences, uses and purposes of a translation are powerful factors which should, and

6 James S. Holmes, 'The name and nature of translation studies' (1972), in Holmes, *Translated! Papers on literary translation and translation studies* (Amsterdam 1988), pp 67–80; G. Toury, *In search of a theory of translation* (Tel Aviv, 1980); G. Toury, *Descriptive translation studies and beyond* (Amsterdam, 1995). **7** Toury, *Descriptive translation studies*, pp 56–7. **8** Peter Newmark, *Approaches to translation* (Oxford, 1981), p. 39. **9** Anna Wierzbicka, *English: meaning and culture* (Oxford, 2006) p. 82. Judgmental attitudes to translators' misdeeds are of course relative. André Lefevere (*Translation/History/Culture* (London, 1992), p. 27) reports that the 16th-century French poet and translator Étienne Dolet, author of a treatise entitled 'On the way of translating well from one language to another' (1540), was burnt at the stake because his translation of Plato contained 'some errors'.

do, exert influence on its textual form. A new focus on strategies, varieties of translation, and varying translation practices enriched our understanding of the 'target text' and its function within its own environment. Deviations from direct literal translation, no longer subject to quick condemnation, were studied with increasing subtlety and historical awareness; indeed, justifiable changes and transformations proved a more engaging focus of study than the more pedestrian matter of noting correct and incorrect solutions. Translation expanded its real and metaphorical grasp to cover an increasing range of human interactions, and was seen more and more as reflecting and incorporating cultural pressures from the world at large. In this more ambitious framework, 'right' and 'wrong' (no matter how nicely they alliterated) could be seen as impoverished and simplistic categories of thought.

We have come to realize that a certain level of 'wrongness' is inherent in all translation activity, and in all cultural transfer. To quote Michael Cronin,

> When we bring cultural or linguistic material from one site, one time, to another, are we always condemned in that act of translation to speak the 'wrong' language, to deform, caricature, approximate, betray the other? Or is the 'wrong' language a 'right' in the sense of the right of writers and cultures to transmute, transform, and endlessly recreate what they have received from other places and other times to sustain the principle of life itself in cultural practice and aesthetic renewal?[10]

Despite all these reassurances, the 'right or wrong' question refuses to dissolve completely, if only because of what Juliane House has called the 'double-bind' relationship inherent in all translations: they have an 'orientation backwards' to the message of a source text, and an 'orientation forwards' towards comparable texts in the target language. Clearly, this Janus-like balance is a tense and delicate business, demanding a high level of skill and competence if one is to avoid tripping up. House's double-bind is perhaps a less painful condition than the one noted by Theo Hermans, who tells how Derrida 'explained, in patient detail, the "double bind" of translation as both impossible and necessary.'[11]

The gains of translation studies since the 1990s, and our contemporary awareness of translation as cultural interaction and not a purely linguistic matter, allow us to pose old questions in a new light. There are many ways of being

10 Michael Cronin, review of Bella Brodzki, *Can these bones live? translation, survival, and cultural memory*, *Comparative Literature*, 62:2 (2010), 189–90 at 189. **11** See Juliane House, *Translation* (Oxford, 2009), pp 6–7; Theo Hermans, 'Hermeneutics' in Mona Baker & Gabriela Saldanha (eds), *Routledge encyclopedia of translation studies* (1st ed., London, 1998) pp 130–3 at pp 132–3.

'right or wrong', many settings in which the issue can be played out in practice and in theory. A translation is right, but for whom? How and where? For how long? And who decides? For translation has come to be seen as crucially involved with questions of power.[12] Every agent in the processes of making, judging or studying translations needs to be evaluated; none of us is neutral, standing outside the process. As bias, ideology and position cannot be eliminated, they must be acknowledged and factored into the discussion. Judges are subject to judgment. Such a multi-faceted approach, reflecting the interdisciplinary nature of translation studies, also seems to fit well with the interactive nature of translation itself.

An old debate, then, takes on new shapes. *Translation right or wrong* started out as an international conference held at Trinity College Dublin in March 2009. The slightly provocative title of the conference evoked a wide response. Out of fifty-three speakers from more than a dozen countries, the organizers have succeeded in assembling nineteen essays covering a wide range of languages, cultures and periods. Our writers offer an interlocking range of contexts, purposes, focuses and media within which general claims of translation quality can be re-examined. There were many fine papers that we did not select or pursue, including some that asked the question 'right or wrong?' directly. This volume has more of a slantwise quality. Translation is studied from a variety of perspectives, traditional distinctions are challenged; the field is broadened out beyond the customary focus on the literary; the distinction between translation and adaptation is interrogated; the impact of new technologies is integrated into translation studies. 'Bad' language, whether used by Nicolas Sarkozy or imagined by Roddy Doyle, may be resisted by translators, and some texts may refuse translation entirely.

ORTEGA Y GASSET: STEPPING OUT OF THE SHADOWS

A question many of our essays address at least by implication is the broad one: what is the role of the translator and what is his or her authority to be? The decisions made in this professional capacity can be scandalously evident – as when, in 1526, William Tyndale rendered the word that had always been translated as 'church' as 'congregation' – or can lie hidden in the shadow cast by the presumed ignorance of the reader. Do we need to trust this presumably knowledgeable guide, or how far should our trust go? Much depends on the translator's status, and on whether any degree of creativity is allowed. In turn, such

12 See Maria Tymoczko & Edwin Gentzler (eds), *Translation and power* (Amherst, 2002).

questions are inflected by the nature of the source text since, as many of these essays show, 'high' and 'low' genres arouse varying expectations, and the role of the translator may differ. Pilar Ordóñez López argues in 'Judging the translator: Ortega y Gasset's characterization of the translator' that Ortega's views reveal the audacious and anticipatory character of his thinking. He described the translator as a 'shy character' who has chosen an 'insignificant occupation' but also asserted the importance of the task. Certainly, two of the most thought-provoking writings on the art and practice of translation are Ortega's 1937 essay 'The misery and the splendour of translation' and Jorge Luis Borges' 1936 essay 'Los traductores de las 1001 noches'.[13] Ortega's conviction of both the impossibility of translation and its necessity prefigures Derrida's position. 'Impossibility' and 'necessity' imply inadequacy and while Ortega avoids getting caught up in the 'right' or 'wrong' of translation, Borges avows the aesthetic and linguistic possibilities of 'mistranslation', even its superiority, and goes so far as to state that even the worst translations have a value and a place.[14]

These writers foreshadowed some of the methodological and theoretical discussions central to the upsurge and consolidation of translation studies from the 1970s onwards: how language moulds and constrains us, the possibilities of communication, the anachronisms of language, writing as creation, the necessity of re-translation, foreignization, and cultural awareness. Ortega promoted the autonomy of translation: 'we must dedicate ourselves more than ever to this task', of restoring the prestige of this 'intellectual work of the first order'.[15] Although Ortega believed that the perfect or right translation was a utopian

13 'The misery and splendour of translation' ['La miseria y esplendor de la traducción'] appeared in five instalments in the newspaper *La Nación* (Buenos Aires) in the summer of 1937. The essay was translated into German in the 1950s and re-edited several times and was retranslated by Katharina Reiss in 1976. Its translation into French (2004), English (1982, 1993) Italian (1984, 2001), and Russian (1994) among other languages, coincided with the growth of translation studies as an academic discipline in its own right. Although Ortega, unlike Borges, was not a translator, as founding editor of *Revista de occidente*, the foremost intellectual journal in Spain from 1924 until the outbreak of the Spanish Civil War, he regularly commissioned translations of the latest foreign writings on science, literature, philosophy, psychology, technology, and the arts. For a study of the impact of *RO* see *Desde occidente: 70 años de 'Revista de occidente'* (Madrid, 1993). For an in-depth study of the ideas of Borges on translation see Ana Gargatagli & Juan Gabriel López Guix, 'Ficciones y teorías de la traducción: Jorge Luis Borges', *Livius: revista de estudios de traducción,* 1 (1992) and Sergio Gabriel Waisman, *Borges and translation: the irreverence of the periphery* (Cranbury NJ, 2005). **14** His notion of mistranslation is bound up with 're-writing' and 'creation'. See also J. Hillis Miller, 'Border crossings, translating theory: Ruth' in Sanford Budick & Wolfgang Iser (eds), *The translatability of cultures. Figurations of the space between* (Stanford, 1996), p. 220. **15** 'The misery and the splendor of translation' in L. Venuti (ed.), *The translation studies reader* (London, 2000), pp 60, 63.

undertaking, he also held that in the process of trying to capture the source text in all its resonances and silences, translators become creators and translation 'a literary genre apart'. But within his powerful reflections on translation and translators it is possible to detect a kind of distress in sections of 'Miseria' – his exile since the beginning of the Spanish Civil War helps us to relate more closely to his view that 'Man, in himself, is nothing but a beast'. Ordoñez López also reminds us that the sometimes controversial views of Ortega, one of the first thinkers to consider the translator, remain as relevant today as they were fresh seventy five years ago. While it may seem paradoxical that Ortega belittled the ability of 'average' translators, accusing them of contributing to their own 'invisibility', Ordoñez López argues that his aim was to encourage translators 'to step out of the shadows'.[16]

THE TRANSLATOR'S STATUS AND FUNCTION

The assertive translator may get a mixed reception. A classicist, a translator and a poet, Josephine Balmer addresses the common sneer at the profession, the reproach of lack of originality, by exploring her own blend of creativity and translation and the reactions it has produced among classicist reviewers. She is alone in this book in writing an essay on the translation of poetry, and in exploring the spillover from translating to writing new poems: poems that are allusive, and which in that sense derive from her reading, including reading for translation. The fact that her originals were Catullus and Ovid surely inflected the critical response to Balmer's work. These are not only classics of Latin poetry but foundational texts of Western culture and elite education, so that critics tended to feel that they already owned these texts and had pre-existing views and traditions of reading them.

Carmen Mangiron examines a very different situation, which also concerns a classic text translated into English, but in this case a Japanese classic, thus one remote from the target culture. The task was initially undertaken by writers who nowadays might be thought poorly equipped, in that they were working into a language that was not their own, and only later was the book translated by professionals who were native speakers of English. Intriguingly, the critical reaction, to a total of five translations over a century, is not measured only by the reception which their work met from established and professional critics; Mangiron includes the informal and enthusiastic exchanges of Amazon customer-reviewers on the internet in her survey. She also points to the comments,

16 Ibid., pp 62, 54.

implied or explicit, of rival translators, and discusses the input of the 'patrons' who commission and publish retranslated versions of the classic. Her study reminds us that the relative prestige of cultures and languages is not easily calibrated. The prestige of Japanese culture was high in the West throughout the twentieth century. However, admiration was narrowly focused, and was combined with a lack of interest abroad in some texts which the natives of the culture regarded as important, and were thus impelled to translate themselves.

The status of the translator is not infrequently complicated by her gender. It has been suggested – and perhaps overemphasized – that women have been translators, adapting a foreign (and male) writer's voice, when traditional society has denied them a voice of their own.[17] Michelle Woods explores the fate of a translator who was also her author's lover, and whose later image is affected not only by her personal relationship with Franz Kafka but by the erasure of her voice, through the destruction of her letters, and her fate as a victim of the concentration camps. Has the mere fact of her being a woman translating a man misled the critics into seeing her as silenced?[18]

TRANSLATING DOWN THE SCALE

The translators mentioned so far have all been dealing with 'high' literature. What happens when we descend to genres that are avowedly or conventionally 'low', aimed at a juvenile readership or primarily concerned with entertaining the reader? Does translation practice change, and are there different measures of 'right' and 'wrong'? Children's literature and crime fiction provide particularly fertile grounds for exploring these questions. Three contributions on children's literature show how translation of the text is just one practice among others that

17 See Margaret P. Hannay, *Silent but for the word: Tudor women as patrons, translators, and writers of religious works* (Kent, OH, 1985); Lori Chamberlain, 'Gender and the metaphorics of translation' in L. Venuti (ed.), *Rethinking translation: discourse, subjectivity, ideology* (New York, 1992), pp 57–74 at p. 59; Sherry Simon, *Gender in translation: cultural identity and the politics of transmission* (New York, 1996), p. 10. **18** The topic of the invisibility of women translators began to be seriously addressed with the publication of a number of articles in the late 1980s and several studies in the 1990s (Rosemary Arrojo, 'Fidelity and gendered translation', *TTR*, 7:2 (1994), 147–63; Luise von Flotow, *Translation and gender* (Ottawa, 1997)). For recent contributions see, for example, Melissa Wallace, 'Writing the wrongs of literature: the figure of the feminist and post-colonialist translator', *The Journal of the Midwest Modern Language Association*, 35:2 (2002): 65–74; Theresa Ann Smith, 'Writing out the margins: women, translation, and the Spanish enlightenment', *Journal of Women's History*, 15:1 (2003), 116–43; *MonTI*, 3 (2011) – special issue on women and translation; Tina Krontiris, *Oppositional voices: women as writers and translators of literature in the English Renaissance* (London, 1992).

produce the final result. Radical adaptation, rearrangement, annotation, attenuation amounting to bowdlerization, illustration both imaginative and downright fraudulent, and target-oriented packaging can all play major roles in deciding what the child will eventually pick up and read. The three essays, as it happens, all deal with 'classics' or even 'instant classics' of different kinds, which are (to varying extents) open to adult as well as child readerships.[19]

In her essay on translating Dante's *Comedy* for children, Virginia Jewiss (a practitioner as well as an analyst in this case) shows how the sometimes unpalatable achievements and doctrines of a medieval author could be presented in digestible form by didactic authors of the Victorian era, or reinvented in a genuinely childlike and imaginative manner in contemporary times. Mette Rudvin also takes a long diachronic sweep, surveying, in her essay on Rudyard Kipling's *Jungle books*, a century of translation history during which Italian translators and publishers wrestled with a writer who was himself oscillating between the cultures of India and England: two countries with which he, and many of his original readers, identified in complex ways. That particular bipartite relationship was one in which Italy, of course, could never share. And to complicate matters further, the Italian translations of Kipling were variously pitched – at adults, adolescents, and very young children – and since 1967 these books have coexisted with an enormously influential Disney cartoon film from America. Rudvin's analysis shows how such a wide variety of factors and pressures could give rise to a series of very different 'jungle books'. Interestingly, some of the early translations have proved unusually long-lived in this process of adaptation.

Emer Delaney, in the third essay on children's literature, details how Richmal Crompton's *William* stories got transported from England to Italy, with some striking alterations – the dark subversive elements that gave the original stories their charm being domesticated (or emasculated) for the Italian market by subtle and treacherous processes of rearrangement, while the author herself had to undergo a sex-change, turning into a retired gentleman, complete

19 Although Jack Zipes has observed that fairy tales and the Bible were the most popular and most translated genres during the eighteenth century, the status of children's literature has continued to fluctuate, with only tardy recognition of its complexity, and with critics still tending to dismiss it as secondary. If authors of children's fiction have fared badly, translators have fared worse, the common perception being that they are 'simply beginners'. Only recently have they moved to centre-stage, with increasing recognition of the unique relevance of translating children's fiction to both theory and practice, as well as to the field of intercultural studies. See, for example, R. Tabbert, 'Approaches to the translation of children's literature', *Target*, 14:2 (2002), 303–35; special issue in *Meta* (2003); Eithne M.T. O'Connell, *Minority language dubbing for children: screen translation from German to Irish* (Oxford, 2003); G. Lathey (ed.), *The translation of children's literature: a reader* (Clevedon, 2006); five articles on children's literature in translation appeared in *Meta*, 53:1 (2008).

with a bearded author image – before going on to speculate as to whether a contemporary set of children's books with a huge adult readership, J.K. Rowling's Harry Potter series, are translated, received and read differently because of their position on the border between child and adult literature. With essays such as these three, situating the translation process in a wide context of different media, audiences and social influences, we can certainly identify instances of 'wrong' translation, but we may also understand what caused them to occur, and perhaps refrain from heaping opprobrium exclusively on the head of the individual translator, who has to work under the constraints of many cultural aspirations.

If children's literature provides a revealing frame for the translator's work, the crime or mystery genre is equally promising. Taking an Anglo-Italian perspective, Jane Dunnett shows that the effects of censorship leave traces on popular literature, and that these can persist over time with works that retain popularity even as societies change. The translated detective story must rearrange whole systems of prejudice and shared assumptions as it enters a new readership; the rascally or unreliable foreigner, especially, has to be fitted into a reassembled scenario of the familiar and the strange. If Agatha Christie too was traduced in translation it is not merely because she was a world best-seller in a popular genre. Her novels make so much, among the apparently trivial details of social life which are their basic elements, of national identities and insecurities, that the translator has a particularly challenging task. Sabine Strumper-Krobb, in a discussion drawing on a wide range of European and American crime writers, shows how the crime novel can highlight the role and status of the translator, by emphasizing the ways in which he or she can be seen as marginal and placeless. The process of translation offers a sheaf of metaphors of inauthenticity and bad faith which fit the genre, but her account shows how these can elegantly collapse into a metaphor for all writing, not just translation, and for the enterprise of the book. The passage of time exposes crime novels as translated literature to new readings in the light of history and political pressure.

With fictions of crime we skirt a transgressive area, and language can be violently transgressive, inviting those half-conscious interventions of self-censorship which persist when more formal machineries of control have been at least partially dismantled. Such interventions crop up especially in those media that deal most directly with the spoken word. Ilaria Parini looks at the ways in which the explosive language and sexual references of Quentin Tarantino's films, the dialect of his imagined criminal milieu, are tamed for Italian audiences. Bart Defrancq examines how newspapers and web writers conveyed outbursts of verbal abuse by actors, 'celebrities' and politicians across the barriers of language, how they reported them in diluted forms or mistranslated or, like the

Victorian editors of ancient texts, opted for the 'decent obscurity' of the original language. But the obscurity of a world language such as English or French must always be relative, and Annjo Klungervik Greenall shows us in her essay on the 'knowledgeable audience' shows how viewers with good linguistic awareness respond to translated subtitles which they judge inadequate in dealing with taboo words.

HISTORY AND POLITICS OF TRANSLATION

We have already mentioned Ortega y Gasset as an important historical figure in foreshadowing contemporary ideas of the translator's status and responsibilities. Apart from Pilar Ordóñez López's account of Ortega's philosophical principles, our 'history and politics' section also contains three more detailed studies based on a searching analysis of textual matches and faultlines.

Translation by its nature reflects the relationship between groups separated by barriers of linguistic ignorance or knowledge. But groups distinguished by language conditions tend also be to be separated in other ways. Power relations complicate language questions, including the categories of right and wrong. Sabine Dedenbach-Salazar Sáenz explores these issues in an essay centred on one significant verb – *muchay* – and its derivatives in colonial South America, showing how attempts to translate this symptomatic term (with its semantic field revolving around love, greeting, worship, veneration) could lead to paradoxical results. The Spanish invaders were grimly convinced of their own rightness – religious, political and linguistic – and determined to spread the true Christian faith to a misguided local Andean population, lost in the axiomatic wrongness of idolatry. Translation, as the engine of contact between these two realities, points up perfectly the delusions and limitations of the colonial enterprise. The Spanish language coined the verb 'mochar' as a loan-word from the Quechua term 'muchay', and used it as a word for the wrongful idolatrous worship of false deities, as opposed to the verb 'adorar' which denotes Christians righteously worshipping their own true God. But in Quechua, the local population was urged to desist from idolatrous worship and turn to worshipping Jesus, the Virgin Mary and the Saints, with the same verb 'muchay' being used for both 'wrong' and 'right' religious practices. This, the essay argues, encouraged the native population to build a bridge to the new religion, but as bridges (like translation) are bidirectional, the traffic was not all one-way and the conquered people could also reverse the process, integrating the Christian deity into the Andean pantheon. Translation, and the mismatch of lexical categories, form the perfect litmus paper to reveal this rather fascinating process of cultural resistance. Of course the 'rights and wrongs' of pure translation criticism, in cases such as this, may tend to be overshadowed by larger questions as to whether such instances of translation form part of a project that is worthy and noble, or vile and inhumane.

When dealing with the rights and wrongs of translation, one may often question whether it is right to translate at all. Some texts, as Anne Markey demonstrates in relation to Patrick Pearse, may apparently both refuse and invite translation. Pearse was much opposed to the development of Irish literature in the English language, on the grounds that literature which is not in Irish is not Irish literature. He then led a rebellion against English rule, was executed and became posthumously consecrated as a national hero by large numbers of Irish people who endorsed his ideology but did not speak Irish, the language which he had adopted as his own. Inevitably, Pearse's Irish-language short stories were then translated into English, thereby undermining his personal linguistic policy. But even if it had been wrong in principle to do this, the distinction between doing it right or doing it wrong still remains open, and Markey uses a comparison of two published texts, together with archival records of manuscript notes, to show how in the case of one translator and his editor, ideological agendas could distort truthful translation by such tried and tested techniques as omission, attenuation and conventional padding. She also shows, along the way, how 'domestication' and 'foreignization' can alter their meanings in a situation where two languages coexist in a small nation that speaks one, loves the other, and needs translation in order to access those elements in the unspoken language which it considers most characteristic of its own identity.

The final essay in this section deals with the role of translation in communicating a historical event that can be compared to the atrocities of the Conquistadores in South America. The event is the Shoah, and the translations in question were made for German consumption. To what extent were the horrors of the Nazi past attenuated to spare the feelings of German readers of Anne Frank's *Het Achterhuis*, translated from Dutch, and Daniel Goldhagen's *Hitler's willing executioners*, translated from English? Simone Schroth examines two translations, and their publishing history, briefly but in depth, showing how the translation scholar's natural expectation that some painful references to Germany might be 'toned down' is indeed borne out by the evidence, but also noting instances where the original was 'toned up' in translation, making certain points more emphatically than the originals. In Schroth's scrupulous evaluation of these controversial texts, 'right or wrong' becomes 'right and wrong', or sometimes 'wrong and wrong' – but could two contrasting wrongs conceivably add up to (more or less) 'right'? It is worth noting that one of the two texts has been retranslated into German: even in the worst of times, accuracy is a value still worthy of our attention.

TRANSLATION NOW

The impact of new technology did not figure very largely at the 'Translation Right or Wrong' conference, and receives limited representation in the present volume; yet its potential for redrawing the field of translation, and its evaluation, is so vast that it merits some reflection in our introduction. Apart from anything else, technology creates new methods of study, new ways of being right, new ways of detecting wrong behaviour, and new cohorts of translators whose professional standards of 'right or wrong' translation demand to be judged differently, because in fact they are not professionals.

James Holmes divided translation studies (TS) into Pure and Applied, the former sub-divided into Theoretical and Descriptive, with eleven sections, and the latter with three.[20] This taxonomy usefully displayed the interconnectedness of a cross-disciplinary field of ever-widening scope, but, as Mona Baker later warned, there were risks of fragmentation from the divisive clash between emerging Cultural Studies and established Linguistics.[21] More recently, Edwin Gentzler has observed what may be valid reasons for a degree of flux:

> [T]he focus in translation investigation is shifting from the abstract to the specific, from the deep underlying hypothetical forms to the surface of texts with their gaps, errors, ambiguities, multiple referents, and 'foreign' disorder. These are being analyzed – and not by standards of equivalent/un-equivalent, right/wrong, good/bad, correct/incorrect. Such standards imply notions of substantialism that limit other possibilities of translation practice, marginalize unorthodox translation, and impinge upon real intercultural exchange.[22]

The whole issue of alternative emerging standards, of 'right or wrong', is further complicated by the fact that translation, once the product of the human mind alone, is increasingly entering the realm of the machine.

Where once an individual or a group of experts, would gather all the resources of experience to produce a fair rendering of an original text, today

20 James Holmes, quoted in María Calzada Pérez, *El espejo traductológico* (Barcelona, 2007), p. 84. The formulation by Holmes appears in diagrammatic form in his article, 'The name and nature of translation studies' in Gideon Toury (ed.), *Translation across cultures* (New Delhi, 1998), pp 10–25 at p. 22, and in a slightly different layout in Toury's *Descriptive translation studies*, p. 10. **21** Mona Baker, 'Linguistics and cultural studies: complementary or competing paradigms in translation' in Angelika Lauer, Heidrun Gerzymisch-Arbogast, Johann Haller & Erich Steiner, *Übersersetzungswissenschaft im Umbruch: Festschrift für Wolfram Wilss* (Tübingen, 1996). **22** Edwin Gentzler, *Contemporary translation theories* (2nd ed., Clevedon, 2000), p. 4.

one is more likely to find the gathering of software and corpora. This accompanies, of course, the present-day scope of translation, which, in catering for a much wider range of clients, has developed an increasing reliance on technology. As Maria Tymoczko suggested in 2005,[23] new technologies are leading to a major shift in translation studies away from the purely literary towards the practical, the professional, the profitable, and even the mass-amateur (subtitling, advertising, manga, anime, and so on). The internet has promoted the creation of advanced translation memory software programs and the rise of web localization as the major activity within translation technologies.[24]

The influence of technology in the discipline can also be detected in the expansion of research centres in the universities, the establishment of professional organizations, the number of international conferences that have taken place over the past decade, and the proliferation of dedicated academic journals and publications.[25] It is clear also that technology applied to literature can open up many possibilities for the critique of translations and for the comparative study of stylistics in translation.[26] However, the Septuagint and the King James version owed more to creative genius with words than to any verbal database and, as this realm of the gentleman scholar declines, translation may be at risk of too much mechanization. That said, there can be no doubt of its value in many areas that would be scarcely viable without modern technology, among them translation plagiarism, international advertising, audiovisual translating, and amateur translation.

This is not, of course, to claim that technology is solely responsible for the surge of interest in translation, which, since its relatively recent emergence from under the umbrella of linguistics has seen considerable expansion in, for example, the area of literary translation studies. But even here, where perhaps the greatest need for individual creativity exists, the field has seen increasing work in stylistics, critique, and plagiarism, all now owing much to recent advances in forensic linguistics.[27]

23 Maria Tymoczko, 'Trajectories of research in translation studies', *Meta,* 50:4 (2005), 1082–97. **24** In 1996 Minako O'Hagan referred to 'teletranslation', *The coming industry of teletranslation* (Clevedon, 1996). Apart from the machine translation facilities provided by Babel Fish, Bing Translator or Google Translate, software tools include SDL Trados Studio, Wordfast, and MemoQ. **25** For example, *The Journal of Translation Technology* (2012), *Jostrans: the Journal of Specialized Translation* (2004), *Tradumàtica* (2001), *Machine Translation* (1997), *Localization Focus: the International Journal of Localization* (1996). In 2010 Peter Lang added a new series to their catalogue entitled *New trends in translation studies* – the focus being the expanding area of the internet, audiovisual media and technologies. **26** An example is the COVALT (Valencian Corpus of Translated Literature) project –www.ventanillaunica.uji.es/LibroNaranja/ENG/pdf/COVALT_eng.pdf. **27** Although these studies have traditionally been related to the judicial system and the law, increasingly forensic linguistics is expanding

PLAGIARISM, AUTHORSHIP, TEXT COMPOSITION

Literary translation plagiarism is among the emerging major areas of increasing activity, and, paradoxically, technology itself suggests a problem: to what extent can authorship of a translation be claimed when much of its text has been mechanically derived? In the past, the translator was more often anonymous, while the 'authority' of an original text was enhanced by ascribing it to a credible figure (who might be an apostle) and much dubious authorship was thereby disguised.[28] To add to the mix of 'authorships', technology has enabled a much closer focus on just what constitutes plagiarism in literary translation, a focus that embraces issues which differ subtly from those within literary plagiarism, issues not only of authorship, but of 'erasure', of 'double-voicedness', of originality/creativity and 'forgery/copy', of meaning and interpretation, of retranslation, and of ethics. Technology helps here, as it does in so many areas pointed out by Alberto Fuertes in his quantitative analysis of anchor phenomena applied to re-translations of literary texts.[29]

And while from the 1950s onwards, structuralism, deconstruction and postmodern literary theories challenged the concept of the author and of originality,[30] identification of the genuine author continued to persist, supported by such laws as that in Britain on intellectual property rights (1911) and the more

its applicability and becoming a focus of postgraduate research in areas related to the detection of plagiarism in other environments and to the attribution of authorship. Pompeu Fabra University (Barcelona) offers a Masters degree in Forensic Linguistics in collaboration with Ashton University Centre for Forensic Linguistics (for an example of research into plagiarism in literary translation, see the 2011 Masters dissertation of Joan Pla Fulquet, 'La detecció de plagi en traducció literària. Anàlisi de tres versions de *El Barón rampante* de Italo Calvino a l'espanyol'. See also R. Howard & A. Robillard (eds), *Pluralizing plagiarism, identities, contexts, pedagogies* (Portsmouth, 2008)). **28** For one of the most surprising cases of concealed authorship and plagiarism in literary translation see Inmaculada Serón Ordoñez, 'Plagiarismo y autoría en las obras de Shakespeare por R. Martínez Lafuente', *Revista de Historia de la Traducción*, 4 (2010), http://www.traduccionliteraria.org/1611/generalnum.htm, accessed 30 Apr. 2012. **29** For an analysis of the strengths and weaknesses of the major linguistic corpora databases in Spain (CORDE, Real Academia Española, and the Corpus del Español, both incorporating a large percentage of literary texts across centuries and genres) see Mark Davies, 'Creating useful historical corpora: a comparison of CORDE, the Corpus del Español, and the Corpus do Português' in Andrés Enrique-Arias (ed.), *Diacronía de las lenguas iberorromances: nuevas perspectivas desde la linguistic de corpus* (Frankfurt, 2010), pp 139–68, www.corpusdelespanol.org/compare-cde-corde.pdf , accessed 23 May 2012. **30** Postmodernist theories promote the notion of 'un-originality' with some claiming that plagiarism is the highest expression of authentic creativity. See Terry Eagleton, 'Faking it: the art of literary forgery', *The Guardian*, 6 June 2002, www.guardian.co.uk/books/2002/jun/06/londonreviewofbooks, accessed 12 May 2012; John Mullan, review of '*The forger's shadow: how forgery changed the course of literature* by Nick Groom', *The Guardian*, 13 Apr. 2002. www.guardian.co. uk/books/2002/apr/13/art, accessed 14 May 2012. See also Fritz Gutbrodt, *Joint ventures: authorship, translation, plagiarism* (Bern, 2003).

recent Spanish legislation that gives the profession legal protection and recognizes the translator's ownership of the form, that is, of the words, if not the ideas.[31] But, despite the fact that current combinations of quantitative and qualitative analyses make it more difficult to conceal translation plagiarism and help translators to win court cases against offenders, Alberto Fuertes recognizes that there are many unresolved difficulties in the detection of translation plagiarism (for example, the high incidence of overlapping vocabulary, the limitation of the tools applied, generic constraints, and the environment of the translator). And, according to Deborah Weber-Wulff, this is still an area where progress is very slow, where there is not yet in place a system which can 'effectively deal with the issue of translated plagiarism'.[32]

All of which offers an encouraging scope for research, and a precise rationale for an increasingly large role for technology in just this contentious area of authorship, where some even claim, in contradistinction to Lawrence Venuti's attempt to promote the visibility of the translator, that a translation is not the unique 'property' of an unaided translator but rather a jointly creative effort with the (absent) originator of the text. Mona Baker has argued that a translator leaves behind stylistic fingerprints regardless of the original,[33] and if Theo Hermans is right to maintain that a translation is a coproduction, that the stylistic voice of the translator is always present, then it follows that plagiarizing involves a translator in appropriating the voice/reading of another. The implications are profound enough for plagiarism to become a central field of research within translation studies,[34] aided by the development of sophisticated software programs,[35] by forensic linguistics,[36] and by a growing interest in the comparative study of translations.

31 For the recent widespread practice of re-printing earlier translations under different names in Brazil and Turkey see 'Plagiarism of translation', *Goodreads*, 18 Dec. 2010, www.goodreads.com/topic/show/454509-plagiarism-of-literary-translation, accessed 5 May 2012; 'Brazilian translator of Jane Austen accused of plagiarism', *The Spectacled Bear*, 23 Jan. 2009, thespectacledbear.wordpress.com/2009/01/23/brazilian-translator-of-jane-austen-novel-accused-of-plagiarism/, accessed 5 May 2012; S. Yavuz, 'Turkish translators seek to be protected by law', *Hürriyet daily news*, 29 Sept. 2010, www.hurriyetdailynews.com/default.aspx?pageid=438&n=translators-want-their-profession-to-be-regarded-as-a-profession-2010-09-29, accessed 7 May 2012. **32** Jonathan Bailey, 'The problem with detecting translation plagiarism', *Plagiarism Today (PT)*, 24 Feb. 2011, www.plagiarismtoday.com/2011/02/24/the-problem-with-detecting-translated-plagiarism/, accessed 25 May 2012. **33** For an examination of style in translations see Mona Baker, 'Towards a methodology for investigating the style of a literary translator', *Target*, 12:2 (2002), 241–66. **34** See Lauren G. Leighton, 'Translation and plagiarism: Pushkin and D.M. Thomas', *The Slavic and East European Journal*, 38:1 (1994), 69–83. On literary plagiarism see, for example, Martha Woodmansee & Peter Jaszi (eds), *The construction of authorship: textual appropriation in law and literature* (Durham, 1994); Pierre Bayard, *Le plagiat par anticipation* (Paris, 2009). **35** For example, CopyCatch Gold and JVocalyse, both developed by David Woolls at the University of Birmingham. **36** See John Gibbons & M.

Within comparative study the issue of localization has become even more acute, with technology allowing more emphasis on international rather than merely local awareness of the text: 'Globally, this is the age of mass communications, of multimedia experiences and a world where audiences demand the right to share the latest text, be it film, song, or book simultaneously across cultures'.[37] And the growing place of localization studies has spurred a new debate on what the process of translation actually involves, with LISA (the largest industry association until it closed in 2011) stating that the aim of localization is to produce texts adapted to look as though they were developed in-country or for a specific market.[38] Nonetheless, not all commentators feel the need for a separate label: '[L]ocalization is only a fancy name for the act of adapting a text for a specific target readership, which is something translators have been doing for millennia'.[39] Whether merely a label, or something more, the act of localizing is a major user of technology, one which may also contribute towards what Anthony Pym calls 'the logics of quantity and democratic participation',[40] with the accompanying caveat that '[t]he dehumanizing tendency of localization discourse is of particular importance to translators (who risk getting lousy jobs) and translation theory (whose recent advances are threatened with immediate extinction)'.[41]

CASES OF LOCAL ADAPTATION: ADVERTISING, SUBTITLING, AUDIENCE RESPONSE AND THE AUDIENCE AS AUTHOR

Localization, whatever its status, is of central importance to the global standardization of marketing, where advertising needs to tailor a product for a particular audience while simultaneously providing the wider appeal that localization can supply.[42] But exactly how this can be carried out must be ques-

Teresa Turell (eds), *Dimensions of forensic linguistics* (Amsterdam, 2008); Jonathan Bailey, 'Translation plagiarism', *Plagiarism today*, 13 Aug. 2005, accessed 25 June 2012. **37** Susan Bassnet quoted in R. Álvarez & M.C. Vidal (eds), *Translation, power, subversion* (Philadelphia, 1996), p. 1. **38** José Ramón Biau Gil & Anthony Pym, 'Technology and translation (a pedagogical overview)' in A. Pym, A. Perekrestenko & B. Starink (eds), *Translation technology and its teaching* (Tarragona, 2006), pp 5–19 at p. 14. For an Irish institution that has done pioneering work in this field, see www.localisation.ie for an overview of the LRC at the University of Limerick. **39** LISA, 'What is globalization?', web.archive.org/web/20110101205931/www.lisa.org/What-Is-Globalization.48.0.html, accessed 25 Apr. 2012. **40** A. Pym, 'What technology does to translating', *The International Journal Of Translation & Interpreting Research*, 3:1 (2011), www.trans-int.org/index.php/transint/article/viewFile/121/81, pp 1–9 at p. 5, accessed 23 Apr. 2012. **41** Anthony Pym, 'Localization: on its nature, virtues and dangers', www.usuaris.tinet.cat/apym/on-line/translation/translation.html (2005), pp 1–10 at p. 7, accessed 23 Apr. 2012. **42** For an extremely sophisticated multime-

tionable when national identity intervenes to the extent, as Kathleen Shields points out, of the 1994 French Loi Toubon which, in response to the encroachment of English, made it compulsory to translate advertising. Simon Anholt succinctly observes that

> [t]ranslating advertising copy is like painting the tip of an iceberg [...] What makes copy work is not the words themselves, but subtle combinations of those words, and most of all the echoes and repercussions of those words within the mind of the reader. These are precisely the subtleties which translation fails to convey. Advertising is not made of words, but made of culture.[43]

The localizer/translator of advertising must not only retain the subtle appeal of an original image and text but also, as Mathieu Guidère notes, take responsibility for the success or failure of the campaign.[44] Not surprisingly, therefore, as Jeremy Munday[45] has remarked, advertising challenges many assumptions about translation theory, which in turn naturally leads to increasing interest in researching the processes involved in correlating text and image, and in comparing cultural, linguistic and rhetorical similarities and divergences.[46]

Alongside advertising translation as a major current concern could be placed audiovisual translation (AVT), once considered peripheral but now one of the more dynamic and expanding areas within translation studies. From the publication of sporadic articles and a few scholarly volumes in the 1990s,[47] the field has grown considerably in the last decade.[48] Where dubbing was once supreme,

dia advertisement by an American translation company to promote its services see, translationllc.com/#/home, accessed 5 June 2012. **43** S. Anholt, *Another one bites the grass. Making sense of international advertising* (New York, 2000), p. 5, quoted in Marieke de Mooij, 'Translating advertising', *The Translator*, 10:2 (2004), 179–98 at 180. **44** Mathieu Guidère, 'Translation practices in international advertising', *The Translation Journal*, 5:1 (2001), www.bokorlang.com/journal/15advert.htm, accessed 5 June 2012. **45** J. Munday, 'Advertising: some challenges to translation theory', *The Translator* 10:2 (2004), 199–219. **46** *The Translator* published a special issue on the translation of advertising in 2004. For a timely and useful publication see Ira Torresi, *Translating promotional and advertising texts* (Manchester, 2010). In Spain over the past decade a series of major studies have appeared – for example Cristina Valdés Rodríguez, *La traducción publicitaria: comunicación y cultura* (Barcelona, 2004); José Dávila-Montes, *La traducción de la persuasión publicitaria* (Lewiston, 2008). **47** For a pioneering special issue on subtitling see *Babel*, 6:3 (1960); Helen Reid, 'Subtitling: the intelligent solution' in P. Hoguelin (ed.), *Translating, a profession; proceedings of the VIII World congress, international federation of translators* (Montreal, 1977), pp 420–8; Jan Ivarsson, *Subtitling* (Shimrishamn, 1992); H. Brondeel, 'Teaching subtitling routines' in *Meta*, 39 (1994), 26–33; A.M. Nornes, 'For an abusive subtitling', *Film Quarterly*, 52:3 (1999), 17–34. **48** For example, C. Taylor, 'Multimodal transcription in the analysis, translation and subtitling of Italian

the emphasis has shifted to subtitling, which, notwithstanding its need for translation strategies of reduction and simplification, of omission, of reformulation and paraphrasing, has had to struggle against the perception that it is merely 'summarization'. Such a perception has been revised in light of the latest research, which has widened out from a focus on the comparative to embracing the study of reception theory, the compilation of databases and corpora, and methodologies for training multimedia translators.[49] Training is crucial since, as Yves Gambier observes, 'new services such as streaming, video and TV on demand, TV on mobile (with new types of very short films), podcasting, etc., will challenge [...] screen translators'.[50]

Francisca García Luque notes that studies of film subtitling have increased while research on the peculiarities of documentaries continues to lag behind, and examines to what extent there are differences between subtitling for films and documentaries.[51] And Annjo K. Greenall's study of spontaneous 'perceptions of good and bad' in subtitles reveals common sense assumptions about 'right' and 'wrong', where norms of appropriateness and acceptability, of what is considered blasphemous or taboo, may involve strategies of substitution, euphemism, equivalence, or even expurgation. As many experts observe, subtitling automatically keeps in mind the 'ideal spectator' for a particular film, an

films', *The Translator*, 9:2 (2003), 191–204; John D. Sanderson (ed.), *Research on translation for subtitling in Spain and Italy* (Alicante, 2005); A. Matamala, 'Main challenges in the translation of documentaries' in J. Díaz Cintas (ed.), *New trends in audiovisual translation* (London, 2009), pp 112–26. Jorge Díaz Cintas, Anna Matamala & Josélia Neves (eds), *New insights into audiovisual translation and media accessibility* (Amsterdam, 2010). **49** The Universitat Autònoma de Barcelona in collaboration with other universities established the LeVis project (learning through subtitling). The research group developed a software package that allows students to insert subtitles into the scenes/frames of a film. The University of León is in the process of creating a database of Hollywood movies called P-ACTRES as a specialized corpus which will include 100 films with their translation into Spanish. Similarly, the University of Bologna has developed, in Forlì, a database of approximately 51 films with the transcripts of dialogues (see Cristina Valentini, 'Developing AVT corpora for a quantitative approach to language transfer in cinematic products', www.arts.kuleuven.be/info/bestanden-div/VALENTINI.pdf, accessed 22 May 2012. **50** Y. Gambier, 'Multimodality and audiovisual translation', *MuTra* – audiovisual translation scenarios: conference proceedings, 2006, www.euroconferences.info/proceedings/2006_Proceedings/2006_Gambier_Yves.pdf, accessed 25 May 2012. **51** See E. Franco, 'Documentary film translation. A specific practice?' in A. Chesterman, N. Gallardo & Y. Gambier (eds), *Translation in context* (Amsterdam, 2000), pp 233–42; E. Espasa, 'Myths about documentary translation' in P. Orero (ed.), *Topics on audiovisual translation* (Amsterdam, 2004), pp 183–97; A. Remael, 'Whose language, whose voice, whose message? Different AVT modes for documentaries on VRT-Canvas Television, Flanders', *TradTerm*, 13 (2007), 31–50; F. Kaufmann, 'Le sous-titrage des documentaires: Défis et enjeux de l'établissement du texte de "départ"' in A. Serban & J.M. Lavaur (eds), *La traduction audiovisuelle. Approche interdisciplinaire du sous-titrage* (Brussels, 2008), pp 69–83.

awareness of equal importance in the area examined by Minako O'Hagan, who reviews different types of subtitling practice – fansub (Japanese anime), scanlation, fanfic, and digisubbing, as well as 'translation crowdsourcing'. Such translations are made free by fans for other fans.

But as some corporations are selecting free translation, and as many fansubs do not translate into their mother tongue, some professional translators may resent what they see as an encroachment. While professional translators may be disturbed by the phenomenon of unremunerated translation, and some anime may be offensive, there are certain advantages to the practice. Message boards allow international communication, the spirit of collaboration is in accord with modern social and educational theories of purposeful cooperative working, it engenders a spirit of critical response to translation, it encourages improved quality standards, and it may enhance linguistic skills. In addition, it can make material available that might never otherwise have been translated. But notions of 'right' and 'wrong' are also being debated by a section of fansubs, who sharply criticize the work of other fansubs when they go beyond translating to 'improving' the graphics with colourful subtitling, bigger fonts, and so on.[52]

Whatever the divisions between professional translators and amateurs, between theory and practice, between established standards and new approaches to 'rightness', the most influential impact on translation will continue to come from technological advances, even perhaps from speech recognition eventually allowing instant translation into any chosen target language. Whatever the prospects, the centrality of translation studies as a major discipline in its own right was firmly recognized by the fact that Catherine Porter, president of the MLA, chose as her 2009 address to the Association: 'The tasks of translation for the twenty-first century'.

TRANSLATION QUALITY: AN ENDLESS DISPUTE?

Quarrels between translators and their critics, or even between translators themselves, will probably never fully abate. The 'retranslation hypothesis', as summarized by Jenny Williams and Andrew Chesterman, claims that 'retranslations tend to be closer to the original than first translations'.[53] This makes intuitive sense, since for reasons of politeness a translated text, on first introduction to

52 A 2008 documentary convincingly argued for the classical 'right' way of translating anime, the author calling on mainstream translation theory ('Rise and fall of anime fansubtitling', http://celestialkitsune.wordpress.com/2008/06/07/rise-and-fall-of-anime-fan-subtitling-documentary/, accessed 5 Apr. 2012). **53** Jenny Williams & Andrew Chesterman, *The map: a beginner's guide to doing research in translation studies* (Manchester, 2002), p. 72.

new readers, might tend to mould itself to their expectations, but once the new text has established itself as a thing of value, perhaps even an object of reverence, its readership may then grow curious to take it on its own terms rather than on theirs. Second translators will naturally wish to support that exploratory ambition, and publishers will wish to suggest that the new version is a superior job; very few retranslations are advertised with the slogan 'now, for the first time, less accurate'. Thus, while a first translation might naturally tend to err by being spinelessly ingratiating, its successor might equally tend to err through prickly insistence on the purity of its alien qualities.

So far, so innocent. However, fresh translations are sometimes accompanied by unkind critiques of their predecessors, who, it seems, have omitted, misunderstood and distorted important elements of the text. The new translators of the latest version of Simone de Beauvoir's *The second sex* (2010) provide a sample of the first translator's failings (1953), suggesting that fundamental concepts have been traduced. 'One is not born, but rather becomes, a woman' (translating 'On ne naît pas femme, on le devient') should apparently have been rendered quite differently: 'One is not born, but rather becomes, woman'.[54]

That formulation might have sounded odd in 1953, thereby making Beauvoir seem faintly ridiculous – the misuse or omission of pronouns and articles traditionally served as a slightly comic or endearing marker of foreigners doing their humble best to speak proper English[55] – but by 2012 the omission

54 Simone de Beauvoir, *The second sex*, translated by Constance Borde & Sheila Malovany-Chevallier (New York, 2010), p. xviii. The original American translation of Beauvoir, dating from 1952, has been subjected to searching criticism by feminist translation scholars for several decades. As early as 1983 Margaret Simons, a philosophy professor who was herself working on a new translation of *The second sex*, not only identified errors of philosophical translation in H.M. Parshley's version but condemned his obliteration of 78 historically significant women from the book, which distorted the balance of Beauvoir's message; Simons discerned 'evidence of his sexism' in the material he chose for deletion, and quoted the author's dismay when informed of these misrepresentations (and Beauvoir's endorsement of Simons' planned retranslation). Given that the Bantam paperback edition of the Parshley translation claimed to be 'complete and unabridged', she has a point against the publishers, but her imputation of base motives to the translator seems a little harsh. See Margaret A. Simons, 'The silencing of Simone de Beauvoir: guess what's missing from *The second sex*', *Women's Studies International Forum*, 6:5 (1983), 559–63. For this and other instances of male translators who 'do not do justice to women writers', see Irene Chen, 'Translating rape', *Translation Journal*, 13:2 (2009), www.bokorlang.com/journal/48rape.htm , accessed 26 June 2012. **55** See, for example, Peter Dickinson, *The lizard in the cup* (London, Hodder & Stoughton, 1972), paperback reprint (London, Panther, 1974), pp 122–23. Capt Thagoulos, a Greek policeman, is explaining his suspicion that a Londoner has come to his country for paedophile purposes: 'He says he is one London businessman; [...] I am policeman many years. [...] His room at Hotel Aeschylus is O.K. [...] But is not satisfactory. Is not the room of the man who comes for holidays. Yes?'

of the indefinite article is endorsed in a gendered context by no less an authority than Google Translate: 'Je suis homme' is rendered as 'I am a man', while 'Je suis femme' becomes 'I am woman'.[56]

Large-scale omissions are another problem. Reviewing the 2010 translation of *The second sex*, Francine du Plessix Gray recalls that it was actually the publisher, Alfred Knopf, who urged the first translator, a retired zoologist from Smith College named Howard M. Parshley, to abbreviate Mme de Beauvoir's 'verbal diarrhoea'. And, Gray continues, Parshley 'provided the necessary Imodium by cutting 15 percent of the original 972 pages'. (This touches on a perennial problem of translation criticism: given the low status of translators within the publishing process, one can rarely be sure that they are fully responsible for their own crimes.) The reviewer approves the restoration of Parshley's cuts in the 2010 edition, but then protests that the new unabridged translation 'doesn't begin to flow as nicely as Parshley's'. She gives examples:

> Writing about the aggressive nature of man's penetration of woman, Parshley felicitously translates a Beauvoir phrase as 'her inwardness is violated'. In contrast, Borde and Malovany-Chevallier's rendering states that woman 'is like a raped interiority'. And where Parshley has Beauvoir saying of woman, 'It is she who defines herself by dealing with nature on her own account in her emotional life,' the new translators substitute, 'It is she who defines herself by reclaiming nature for herself in her affectivity'.[57]

Judith Thurman, introducing the new edition of Beauvoir, hails it as a 'magisterial exercise in fidelity'. But a similar claim of fidelity had been made, apparently in absolute good faith, by the first translator:

> I have conceived it my duty as translator to adhere faithfully to what she says and to maintain to the best of my ability the atmosphere she creates. Thus my intention has been in general to avoid all paraphrasing not required by language differences and to provide a translation that is at once exact and – with slight exceptions – complete. [...] I have also done some cutting and condensation here and there with a view to brevity.[58]

56 translate.google.com/, accessed 16 July 2012. **57** *New York Times Sunday book review*, 27 May 2010, available online at www.nytimes.com/2010/05/30/books/review/Gray-t.html?ref=books (accessed 26 June 2012). Gray's reference to 'flow' bears out perfectly Lawrence Venuti's protest that 'fluency' is seen by uninformed reviewers as the dominant criterion for successful translation: see *The translator's invisibility* Ch. 1. **58** Simone de Beauvoir, *The second sex*, translated and edited by H.M. Parshley (London, 1953, reprinted London, 1997), translator's preface, p. 11. For an impressive and balanced survey of the whole translation process which Professor Parshley (1884–1953) diligently forwarded during

Clearly, fidelity means different things at different times. The present volume, as already mentioned, will touch on Ortega y Gasset's view that one can be unfaithful to the free spirit of an author by failing to be just as free in one's own translation. But when does rightful freedom shade into wrongful interference?

The practice of criticizing one's predecessors has interesting consequences, inter alia, for the relationship between the translator and the original foreign-language text. Theo Hermans records that when David Luke published a new translation of Thomas Mann's *Death in Venice*, he added a preface which included several pages cataloguing alleged errors in the earlier translation of Mann's novella by Helen Lowe-Porter. Hermans comments:

> As a result, Luke's own rendering pitted itself not only against Mann's German original but equally against Lowe-Porter's English version. [...] This second intertextual dimension, that of the translator in critical dialogue with another translator, betrays the presence of a speaking voice that is not reducible to that of the original author.[59]

Such three-cornered dialogues, which can be extended into various dimensions of reader response, may well become the norm for future translators of influential texts. Already in China, translators of literary works from English are confronted with detailed discussions of their work by readers, on dedicated websites, and the debate over possible failings and potential improvements seems to be taken in good part by translators and readers alike.[60]

When speaking of translation, do the opposing categories of right and wrong still serve any useful purpose? Many accusations of wrongness are themselves

the final years of his life, see the MA thesis (2009) by Anna Bogic, University of Ottawa, 'Rehabilitating Howard M. Parshley: a socio-historical study of the English translation of Beauvoir's *Le deuxième sexe*, with Latour and Bourdieu', available under a 'Creative Commons Attribution-NonCommercial-NoDerivs 3.0 Unported License' at www.ruor.uottawa.ca/fr/bitstream/handle/10393/19600/Bogic,%20Anna%20-%202009%20-%20Rehabilitating%20Howard%20M.%20Parshley.%20A%20Socio-historical%20Study%20of%20the%20English%20Translation%20of%20Beauvoir%E2%80%99s%20Le%20deuxi%C3%A8me%20sexe,%20with%20Latour%20and%20Bourdieu.pdf?sequence=1, accessed 26 June 2012. Luise von Flotow provides a critique of Parshley's procedures and a broad reflection on the processes of translation and retranslation in 'This time "the translation is beautiful, smooth, and true": theorizing retranslation with the help of Beauvoir', *FLS*, 36 (2009), 35–49. **59** Theo Hermans, 'Paradoxes and aporias in translation and translation studies' in Alessandra Riccardi (ed.), *Translation studies: perspectives on an emerging discipline* (Cambridge, 2002), pp 10–23 at p. 15. Lowe-Porter's errors, recorded by Luke, include misreading of similar words in German, which sounds wrong by any standards. But how far do individual lapses detract from the overall meaning? **60** As reported by the translators Jian Lu and Zhou Jianing, at a literary translation seminar, Trinity College Dublin, 5 April 2012.

wrong, either because the critic is less skilled than the translator, or because he or she has set up an arbitrary criterion that the translator was under no obligation to respect. The underlying fallacy is often the assumption that there could be just one 'right' translation of word or a text. Susan Bassnett and André Lefevere have observed that translation is 'a rewriting of an original text'; all rewritings, they believe, 'reflect a certain ideology and poetics and as such manipulate literature to function in a given society in a given way'.[61] But as well as being a rewriting, a translation is also a reading, or a rereading, of a text, and the act of reading normally attracts less daunting standards of authority than those which may apply to a writer. There is room for more than one understanding of a text, and (at least in principle) a reader who is dissatisfied with the translator's reading of an original can have access to alternative translations. If critics believe themselves to be truly qualified to improve on the translator's efforts, then their personal problem is by definition already solved. It is only the rest of us ignorant folk who need to be saved from mistranslations.

Nevertheless, the categories of right and wrong have proved hard to eradicate, and the question of whether a translation is correct or misleading is not fully disallowed by even the most sophisticated readings contained in the present volume.

TRANSLATOR ETHICS: THE VIRTUE OF HOPE

We need to return to the focus of this book's first article: the working translator. Edward Koren drew a cartoon for the *New Yorker* (20 December 1982), in which a genial devil reassures a glum group of souls as they arrive in Hell: 'You'll find there's no right or wrong here. Just what works for *you*'. Is such relativism also open to the living, breathing translator? Is she entitled to reach for absolute truth? And failing that, can she continue to strive, to 'fail again, fail better' in pursuit of such an elusive goal?

Some authorities believe that subjective feelings are indeed a potential guide to translation quality. In *Becoming a translator*, Douglas Robinson pictures, with tongue-in-cheek intensity, the intuitive process of finding just the right word:

> All of a sudden it comes to you, out of nowhere, it seems, and your fingers type it. How do you know it's right? Well, you just know. It feels right. It feels intuitively right [...] You turn it around in your head three

61 André Lefevere, *Translation, rewriting and the manipulation of literary fame* (London, 1992), General editors' preface, p. vi.

> or four times, sampling it on your tongue, and no matter how you probe it, it still feels right. So you trust your intuition (or your experience) and proceed.[62]

And then comes the morning after. As Robinson points out, you may subsequently realize that there are serious problems with the word or phrase that you have found, and you discover another solution, but this one feels somehow wrong as well, and no amount of reassurance from your dictionaries will convince you that either of your alternatives is the right one. At which point our guide helpfully comments: 'Welcome to the world of translation – a compromised world of half-rights and half-wrongs.'

Half-right and half-wrong may in fact be a perfectly acceptable professional outcome, if the first duty of translation is to avoid egregious mistakes (like the *primum non nocere* of medical ethics); the translation process could perhaps be seen as analogous to Philip Larkin's 'Talking in Bed', where one must search for 'Words at once true and kind,/ Or not untrue and not unkind.' Yet a translator is entitled to aspire, once in a while, to the moment of grace when the right word appears. The French translator Pierre Leyris described how, having arrived at an impasse in translating a phrase by Stephen Crane, 'the dull fall of dirt on wood', he could not come up with the right word for 'dirt':

> The following night, half asleep, but aware of a drift of trivial unconscious thoughts completely unrelated to his translation, the word *fange* suddenly presented itself, perfectly appropriate for the problematic line in question. He leapt from his bed to note it down.[63]

Of course it takes skill and discernment to recognize the gift of the right word when it arrives. In a recent novella, 'Translator translated', Anita Desai describes the challenge facing a sensitive Indian academic who is commissioned to translate a book from Oriya, her childhood language, into English. The project is very close to her heart, and the strength of her hidden feelings weighs upon her. The action of translating, however, begins to relieve that weight:

> As soon as I took out the little paperback – its pages were coming loose from the binding, I noticed – and pulled a piece of paper to me and

62 Douglas Robinson, *Becoming a translator: an introduction to the theory and practice of translation*, 2nd ed. (London, 2003), p.102. **63** Phyllis Gaffney, '"The achieve of, the mastery of the thing!" Pierre Leyris' verse translations of Gerard Manley Hopkins' in Jean Boase-Beier & Michael Holman (eds), *The practices of literary translation: constraints and creativity* (Manchester, 1999), pp 45–58 at p. 58.

> began to translate the first line, it was as if I had been given a magic key that would open the rest. *'It started to rain. It was getting dark.'*

That literal version is immediately rewritten into a more evocative phrase: *'Rain began to fall. The village was in darkness.'* The power of that transformation is instantly communicated to the reader of the novella:

> Yes, and yes. How easy to see that these words worked, the others did not. I hurried on, hurried while that sense lasted of what was right, what was wrong, an instinct sometimes elusive which had to be courted and kept alert. Selecting, recognizing, acknowledging.

Soon the translator is lost in her instinctive knowledge of the writer's background. 'I was also the one who knew what she meant, what worlds her words evoked. They were not mine but they were my mother's'.[64] Later in the novella, a heavy personal and professional price is paid for this over-familiar mingling of languages. The reader learns the danger of eliding the conceptual distance between the author's voice and that of her translator. And yet, 'Translator translated' amounts to much more than a warning; it is a celebration of foolhardy courage, and nothing quite extinguishes the translator's first transitory joy of knowing 'what was right, what was wrong', of being able to reshape *'It started to rain. It was getting dark'* into *'Rain began to fall. The village was in darkness.'* That minute act of intralingual translation trips the reader, too, into a symbolic sense of creative possibility, as though we ourselves were also free to make an interlingual move between the languages in the story, English and Oriya. An illusion, of course, but necessary to our reading of the story. Although translation is ultimately a risky business, the translator is bound to keep hoping – the goal may be wrong but the search is right – and translation, as a practice, is ultimately built upon the transient but fundamental pleasure of knowing right from wrong, which, like the knowledge of good and evil, may, in an imperfect world, be an effort worth the trouble it entails.

64 Anita Desai, 'Translator translated' in *The artist of disappearance: three novellas* (London, 2011), pp 41–92 at pp 59–60.

PART I

TRANSLATION AND GENRE: HIGH AND LOW

Translators are the shadow heroes of literature, the often forgotten instruments [...] who have enabled us to understand that we all, from every part of the world, live in one world.

Paul Auster, *To be translated or not to be* (2007)

Whose Classics? Transgressing and recreating ancient Greek and Latin texts

Josephine Balmer

In his *Histories* Herodotus describes the Persian king Darius' ill-fated campaign against Scythian tribesmen in *c*.B.C.E. 512 (4.128–134). As Darius lines up his army to fight the elusive Scythian forces, he demands that they either meet him in battle or acknowledge him as their new ruler. The Scythians respond by sending four gifts: a bird, a mouse, a frog and five arrows. These confound the Persians. Are they traditional tokens of surrender, as Darius chooses to believe? Or is their meaning, as one of Darius' advisors argues, that if the Persians do not retreat, melt away into air like birds, burrow into the ground like mice or leap into water like frogs, then they will be slaughtered by Scythian arrows?

During the debate, the Persians' confusion only deepens. As the Polish traveller-reporter Ryszard Kapuściński notes of this story in his memoir *Travels with Herodotus*:

> Frequently [...] external circumstances do not conform, or fit, with the structure of our webs, and then we can misread the unfamiliar reality, and interpret its elements incorrectly. On such occasions we move about in an unreal world, a landscape of dead ends and misleading signs.[1]

Kapuściński could be referring to the work of classical translators, attempting to unravel their web of associations from the far-distant past, from vanished civilizitions and dead languages, that lost, unreal world of dead ends and misleading signs. Theirs is an art of illusion, of allusion, of substituting one signifier for another, of meaning within meaning, interpretations that keep revealing another hidden and locked within, like nesting dolls or the paradoxical never-ending horizon of an Escher painting. In addition, such conditions and confusions impact not just on the way in which we approach the texts we translate – or the poems or novels or plays we create from or through them – but also on how we approach the work of others, how we formulate our own judgments and analyses, our own reception of their new texts. How we evaluate what is right or wrong.

1 R. Kapuściński, *Travels with Herodotus* (London, 2007), p. 142.

Clearly, as is often pointed out,[2] there are issues of responsibility towards monolingual, non-practitioner readers, who might well expect a level of linguistic competence. This is particularly seen to be the case with dead languages, such as Latin and ancient Greek, in which translation is often the only gateway through which a reader might enter not only a particular work but an entire culture – fragmented, unknowable, it seems, to all but its dedicated scholars. As one literary critic recently argued: 'if students are to become reliant on English versions of Ancient texts then they should be the best possible interpretations of that culture at all levels of translation, from the textual through the contextual to the cultural'.[3]

Yet for classical translators, working on reconstructed ancient worlds, the difficulty lies in deciding which culture, or rather which version of it, to interpret. Or even, given the tenuous and often fragmentary survival of many of its great works, which text.[4] For in such tenuous circumstances, how can they carry the burden of providing the unambiguous and indisputable interpretations that might often be assumed or demanded? As Clive Scott has argued 'we are wrong to allow literary translation to be [...] designed for readers who are ignorant of the source language', which, he believes, not only endows the translator with too much unquestioned authority but ignores reader-response theories, 'producing a translated text without really knowing what constitutes a proper use of the reader's intelligence and imagination'.[5]

Nevertheless, the question 'Whose Classics?' might seem arcane today. Can classical subjects be deemed to belong to anyone any more? Or is it the case that, with available classical education often confined to public, fee-paying schools, they are once again, as in previous centuries, the domain of wealth and privilege?[6] Yet the same vital questions remain: what sort of sense of ownership do we feel towards such canonical works, the bedrock of western cultural history? How do we go about protecting any such ownership? And how might we set about appropriating it? Who decides – or how might one decide – the means by which we read such texts, both in their original, filtered through scholarly commentaries and critical apparatus, or in translation, filtered through the literary, ideological and personal channel of their translator?

Even in these times of shrinking Classics departments and disappearing school syllabi, such issues are still contentious. Peter Green, the acclaimed trans-

2 See, for instance, A. Lefevere, *Translation, rewriting and the manipulation of literary fame* (London, 1992), pp 49–50; p. 90. **3** S. Smith, 'Accessibility: a Catullus for now?', *Poetry Review*, 95:1 (2005), 98–102 at 98–100. **4** See J. Balmer, 'What comes next: reconstructing the classics' in S. Bassnett & P. Bush (eds), *The translator as writer* (London, 2006), pp 184–95 at pp 188–9. **5** C. Scott 'Our engagement with literary translation', *In Other Words*, 32 (2008), 16–29 at 16–17. **6** See F. Waquet, *Latin or the empire of a sign: from the sixteenth to the twentieth centuries* (London, 2001).

lator of Latin poetry, has deemed classical translation – his own art – to be no more than 'crutches for those who cannot read the original'. To Green, the relatively new discipline of translation studies constitutes no more than 'post-structural efforts to boost [translation's] status'.[7]

On the other hand, a younger generation of scholars have questioned classical scholarship's traditional emphasis on philology over literary-textual analysis and theory; as Thomas Van Nortwick points out, 'anxiety about standards can be a device for hoarding power'. Acting on Van Nortwick's plea for classical works to have 'significance beyond the museum',[8] many scholars have embraced contemporary reception studies, as in Edith Hall's 2008 *The return of Ulysses*, which presents a cultural history of Homer's *Odyssey* from Attic tragedy through Cavafy and Joyce to the films of the Coen Brothers. Yet many still perceive it to be the solemn duty of classicists and classical translators to protect such sacred ancient works against the onslaughts of dumbed-down contemporary popular culture. Take, for example, this critical appraisal of a recent classical translation from the British journal *Poetry Review*:

> [the volume] [...] crosses the boundary from creative representation to a dangerously twisted caricature [...] moving it away from its cultural roots, crushing it into a shape that resembles its own [...] [it] fulfils all the accessibility criteria whilst failing those of authenticity. It is an indictment of where we are now and a weakness of our own literary culture [...][9]

I have to admit here that the volume in question was my own 2004 translation of Catullus' shorter poems, *Poems of love and hate*. I had thought my versions fairly conservative, at least alongside other radical reworkings such as Louis and Celia Zukovsky's 1969 'phonic' interpretations or even Peter Whigham's free verse versions for Penguin Classics in 1966. And certainly the reviewer here admitted to approving of my translations themselves. What had invoked his fury, however, was my decision to reorder the traditional – if often controversial – numbering of Catullus' poems, from an arrangement by metre in the surviving fourteenth-century manuscripts, to one by theme, as well as my use of section and poem headings.

I was in good company. When Ezra Pound's *Homage to Sextus Propertius* first appeared in 1919, containing radical versions and re-workings of the Roman elegiac poet, one distinguished American classicist declared that 'if Mr Pound

7 P. Green, *Ovid: the poems of exile* (London, 1994), p. viii. **8** T. Van Nortwick, 'Who do I think I am?' in J. Hallett & T. Van Nortwick (eds), *Compromising traditions* (London, 1997), pp 16–24 at p. 22. **9** S. Smith, 'Accessibility', 12.

were a professor of Latin there would be nothing left for him but suicide', while another critic accused his work of being 'so changed and twisted that hardly a shadow of the original Propertius has a chance to emerge'. It was as if, as J.P. Sullivan notes in his fascinating study of Pound's work, '*Homage* were the only translation of Propertius in English and the reader were in danger of being cheated'.[10]

Meanwhile Pound himself, Sullivan reports, appears to have felt so battered by such adverse reaction to the work that he began to insist it should no longer be termed a 'translation'.[11] More recently, Ted Hughes' 1997 version of Ovid's *Metamorphoses* in *Tales from Ovid*, whilst highly-praised in most quarters, was attacked by some classical scholars, including Peter Green, for its condensing and restructuring of its original source, not to mention Hughes' use of Poundian anachronisms. Ironically, the work was also the subject of some controversy when it was short-listed for – and later won – that year's Whitbread Poetry Prize, as translations were normally ineligible.[12]

We are faced with the problem of the Scythian gifts, with the issues of perception and interpretation. To return to Catullus' poetry, I had felt fairly agnostic about its textual ordering, adopted from Renaissance editions, themselves copies of copies of a single surviving manuscript that had turned up in Verona – the poet's home city – in the fourteenth century, and then almost as mysteriously disappeared again. I was not alone in my scepticism; in 1934 A.L. Wheeler had concluded not only that the collection as we have it today could not have been put together until after Catullus' death but also that its arrangement 'has greatly obscured the poet's own purposes and methods'.[13] Later, in 1999, John Godwin more cautiously noted that if the poems do appear to be ordered with care, then we still cannot be sure who was responsible for that ordering.[14] Most recently, in 2010, J.L. Butrica argued that the Catullus manuscript represents 'one man's Catullus [...] simply whatever the Verona codex happened to contain'.[15]

My aim, as with my previous translations of Sappho and other classical women poets, had been, on the one hand, to maintain the poems' archaic mysteriousness – a sense of their textual difficulties – while, at the same time, enabling the general poetry reader both to engage with and also to embrace that strangeness.[16]

10 See J.P. Sullivan, *Ezra Pound and Sextus Propertius: a study in creative translation* (London, 1964), pp 6–7, 11. **11** Ibid., p.11. **12** See J. Balmer, 'Forget Homer: salute the translator', *New Statesman*, 21 Feb. 1997. **13** A.L. Wheeler, *Catullus and the traditions of ancient poetry* (Berkeley, 1934), pp 5–6. **14** J. Godwin (ed.), *Catullus: the shorter poems* (Warminster, 1999), p. 19. **15** J.L. Butrica, 'History and transmission of the text' in M. Skinner (ed.), *A companion to Catullus* (London, 2007), pp 13–34 at p. 24. **16** See J. Balmer, *Catullus: poems of love and hate* (Newcastle upon Tyne, 2004), pp 24–7.

To this end, I decided to employ such strategies as juxtaposition and recontextualizition, grouping the poems by theme, as I had done with my previous translation of Sappho, minimizing the need for repetitive explanations and helping to fix an impression of the poems' intricate web of references, not to mention its diverse cast of picaresque characters: the refined Suffenus who writes poetry with all the sophistication of a 'goat-milker', Egnatius who cleans his teeth in the alarming 'Spanish' manner, Rufus with his goat-like armpits or Arrius and his endless haspirated haitches. In addition, I used section and poem headings – what the poet Don Paterson has called 'small mnemonic handles' – again to aid readers, and allow them to leave the volume's inevitable footnotes as optional rather than essential reading.[17]

But to many others, the ordering of Catullus' poetry represents something else, something more, a precious connection to Catullus' own hand, his poetic will, a tenuous, perhaps almost mystical, link to the Roman poet himself, hanging by a thread as the barbarians – of time and change and even of 'accessibility' – advance, cutting off the classical past, perhaps forever. In other words, we can all receive the Scythian gifts but, like Darius and his advisors, we read them in very different ways. As Yeats wrote of his dry Catullan Scholars, long-divorced from their subject's youthful virility: 'Lord, what would they say/ Did their Catullus walk that way?'[18]

Of course, in any appropriation of a source poet's work, the framing of the target volume becomes crucial, not just internally but, as discussed above, in its external context as well, in the way in which it is positioned for its target audience.[19] Anne Carson's radical rewritings of Catullus often reduce the original source text to one or two base elements as, for example, in her version of poem 70, in which the last eight lines read as follows: 'River/ River/ River/ River/ River/ River/ River/ River river river river river river river'.[20]

Clearly this approach can prove more palatable when framed within a poetry collection such as Carson's 2000 volume *Men in the off hours* than they would do in a Loeb dual text or a Penguin Classics edition. Nevertheless this might be merely a matter of perception. As Carson has commented of her Catulluses: 'they bear about the same relationship to translation as Francis Bacon's paintings do to mug shots. He says they are very close.'[21] Indeed, when working on my own versions of Catullus in *Poems of love and hate* – positioned

17 D. Paterson, *Orpheus: a version of Rilke* (London, 2006), p. 78. **18** W.B. Yeats, *The poems*, ed. A.N. Jeffares (London, 1989), p. 243. **19** Lefevere, *Translation, rewriting and the manipulation of literary fame*, pp 11–25. **20** A. Carson, *Men in the off hours* (London, 2000), p. 41. See also J. Balmer, 'Subverting the national: the classical model', *In Other Words*, 22 (2004), 37–42 at 38–40. **21** Carson quoted by J. Haig Gaisser in *Catullus in English* (London, 2001), p. 252.

by its publisher Bloodaxe as a literate yet 'standard' verse translation for the general poetry-reading public – Carson's versions proved invaluable, like detailed studies of a small corner of an old master painting, serving to underscore the artistry and technique of the whole.

There is also a further similarity between Carson's versions of Catullus and my own: they are both written by women. For Catullus is not a poet that many women have chosen to engage with, at least not in English; in Julia Haig Gaisser's 2001 anthology, *Catullus in English*, only five out of more than 100 translators are women. This is hardly surprising, perhaps, given the threat of sexual violence implicit in much of Catullus' verse, often expressed in scatological Roman street slang. In addition, his frequently foul-mouthed rage against his female (and indeed male) lovers have often alienated readers; 'as for the women, let's try to define them', muses poem 97, 'they would lick the arse of diarrhoead hangmen'.[22] To Harold Nicolson, reading Quentin Hogg's translations in 1957, such poems were 'vindictive, venomous and full of obscene malice'.[23] More recently, women have begun to approach such work as textual editors or commentators,[24] but still rarely with the creative and empathetic response required of a poetry translation. So how does a woman reader/poet/translator engage with such work, let alone appropriate it for herself? As we have seen, Carson's solution is the systematic breakdown of Catullus' verse form. For myself, the answer lay more in the semantic tone of my translations – a form of dramatic irony.

In poem 110, for example, Catullus attacks a treacherous prostitute who, having promised him sexual favours then later withdraws them – a betrayal he describes in terms of a legal crime or an outrage. My version, however, looks to a very different source, the teasing innuendo of English Music Hall tradition or even the saucy, seaside postcard – bawdy, yes, but stripped of sexual menace:

> Obliging girls, Aufillena, are always prized,
> they do what they say and they reap their reward;
> but you've lost my favour: you promised and you lied,
> doing something wrong but doing nothing untoward [...][25]

Similarly, poem 32, in which the poet is trying to arrange an afternoon assignment with Ipsitilla, ends with a sexual pun centred on *pransus*, originally a military metaphor which meant 'having breakfasted (or lunched)' and also, since soldiers march on their stomachs, 'ready for action' – in all senses. In addition, the

22 Balmer, *Catullus*, p. 91. **23** Quoted by T.P. Wiseman, *Catullus and his world* (Cambridge, 1988), p. 240. **24** See L. & P. Watson, *Martial: select epigrams* (Cambridge, 2003), E. Gowers, *Horace: satires I* (Cambridge, 2012) and A. Richlin, *The garden of Priapus: sexuality and aggression in Roman humor* (New Haven, 1983). **25** Balmer, *Catullus*, p. 51

poet is *satur,* 'full' and *pertundo tunicamque palliumque,* literally 'boring through both cloak and tunic'. To translate such jokes in kind, it was necessary to adopt Octavio Paz's mimetic approach rather than a mere semantic one: 'just say you're game, just say you will/ you see, I've eaten, had my fill,/ yet still my lunchbox is bulging'.[26] It might be a high-risk strategy to employ contemporary euphemisms or colloquialisms in a translation of ancient poetry. Yet Catullus himself borrowed his own age's slang – or invented new usage of his own.[27] 'Lunchbox' first appeared in the 1990s, as a term for 'an area of man's anatomy accentuated when he wears tight shorts'.[28] My English might seem less violent than Catullus' Latin. And compared to those of other male translators such as Peter Green in 2005 ('I'm full, flat on my back and bursting/ up, up, up, through undershirts and bedclothes'),[29] my solution is more flippant, less sexually threatening, more satirical than overtly hostile, more emasculating. As I noted in my preface to the volume: 'perhaps, as a woman, I could not take Catullus' belligerent posturing so seriously. But then neither, one suspects, did Catullus.'[30]

At the same time as translating Catullus, the question of how to find new ways of interpreting and misappropriating classical texts – and perhaps also a 'safe' place to do so – led me to start work on a second volume, a volume of poetry, '*Chasing Catullus*', which was sub-titled '*poems, translations & transgressions*'. Here I wanted to explore further the relationship between translation and creative writing; to find new ways in which original and translation might interact; to present 'a journey into the border territory between poetry and translation'. As such, the volume offered a range of interpretative positions 'from straightforward translation to versions based on or inspired by an original as well as [...] "transgressions" – versions which shamelessly subvert a source text's original intent or meaning'.[31]

One such version, commissioned for the now defunct journal per*versions*, was 'Fresh meat', inspired by a textual interpolation in Homer *Iliad* 22 – that is, a later addition by a copyist or scribe, in itself an early form of a transgressional version. Here, as the Greek warrior Achilles and the Trojan champion Hector face each other in mortal combat, Hector debates suing for peace but, realizing the two were not 'young lovers exchanging confidences', he concludes that Achilles would kill him where he stood 'naked like a woman, when I had stripped off my armour'. I was struck by the sub-text of desire here between Hector and his Greek adversary, which turns traditional readings of the scene inside out:

26 Paz in E. Honig, *The poet's other voice: conversations on literary translation* (Amherst, 1985), p. 155; Balmer, *Catullus*, p. 50. **27** G.P. Goold, *Catullus* (London, 2001), p. 6. **28** D. Rowan, *Glossary for the nineties* (London, 1998), p. 23. **29** P. Green, *The poems of Catullus* (London, 2005), p. 79. **30** Balmer, ibid., p. 24. **31** Balmer, *Chasing Catullus* (Newcastle upon Tyne, 2004), pp 9–10

But we were warriors
not lovers lying side by side in hazy summer fields,
talking out our lives as dandelion or parsley seed
drifted down in search of former flower. And I knew – I knew
he would have killed me where I stood, naked and trembling, trapped
like a woman, when I had shed the armour from my skin [...][32]

Such transgressional approaches have clear precedents, most notably Pound's *Homage to Sextus Propertius*, while any recontextualistion of the *Iliad* must call to mind Michael Longley's inspirational versions, particularly his poem 'Ceasefire', collected in his 1995 volume *The ghost orchid*. In 'Fresh meat', I wanted to explore how translation and original could interact in ways that went beyond the standard imitation or the stray version in a 'poetry volume'. It was not just a case of 'free' translation. Rather, I wanted to create a version of the *Iliad* that could not exist without the classical translator's close knowledge and understanding of the original text and so could present a way of harnessing the dream world Kapuściński had found in Herodotus, unravelling its misleading signs, without diminishing their strangeness, their mysterious impact.

But, as in Herodotus, and indeed the *Iliad*, such gifts can also be dark and grief-laden. While I was working on *Chasing Catullus* my young niece became terminally ill. In the subsequent fog of bereavement, I found comfort in classical literature and its translation, which enabled me to articulate private or difficult events through the voices of classical myth and literary reference, a vocabulary through which I could say the unsayable. These poems later formed the central section, the dark heart of the collection, adopting the shape of a diary sequence. *De raptu Proserpinae*, for instance, is a short extract from Claudian's fifth century AD late Latin epic (3.231–44) based around the myth of the abduction of Proserpina by Hades, god of the Underworld: 'At first light she picked her flowers:/ the earth shivered with dew, violets slaked/ their new-born thirst'.[33] My fairly faithful version was remade into a new poem, recontextualized and appropriated, as with the Catullus translations of *Poems of love and hate*, by a new sub-title, '2/8: 6.47AM'. As in many other poems in the sequence, the act of appropriating these different classical 'selves' allowed me to communicate the horror of loss and grief without directly narrating it, providing, as Charles Beye has commented of classical scholarship, 'a place to hide', a slippage of self-construction and self-image.[34]

Again, as with Catullus and my previous translation volumes, juxtaposition played an important part, both in the structure of the collection and within

32 Ibid., p. 41. **33** Ibid., p. 28. **34** C. Beye, 'A Response' in Hallett & Van Nortwick (eds), *Compromising traditions*, pp 153–67 at p. 154.

individual poems. For instance, in the volume's sequence, *De raptu Proserpinae* is followed by an original poem, 'Demeter in Winter', harking back to the former's subject matter while offering a contemporary incarnation of the Greek corn goddess as she grieves for her lost daughter throughout an eternal winter: 'Then I have to know/ again how I could lose her, cell by cell,/ how she could slip away, how she could fade –/ that first uncertain fall of rain-washed snow.'[35]

For Pound such adopted voices were masks or 'personae', a means of speaking through another text.[36] Such poems not only translate but interact with their source text, re-enacting as well as voicing otherwise unapproachable or uncomfortable emotions such as grief or guilt. Here, translation becomes a part of the transformed poem's metaphoric landscape – or perhaps, as Charles Tomlinson expresses it, quoting Georges Braque: 'no longer concerned with metaphor but metamorphoses', transforming their objects, as Tomlinson continues 'into a less predictable, a more variously multi-faceted image'.[37] We are back to Herodotus' Scythian gifts again. As I noted in my Preface to *Chasing Catullus*, my aim in the collection had been not only 'to blur the distinction between original and translation, but to make it unimportant, until the reader – or even the writer – cannot distinguish between the two'.[38]

In my 2009 volume, *The word for sorrow*, I wanted to broaden the parameters of such metaphoric landscapes to give voice not just to private but wider national tragedies such as the carnage of the First World War. At the same time, rather than employing a variety of different source texts and authors as in *Chasing Catullus*, I was drawn to a single work, the Roman poet Ovid's harrowing exile poems *Tristia*, a work, which if often neglected by scholars, has proved enticing to poets such as Mandelstam or Brodsky and more recently also to the novelists David Malouf and Christoph Ransmayr.[39] For here, it seems, is the one instance where the mask of classical literary artifice slips to reveal the person behind the persona as Ovid details the heart-wrenching hardships and deprivations of an urbane poet exiled from Rome to the wintry Black Sea city of Tomis, at the end of his known world.

As the Preface to *The word for sorrow* describes, my own appropriation of *Tristia*, however, came about almost by chance: one rainy spring morning, I was working on the text using Perseus, Tufts' online classical library and resource, when an electrical storm forced me to log off. I turned to an old second-hand

35 Balmer, *Chasing Catullus*, p. 35. **36** Sullivan, *Ezra Pound and Sextus Propertius*, pp 24–34. **37** C. Tomlinson, *Metamorphoses: poetry and translation* (Manchester, 2003), p. 127. See also J. Balmer, 'Jumping their bones: translating, transgressing and creating' in S. Harrison (ed.), *Living Classics* (Oxford, 2009), pp 43–64 at pp 52–9. **38** Balmer, *Chasing Catullus*, pp 9–10. **39** See R. Lyne, 'Love and exile after Ovid' in P. Hardie (ed.), *The Cambridge companion to Ovid* (Cambridge, 2002), pp 288–300.

dictionary, bought at a summer fête as a school student. Here, as if for the first time, my eye was drawn to the name of its original owner, etched on the fly-leaf with a date, early in January 1900, 'dual initials', as I later wrote in the poem 'Hail', 'double-barrelled surname [...] scrawled in schoolboy boredom, thunder-stiff/ blood-brown ink, faint as an old man's vein [...]'.[40]

A subsequent Google search revealed that my dictionary's original owner had been posted to the Dardanelles (which, by coincidence, Ovid had just described crossing in the poem I had been translating). He had subsequently served in 1915 at Gallipoli (where an estimated 100,000 Allied and Turkish soldiers had lost their lives). And so *The word for sorrow* came into fruition, versions of Ovid's *Tristia* interspersed with original poems exploring the history of the old dictionary used to translate them – a work, like *Chasing Catullus*, exploring an interplay between translation and original poem, text and translator, affording ancient grief a modern resonance.

Ovid's grief, though, is trickier than most – impenetrable, mysterious, deliberately leading us, tongue firmly placed in cheek, into Kapuściński's 'landscape of dead ends and misleading signs'. So much so that some scholars even claim that his exile is an elaborate literary hoax, conjured up in the comfort of the poet's Italian country estate.[41] In order not just to convey but, again, to appropriate this irony – to distinguish my 'Ovid' from the Ovid of literary tradition, my own construct from that of the western canon – I referred to the Roman poet throughout by his cognomen 'Naso', the name he calls himself in his poetry.

And, as in *Chasing Catullus* and the translation volumes, each version is then reclaimed for the collection, recontextualized with often ironic new titles. For instance, Ovid's surely semi-comic description of Tomis in winter in *Tristia* 3.10 became 'Naso Sees Hell Freeze Over'. Or, again, 4.10, his famous autobiographical poem, became 'Naso's Back Story'. While 4.1, in which, like Darius' Persians, the poet finds himself taking up arms against wild eastern tribesmen, became 'Naso Sees Action'. For, providing his account of exile can be taken at face value, Ovid had more knowledge of the Scythians and their gifts than most Roman poets, as he describes them sweeping down on Tomis:

> Our fierce enemy brandish arrows dipped in venom,
> encircle the walls with snorting horse, breath frozen.
> Should we dare to leave our ramparts, venture out alone,
> they fall on us like wolves on sheep outside the fold [...]
> And if my Muse still dances to those same old tunes,

40 J. Balmer, *The word for sorrow* (Cambridge, 2009), pp xiii, 4. **41** See Gareth Williams' overview in Hardie, *The Cambridge companion to Ovid*, pp 233–48 at p. 235.

> I write for myself, read to myself: what else can I do? [...]
> Many lines are inscribed although all are condemned –
> still I send them home in the hope you will read them.[42]

The tension between irony and agony in *Tristia* is no doubt a factor in the work's subsequent troubled reception. Yet there was much to inspire here too. Ovid's lightness of touch, his constant changes in register from comedy to despair, were exactly what was required for my own poems too; letters home from soldiers in Gallipoli I had researched were full of the same sharp changes in tone, from horror one minute to jaunty, often inane, comments the next; making the best of it, not wanting to upset loved ones with too much reality.

As in *Chasing Catullus*, too, juxtapositions and pairings were crucial so that the poems, both new and translated, again formed a symbiotic relationship. For instance 'Naso Sees Action' is followed by an original poem, 'Welcome Note', in which my dictionary owner, wounded after battle, writes a letter home from hospital in Alexandria. The poem is loosely based on real letters by Gallipoli soldiers although Ovid himself also seeps into the text in the last stanza via the opening lines of *Tristia* 4.8 in which he mourns his own changed appearance: 'I looked in the mirror and hardly knew myself:/ an old man looking back, black hair bleached/ to white'.[43]

Alongside these parallel stories of Ovid – Naso – and my dictionary owner, there was also a third narrative. For just as Ovid's ironic poetic voice interposes itself into his narrative so could my own, offering a third story of discovery running like an undercurrent beneath, as I traced each story like a detective, offering something beyond a simple Gallipoli/Tomis or text/dictionary equation. Here the dictionary itself provided a leitmotif, decoding the past like a text. As I wrote in the poem 'Among the Graves, Green Hill', describing my visit to an overgrown and forgotten soldiers' cemetery on Gallipoli:

> I wish now I'd spoken out, roll-called the names,
> taken one small thing, at least, home to Gloucs:
> rosemary sprig to dry, daisy or phlox to press
> between **calamitas.** *hurt* and *healed*. **consanatus.**[44]

Ovid himself is harder to decode – tricky, sinuous, he slips through the fingers like sand whenever we try to pin him down. We will never know if we can believe his descriptions of winter exile in *Tristia* 3.10 – the dolphins caught mid-leap beneath the frozen seas, for instance, reminding us now of Virginia

42 Balmer, *The word for sorrow*, p. 32. **43** Ibid., p. 33. **44** Ibid., p. 21.

Woolf's satirical description of the Great Frost in *Orlando*. Or his insistence, as 3.14 claims, that his Latin is now 'Scythian-scarred [...] quivers with barbarian'.[45] Similarly in Herodotus, the Persian king Darius never discovers the truth about his own gifts from the barbarians. As the two armies line up against each other, the Scythians start chasing a passing hare before they will engage in battle, a humiliating show of disdain for the Persians. That night, under cover of darkness, a rattled Darius orders his troops to retreat. And the mystery of the Scythian gifts is never solved. For Herodotus, the point of interest was not so much what these unfathomable signs might mean as in the fact that they vary so much from culture to culture, world to world. What mattered to him was not interpretation but difference.

And if with projects such as *Chasing Catullus* or *The word for sorrow,* there is always the risk of being accused of ransacking ancient literature like a grave robber – taking 'their' Classics, editing them, paring them down, gutting them, transgressing them, perverting them, turning them upside down, making them accessible or contemporary, making them even stranger – then such assaults are nothing new. Throughout the centuries from Golding, Jonson, Dryden, Pope through to Pound, Heaney, Harrison, Logue, Longley, and Hughes, such appropriations have helped us to appreciate, if not always understand, the mysterious poetic landscape of the ancient world. Its strangeness. Its difference.

Meanwhile, the text is certainly strong enough to withstand such assaults. For through each new reading, each new re-writing, our classical sources only gain in stature, transformed again as they have been so many times, into a new and different work, a net to catch each dream-like reading which might sag but never breaks. As Kapuściński concludes of Herodotus: 'The past does not exist. There are only infinite recordings of it'.[46] And so we can embrace the difference between us; the different signs we might read in the same texts, the different choices we might make in their subsequent interpretation, the different gifts we all might receive. For throughout the centuries, these various, multi-faceted translations – and appropriations – of classical texts have fed the imagination – fluid, dynamic, performing an act of critical resuscitation, breathing new life into ancient works like a necromancer. In addition, as I discovered for myself, by transforming the text, the translator, too, can be transformed as a writer, finding her own voice by re-voicing those of the past. As Raphael Lyne astutely comments of *Tristia*, the 'appeal of the exile persona may be that it enables writers to express both the problems they have which parallel Ovid's, and the sense of separation that they have from their source'.[47] As Lyne suggests, such source

45 Ibid., p. 27. **46** Kapuściński, *Travels with Herodotus*, p. 262. **47** Lyne, 'Love and exile after Ovid', p. 298.

texts can both entrap us and set us free. In Clive Scott's words: 'each entry into the text is likely to produce new configurations of the text's space and time'.[48] As *The word for sorrow*'s title poem concludes:

> We are all translating the same story
> search same words in same thesaurus.
> What drives us on, keeps us to our path,
> in every version is not gain but loss.[49]

48 Scott, 'Our engagement with literary translation', p. 26. **49** Balmer, *The word for sorrow*, p. 47.

Translator, writer, and wronged? Milena Jesenská unconstructed

Michelle Woods

Milena Jesenská and Franz Kafka were lovers for six months although they only met twice; once in Vienna and once in the border town of Gmünd. Their affair began in April 1920 when Jesenská wrote to Kafka regarding a story of his that she was translating into Czech, beginning a blizzard of letters over the summer months that became a scene of what Elizabeth Boa defines as 'textual intercourse'.[1] Following Kafka's death in 1924, Jesenská wrote to Kafka's executor, Max Brod, requesting that he 'please make sure my letters which belonged to Franz are burned; I trust you will do so, though of course this is nothing important'.[2] What survives are only Kafka's letters to Jesenská (Brod omitting to burn Kafka's work on his request), which were published in 1952 as *Letters to Milena*, and in a revised edition in 1990. Much has been made of Jesenská's connection with Kafka – she is the subject of numerous biographies – but almost nothing has been written about her role as the first translator of Kafka's work, and, importantly, the translator of his work into his other native tongue, Czech.[3] This may be because translation itself has been regarded as 'a secondary art' (as another of Kafka's translators, Edwin Muir, put it), but also because critical interest in Jesenská has focused on Kafka's construct of her in his writing, thereby concentrating on her as a love interest rather than on her work.[4]

In this essay, I want to suggest that Jesenská the translator has been wronged, deliberately, in order to further a critical *idée fixe* which makes her merely a textual construct in Kafka's eyes. I want to do so by suggesting that the abundant physical imagery in the letters is not just a metonymic escape from a physical relationship on Kafka's part, but an articulation of Jesenská's linguistic re-embodiment of Kafka's stories and the physical transformation of his stories

1 Elizabeth Boa, *Kafka: gender, class, and race in the letters and fictions* (Oxford, 1996), p. 62. **2** Franz Kafka, *Letters to Milena* (New York, 1990), p. 252. **3** The three biographies are: Margarete Buber-Neumann's *Kafkas Freundin Milena* (Munich, 1963); Jana Černá's *Adresát Milena Jesenská* (Prague, 1969; English translation by Gerald Turner London, 1988); and Mary Hockaday's *Kafka, love and courage* (New York, 1995). The two novels are Maggie Ross' *Milena* (London, 1983), and Alina Reyes' *Nus devant les fantômes* (Paris, 2000). **4** Edwin & Willa Muir, 'Translating from the German' in *On translation*, ed. R. Brower (New York, 1996), pp 93–6 at p. 93.

from one language (Prague German) to another (Czech, written by a Czech in exile in Vienna). This linguistic re-embodiment of Kafka's language highlights Jesenská as a translator rather than merely a textual construct, a translator who was central to Kafka's thinking on language and identity and who was herself an embodied agent in the early dissemination of his work.

During the period of their affair, Jesenská published the first Czech translations of 'The stoker' ('Topič'), as well as selections from the 1913 story collection, *Contemplation*, including 'Being unhappy' ('Nešt'astný'), 'The sudden walk' ('Náhlá procházka'), 'The excursion into the mountains' ('Výlet do hor'), 'The plight of the bachelor' ('Neštěstí mládence'), 'The businessman' ('Kupec'), 'The way home' ('Cesta domů'), 'The men running past' ('Ti, kteří běží mimo'), as well as 'A report to an academy' ('Zpráva pro akademii') in the Czech literary magazines, *Kmen* and *Tribuna*. In 1923 she published her translation of 'The judgment' ('Soud').[5] She also translated *The Trial* and *Metamorphosis* and intended to publish these, alongside *Contemplation* and 'The Stoker' in a book with S.K.Neumann's imprint Edice Červen, but the publication never transpired.[6] In June 1924 she wrote an obituary of Kafka for the Prague daily *Národní listy*, in which she noted that 'few people knew him' in Czechoslovakia, underscoring the importance of her translations, as they were an introduction to Kafka's work for the Czech-speaking majority of his homeland (published two years after Czechoslovak independence from the Austro-Hungarian Empire). Confident of his literary importance, she assured readers in her obituary that Kafka had 'written the most significant books of modern German literature'.[7]

By that time, Jesenská was by far the better known of the two in Prague. She translated widely for various papers, not only translating Kafka, but also Franz Werfel, Leo Tolstoy, G.K. Chesterton, Gustave Flaubert and Rosa Luxemburg, among others. Her *feuilletons* from Vienna for *Tribuna* had begun her career as a groundbreaking female journalist; her articles on women's issues in *Národní listy* constituted an influential public voice for the newly emancipated generation of Czech women. Following the Nazi invasion of Czechoslovakia in 1938, she wrote courageous anti-Nazi articles in the political paper, *Přítomnost*; when that paper was banned she wrote for and distributed an underground paper, *V Boj*. Arrested in 1939, she was deported to Ravensbrück concentration camp, and died there in 1944. After the war, a fellow inmate contacted Jesenská's teenage daughter, and, when she came to visit, brought evidence that

5 See: *Kmen* (Prague) 4 (1920) Nr. 6 (Apr. 22), 61–72; *Tribuna* (Prague) 2 (1920) Nr. 166 (July 16), 1–2; *Kmen* 4 (1920) Nr. 26 (Sept. 9), 308–10; *Tribuna* 2 (1920) Nr. 227 (Sept. 26), 1–4; *Cesta* (Prague) 5 (1922/23) Nr. 26/27 (Dec./Jan. 1923), 369–72. **6** Kafka, *Letters to Milena,* p. 250. **7** Ibid., p. 271.

Jesenská had died in the camp. 'On the table before my eyes lay a piece of her body,' Černá wrote in her memoir of her mother, 'a segment of her smile, a part of the mouth that had once talked to me'.[8] All that was left of Milena Jesenská was a tooth.

The physical metonym of Jesenská is emblematic of her absence in reconstructions of her. The 'many white spaces' in her biography have given rise to 'guesses and gossip' about her that have established a 'Milena myth',[9] but most striking of all, in the numerous biographies and memoirs of her, is the short shrift given to her translation work, and the overall sense that, as Marta Marková-Kotyková writes, Kafka was not interested in her translations of his work and did not comment on them.[10]

The given critical assumption is that Kafka was more interested in his fantasy of the famously beautiful Jesenská and that he deliberately constructed a textual 'Milena' to satisfy his own needs.[11] Kafka, Elizabeth Boa writes, 'treats Milena as an inner aspect of himself' and in doing so, 'Kafka refused Milena a voice'.[12] In a similar Freudian analysis, Hartmut Böhme argues that the letters should 'be regarded more as a highly condensed association between Kafka and his inner objects than as an act of genuine communication' adding that the 'real, rarely seen, distant Milena is the projection screen for K's narcissistic neurosis: "Mother Milena" as he writes, "nothing more, silence, deep forest"'.[13] For Böhme, Jesenská represents the 'narcissistic longing for an archaic mother'.[14]

Such assumptions tend to read the *Letters* as they have come down to us, without Jesenská's replies and with the silence that now implies, rather than as Kafka's responses to actual letters and to an actual woman, his translator. Kafka, in fact, explicitly addresses the problematics of constructing another's identity. 'I can't talk about some Milena in Vienna' Kafka writes to Jesenská, 'and then go on saying that "she" thinks and says and does this or that. After all, you are neither "Milena" nor "she" – that's utter nonsense – and consequently I can't say a thing. This is so obvious it doesn't even make me sad'.[15] The wry humour, 'it doesn't even make me sad', enunciates a deliberate ludic engagement in the *Letters,* often connected to physical images (true also of Kafka's fiction) of mouths, lips, hands, faces and the voice. There is a flirtation but the 'textual intercourse' does not construct an objectifying fantasy of 'Milena'; rather, it physicalizes their actual link through language and through translation. Kafka is

8 Černá, *Milena Jesenská* (1988), p. 17. **9** Alena Wagnerová, *Milena Jesenská* (Prague, 1996), p. 188. **10** Ibid., p. 52. **11** Julian Preece, 'The letters and diaries' in Julian Preece (ed.), *The Cambridge companion to Kafka* (Cambridge, 2002), pp 111–30 at p. 111. **12** Boa, *Kafka: gender, class, and race,* pp 87–8. **13** Hartmut Böhme, 'Mother Milena: on Kafka's narcissism' in Angel Flores (ed.), *The Kafka debate: new perspectives for our time* (New York, 1977), pp 80–99 at pp 84, 88. **14** Ibid., p. 88. **15** Kafka, *Letters to Milena,* p. 104.

interested in Jesenská's language, in her translation and her re-embodiment of his prose in the Czech language.

Kafka's self-awareness of the propensity to construct the image of an other via language and via our own needs and desires allows a space from which we can see the professional Jesenská, who, as a translator, was negotiating her own identity in exile in Vienna through both the Czech and German languages. Forced to translate out of financial need, she chose an author much admired by her husband, Ernst Pollak. After causing a huge scandal in Prague by having an affair with Pollak, a German-speaking Jew, who was part of the *Prager Kreise*, she married Pollak and left for Vienna. The marriage was a deeply unhappy one, with Jesenská isolated on the fringes of the literary Viennese café circles, dismissed as Pollak's young Czech wife and viewed as 'lost', 'foreign', and 'on the periphery'.[16] Jesenská spoke little or no German when she arrived in Vienna (Pollak, like Kafka, spoke Czech), and may have been aided in her initial translations by Pollak, and later, by her lover, Count Schaffgotsch. But translation allowed her, in a city where she felt culturally and linguistically alienated, to return home via the Czech language, albeit from a changed perspective. Her ventures into translating German-speaking Czech writers, such as Kafka, but also Franz Werfel, allowed a negotiation of the linguistic identities – both Czech and German – that she faced daily.

Both Kafka and Jesenská were interested in the physical presence and causalities of language, or, to be more precise, in the meeting of languages and the effect this has on identity. The discourse in the *Letters*, though handed down to us as a one-sided correspondence, suggests an identification between the two through language at its abstract and physical (in terms of sound and sight) borders. Thinking of Jesenská as not simply an invention of Kafka's, a satiation of his needs for both intimacy and distance, allows us to view her, and him, as negotiatiors of identities through language, giving us a more nuanced calibration of Jesenská's identity as a woman and a translator in life and in Kafka's prose than critics have supposed. The repeated physical imagery that I will analyse here – of hands, mouth, blood and voice – provides a discourse on translation that is intimately connected to questions of identity and how it is constructed and deconstructed by the use of language.

HANDS

Kafka plays with, and subverts, the traditional asymmetric relationship between the author and the translator, focusing on the issue of fidelity and dominance,

16 Wagnerová, p. 75.

imbued as these are also with patriarchal underpinnings, 'the gendering of translation by [the] language of paternalism' with translations seen as the passive, feminized text which 'like women, should either be beautiful or faithful'.[17] In response to the translations Jesenská sends him, Kafka confronts fidelity and dominance head-on, sexualizing his discourse, but with a wry humour that enables him both to praise fidelity, imagine Jesenská as a kind of dominatrix and place himself as the lead guide through his prose, but at the same time to undermine these images. In his letter of 30 May 30 1920, he writes: 'What is particularly beautiful about your translation, that it is faithful', but he quickly adds 'go ahead and scold me on account of this "faithful"' suggesting that both of them realize the frailty of the term. He then goes on:

> I know you can do everything, but maybe you scold best of all. I'd like to be your pupil just so you would constantly scold me; I'm sitting at my desk, scarcely daring to look up, you are bent over me and your index finger is glittering in the air, finding fault, isn't this the way it is?[18]

Kafka evinces this sexual fantasy, with her embodied index finger, but he also places her – the translator – in a position of dominance and continues to suggest her role in the translation process as the one who will bring his language elsewhere. He continues:

> As I was saying, your translation is faithful, and I have the feeling that I'm taking you by the hand through the story's subterranean passages, gloomy, low, ugly, almost endless (that's why the sentences are almost endless, didn't you realize that?), almost endless (only two months, you say?) hopefully in order to have the good sense to disappear into the daylight at the exit.[19]

Here, Kafka, gets to the heart of his stylistic aesthetic, and does so with humour, adding the parentheses to lengthen his thought as a kind of pastiche both of his work and his falling in love (the wry, heartsick 'only two months, you say', being the length of their relationship to date). More importantly, though he leads her 'by the hand' he sees Jesenská's translation as bringing his work out of the cave – in which case, her translation is an illumination of his work – or up from the underworld, with Kafka as a Tiresias figure and Jesenská

17 Lori Chamberlain, 'Gender and the metaphorics of translation' in L. Venuti (ed.), *Rethinking translation: discourse, subjectivity, ideology* (New York, 1992), pp 57–74 at p. 59 and Sherry Simon, *Gender in translation: cultural identity and the politics of transmission* (New York, 1996), p. 10. **18** Kafka, *Letters to Milena*, p. 20. **19** Ibid., pp 20–1.

as Odysseus – in which case, her translation might be a homecoming of sorts; Kafka's German text made Czech. Importantly, Kafka passes his texts to Jesenská, allowing her to bring them 'into the daylight at the exit'. The physical translations are a mode of contact: 'Please send me the translation,' Kafka writes, 'I can't get my hands on enough of you' and he insists, elsewhere, on 'holding on to the translation for a little while'.[20] In another letter, he asks: 'Won't you reach out across these stories to me, and leave your hand with me for a long, long time?'[21]

MOUTH

The passages quoted above come directly after Kafka writes about the insecurity of Jewish identity – again using physical terms, [Jews] 'believe they possess only whatever they hold in their hands or grip between their teeth' because of their 'insecure position' and he tells her about the racism experienced by his sister, Ottla, who married a non-Jew, Joseph David. One of David's relatives warns him not to marry a Jew, citing Jesenská's unhappy marriage to Ernst Pollak, a German Jew, as an example of what the Jews are like.[22] The well-born and famously beautiful Jesenská eloped to Vienna with Pollak and was disowned by her father because she crossed cultural and religious lines. The notion of sexual and racial impurity shares a sense of cultural impurity from both the move to Vienna and the move to another language, particularly German. Prague was strictly divided between linguistic communities and Jesenská's father, a Czech nationalist, would have regarded this as a betrayal. That Jesenská became a translator may not be surprising as the profession is 'haunted by a hermeneutics of suspicion that would see interpreters as dubious cultural transgressors' because translators 'are a disruptive presence in that their return to their native language has the capacity to unsettle that language'.[23]

In the postscript to the 20 May letter, Kafka dwells on one of Jesenská's questions, pertaining to his identity; she had asked whether he was Jewish. He directly associates the import of the question to the Czech language in which it is asked:

> Milena is still going on about anxiety, striking my chest or asking: *jste žid*? [are you a Jew?] which in Czech has the same movement and sound. Don't you see how the fist is pulled back at the word 'jste,' so as

20 Ibid., pp 108 and 137. **21** Ibid., p. 116. **22** Ibid., p. 20. **23** Michael Cronin, *Across the lines: travel, language, translation* (Cork, 2000), pp 75, 65.

to gain muscle power? And then in the word 'žid' the happy blow, flying unerringly forward? The Czech language often produces such side effects on the German ear.[24]

Kafka embodies the Czech language and in doing so estranges it; it is Czech heard not only to the German ear, but to the German Jewish ear, for whom Czech is the language of the domicile. He then focuses on another word that she had used: *nechápu* [I don't understand], writing:

> A strange word in Czech and even in your mouth it is so severe, so callous, cold-eyed, stingy, and most of all like a nutcracker, pronouncing it requires three consecutive cracks of the jaw or, more exactly, the first syllable makes an attempt at holding the nut, in vain, the second syllable then tears the mouth wide open, the nut now fits inside, where it is finally cracked by the third syllable, can you hear the teeth?[25]

By focusing on the physicality of the word, concerned with the issue of non-understanding, Kafka again highlights its foreignness and strangeness – the word is strange in its own domestic language, and 'even' in Jesenská's mouth. Kafka peppers his letters, written in German, with Jesenská's Czech words, the remnants of what we have from their dialogue; the placing of these words in his discourse also appears to be a testing out of the language, appearing to savour it just as his stories are being transferred into Czech. Jesenská began her correspondence writing in German but Kafka asked her to change language 'because, after all, you do belong to that language, because only there can Milena be found in her entirety (the translation confirms this).'[26]

Kafka locates Jesenská's identity in the Czech language but also in the Czech language of her translations of his work; at the place where the languages meet. However he also enjoys her estranging of the German language: 'most of the time [your German] is amazing' he writes 'and on those occasions when it does falter, the German language becomes pliant just for you, of its own accord, and then it is particularly beautiful, something even a German doesn't hope for; a German wouldn't dare write so personally'.[27] In another letter, 'I have never lived among German people,' Kafka writes, 'German is my mother tongue and therefore natural to me, but Czech feels to me far more intimate, which is why your letter dispels many an uncertainty, I see you clearer, the movements of your body, your hands, so quick, so determined, it's almost a meeting'.[28] Kafka's reference to his own unstable identity – as a German-speaking Jew in a now

24 Ibid., p. 21. **25** Ibid. **26** Ibid., p. 8. **27** Ibid. **28** Ibid., p. 14.

officially dominantly Czech-speaking capital (Prague, after Czechoslovak independence in 1918) – and to Jesenská's – a Czech speaker writing from an old German-speaking capital (Vienna, the capital of the newly defunct Austro-Hungarian empire), married to a Jew – allows a common ground in writing, where there is 'almost a meeting'. The two of them, in other words, are already living translated lives; living in one language, *writing in one language*, and surviving in another. Jesenská, for Kafka, is only fully present in Czech, but even then her identity is elusive: 'almost a meeting,' he writes, 'although when I try to raise my eyes to your face, then in the flow of the letter – what a story! – fire breaks out and I see nothing but fire!'[29]

BLOOD

In a letter on 20 June Kafka brings up a scandal involving his friend Willy Haas and his lover and suggests that the outrage over the affair feeds into stereotypes of cannibalistic Jews: 'that the Jews are necessarily bound to fall upon you Christians, just as predatory animals are bound to murder'.[30] He comes back to the imagery when defending Brod's Zionism to Jesenská, arguing that both Brod and Kafka have to construct their homeland, that it is constantly on their minds even as they write 'the book which you will translate', pointing to her role in helping to construct a new homeland, a new identity.[31] He then imagines her working and employs the cannibalistic stereotype: 'I see you bent over your work, your neck bared, I'm standing behind you, but you don't know it – please don't be frightened if you feel my lips on the back of your neck'.[32] The faintly vampiric imagery of Kafka leaning over towards her neck, unseen, again subverts the notion of the translator somehow feeding off the original work; here, the author needs the translator, both sexually, but also suggestively in literary terms – the translation is the new blood of the work, as Walter Benjamin argued, its 'afterlife'. Kafka uses this imagery himself; finally reading her translation of 'Unhappiness', he writes:

> I'm not even concerned about what's inside, but I hear the voice, my voice! [...] I don't know how it happens, after all I only read it with my eyes, so how did my blood find out so quickly, so quickly that my veins are already hot from circulating its words?[33]

Elsewhere in the letters physical blood permeates the prose in the spectre of Kafka's tuberculosis and his concern over Jesenská also being ill in the summer

29 Ibid. **30** Ibid., p. 51. **31** Ibid., p. 123. **32** Ibid. **33** Ibid., p. 129.

of 1920 and spitting up blood (blood is the messenger of death in its literal physical presence, but figuratively it offers rebirth), and reference to mixed blood.

VOICE

As Jesenská's letters no longer exist, it is easy to suggest, as Boa does, that Jesenská is silenced. Yet, she does remain not only in the translations, but also in the remnants of her words in Kafka's letters, the stubborn Czech trace of her. Contrary to Boa's and Böhme's assertions that Kafka was only interested in the construct of 'Milena', Kafka appears keenly sensitive to allowing Jesenská to articulate herself. He constantly urges her to send him her translations and her journalistic feuilletons, praising her writing at all opportunities and continuing to read her articles after their affair ends; his last request to her in 1923 shortly before he died was for her to send her articles. He tells her that he enjoys reading her translations of other writers, because of his worry that he hears too much of his own voice, 'the voice of the old grave, the voice I know only too well'.[34] 'I wanted to hear from you' he writes through his disappointment when he 'pulled the translation out of the large envelope'.[35] 'Why did it have to come between us?' he asks, with the sense that his voice might drown out hers but 'Then I realized that this same voice had also come between us, as a mediator'.[36] In other words, he does not see his voice as erasing hers but as a starting point, a mediation. The act of translation allows a cross-fertilization of voices; the translations articulate Jesenská as much as they do Kafka.

In June, Kafka has two dreams about Jesenská: in the first, she talks non-stop 'bang bang bang', he writes, but he only catches a couple of sentences, noting that she is speaking in Viennese argot. In the dream he isn't interested in what she looks like: 'your words were all I cared about'.[37] In the second, 'I was very unhappy' he writes, 'not because you were warding me off, but because I was treating you like some mute woman, ignoring the voice that was speaking out of you directly to me'.[38] While we, as contemporary readers might be deprived of Jesenská's voice, Kafka was not, and, in his support of Jesenská and her work as a translator and a writer, he seems ahead of his time in acknowledging the input she made and in respecting her voice and the benefits it gave his work.

The narrow interpretation of Kafka's intent in the *Letters* to construct a fantasy figure of Jesenská perhaps tells us more about what we desire from the *Letters* and from our notions of both Kafka and Jesenská. The story of the doomed love affair – doomed because of Kafka's inability to sustain a physically

34 Ibid., p. 7. **35** Ibid. **36** Ibid. **37** Ibid., pp 48–9. **38** Ibid., p. 50.

present relationship with a woman – seems, on the surface, more arresting than a narrative about two people falling in love over a translation. Yet the recognition in Kafka's *Letters* that he had met someone who understood the frailty and possibilities of identities at the borders of different cultures and languages that are, in turn, articulated by language, means a recognition also of Jesenská's professional worth as a translator. Not only does she bring his words back into the other language of his home town, Prague, but she understands the process and importance of doing so. Jesenská, the first person ever to translate Kafka's work, finds her independent self, her voice, as a professional translator and writer in the act of translation. In her *Letters* we may not be able to hear her voice physically (as her letters were destroyed), but Kafka does, and in his echoes, his metonymic reconstruction and deconstruction of Jesenská, we can see the process by which they both negotiate their identities.

The five lives of *Botchan*: a comparison of the English translations of Natsume Sōseki's classic

Carmen Mangiron

Natsume Sōseki's *Botchan* (1906) is considered a modern classic of Japanese literature and has been translated into several languages, including English, French, German, Spanish, Catalan, Hungarian, Romanian and Bengali.[1] In the case of English, there are five translations, a remarkable figure for a Japanese literary classic. What are the reasons behind the existence of five different translations of the same original? What are the main differences between them? There is of course a story behind any translation, and extratextual socio-cultural factors play an important role. Factors such as the translator, patronage,[2] time, place and literary and translation norms contribute to the decision to translate or to retranslate a literary work. These factors also influence, overtly or covertly, the translator and his/her work. In this essay I will compare the five different English translations of *Botchan,* by Yasotaro Morri, Umeji Sasaki, Alan Turney, Joel Cohn and Matt Treyvaud.[3] I will analyse the sociocultural factors surrounding the translations, the language and style used, the treatment of culture-specific references, the global translation method and the reception of the translations.

NATSUME SŌSEKI

Natsume Sōseki, pen name of Natsume Kinosuke (1867–1916), is considered one of the best Japanese novelists of the twentieth century. He studied English literature at Tokyo Imperial University and spent over two years in England,

1 See the Unesco Index Translationum, portal.unesco.org/culture/en/ev.php-URL_ID=7810&URL_DO=DO_TOPIC&URL_SECTION=201.html, accessed 24 Aug. 2011. **2** The term 'patronage' was introduced by Lefevere in *Translation, rewriting and the manipulation of literary fame* (London, 1992) to refer to the forces that regulate cultural exchange and influence the translator and his/her work, such as governments, publishers, educators, etc. **3** Natsume Sōseki, *Botchan* (Tokyo 1906/1992); *Botchan*, translated by Yasotaro Morri (Tokyo, 1919), available at www.gutenberg.org/dirs/etext05/btchn10.txt, accessed 6 Mar. 2012; *Botchan*, translated by Umeji Sasaki (Tokyo, 1922); *Botchan*, translated by Alan Turney (Tokyo, 1972); *Botchan*, translated by Joel Cohn (Tokyo, 2005); *Botchan*, translated by Matt Treyvaud (Tokyo, 2005), available at no-sword.jp/botchan/, accessed 6 Mar. 2012.

which he considered the worst of his life. When he returned to Japan he started working as a lecturer at Tokyo Imperial University, a position from which he resigned in 1907 to devote himself to his literary career. He wrote fifteen novels, the last one unfinished, all of them highly acclaimed by literary critics, particularly *Kokoro* (1914), considered by many as his masterpiece. Sōseki's novels are characterized by a deep realism. They portray human alienation, egotism, the difficulties in human communication and the search for moral values. He also explored the clash between Eastern and Western cultures, which first manifested itself in Japan after the Meiji Restoration in 1868 and spread rapidly through the country, causing the loss of some traditional Japanese values.[4]

Botchan is a short, light-hearted novel, published in 1906, which narrates the adventures and misfortunes of a young mathematics teacher from Edo, as Tokyo was formerly named, who accepts a post in a rural town in the island of Shikoku. The title of the novel refers to the nickname given by one of the house servants, Kiyo, to the protagonist, as the term *botchan* can be translated as 'young master'. Once Botchan arrives at his destination he is subjected to mischievous behaviour by students and soon gets involved in the intrigues of his fellow school teachers. It is a partly autobiographical work, as at the age of thirty-one Sōseki took a job as a teacher in a school in Matsuyama, in Shikoku.

Botchan is an impulsive and restless young man, rash but honest, and an ardent proponent of the fast disappearing traditional, samurai-like Japanese values. Through Botchan's eyes, Sōseki humorously criticizes Japanese society of the time, particularly intellectuals who adopted Western values unquestioningly and were viewed as hypocritical by the author.

EXTRATEXTUAL FACTORS SURROUNDING THE ENGLISH TRANSLATIONS OF BOTCHAN

The five translations of *Botchan* into English, spanning an eighty-six year period, are by Morri (1919), Sasaki (1922/1968), Turney (1972/1992), Cohn (2005) and Treyvaud (2005). In view of the fact that the amount of Japanese literature translated into English is still very small in comparison to the number of works translated from English into Japanese,[5] it is remarkable to find five translations of this modern classic into English. One of the reasons behind the multiplicity

4 See J. Thomas Rimer & Van C. Gessel (eds), *The Columbia anthology of modern Japanese literature: from restoration to occupation, 1868–1945* (New York, 2005). **5** According to the Unesco Index Translationum database, 2,728 Japanese literary works had been translated into English by 2008, while the amount of English works translated into Japanese is 96,098. (See note 1 above.)

of English translations of *Botchan* is related to its status as a canonical text in the source culture. Canonical texts, such as the Bible and Greek classics, are often retranslated to update the language and make them accessible to contemporary readers. John McCarthy affirms this is due to the 'temporal disparity' factor, as 'the further in time a translation is from its source text, the greater the differences will be linguistically and culturally, though not, perhaps, spiritually, between the two texts', while Clifford E. Landers suggests that translations lose half of their vitality and ability to communicate to a contemporary reader every thirty or forty years.[6] In fact, this does not only apply to translations, but also to the original texts, as Japanese language and customs have also evolved over the last hundred years, and many expressions which appear in the novel are no longer in use. For these reasons, contemporary editions of *Botchan* are edited to update the language and include footnotes to explain cultural references and intertextual allusions that may be obscure to the contemporary Japanese reader. For example, on page 28 of the edition I have used, there is a note from the editor to explain that the term 茶代 (*chadai*, literally 'tea fee') refers to a small amount of money that was given to restaurants and guesthouses by the customer to express gratitude – a form of 'tip' in modern parlance.

Another of the reasons for the existence of several translations is related to the sociocultural and economic factors that determine their production. The first English translation of *Botchan* made by a native English-speaker was not published until 1972, sixty-six years after the novel was published in Japan. According to Edward Fowler, publishers in the United States did not take an interest in Japanese literature until the mid-1950s, a decade after the end of the Second World War, when they started translating a few works that presented an elusive, melancholic, and exoticized version of Japan that appealed to the American audience. Three authors, Tanizaki, Kawabata and Mishima, became a 'metonymy for the entire corpus of Japanese fiction', what we could consider the 'high-brow' canon. Interest in Japanese literature in the US started to decrease in the mid-1960s, but a few Japan-based publishing companies, such as Kodansha International, Charles E. Tuttle and the University of Tokyo Press took up the slack and began to publish a more varied, extensive selection of Japanese literature that presented a different perspective on the Japanese canon.[7] *Botchan* does not present the idyllic and exotic image of Japan that US publishers and audience were used to, so this could explain why it took so many years

6 John McCarthy, 'Why two translations?', *Donaire*, 14 (June 2000), 18–24 at 18; Clifford E. Landers, *Literary translation: a practical guide* (Clevedon, 2001), pp 10–11 **7** Edward Fowler, 'Rendering words, traversing cultures: on the art and politics of translating modern Japanese fiction', *Journal of Japanese Studies*, 18 (1992), 1–44 at 8 and 14.

to produce a translation made by a native speaker of English. The fact that Sōseki's work presents a critical view of the rapid modernization taking place in Japan due to Western influences may also have contributed to its exclusion, together with the fact that *Botchan* is one of Sōseki's early novels and, by Western standards, it presents a rather simple plot and thinly developed characters. Its success with a young audience in Japan may also have led US publishers to consider it 'low-brow' and hence not worthy of translation.

In what follows I will examine the extratextual factors surrounding the five translations, including the people or organizitions who commissioned the translation and their possible motives, the translator, and the date of publication.

MORRI'S TRANSLATION

This is the oldest translation, published in 1919, thirteen years after the original. It is an inverse translation, that is, a translation made into a non-mother tongue by a Japanese translator, at a time when there would not have been many translators from Japanese into English. The translation was reviewed by a native speaker and editor, J.R. Kennedy, and Morri included a prologue where he expressed his view on translation, emphasizing the primacy of the original, the need for fidelity and the difficulty of maintaining the colloquial, vivid style of the original. He also explains in the prologue that he resorted to the use of language that might 'provoke disapproval from those of the "cultured" class with "refined" ears' (p. 3).

SASAKI'S TRANSLATION

Sasaki's translation was published in 1922, only three years after Morri's. It is also an inverse translation, reviewed by a native speaker, a university professor, Prof. E.W. Clement, as explained by Sasaki in the prologue, where he primarily discusses Sōseki's work. There is no information in the prologue about the reasons that led to the production of his new translation, although he thanks Mrs. Sōseki for having allowed him to translate the novel. This may indicate that the translator was the initiator, although it is unclear why this translation was made only three years after the first one, as the period of time is not long enough for any substantial change in norms to have taken place. Perhaps Morri's use of colloquial language was not considered appropriate by Sasaki, as he uses a much more formal register and vocabulary, as will be seen when the style of the different translations is compared.

TURNEY'S TRANSLATION

Turney is a British professor of English literature based in Japan, who has translated several Japanese literary works and is a specialist in Sōseki. He was approached by the Japanese Commission for UNESCO. The original idea was to include several essays about Sōseki's work together with a translation in a book commemorating the centenary of Sōseki's birth in 1967. This is an example of patronage, as the translation was commissioned by a government body with the aim of making available in English a work belonging to what was considered to be the Japanese literary canon. Turney has informed me in a personal communication that he believes the sponsors wanted a native English speaker in order to produce an idiomatic translation. However, after he had completed the translation, the sponsors decided not to include it in the book. Turney tried to look for another publisher, and approached Kodansha, but he was told there was no market for the translation. It was not until four years later, in 1972, when Turney approached Kodansha again, that his translation was given a green light.

COHN'S TRANSLATION

Cohn is an American professor of Japanese literature based in Hawaii, who specializes in modern Japanese literature and the use of humour in Japanese works. His translation was also the result of patronage; in this case it was the Japanese Literature Publishing Project (JLPP), an initiative from the Agency of Cultural Affairs of Japan. The aim of the project is 'to promote understanding of Japan in the world and its contribution to world culture and to elevate the standards of Japanese literature'.[8] In the case of *Botchan*, a new translation was commissioned in order to reflect contemporary language so as to appeal to a new generation of readers.[9] Cohn includes a prologue to the translation where he discusses Sōseki's work and provides information about the use of language and dialects, as well as some of the culturally specific references found in the book. This is done to facilitate the target audience's understanding and engagement with the book.

TREYVAUD'S TRANSLATION

Treyvaud is an American writer and translator living in Japan who set out to do a thirty-evening speed translation without revision, which he published in his

8 Japanese literature publishing project, n.d., available at www.bunka.go.jp/1bungei/nihon-bungakuhonyaku_english.html, accessed 25 Aug. 2011. **9** (Kijo Hoshino, member of the JLPP, personal communication).

blog. He wanted to capture the spirit of the original and its entertainment value in his translation. This is a type of 'fan translation', an expression used to refer to unofficial translations made by enthusiasts, particularly in the field of audio-visual translation. Fan translations are prompted by the lack of an official translation or by dissatisfaction with the official one. Treyvaud affirms in his blog that he did not find the existing translations satisfactory, so he decided to do a new one. Treyvaud's translation was subsequently revised and has been available since 2009 as an e-book from Amazon Kindle.

I will now briefly compare the translations, focusing on three aspects: the language and style, the treatment of cultural references and the global translation method applied by the translators to their text. Due to the scope of this paper I will limit to five the number of relevant examples that illustrate the main differences between the translations.

THE LANGUAGE AND STYLE OF THE TRANSLATIONS

Sōseki's language in *Botchan* has a distinctive oral and colloquial feel, with the use of colloquial expressions and informal verb endings. For example, the term 馬鹿 (baka, 'stupid') is used on more than one occasion as is the informal expression 仕方がない (shikata ga nai, 'it can't be helped'). In the first example below, Morri uses the informal, albeit old-fashioned, expression 'Great Scott!' and the colloquial expression 'hole' as in dingy dwelling, in an effort to reflect the casual register of the original. Sasaki's translation is rather formal, wordy and quite stiff, and in most cases is much longer than the original as well as longer than the other translations. Examples of his style include expressions such as 'A fool I surely was' and 'This was the prevailing thought [...]'. Sasaki's translation lacks idiomatic quality, betraying the fact that it was written by a non-native speaker. Although this is also the case with Morri's translation, his rendition is more idiomatic, due to the use of colloquialisms and slang terms. Inverse translations are no longer frequent, but at the time when these translations were made they were probably the only option available for translating Japanese literature into English. On the other hand, Turney's translation, using British English, is idiomatic and beautifully written; however the style is also rather formal, unlike that of the original. Cohn's translation is more colloquial, with expressions such as 'Who the hell [...]'; it is clearly marked as American English, although the style is still rather literary in many instances. Treyvaud's translation is very idiomatic, with some bad language that reflects cool US street speak. It is a transgressive and liberated translation, not subject to the scrutiny of an editor and not subject to translation norms, which uses colloquial expressions such as 'kidding' and vulgar language, as in 'fucking'. The following example illustrates the main differences between the translations:

Table 1. The language and style of the translations – I

Author/Translator	*Example*
Sōseki (original; literal translation provided in brackets)	人を馬鹿にしていらあ、こんな所に我慢が出来るものかと思ったが仕方がない。(p. 25) (*They* are *making a fool out of people, they thought I could stand a place like this, there is nothing I can do*.)
Morri	Great Scott! I wouldn't stay in such a hole, I thought [...] (p. 8)
Sasaki	A fool I surely was to have been sent so far down to such a miserable place, where no human being could comfortably stay even a day. This was the prevailing thought then [...] (p. 28)
Turney	What a fool they'd taken me for to bring me here! No one could stand a place like this. (p. 23)
Cohn	Who the hell did they think they were, sending me to a place like this? How was I supposed to stand it? (p. 26)
Treyvaud	You've got to be kidding me! I'm supposed to fucking live here?, I thought [...] (online)

In the next example, Sasaki's style is again the more formal, with longer sentences, while Cohn and Treyvaud's translations are the more colloquial, following the style of the original most closely. In addition, it should be noted that both Cohn and Treyvaud decided to explicate the information about *kabuki* plays implicit in the original by including the information that *kabuki* plays feature all-male casts, with female roles acted by male cast members. While this information would be inferred by Japanese readers, these two translators felt the need to make it explicit for their target readership.

Table 2. The language and style of the translations – II

Author/Translator	*Example*
Sōseki (original; literal translation provided in brackets)	この兄はやに色が白くて、芝居の真似をして女形になるのが好きだった。(p. 12) *(This brother was disgustingly white, and he liked pretending it was a play and he was a female.)*
Morri	This brother's face was palish white, and he had a fondness for taking the part of an actress at the theatre. (p. 4)
Sasaki	This brother had a complexion unpleasantly white, verging almost on paleness; he was very fond of theatrical performances, and would play the part of a female. (p. 15)
Turney	He was terribly white-skinned and liked to pretend to be an actor, taking the female parts. (p. 8)
Cohn	His face was so pale it was creepy, and he liked to act out scenes from Kabuki plays – especially the female roles. (p. 15)
Treyvaud	He was disgustingly fair-skinned, and he loved putting on pretend *kabuki* plays, always taking the female parts. (online; 'kabuki' and 'female parts' are marked as hyperlinks)

THE TREATMENT OF CULTURAL REFERENCES

As *Botchan* is set in Japan at the beginning of the last century, there are abundant culture-specific references (CSRs) that are obscure to an English speaking target audience without specialized knowledge about Japanese culture. According to Jan Pedersen, such references represent 'translation crisis points', which he defines as 'turning points at which the translators have to make active decisions'.[10] When encountering a CSR, translators should assess its function and relevance, as well

10 Jan Pedersen, 'How is culture rendered in subtitles', *MuTra 2005 – Challenges of multidimensional translation: conference proceedings*, 2005, pp 1–18 at p. 1. Available at www.euroconferences.info/proceedings/2005_Proceedings/2005_Pedersen_Jan.pdf, accessed 15 July 2012.

as consider whether it poses a comprehension problem for the target audience, or in Leppihalme's terms, a 'cultural bump'.[11] There are four main strategies for dealing with a CSR: preserving it, either without manipulating it or by explaining or describing it to facilitate its comprehension; omitting it if it would require a long explanation or a major comprehension effort by the receivers; neutralizing it, by removing the specific reference to the original culture and either generalizing or particularizing the reference; and adapting it by replacing it with a reference to the target culture.[12] Preservation is a strategy often used for a foreignizing, source-culture oriented translation, as it allows the sociocultural content of the original to be retained. Omission and neutralization lean more towards the target culture pole, as they remove the source culture specificity to make the references easier to comprehend by target readers. Adaptation, on the other hand, is the most extreme form of domestication, as a reference to the source culture is replaced by a target culture equivalent. It is important to deal with CSRs consistently, according to the global translation method chosen, in order to present a homogeneous textual world that does not present a distorted image of the source culture to the target audience.

The following table contains two examples that illustrate the treatment of CSRs by the different translators. Both examples belong to the cultural category of food, one of the areas where there tends to be major differences among cultures.

These examples illustrate Morri's tendency to neutralize and adapt the original CSRs, without even trying to describe them, as he uses the same term 'sweetmeats' (inconsistently spelt in these two occasions) as a translation for a type of biscuits and a type of soup and a rice dish. Sasaki does not use a consistent method, as he adapts the first two references to Japanese sweets, using the terms 'doughnuts and crackers', which were largely unknown in Japan in the early 1900s. However, in the second example he simply borrows and transcribes the terms *oshiruko* and *ozoni*, which would be opaque for the target readers. Turney, on the other hand, preserves the CSRs, transcribing them and adding information of encyclopaedic nature, more information than strictly needed to understand the CSRs. Cohn uses a generalization in the first example, using the hypernym 'sweets' and removing the reference to Japanese culture, while in the second example he preserves the references by means of describing the particular food. Treyvaud decides to preserve the CSRs, by describing them in the first example and borrowing the Japanese terms in the second, where he uses capital

11 Ritva Leppihalme, *Culture bumps: on the translation of allusions* (Helsinki, 1994). **12** See Carme Mangiron, 'El tractament dels referents culturals a les traduccions de la novella *Botxan*: la interacció entre els elements textuals i extratextuals' (PhD, Universitat Autònoma de Barcelona, 2006), available at www.tesisenxarxa.net/TDX-0124108-125537/index_an.html, accessed 6 Mar. 2012.

Table 3. The treatment of CSRs in the translations

Author/Translator	*Example* 3.1	*Example* 3.2
Sōseki	金鍔や紅梅焼 (p. 15) *(Kintsuba or Kōbaiyaki)*	汁粉、お雑煮 (p. 123) (*Shiruko, ozōni*)
Morri	cakes or sweetmeats (p. 5)	sweet meats (p. 37)
Sasaki	doughnuts and crackers (p. 18)	*Oshiruko* and *Ozoni* (p. 118)
Turney	Kintsuba cakes shaped like sword-guards, or Kōbaiyaki biscuits in the form of plum blossoms. (p. 11)	*shiruko* – red-bean soup with rice-cake in it – and *o-zōni* – vegetables and rice-cake boiled in soy. (p. 135)
Cohn	various kinds of sweets. (Cohn, p. 17)	Sweet bean soup and rice cake soup (p. 108)
Treyvaud	roasted red-bean jam cakes and sweet rice crackers (online, marked as hyperlinks)	SHIRUKO and ZOUNI (online, marked as hyperlinks)

letters to highlight the fact that this is a sign in a restaurant. In his text, all four CSRs are marked as hypertext links, so when readers click on them they are taken to a webpage with extra information. Electronic texts like this provide new ways for readers to receive texts in a non-linear form, facilitating access to other texts and additional information to complement their reading and understanding of the main text, including images of the type of food referred to.

THE GLOBAL TRANSLATION STRATEGY

A close analysis of the five translations reveals that Morri's translation tends towards the adaptation of the sociocultural content of the original and strives to use idiomatic language, although the language is still rather literal and sounds quite dated to a twenty-first century audience. Sasaki's translation, on the other hand, is literal and unnatural, and it presents a tension between a source and a target culture oriented approach, adapting some CSRs but preserving some obscure ones without any explication that would help target readers to comprehend them. For this reason, he presents a culturally heterogeneous world that mixes source and target culture elements to an extent that can puzzle readers, and present a distorted image of Japanese culture. Despite the differences in language use, register and style, Turney, Cohn and Treyvaud's translations all use idiomatic language and present a source-culture oriented approach that aims to reproduce the sociocultural content of the original accurately by preserving the original CSRs and explicating them, describing them or borrowing the Japanese terms if they consider they will be understood by the target readers.

Another strategy is the use of footnotes. Morri uses twelve footnotes to include additional information about CSRs, revealing his presence and breaking the convention of the translator's invisibility currently prevalent in the English-speaking publishing world. Sasaki uses ten footnotes, one of them to include what Virgilio Moya calls a 'confession of ignorance', an expression he uses to refer to a translator's intervention in the text to explain that s/he is unable to translate a particular expression, as described in the example below.[13] Turney and Cohn do not use any footnotes, following one of the current norms of translation into English, which avoids the use of footnotes, as it is perceived that they break the rhythm of the narrative and the invisibility of the translator. Lawrence Venuti has objected to this invisibility of the translators imposed by publishing companies, and urged translators to rebel against this 'domesticating' approach that effectively implies 'an ethnocentric reduction of the foreign text to target-language cultural values, bringing the author back home'.[14] Although Venuti urges translators to use footnotes and reproduce when possible stylistic features of the original text, this is still not the case in many translations into English, as in the case of *Botchan*. Interestingly, the older translations make use of some footnotes, while the more recent translations in print do not. This may indicate that the use of translator's notes was more acceptable in the English-speaking publishing world at the beginning of the 1900s, although this hypothesis should be confirmed by examining the use of footnotes in other works translated around the same time. Treyvaud, on the other hand, includes one hundred and eleven hyperlinks in his e-translation, which would be the equivalent to footnotes in a translation in paper format, with the advantage that the reader can opt to check the hyperlinks or not. In addition, a hyperlink can contain much more information than a footnote, including pictures, which are useful for readers when dealing with CSRs.

A problem which may elicit a confession of ignorance is posed by wordplay, as in the example below.

13 Virgilio Moya, *La traducción de los nombres propios* (Madrid, 2000), p. 106. **14** Lawrence Venuti, *The translator's invisibility: a history of translation* (London, 1995), p. 20.

Table 4. The translation of a play-on-words

Author/Translator	*Example*
Sōseki (original; literal translation provided in brackets)	第一先生を捕まえてなもした何だ。菜飯は田楽の時より外に食うもんじゃない」とあべこべに遣り込めてやったら「なもしと菜飯は違うぞな、もし」と云った。いつまで云ってもなもしを使う奴だ。 (*When I tried to make them quiet by saying*: '*First of all, how come you address your teacher with* na moshi*?* Nameshi *is what you eat outdoors at the time of* dengaku [rice planting celebrations]', *one of them said* 'Namoshi *and* nameshi *are different*, namoshi'. *These guys always used* namoshi.) (p. 19)
Morri	'Shut up. They're the same thing. In the first place, what do you mean by answering your teacher "A-ah say"? Ah-Say or Ah-Sing is a Chink's name!' For this counter-shot, he answered: 'A-ah say and Ah-Sing is different, – A-ah say.' They never got rid of 'A-ah say.' (p. 56)
Sasaki	'Moreover, "don't you see?" is an extremely impolite expression to your teacher. What is your Namoshi? Nameshi is eaten only when you take dengaku*.' At this rebuff, he said that Namoshi and Nameshi are not the same. This fellow would not give up his dreadful Namoshi to the last. (p. 58)
Turney	'And while we're about it, stop finishing every confounded sentence with "like". It sounds like "tyke", and if that's what you are trying to call me come straight out with it and don't mumble'. I thought that would shut him up, but no. '"Like" and "tyke" are different, like,' he said. Like, like, like! That's all you ever heard out of them. (p. 61)
Cohn	'And who do you damned jackasses think you are sticking that stupid na moshi on the end of everything when you are talking to a teacher? It just makes you

	sound mushy – that's all it's good for!' That ought to show them who's boss, I thought – but they came right back with 'Na moshi isn't the same as mushy – na moshi.' It was hopeless – they couldn't stop saying na moshi even if they tried. (p. 53)
Treyvaud	'And what's with all this "like" crap? I don't care if you like it or not!' 'Naw, thait's a different kind of like, like –' began one. 'Shut up!' (online)

In a comment on the above example, Sasaki confesses he has not been able to translate the play on words, based on the term *nameshi*, a rice dish, and *na moshi*, a dialectal expression the locals from the island use to end all their sentences: '*Here is a play on words, namoshi and nameshi. It is entirely beyond my power to render them into appropriate English.' (p. 26). Despite the fact that it was not possible to translate the play on words literally, all the other translators managed to translate it functionally, that is, introducing a new play on words in the target language that would have a similar effect on target readers. Morri has replaced the original play-on-words with another one based on 'A-ah-say' and 'Ah-Sing', and he uses the term *Chink*, which would nowadays be considered politically incorrect; but this probably was not the case in the early twentieth century. Turney plays with the terms *like* and *tyke*, while Treyvaud uses two different forms of the word *like*, the verb and the conjunction. It is also worth highlighting Cohn's effort to break with the translator's invisibility and retain some of the Japanese flavour of the novel by using the dialectal expression 'namoshi' in this fragment, where he contrasts *namoshi* with *mushy* to reflect the original play-on-words. Cohn uses the expression *na moshi* at the end of some sentences in the book in order to give English-speakers a flavour of the original language and dialect, a decision he explains to the readers in his prologue.

THE RECEPTION OF THE TRANSLATIONS

Translation reviews, as well as providing a good yardstick to measure how a translation is received in a target community, allow us to extrapolate information about the literary and translation norms that prevail in a target community at a given time. Despite the fact that reviews are traditionally written by critics and appear in newspapers, magazines and journals, the spread of the Internet has allowed users to include their own reviews in websites, such as book-selling sites like Amazon.com, or posts in blogs. Interestingly, the lengthier and more elaborate expert reviews in journals, magazines or specialized websites and blogs on occasion devote more attention to the literary qualities of the original work, such as its style and themes, than to the quality of the translation. The brief and informal reviews by customers who bought the book on websites such as Amazon.com, however, tend to focus more on the quality of the translations, mainly focussing on whether the language is contemporary and easy to read, which once again points to the convention of using idiomatic and fluid language in translations into English today. It should also be observed that reviews, whether done by experts or amateurs, are subjective, and therefore, one can often both find positive and negative reviews for the same book or translation, depending on the aspects the reviewer has chosen to focus on. While there are obviously considerable differences between expert and amateur commentaries and reviews in terms of length, quality, style, the target audience and the amount of attention awarded to the translation, and the impact of the reviews, both types of reviews provide information about how a particular translation has been received in the target community.

The five translations of *Botchan* have had varied responses from English speaking audiences. Morri's translation obtained mixed reviews. A contemporary reviewer in Amazon.com states that it is 'extremely bad', while the East Asia Digital Library of the University of Oregon refers to this work as 'one of the better translated novels of the many that were translated during the 1910s and 1920s'.[15] Obviously, to judge this, or any, translation objectively, the time when it was produced and the language and translation norms prevalent at the time must be considered. Sasaki's translation has mainly received negative reviews by contemporary readers because of its unnatural and unidiomatic language. A reviewer writes in Amazon.com '[i]t is easily the worst 20th C translation I've ever read',[16] and Turney, Cohn (personal communication) and Treyvaud in his blog also give their judgment that Sasaki's translation is very unnatural. The novelist Todd Shimoda also writes in his blog that 'as one may expect, the prose in that translation [Sasaki's] sounds stilted today', as it was published in 1922.[17]

15 Philip Roncoroni, Customer review, available at www.amazon.com/Botchan-Master-Darling-Kin-Nosuke-Natsume/dp/1434603660, accessed 6 Mar. 2012; East Asia Digital Library of the University of Oregon, available at e-asia.uoregon.edu/, accessed 30 Sept. 2010. **16** Patrick Robbins, Customer review, available at www.amazon.com/review/R17BWLE-JWFQToO/ref=cm_cr_pr_viewpnt#R17BWLEJWFQToO, accessed 30 Sept. 2009. **17** Todd Shimoda, 'Review: *Botchan*', Todd Shimoda's writer blog, 28 Feb. 2010. Available at

However, a literary journalist, Jessica Schneider, stated in a review in the *Seattle PI* newspaper that in Sasaki's translation 'there are a few instances of spelling errors and the occasional incorrect word selection, but they are minor and don't distract from the overall narrative'.[18] On the other hand, Turney's translation has received positive commendations from readers and critics. One customer at the Amazon.com site recommends: 'Make Sure You Get the Alan Turney Translation !!!!'[19] while the Japanese literature scholar Oliver Statler stated in the blurb on the cover of the translation that 'Turney's new version is lucid and lively [...] At last Botchan is fun to read in English'. Cohn's translation also has been praised by readers in Amazon.com and by critics, such as Thiessen, Janairo and Shimoda.[20] As this is the most recently published translation in book form, most reviews currently available refer to it. In addition, Cohn's translation won the Japan–U.S. Friendship Commission Prize for the Translation of Japanese Literature awarded by the Donald Keene Center of Japanese Culture, Columbia University, in 2006. Finally, although there are no published reviews of Treyvaud's translation, it has also received positive feedback by the readers of his translation in his blog, who, in general, consider it funny and enjoyable.

CONCLUSIONS

Extratextual sociological parameters have played a key role in the production of the five English translations of the Japanese classic *Botchan* and have influenced the translation process and product. For example, the phenomenon of 'patronage' played a central role, particularly in the production of Turney's and Cohn's translations, as they were originally commissioned by Japanese cultural authorities to promote Japanese literature in English. The translators have also left their personal imprint in their work, which reflects aspects such as their origin, competence, and preferred translation method and strategies. In addition, temporal disparity and the evolution of language and translation norms over the years have made it necessary to update the language and style of the translations of *Botchan* in order to bring them closer to contemporary target readers.

www.shimodaworks.com/blog/index.php?action=display&entryID=46, accessed 28 Aug. 2011. **18** Jessica Schneider, 'Book review: *Botchan* (Tuttle Classics) by Soseki Natsume', *Seattle PI*, Tuesday, Apr. 26, 2011. Available at www.seattlepi.com/ae/books/article/Book-Review-Botchan-Tuttle-Classics-by-Soseki-892977.php, accessed 28 Aug. 2011. **19** Play2632ball. Customer review, available at www.amazon.ca/gp/cdp/member-reviews/A1XR5U7E7O3SCO/ref=cm_pdp_rev_more?ie=UTF8&sort_by=MostRecentReview#R1TNYDTX3T92QC, accessed 28 Aug. 2011. **20** Cherie Thiessen, 'Cross cultural experience', *January magazine*, 2005. Available at www.januarymagazine.com/fiction/botchan.html, accessed 28 Aug. 2011; Michael Janairo, '"Botchan" only improves in translation', the *Times-Union*, 16 Oct. 2005.

This case study indicates that literary and translation norms have shifted over the last hundred years in English-speaking territories. While the older translations of *Botchan* tend to domesticate the sociocultural content of the original, the more recent translations tend to preserve it and to add information as required in order to facilitate readers' comprehension. The attitude towards the use of notes in literary translation also seems to have changed, as the older translations by Morri and Sasaki include footnotes, while the more recent ones in print do not (Turney, Cohn). Treyvaud's translation, in e-book format, includes a high amount of hyperlinks to websites containing information about Japanese CSRs. Electronic texts provide new ways of reading texts in a non-linear fashion, and allow translators to make use of resources available on the Internet to provide readers with additional information about the source culture, including images, which can contribute to a better understanding of the original work.

In relation to language and style, translators have striven to use a vivid, natural language and fluid style to help Sōseki's voice reach the target readers, although in Morri's and Sasaki's case this was not always possible as they were not native speakers, and their translations sound stiff and old fashioned to a contemporary audience. All this evidence supports Venuti's claim that translation norms in English tend to favour the invisibility of the translator, using fluid and natural language, and avoiding footnotes, to disguise the fact that the text is a translation, despite the fact that notes can be useful to help readers gain knowledge about the source culture. Further research focussing on other Japanese literary works translated into English around the same periods would be needed to confirm whether the data obtained can be extrapolated. However, it is clear that extratextual factors and their possible impact should be always integrated into the analysis and assessment of any translation, as translations cannot be dissociated from the agent who produces them and from the context in which they are produced.

Hell for kids: translating Dante's *Divine Comedy* for children

Virginia Jewiss

Dante's *Divine Comedy* might seem strange territory for children. A medieval epic poem that graphically portrays the horrors of damnation, debates philosophical questions, and engages in rarefied theological matters of purgation and salvation as it leads its protagonist through Hell, Purgatory, and Heaven does not immediately seem suitable material for young readers. Yet the poem's canonical status, together with its explicit moral agenda, sustained use of allegory, and adventure in an otherworldly setting have inspired authors to adapt the poem for well over a century. This essay considers four of the many English translations of the *Divine Comedy* for children. 'Translation' is used in a broad sense here, to convey something well beyond the normative question of language. I draw in particular on Zohar Shavit's definition of translation as 'a semiotic concept', namely 'the process by which the textual models of one system are transferred to another'.[1] In this case the transfer is primarily one of genre: from high to low, or from adult literature to children's story. In order to illustrate the stylistic, thematic, and structural range of the genre, as well as the most significant changes it has undergone, I have selected two of the earliest versions, both of which appeared at the end of nineteenth century, and two versions published in 2008, one of which I wrote myself.

A Dante scholar and translator, I first became interested in children's versions of the *Divine Comedy* when an expectant mother asked if I would write one. What began as a favour quickly became fodder for serious reflection. Should one tell children about death, damnation, divine judgment, and gruesome punishments, and if so, how? Where is the line between pleasurable fear and terror? What happens to a classic work of literature when it is distorted and oversimplified for a young audience? To the reader? How much of the original can be left out or altered before the new version loses meaningful contact with the old? And finally, what did I want the *Divine Comedy* to say to children? These questions not only guided my own writing; they also frame my discussion of the other versions under consideration here. The adaptation of such a learned – and lengthy – work into a story for children obviously calls for radi-

1 Zohar Shavit, *Poetics of children's literature* (Athens, 1986), p. 111.

cal transformations and truncations, and countless choices regarding content, style, and tone must be made.

The *Divine Comedy* enters the English child's universe in 1887, with the publication of Rose E. Selfe's *How Dante climbed the mountain. Sunday readings with the children from the 'Purgatorio'.*[2] As the title makes explicit, Dante's poem is placed within the framework of Sunday School lessons. Thus it comes as no surprise that it becomes a sort of spiritual guide that offers help on the 'pilgrimage through life'.[3] The overtly religious nature of the translation is announced in the preface, written by the lord bishop of Ripon, William Boyd-Carpenter.[4] He claims that 'all the highest and best truth is the common heritage of the great and the small', but it needs to be simplified or adapted for the smallest members of society.[5] He assigns an almost ministerial role to the translator and foregrounds the salvational dimension of the poem by casting Selfe's project in blatantly Eucharistic terms; she is the 'friendly hand' that will 'break and distribute' the truth of the *Divine Comedy* to feed the young.

Selfe limits the poem's potential for spiritual guidance to Dante's journey up the mountain of Purgatory. The bishop justifies her selection of the second canticle as follows:

> Miss Selfe [...] opens to children the scenes of the 'Purgatorio'. The aim appears to me right and fit. One would not too early familiarize childhood with the weird and terrible scenes of the 'Inferno'; and the 'Paradiso' would be beyond their powers; but the story of the Purgatory is within their grasp, and is full of clear, bright teaching; rightly used, it becomes a sort of 'Pilgrim's Progress', full of deep truth and life-lessons.[6]

He articulates what will come to be the dominant opinion of other early translators: Hell is too scary for children, and Heaven too lofty, but Purgatory is just right. So how does Selfe break and distribute the truth of Purgatory for them? She makes little use of Dante's rich poetic language and no attempt at verse. Her at times condescending prose is accompanied by a selection of Gustav Doré's engravings, although she never engages with them directly.[7] Her

2 R.E. Selfe, *How Dante climbed the mountain: Sunday readings with the children from the 'Purgatorio'* (London, 1887). **3** Ibid., p.3. **4** Like Selfe, Boyd-Carpenter also wrote on Dante for adults. He contributed the introduction to William Warren Vernon's *Readings on the Paradiso of Dante* (London, 1900), and his William Belden Noble lectures were printed with the title *The spiritual message of Dante* (London, 1914). Selfe translated *Selections from the first nine books of the chroniche fiorentine of Giovanni Villani translated for the use of students of Dante and others* (London, 1896). **5** Selfe, *How Dante climbed the mountain*, p. iii. **6** Ibid., pp iii–iv. **7** Doré's illustrations, which he published between 1857 and 1867, also begin to appear in

pace is measured at first, but then changes dramatically: she takes several pages to paraphrase the action of the first two cantos, in which Dante is lost in the dark wood and encounters Virgil, but she accelerates when they begin their descent. The next thirty-two cantos are compressed into a few sentences:

> Through the first part of their journey I do not intend to follow the travellers. It was a very dark and terrible road over which they had to pass, and Dante's heart many times failed him for fear, even though he loved and trusted his guide and master so entirely. But through the darkness and the terrible sights and sounds, Dante knew that God was leading him and teaching him, as He so often does lead us through what is painful and hard to understand, to the fuller knowledge of His truth, and justice, and righteousness.[8]

What exactly God was teaching and how Dante knew is left to the reader's imagination. Selfe edits out the justice of Hell and the joy of Heaven, honing Dante's journey into an education through purposeful suffering. Her account is laden with bleak reminders of the suffering that awaits us in this life and the next, and bolstering defences of authority figures, including parents, teachers, and God:

> We cannot too early realize that if we do wrong we must surely suffer for it, and I think, if we read the story rightly, we shall have quite a new idea about pain, and the help it may be to us. [...] When we are children, some of this purifying pain comes to us through our parents and teachers, in the form of punishment for our wrong-doing, and these punishments, though hard to bear at the time, should really be welcomed by us as the painful consequences of wrong, and as helping us to resist temptation another time.[9]

In her heavy-handed, moralistic rendering of Dante's *Purgatorio*, Selfe nonetheless tames the potent descriptions of punishment found in the original. For example, the envious – whose eyes are sewed shut with iron, causing them to weep rusty tears – here merely have their eyes 'closed, for these poor souls are all blind, and down their cheeks flow floods of salt tears.'[10] Yet in her vision

translations for adults at the same time. They accompanied later editions of Henry Francis Cary's translation, which first appeared in its entirety in 1815 under the title *The vision of Dante*, and were also included in some editions of the Henry Wadsworth Longfellow translation, which first appeared in 1867. **8** Selfe, *How Dante climbed the mountain*, p. 26. **9** Ibid., pp 18–19. **10** Ibid., p. 63.

of life's pilgrimage, suffering is so tightly connected with learning that when it ends, so does her story. Thus when Dante reaches the mountaintop, she says:

> You remember that in the 'Pilgrim's Progress', when Christian enters the gates of the Celestial City, we do not follow him further. With music sounding, and light shining upon him, he disappears from our sight within the walls of the City of which the Bible tells us that we are all to be citizens.
>
> So now I do not propose that we should ascend with Dante to heaven. All the suffering is over.[11]

This is just one of many references she makes to John Bunyan's *Pilgrim's Progress*. Shavit notes that translations for children tend 'to relate the text to existing models in the target system'.[12] Selfe grafts the *Divine Comedy* onto *Pilgrim's Progress*, which was still vastly popular reading – for children and adults – two hundred years after it was written. What is more, she maps Dante's otherworldly landscape onto Bunyan's. Hence the mountain of Purgatory is called both 'Hill Difficulty' and 'Mount of Blessing'. In fact, the familiarity and accessibility of Bunyan's vision, which, she notes 'I expect you have all read and enjoyed'[13] forms the basis for her own work: unlike *Pilgrim's Progress*, which 'you can read [...] for yourselves', she explains that Dante's vision is long, in Italian, and 'written in such an old-fashioned way' that it is difficult even for adults to read. It also contains 'very many thoughts and conversations [...] which children could not possibly hope to understand'.[14] Young readers are thus made aware that a 'high' version of the story they are about to hear exists, but is beyond their reach. In the same fashion, they are also reminded of their own spiritual and interpretive limits. For all her efforts to bring the *Divine Comedy* closer to her readers, the shadow of the high and unattainable original actually makes Dante's work recede into the distance.

Five years after Selfe's version appeared, Elizabeth Harrison published her own prose translation for children entitled *The vision of Dante, 'A story for little children and a talk to their mothers'*.[15] A pioneer in children's education, an authority on early childhood development and psychology, a student of the Montessori method, and principal of the Chicago kindergarten college, Harrison was particularly attuned to the special needs of children. She wrote numerous works for them as well as a series of compelling tracts for adults argu-

11 Ibid., pp 106–7. **12** Shavit, p. 115. **13** Selfe, *How Dante climbed the mountain,* p. 2. **14** Ibid., p. 3. **15** E. Harrison, *The vision of Dante: a story for little children and a talk to their mothers* (Chicago, 1892). Rather than using the standard title for Dante's work, Harrison adopts the title used by Cary in his 1815 translation.

ing the importance of literature in early education. Like Selfe, she was also passionate about the *Divine Comedy*. She held that it contained a 'pictorial truth', in which 'the nature of every sin is pictured forth by its symbolic punishment.' She makes bold claims for the value of the poem in child-rearing: 'I know of no study more helpful to mothers than this same study of Dante'.[16] Both in her 'talk to mothers' and an essay entitled the *Relationship between the kindergarten and great literature: Dante,* she celebrates the poem's potential to expose children to – while simultaneously protect them from – evil. It is a place where they can experience vice vicariously, and therefore avoid it for real: 'Thus the Divine Comedy becomes the shield of Perseus in which the terrible gorgon head of evil may be seen and comprehended without withering or turning to stone the life that comes in contact with it'.[17]

Readers expecting to see Gorgon heads of evil will be disappointed, however. Hell's horrors are not vicariously experienced or even recounted in Harrison's *The vision of Dante.* Instead, she tells 'a wonderful story' that 'has been told over and over again for six hundred years, yet people keep reading it, and re-reading it, and wise men never tire of studying it'.[18] Like Selfe, Harrison explicitly evokes the 'high' version of the text as something her readers can look forward to when they are more mature intellectually and spiritually. Their work has many other elements in common. Here too the narrative focuses on Purgatory, where Dante learns about pride, envy, and gluttony, and stops just short of Paradise. Despite her title, she notes that 'No words of mine could make you see that glorious vision as Dante then beheld it'.[19] And while she clearly appreciates the beauty of Dante's verse, she narrates in simple prose, with scant reference to the linguistic richness of the original.

Rather than review other commonalities between Harrison's and Selfe's translations, I would like to focus on its most interesting and unique aspect. When Dante meets Virgil, he explains that

> they must go down through a deep, bad smelling and dark hole in the ground, and must meet with many disagreeable things and crawl through much dirt and filth [...] The dark pit through which they were to pass was the shape of an immense funnel, or a cone turned upside down. It was so large that it reached from the surface down to the very centre of the earth [...] yet as they slowly travelled down its rocky sides the place grew darker and narrower, and the air more stifling, and the smell was worse than anything of which you have ever dreamed. At times Dante nearly fainted, but Virgil put his arms around him and held him up until

16 Harrison, *Vision,* pp 21–2. **17** Ibid., p. 21. **18** Ibid., p.1. **19** Ibid., pp 16–7.

> he revived. I will not stop to tell you of all the horrible experiences they went through. By and by when you grow to be men and women, you can read the whole poem for yourselves.[20]

Harrison slides right through hell and out the other side without even one pictured form of truth. In her world, cleanliness is next to godliness, and dirty Hell is no place for children. Her story really begins when Dante and Virgil emerge from the darkness, Cato appears to direct them up the mountain. 'But' Harrison explains, 'Virgil must first get the grime and dirt off Dante. You know we can not very well go into dirty places without having some of the cinders and ashes and other filth stick to us'.[21] This finger-wagging reminder is followed by a detailed account of Virgil's washing of Dante's cheeks. Dark, dirt, blackened dirt, grime, filth, cinders, ashes: these are the terms Harrison uses to picture Hell, which sounds more like a chimneysweeper's nightmare, more like something from William Blake or Charles Dickens, than Dante's journey to the otherworld. The seasoned voice of the kindergarten teacher can be heard in her insistence on hygiene, as can the grim reality – which the politically active Harrison battled fiercely – of children working in dark and dirty factories.

On both sides of the Atlantic, Dante enters the 'canon' of children's literature through the gates of Purgatory. Other versions gradually allow him to foray into Hell and Heaven, but Purgatory remains the prime destination and didactic core well into the twentieth century. Part spiritual guide, part sermon, and part promise for future enlightenment and bliss, the young are admonished about their behaviour, instructed about the consequences, and tantalized by the prospect both of reading the true poem and seeing God some day. Why Dante enters the children's canon at this particular moment is a fascinating question that extends well beyond the parameters of this contribution. Developments in children's education and literature, the rising fortune of Dante in English through new translations for adults, and the way in which Purgatory – the land of work – resonated in the Anglican and Protestant work ethic all contribute to all contribute to the poem's adaptation as children's literature.

Contemporary versions take a radically different approach in recasting the *Divine Comedy*. John Agard's *The young Inferno* and my *Dante's journey, an infernal adventure* show a dramatic shift in moral geography, tone, and purpose. In both, Hell has become acceptable terrain for kids. And fear – together with death, punishment, and monsters – is now the stuff of children's books. While these versions were composed with no knowledge of each other, they make some surprisingly similar moves. Dante gets a lot younger: in both books, the

20 Ibid., pp 4–5. **21** Ibid., p. 6.

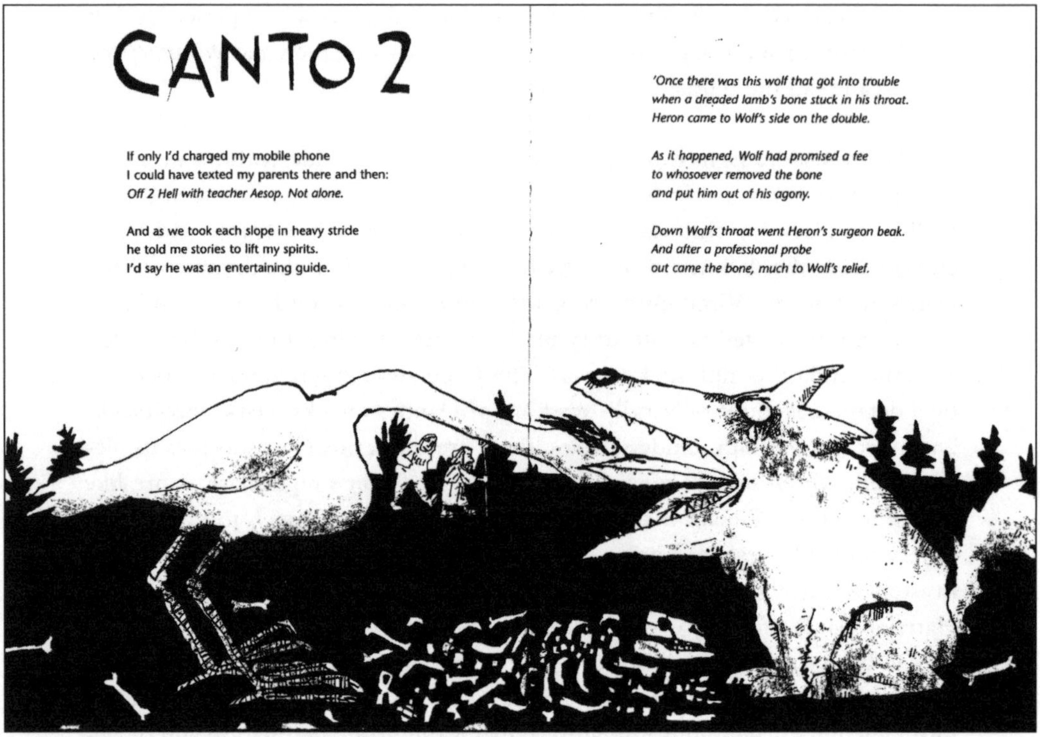

Fig. 1. John Agard's *Young Inferno*

protagonist is the same age as the reader. The autobiographical stance of the original is retrieved. The illustrations now carry as much weight as the words and are an integral part of the narrative. And finally, prose gives way to a poetic form that is highly attentive to and playful with the language and structure of Dante's verse.

Agard's translation, with illustrations by Satoshi Kitamura, begins where Dante does, *in medias res*:[22]

> In the middle of my childhood wonder
> I woke to find myself in a forest
> that was – how shall I put it – wild and sombre.

These lines are instantly recognizable as a clever translation of Dante's 'Nel mezzo del cammin di nostra vita/ mi ritrovai per una selva oscura'. (*Inf.* 1:1–2) In fact, Agard's rhyme scheme throughout is reminiscent of Dante's *terza rima,* and

22 J. Agard, *The young Inferno* (London, 2008), p. 1.

Fig. 2. John Agard's *Young Inferno*

his thirteen cantos are a further nod to Dante's tripartite structure. And though he states that his is 'in no way a translation', his lexicon, rhythm, and imagery brilliantly evoke Dante's own poetic appropriations and transformations.[23] Like Dante, he treats his readers to multiple registers (including text messaging) and even claims that his daughter's hip-hop music seeped in as he wrote.

While Agard's first lines signal his indebtedness to the original, he boldly mistranslates or transforms other elements to bring the text closer to his reader. The teenage Dante wears a hooded sweatshirt with the letters HELL emblazoned on it, and the gate of Hell is now a movie theatre, with Dante's famous inscription appearing on the marquee. The monstrosities of Hell are also modernized: a guitar-playing Frankenstein makes an appearance in Canto 4, as do George W. Bush and Tony Blair in Canto 10. But the most significant deviation, one that impacts the entire narrative, comes right at the beginning: Dante's trusty guide Virgil is replaced by Aesop. The surprising appearance of the famous writer of fables actually heightens the narrative potential of the three beasts that block

23 Agard, *The young Inferno*, 'Introduction' (unnumbered).

Dante's path and allows Agard to incorporate far more animals, a traditional element of children's literature, than can be found in the original. He weaves Aesop's fable of the Heron and the wolf into Canto 2 – a blatant violation of the letter of the original text that nevertheless perfectly captures its spirit (see Fig. 1). I like to think that Agard is acting like the heron: he bravely sticks his neck into the mouth of tradition and extracts a piece. The italic type and the language – the traditional 'Once upon a time' becomes the more slangy 'Once there was this wolf' – makes it clear that this is a story within a story. But that long neck stretching across two pages suggests that the story will not be neatly contained, and that new meaning can come from old bones. Agard's fable, like Aesop's, concludes with a moral: 'Ingratitude wears both beast and human mask'. But young Dante, in imitation of his medieval predecessor, challenges inherited interpretations:

> 'Please, sir, I have a question to ask:
> Shouldn't the heron have done that kind deed
> without thought of payment or reward?
> Doesn't the wolf deserve to be pitied?'[24]

Young Dante's alternative reading causes Aesop to revise his own: 'It just shows that neither beast nor man can be divided into black and white'.[25] And with that, we are returned to familiar Dante territory and to the very letter of the original. The phrase 'black and white' is taken directly from Dante, and recalls his language of division, which he uses in reference to the Black and White Guelphs, the warring political factions of his day.[26] The impossibility of dividing things into black and white speaks to the difficulty of interpretation – of Aesop's fable, certainly, but also of texts and experiences in general – and invites both the protagonist and the reader to participate in the interpretive process. Where does Dante's poem end and Agard's begin? How does one draw meaning from the other? A further interpretation game is played out in Kitamura's black and white illustrations, where clouds and plants metamorphose into haunting images of death. (see Fig. 2)

Agard highlights the joyful fruits of misinterpretation in the final canto of his *Young Inferno*. After reaching the bottom of Hell, Aesop and Dante part ways, with Dante returning to the Upper World. Not surprisingly, in this non-religious adaptation, the once fertile Purgatory disappears, and Dante returns to the earth. He arrives through a trap door that opens onto a library, a playful reminder of the high text that is Agard's inspiration and an invitation to the reader to continue the literary journey undertaken in his poem. Young Dante sees a girl with an 'otherworldly look' who is 'lost to the world in a book'.

24 Ibid., p. 10. **25** Ibid., p. 11. **26** See in particular *Inferno* 24 and 25.

Bewildered at the sight, Dante mutters, 'Are you the good fairy?' to which she responds, 'no, my name isn't Mary'.[27] Her name, of course, is Beatrice, and their confused, rhyming exchange underlines the potential of poetry to bring forth new meaning from misunderstanding. The book ends with them exiting the library and walking toward a flower shop. Young Dante speaks of her in a romantic language that recalls both the *Vita nuova* and Petrarch's *Canzoniere*, remarking 'She made that library a paradise.' Agard thus weaves other medieval literary threads into his own Dantesque verse while hinting at the role Beatrice will play in the *Divine Comedy*.

While Agard's transformative translation targets young teens, mine is aimed at what is probably the youngest Dante audience ever: four- to ten-year-olds. *Dante's journey, an infernal adventure* is certainly the shortest version in print: it is comprised of eleven sets of three rhyming couplets plus one final couplet for a total of thirty-four, in homage both to Dante's *terza rima* and the number of cantos of the *Inferno*.[28] The verse form and metre are reminiscent of countless other children's books. And just as nineteenth-century translators relied on Bunyan's *Pilgrim's Progress* to lend narrative familiarity to Dante's strange journey, I leaned on contemporary favourites to bring Dante into a child's world: like Max in Maurice Sendak's *Where the wild things are*, little Dante is sent to his room for misbehaving and ends up in a mysterious forest. And thanks to Bill Watterson's cartoon strip *Calvin and Hobbes*, Dante's favourite stuffed animal Virgil is actually alive and wiser than his human companion. 'Junior' versions of the poem have long existed, but rather than producing another such semi-scholastic rendition that is shaped by how the *Comedy* will be taught in school, I strove for something that conveys the adventure and immediacy of the poem. Thus there are no lustful here, no sodomists, simonists, or suicides, even though they are central to the 'high' version of the poem, and are among the moments I emphasize most when I teach Dante to university students. Rather than remind my young readers of what they are missing, I present topics they are all too familiar with: greediness, anger, violence, lying, and meanness.

I first wrote *Dante's journey* in Italian, and then, at the request of the publisher, composed an English version. Translating myself presented a series of unexpected challenges, especially because the Italian version incorporated so many linguistic echoes of the original. The Italian version could not but open with a reference to Dante's famous 'Nel mezzo del cammin' (hence I begin with 'Nel mezzo della notte') and end with the word *stelle*. Such a direct lexical relationship with the original can only be approximated in English, how-

27 J. Agard, pp 70–1. **28** V. Jewiss, *Dante's journey, an infernal adventure,* illustrations by Aline Cantono di Ceva (Florence, 2008).

7

Then Virgil told Dante, "Look, there in the gloom,
Deep in the valley the wrathful still fume.

On earth they were angry, quick to see red,
But tantrums serve little now that they're dead.

Hot-headed, irascible, fiery folk
Are punished this way—they go up in smoke."

Fig. 3. Virginia Jewiss's *Dante's Journey*

8

"Who'd take a bath in this hot, crimson stream?"
Asked Dante, perplexed, as he peered through the steam.

"Those who were violent, malicious, or cruel,
Now stew in their own juice, so don't be a fool.

If you harm other people you hurt yourself too,
And could find yourself in this bubbling brew."

Fig. 4. Virginia Jewiss's *Dante's Journey*

ever. In both languages I strove for a poetic playfulness that highlights Dante's system of *contrapasso*. Thus the angry souls go up in smoke and the violent stew in their own juice. (see Figs 3 and 4) The illustrations by Aline Cantono di Ceva visualize the linguistic puns, and many enact their own form of visual translation by playing off of Doré's well-known images of the *Inferno*. With the help of Virgil, Dante comes to realize that home is 'a real paradise' and they return from Hell to the warmth of their bed on earth.

Despite their distance from the early versions, both contemporary translations work on the same basic principle that was operative there: Dante's poem does contain 'simple truths' that can be distilled into simple lessons. Although the religious dimension is now completely absent and the tone is much more playful, the moral imperative remains central. Hell proves to be an ideal place for children to learn, and hopefully their memory of the low version will only increase the pleasure of the high one that awaits them.

The representation of colonial values in Italian translations of *The Jungle books*

Mette Rudvin

INTRODUCTION

This study examines how the subtext of Rudyard Kipling's colonialist world-view emerges in a selection of Italian translations of *The Jungle book* and *The second Jungle book* (1894–95).[1] Rather than focussing on the translator's individual agency in the textual transfer, or the differences between (actual or implied) source and target text readership, the essay aims to detect trends governing the production of the translated text that relate to those colonial elements imbued in the original.

A close analysis of the Kipling translations shows how their subtexts change significantly according to the presumed age-group of the readership (adult, adolescents and young adults, and young children). A low degree of adaptation emerges in the editions for adult readers. In the editions specifically aimed at adolescents, adaptation is slightly more prominent and we see significant changes at the inter-semiotic level through additional text-types (questions, discussions, prefaces, appendices) and atypical illustrations (including photographs); these additions are deeply pedagogical in function. Unsurprisingly, the third category of texts for very young children shows a high degree of adaptation and is particularly susceptible to modifications on the part of translators, illustrators and editors. The trend seems to be that the reluctance of the translators and illustrators to interfere with the text decreases along with the age of the readership, which in turn increases the translators' visibility.

Like most books in this category, the increased textual freedom found in the Italian adaptations of *The Jungle books* for young readers mirrors the prevailing perception of children's literature and of childhood in the specific time and place of the translation, this perception being governed by the text producer's (translator's) own child-image,[2] as well as the cognitive parameters and the textual skills

1 For convenience, the combined text of these two volumes will be referred to collectively as *The Jungle books*; they are sometimes published together under that title, e.g., in the Penguin Modern Classics series: Rudyard Kipling, *The Jungle books*, ed. Daniel Karlin (London, 2000). **2** See Riitta Oittinen, *I am me – I am other: on the dialogics of translating for children* (Tampere, 1993).

and expectations of this readership.[3] As Emer O'Sullivan says, 'an adult implied author creates an implied reader based on her/his (culturally determined) presuppositions as to the interests, propensities and capabilities of readers at a certain stage of their development' – and, because of the 'asymmetrical nature' of the communication format where adults act on behalf of children – the translator is often more tangible in translated children's literature than in literature for adults.[4] In the Kipling corpus selected for analysis, we will find numerous tangible traces of a text-(re)producer's imprint at various textual levels.

One of the basic assumptions of the present essay is that translations are coloured in their very nature by the knowledge basis and personal bias (conscious or unconscious) of the agents involved in the text-reproducing process (which includes strong market forces with high financial stakes). One of these biases seems to be the literary and social role of the author in the respective source and target literary communities (the respective polysystems).[5] Kipling's significant role in world literature may have influenced the translation process by allowing only a very cautious and limited degree of textual 'manipulation' in the adult and young adult/adolescent categories, although this inhibition does not apply to translations aimed at very young readers.[6] The caution that applies

3 Although they are crucial for an in-depth analysis of literature for young children, illustrations – in either original or translated editions – will not be addressed in such a brief study. This topic is examined by the author in another paper which provides greater detail regarding both visual and textual data as well as many examples of illustrations. It also addresses in much more detail the interpersonal relations between the Jungle characters that are deeply embedded in the colonial world-view (especially hierarchy, authority, nature, hunting, the Law of the Jungle) and how the stories relate to Kipling's own personal life and rapport with India, in the light of children's literature as a modern literary construction (Mette Rudvin, 2011, 'Colonialism, children's literature and translation. The colonial gaze: a reading of the text and illustrations in Italian versions of *The Jungle books*', *Ceslic occasional papers* (Bologna, 2011), available at amsacta.unibo.it/3176/; accessed 10 June 2012). Also presented in 2006 at the second conference of the international association for translation and intercultural studies, Cape Town, South Africa. **4** Emer O'Sullivan, 'Narratology meets translation studies, or, the voice of the translator in children's literature', *Meta: Translator's Journal*, 48:1–2 (2003), 197–207 at 199, 198. Available at www.erudit.org/revue/meta/2003/v48/n1-2/006967ar.pdf , accessed 10 June 2012. **5** The polysystem theory was initially developed by Itamar Even-Zohar in 'The position of translated literature within the literary polysystem' in James S. Holmes, José Lambert & R. van den Brook (eds), *Literature and translation* (Leuven, 1978), pp 117–27 and later re-applied with great success to translation studies by Gideon Toury in *Descriptive translation studies and beyond* (Amsterdam, 1995); the term is widely used today in translation studies to indicate the aggregate, or set, of relationships between the domains of literature, language, art, economics, politics, and other collective cultural constructs that interact and impact on each other, creating a dynamic interrelationship between cultural systems (polysystems). **6** In an article on the translation of Salman Rushdie's children's book *Haroun and the sea of stories*, I have previously argued that the status of the author affects translational strategies (Mette Rudvin & Francesca Orlati, 'Dual readership and hidden subtexts

when translating for older age-groups might also be due to the knowledge that the eyes of a global readership will be merciless in their evaluation of omissions, additions and other changes to the text, although, as we will see, that consideration does not seem to restrict the use of other semiotic strategies in the use of extra-textual material such as notes, appendices and photographs in translations made for adolescents.

'AMBIVALENT' TEXTS

A proper analysis of Kipling's *Jungle books* can find a fruitful foundation in Zohar Shavit's work on Lewis Carroll, and the theoretical framework that she establishes for reading his books as 'ambivalent texts'. *Alice's adventures underground* (1864), *Alice's adventures in wonderland* (1865), and the adapted version for young children – *The nursery Alice* (1890) – form a text series which lends itself particularly well to a discussion of norm-breaking text-production (through satire), double readerships, innovation and the creation of new textual models; Shavit discusses all of these in considerable depth.[7] Thirty years after *Alice*, *The Jungle books* also came to occupy a key position as an 'ambivalent text' both in the adult literary polysystem and also as a children's book (and also through spin-off 'paraphernalia' from the text and subsequent illustrations, for example Kipling's friend Lord Baden-Powell's adoption of the Jungle wolf pack for his Boy Scout 'Cubs'). Unlike Lewis Carroll, Kipling did not recreate the fantasy story or the fairy tale (Shavit speaks of the 'invasion' of fairy tales into English children's literature in the mid-nineteenth century)[8] and his aim was neither satirical nor nonsensical; on the contrary *The Jungle books* present a serious, earnest text upholding the rather severe imperial values of sacrifice and duty that the author subscribed to with such commitment. Shavit refers to the 'ambivalent status' of a text that is synchronically written for (and/or received by) both adults and children, and thus belongs to two canonized systems at the same time.[9] She observes how texts that have a dominant position in the canonized system for young children will usually have to be rewritten, abridged and simplified to

in children's literature: the case of Salman Rushdie's *Haroun and the sea of stories'* in J. Van Coillie & Walter P. Verschueren (eds), *Children's literature in translation: challenges & strategies* (Manchester, 2006), pp 157–84). **7** See Zohar Shavit, 'The ambivalent status of texts: the case of children's literature', *Poetics Today,* 1–3 (1980), 75–86; Michael Steig, '"The ambivalent status of texts". Some comments', *Poetics Today*, 2–1b (1980/81), 193–7; Zohar Shavit, '"The ambivalent status of texts": a rejoinder', *Poetics Today,* 2–1b (1980/81), 199–202; Zohar Shavit, *Poetics of children's literature* (London, 1986). **8** Shavit, *Poetics of children's literature*, p. 76. **9** Shavit, 'Ambivalent status', 75–6.

become readable as texts for children. This very ambivalence provides the writer (and translator, one might add) with a wide range of possibilities to 'manipulate' the text and also allows him/her to alter or break with prevailing existing norms in the children's system.[10] An 'ambivalent text' can thus bring new models into the centre of the polysystem.

The dynamic interplay that emerges between the two textual models (especially through intertextual references and irony) will be more easily understood by adults rather than by child readers; the text is thus read and experienced in very different ways by the different readerships. The full potential of the text for adult readers lies precisely in its duality and complexity, appealing both to cognitive sophistication and the remembrance of childhood, while for child readers the reading experience is less ambiguous and intersects with the visual processing of illustrations either in the original or through adaptations and abridgements. There are a number of significant issues that might be explored in relation to the 'ambivalent status' of *The Jungle books* as a text both for children and adults (in the original and in translation), for example the degree of innovation that is – or is not – introduced by the text, and the interaction and tension between the two textual models and how this affects their recognition, acceptance and status by their readerships. For reasons of space, however, I will restrict this discussion to a very few brief observations that are pertinent to the issue of translation. We will see how Italian translations of *The Jungle books* follow, creatively play upon, and are at the same time limited by this very doubleness or ambivalence that impacts not only on the original text and its readership, but on the entire translation/re-writing process.

MOWGLI, COLONIALISM AND CHILDHOOD

The image of the child and of childhood in Europe and the United States, as well as the function of children's literature, have changed drastically over the last two centuries.[11] *The Jungle books* have also undergone changes in status and function. In Kipling's day *The Jungle books* filled several functions in the literary polysystem, one of which was pedagogical: the text was instrumental in the inculcation of Victorian morality and values (primarily loyalty, stoicism, friendship, obedience). As a text that appealed also to adults, both for its artistic qualities and for its representation of Victorian values, it strengthened what might be called a cross-over writing form.

10 Shavit, 'Ambivalent status', 75, 77. **11** See, for example, Hugh Cunningham, *The invention of childhood* (London, 2006) or Jacqueline Rose, *The case of Peter Pan or the impossibility of children's fiction* (London, 1984).

It is a well-known fact that Kipling's tormented nostalgia for his childhood in India deeply influenced his work. Sullivan speaks of his obsession with his original lost home.[12] Tropes of colonialism and childhood interact in a highly complex narrative network of private memories and public ideology in the Mowgli stories. Indeed, it is not unreasonable to claim that Kipling's nostalgia and love for his childhood India led to the creation of *The Jungle books* as a *Bildungsroman*. His own painful cultural displacement during his most formative and vulnerable years seems to have been catalytic in creating the inbuilt tension that is so characteristic of Mowgli. Mowgli's inner tension is generated by a refusal to become socialized into adulthood, a refusal to accept the loss of his Edenic jungle, a refusal to accept his role as a human being who is superior to his beloved animal friends and protectors. Until it becomes inevitable, Mowgli refuses to become English and leave his beloved India/Jungle. In the translations for young children, these essential motifs of the *bildungsroman* are heavily sacrificed.

THE JUNGLE BOOKS IN ITALIAN TRANSLATION

The remainder of this essay is mostly concerned with exploring how the salient traits of Kipling's subtext are maintained in the Italian translations. The *Jungle book* stories exemplify situations in the human world, thus constructing an 'animal metaphor' of the world of the adults. This concern reflects Kipling's concept of the children's book as an educational tool, and also reflects the position that this genre occupied in British society at the time, a position that enabled such texts to promote current values. In Italy, *The Jungle books* have been one of the most successful examples of children's literature (since the late 1960s especially through the Disney film version), serving both as entertainment for juvenile readers and also as a channel through which to teach and promote the English literary canon. Some of the translations that have been examined also reveal another important function, namely to introduce India to Italian children, again in a markedly didactic fashion. It is interesting to note the way in which India is presented, which varies greatly from edition to edition. Where some editions favour a more standard colonial representation, others present a watered-down representation of India with a very vague geographical identity, while yet others furnish a highly detailed ethnographical representation. These differences will be discussed in virtue of how they relate to the age of the presumed reader.

The Italian translations analysed in this article belong to the following three categories (allowing for overlaps between categories): (a) 'adult' unabridged ver-

12 Zohreh Sullivan, *Narratives of empire* (Cambridge, 1993), p. 43.

sions (b) versions for adolescents, and (c) versions for very young children (the list of editions at the end of the essay provides full publication details).

UNABRIDGED VERSIONS FOR AN ADULT READERSHIP

The first Italian translation of *The Jungle books* (*I* and *II*) by Pittola dates to 1903. One of the canonical translations, it was reprinted regularly until recent years. Another canonical translation is the one by Pozzo Galeazzi dating from 1951, also republished frequently. Catani's 1971 translation was followed by Conetti's 1993 translation which contains her own introduction to the volume. Another translation by Fatica was published in 1998. These translations, unsurprisingly, stay close to the source text, which may have something to do with the authoritative status of the Nobel prize-winning author and the translators' resulting reluctance to make major alterations.

The re-issue of the 1951 Pozzo Galeazzi translation in the mid-1990s seems to be aimed at both an adult and an adolescent readership. The detailed scholarly footnotes by a respected Indologist describing various aspects of Indian culture, history and language could suggest the inclusion of an adolescent readership. Conetti's translation is likewise a close and conservative one, with some exceptions (for example, the celebrated poems at the beginning of each story which have on the whole a more informal register than the earlier translation by Pittola).

These translations display some peculiarities: (a) omission of the marked definite article that Kipling uses for animal categories to give them a special status and place in his micro-cosmos and to elevate their function to a symbolic level; (b) a very slight domestication of overtly culture-specific elements such as the ubiquitous Hindi-Urdu exclamation *arré!* (*Ahi! Ahi!* in Conetti); (c) although the translations are close, none of them, not even Pittola's 1903 text, have chosen to imitate or maintain the marked social deixis ('thou'), or the archaic syntax and lexis; this aspect has been standardized and domesticated in all the translations examined; (d) the translations of playful metaphors are on the whole rather unimaginative ('cobwebs and moontalk', for example, becomes *assurde fantasie*, 'absurd fantasies').

UNABRIDGED VERSIONS FOR ADOLESCENTS AND YOUNG ADULTS

Padoan's (1987), Pieroni's (1991) and Arduino's (1996) illustrated editions are aimed at a young adolescent readership, and have a strong pedagogical function that combines the adventure story with the teaching of values through a metaphorical narrative. The editorial/translational tendency of targeting this particular readership, frequently intensifying the pedagogical function, would seem quite deliberate. Prefaces, footnotes and translation commentaries tell us about the translators' love for nature and animals, which motivated these translators to read (and later translate) *The Jungle books*.[13] These are interests typically associated with adolescent or pre-adolescent male reader-groups (the translators are all male). Adventure stories that privilege values such as courage and loyalty comply with the Victorian tradition of the adventurous boy-hero epitomized by Rider Haggard's books and reflected in the Law of the Jungle, with its ubiquitous emphasis on acts of loyalty, courage and friendship.

Arduino's translation is a school edition which even has essay questions for the reader. The educational aims of this version are realized mainly through the illustrations – sketches, watercolours and photographs – which, rather than simply accompanying the text, try to depict and teach something about India. This translation and its illustrations seem specifically designed to present India to schoolchildren.

The didactic function is very strong also in Pieroni's translation, illustrated by Mignon. This edition is aimed at a (pre-)adolescent readership for use in a school setting, signalled primarily by the illustrations but also by the questions and discussions on key issues (such as nature) in a small appendix. Though reflecting in many respects the complexity of *The Jungle books*, this edition as a whole seems to downplay the Indian *topos*. In his editor's preface to the Pieroni edition, Roberto Denti foregrounds the 'young adult' themes of nature and the animal world with their values of endurance and perseverance ('I loved to read *The Jungle books* as a child because I loved the animals'). The much-favoured Victorian motif of the wolf-child is mentioned; India is not. The subcontinent is thus rendered as a sort of fictional stage for a didactic, metaphorical representation, rather than as a real country.

Judging by Scarato and Spaliviero's illustrations in the Padoan translation, this text is also aimed at a pre-adolescent to young adult readership. As I have noted elsewhere,[14] the text actually introduces material additions to the text by explaining what is happening and what Mowgli is thinking and doing (the 'voice of the translated narrator,' which will be discussed below). The translator thus expands upon the characters' actions and qualities, inserting new elements into the text and at the same time limiting the scope of interpretation.

13 The inference seems to be that just as authors of children's books are governed by their own perception and memory of childhood, so also are translators. **14** See Rudvin, 'Colonialism, children's literature and translation'.

This, as Peter Hunt observes, is typical of literature for children and reflects the belief that children are unable to capture covert meaning, implicit signification, irony and subtexts.[15]

In the Padoan translation, the editor's preface and translator's commentary both emphasize the connection between adolescence and nature/animals (indeed this edition is almost an illustrated nature-book): the editor and translator discuss the love they felt for animals during their own childhood, and stress how well Kipling 'understands animals and nature'. The age-group and the animal focus are even more sharply emphasized in the full title of a second illustrated edition using Padoan's translation that appeared in that same year: *I miei animali da I libri della giungla* ('My animals from *The Jungle books*', 1987). This focus on nature and animals suggests that the translators have not maintained the author's sense of the metaphorical and arguably mystical aspect of nature, with Mowgli as a potential Pan-figure (which we find in a related text).[16] Through supplementary elements added to the text, rather than through the translation itself, the function of the maturation story is sacrificed in favour of a boy's adventure story. The boy's final, definitive leap to adulthood and 'humanness', so poignantly presented by Kipling in the last chapter, is not given the prominence that it possessed in the original.

VERSIONS FOR YOUNG CHILDREN

In books for young children, the importance of the illustrations is so crucial that it is hard to draw any conclusions about the text without also mentioning them.[17] The illustrated editions of *The Jungle books* for young children in Italian translation are perhaps best represented by Masini's 1996 translation and De Benedetti's 1983 translation. The illustrated 1989 version for young children using Pasini's translation is also intended for a young readership, as is Marrucchi's 1937 translation reissued in 1994 with illustrations by Mirek in economical black-white sketches in a simple, naive, style.

In this category, however, we also find some of the early canonical 'adult' translations mentioned above in expensive hardback editions, accompanied by high-quality colour illustrations meant for young children. These editions are particularly interesting because they embody a double function, aiming to maintain both the status and 'aura' of the early translated text while also fulfill-

15 Peter Hunt, *Criticism, theory and children's literature* (Oxford, 1991). **16** Rudvin, 'Colonialism, children's literature and translation'. **17** See, for example, Oittinen's approach in *Translating for children* (New York, 2000).

ing the visual expectations of young readers. The most representative of these are the 2005 edition of Pozzo Galeazzi's 1951 translation published in 2005 (*Il libro della giungla*) splendidly illustrated by Vinci, and the 1960 (*Il 2° libro della jungla*) edition of Pittola's 1903 translation with simple sketches by Bernardini and evocative, languid watercolours by Vagaggini that supply a complex subtext for a slightly wider age-group. The preface to Pittola's translation is the one which best captures the complexity of the text and of Mowgli's strained love-authority relationship with the animals and his power over them; it mentions India positively albeit stereotypically ('a magnificent, mysterious landscape') and discusses the *Bildungsroman* angle. The translated texts are challenging in that they employ a high register with elegant and at times old-fashioned words and expressions that add an authoritative austerity to the text (that is, *disputa* rather than *lotta* for 'fight', the more literary adjectives '***acerrimo*** *nemico*' – 'arch-enemy, bitter enemy' and '***scabroso*** *sentiero*' – 'difficult, thorny, or awkward path', in the Pozzo Galeazzi translation). These versions are therefore an interesting combination of challenging texts alongside illustrations meant for young children.

Much work and money has been invested in these editions by editors, translators and illustrators. Although directed at a young readership, these expensive hardbacks could thus be seen as an indication both of the status of Kipling's text as a classic in the Italian polysystem, and of the importance that literature for children has recently attained in the global literary polysystem.

TRANSLATION STRATEGIES IN TEXTS FOR YOUNG CHILDREN

Simplification of register and lexis

The abridged Italian versions for very young children feature the typical textual adaptations made in order to summarize and simplify the main points and issues of the stories for a readership presumably unable to enjoy more complex narratives. Masini's translation is quite close, but more lively and with a more varied lexis than some of the others (such as De Benedetti in which the text has been modernized and rendered informal, the syntax unmarked). Here too the translator accepts the current norm of children's literature in the target text, and produces shorter sentences, simpler syntax and current usage rather than the dated language that in the original text creates a sort of internal Jungle diglossia. For example, 'Now get hence' becomes '*Ora vattene*', 'Now leave' (p. 18). 'Thee' and 'ye' are as elsewhere rendered simply with the familiar '*tu*' form. The adjustments further involve simplification of the language (syntax, lexis) and a lowering of the ceremonial, formulaic, almost ritualistic register found in the original. The exception to this general trend can be found in the hybrid editions already mentioned: the ones that combine canonical translations with high-quality illustrations aimed at a young readership.

In the abridged versions for young children we find the narrative features described by Hunt[18] as being typically used by authors of children's literature to accommodate the presumed cognitive level of children: short sentences, no hypotaxis, simple register and lexis, no marked syntax, a narrow range of grammatical and lexical patterns, standard set phrases rather than idiosyncratic and original language use, and contemporary rather than dated language. Again we see how the perception of children and childhood in a particular time and place impacts on who the text producer (publisher/writer/translator) sees as his/her target readership, taking into account questions such as their reading preferences and their cognitive and linguistic capabilities, how far they can be stretched, to what extent the material is suitable, and so forth. As O'Sullivan says, these same questions are asked also by the translator and the publisher.[19]

Explaining and clarifying

Another typical characteristic of books for children is 'clarification', where the author explains what lies between the lines and may be misunderstood. By speaking/thinking for the child, addressing the readership directly as if s/he were physically present, the author creates a tangible bond between author and reader and a climate of safety and familiarity. The presence of a highly visible narrator of the story (rather than author of the book) thus becomes important. As Hunt (see especially chapter 5) remarks in his analysis of a range of texts for children, this can be done by using a closed/finalized speech pattern where the narrator speaks and thinks for the child, thus impeding other avenues of interpretation; in books for adults there would be a higher threshold for 'open speech'.

The relevance of this visible narrator specifically for translated literature has been addressed by O'Sullivan who shows how translators sometimes have more scope to 'speak' directly to the implied child readers through the 'voice of the narrator of the translation'.[20] It is particularly evident in children's literature because of the 'asymmetrical communication structure' mentioned above between the (implied) adult author/producer/translator and the child (implied) reader.[21] The translator may add clarification, guidance or explanations through the narrator's voice, or may add an interpersonal observation like 'of course', thus commenting directly on the thoughts or actions of the characters and creating a

18 See esp. Hunt, *Criticism, theory and children's literature*, Chapter 6 and also Rudvin, 'Colonialism, children's literature and translation'. **19** O'Sullivan, 'Narratology', 205. **20** Ibid. **21** O'Sullivan, 'Narratology', 205, 202.

direct rapport between reader and text or text-producer (in line with the general tendency to increased explanation and clarification that Hunt addresses). In this way, O'Sullivan shows, the narrator in the source and target texts are different, the translated narrator overriding the source narrator. Again we see how the text producer's voice (through the narrator) is 'based on assumptions as to the interests, propensities and capabilities of readers at that stage of their development'.[22]

In my corpus, the narrator's voice seems to be more evident in the cultural explanations that we have seen in the youngest target group of *The Jungle books* where a general domestication strategy would seem to prevail, the assumption being that the implied reader cannot cope with a 'foreign' setting.[23] In versions for very young children we find examples of how, through translation, the voice of the narrator becomes more intrusive and has been adjusted to fit into the translator's own prevailing image of child and childhood (for that specific age-group).[24] There is also a tendency to make inter-textual referencing clearer – for example, 'Adesso dobbiamo tornare al primo racconto', 'now we must go back to the first story' (Padoan p. 59) – so that the reader is reminded of what happened in the previous chapters, thus reinforcing the above-mentioned bond between author/translator and reader, and creating a safe, familiar setting.

Simplification of content

In the editions for very young children, Mowgli's thoughts, attitudes, self-appraisal and inner monologues (especially his scathing reproach of the villagers and the monkeys) are removed in the abridged versions, as is anything deemed redundant to the primary plot (for example, geographical, territorial, logistical or pictorial detail), sacrificing essential parts of the plot and its subtext, not least the Law of the Jungle and its inherent Victorian world view. For example, one sentence deemed redundant in the De Benedetti translation – deeply symptomatic of how Kipling justifies Victorian values of social and natural hierarchy through the Jungle Law – is 'The Law of the Jungle, which never orders anything without a reason, forbids every beast to eat Man except when he is killing to show his children how to kill [...]'.[25] De Benedetti's version has undergone major adaptations and much of the text has been surgically removed. Whole paragraphs that are considered redundant are summarized, more for example than in Masini's text, and speaker attributions are regularly sacrificed as are logistics and other detail. Irony is largely removed. Although the formal register is often sacrificed in her translation, Masini has at times tried to maintain the irony

22 Ibid., 204. **23** Ibid., 205. **24** See Rudvin, 'Colonialism, children's literature and translation'. **25** Rudyard Kipling, *The Jungle book*, introduction Christopher Paolini (London, 2009), p. 6.

in the dialogues between the animals, sometimes clarifying it by adding explanations: 'chiese Tabaqui, insolente', 'Tabaqui asked *insolently*'.[26] The De Benedetti edition sacrifices irony even more completely. Anthropomorphism replaces a very strong sense of the animals being real. Cultural differences are homogenized: very few Hindi/Urdu words are maintained, except the names. In the illustrations, much of the Indian landscape and milieu has also been removed, and Mowgli is generally white. It is of course impossible to know to what degree such adaptations are the translator's own decisions or made by an editor or publisher.

Generally, the morally didactic elements of the rules, laws and behaviour of the Jungle and its animals are emphasized, but the long explanations of the Law of the Jungle and the attributes of the animals, essential to the plot and narrative style of *The Jungle books*, have been drastically shortened, possibly because they would be considered too tedious for young children. We see here how the voice of the narrator is reconstructed at one level (and becomes the translated narrator), while at another level it is silenced, in accordance with the norms of the prevailing target system at that particular time for that particular translator.

Such elements of domestication and adaptation are very much in line with what Hunt illustrates as an example of prevailing definitions of children's literature:[27] lack of historical detail or context; a timeless setting; an optimistic rather than depressive outlook; the prevalence of adventure and the concrete rather than the abstract, the indeterminate or the ambiguous. Movement and action prevail over stasis, inaction or reflection.

Downplaying of violence and tension

Throughout these abridged versions, and in many of the illustrations of the non-abridged versions for young children, conflict and tension, violence and threatening behaviour are much reduced, as is any trace of fear related to the animals – a key component in the original text.[28] We see a focus on themes such as childhood, friendship and familial relationships as opposed to themes such as death, violence, aggression or fear. It is clear that the translation strategies for the third (abridged) category are in line with the prevailing view of what is appropriate for young children, but not in line with the original text or the strategies employed in the first two categories.

Many aggressive and violent elements are softened by removing the characters' most negative attributes: both Shere Khan and Tabaqui, for example, are

26 Rudyard Kipling, *Il libro della giungla,* trans. by Beatrice Masini (Milan, 1996), p. 10. **27** Hunt, *Criticism, theory and children's literature*, p. 63. **28** For example the chapters 'Letting in the jungle' and 'Red dog'.

less menacing in their looks and words.[29] In Masini's translation Tabaqui the jackal's menacing '"All thanks for this good meal", he said, licking his lips' is jettisoned and Shere Khan's equally menacing 'Ye choose and ye do not choose! What talk is this of choosing?', where his authority is first threatened, becomes '*Volere? Voi volere?*' 'Want? You, want?'[30] In the De Benedetti edition even Shere Khan's lameness and hunger and the resultant danger of this condition are removed. As in so many of the other adaptations the underlying suspense, fear and aggression are substituted by a safe, secure environment in which Mowgli becomes a cute, cuddly baby-boy.

In downplaying the fear and aggression in the interpersonal rapport between the jungle animals, the source text's prime emphasis on the Jungle Law and its inbuilt hierarchy is sacrificed. Also, the potentially threatening nature of Mother Wolf, Raksha ('the Demon') has been sacrificed in some of the abridged texts (for example, De Benedetti, Marrucchi), and she is depicted instead as safe and secure, a maternal haven rather than a ferocious jungle animal protecting her young – 'her young' would include of course Mowgli. The very use of 'Mamma/Papà' (*Mummy/Daddy*) and 'Babbo' (*Daddy/Dad*) for Mother and Father Wolf assigns to them this same 'safe' parental role. These adaptations also lead to a skewed representation of the Law of the Jungle that demands obedience and strict compliance with order, structure, rules, hierarchy and authority. The importance of the supreme Jungle law of killing only for food or necessity, not for pleasure and not Man,[31] the mitigating factor in this harsh fight for survival, is also reduced in many of the texts in this category. Furthermore, in the De Benedetti edition, even Death is humorous and unthreatening.[32] So too is Mowgli, a reading which goes very much against the spirit of the text, but is in keeping with modern views of what literature for young children should contain or not contain.

More than a century after their publication, it is impossible to establish exactly which readership Kipling had in mind when writing these stories[33] and if he felt that the underlying violence of a story like 'Red dog' was suitable for very young readers.[34] Even today the nature of the de facto readership remains

29 Incidentally, in the Masini text, as in so many others, Shere Khan becomes 'she' rather than the 'he' of the original. It is hard to tell what the motivation is for this, perhaps it is simply due to the convention that felines are female, or yet another down-toning of a – possibly – more threatening male figure, or even a downplaying of the representation of Mowgli's alter-ego. **30** Masini, p. 18. **31** E.g. Kipling, *The Jungle books*, p. 190. **32** See Rudvin, 'Colonialism, children's literature and translation'. **33** The *Just so stories* collection is much more easily categorized as 'children's stories'. **34** In the same way it is very difficult to know whether the violence contained in the tales of the Brothers Grimm really was accepted as suitable for young children at the time and what the function of this violence

elusive, given that it is adults who choose and buy children's books and who either read these stories to children or encourage them to read them themselves.

Downplaying of the maturation story

Mowgli's relationship with the animals, which varies profoundly with the different species, is a key element in the maturation motif, and this part of the story practically rests on the whole tiger–boy duel. Mowgli's fearless challenging of Shere Khan is jettisoned in many of the translations; for example in the Masini version the removal of a sentence between chapters 1 and 2 sacrifices Mowgli's first, unafraid look at Shere Khan, so important to the theme of his authoritative, superior, 'colonial gaze'. The maturation theme ties in closely with the use of suspense discussed in the preceding paragraph in that Mowgli's overcoming of fear and his domination of the animals are part and parcel of his coming-of-age process.

CONCLUSIONS

On the basis of the editions examined here there seems to be a general tendency in the editions using close translations to maintain the features that most typically informed Kipling's own world-view. We have seen that there is a significant difference between the level of textual adaptation in the editions for adults and adolescents and the editions for young children (except for Pozzo-Galeazzi and Pittola, as already noted). A continuum tracing the degree of adaptation follows the age of the assumed reader: the translations for the oldest age-groups are wary of adaptations (possibly due, it has been suggested, to the author's status in world literature). The middle group maintains a higher degree of foreignization; it does accommodate adaptation but mainly through extra-textual sources and mainly for didactic reasons. As expected, the abridged versions for young children contain the highest degree of adaptation – and translator visibility – and it is here that the author's world-view has been most obviously abandoned. The Victorian ideals of authority, obedience, hierarchy, independence, so fundamental to the original text and readership, are sacrificed in these editions along with the complex sociocultural interpersonal network that prevails in the Jungle. The downplaying of danger, violence, death, fear, conflict, aggression and tension, especially in the relations between Mowgli and the animals, follows a general tendency not to frighten children, a tendency that is in line with a modern view, or indeed a

was, during the period when they were diffused orally and later when they were collected, adapted, written down and published.

modern construction, of childhood. Other values that could be considered more appropriate and 'safe' for young children have been retained: the family (the Wolf pack), loyalty and friendship. Through this process, however, these translations sacrifice the tension that is so fundamental to Mowgli's coming-of-age process and which makes this story a true masterpiece.

Drawing on a range of textual and extra-textual strategies, the textual freedom that seems to be a feature of translating for young children explodes Kipling's original text into a variety of readings and interpretations. It is hard to say whether or not these translations have actively shaped the wider polysystem, whether or not they have had an innovatory or consolidating force in shaping the views of text producers and readers concerning childhood and children's literature, or indeed their views on Kipling, on Kipling's world-view (colonialism) and on his local environment (India). Those elements that seem to have had a more lasting impact on the Italian literary and educational systems are the didactic versions for adolescents and the illustrations in the versions for young children. Certainly the Disney cartoon version of the book has had an enormous influence on the perception and popularity of the book in large parts of the world, not just the UK or Italy. Although this does not directly concern the present discussion, it seems likely that this is a self-generating process whereby films and film paraphernalia impact reciprocally on text, translation and printed illustrations.

As we have seen, Kipling's own vision, deeply embedded in (his own) time and place, has receded and been replaced by a new time and a new place. This explosive ability to generate and multiply is a feature of abridged literature for children that, although 'disloyal' to the original text, allows that same text to speak to, and live through, future generations of readers across the world.

ITALIAN TRANSLATIONS CITED

The translations of The Jungle books *are listed under the names of their translators. Only editions discussed in the text are mentioned; for a full list of translations, see Rudvin,* Colonialism, children's literature and translation, *in the general bibliography.*

Arduino, Giovanni, *Il libro della giungla*, ill. C. Broutin; Piemme 'Battello a Vapore' (Casale Monferrato 2001, 1998, 1996).

Catani, Fausto, *Il libro della giungla*; Editrice Ancora (Milan, 1971).

Conetti, Lidia, *Il libro della giungla* and *Il secondo libro della giungla* in *Rudyard Kipling romanzi*, introduction by Lidia Conetti; Mondadori (Milan, 1993).

De Benedetti, Maria Paola, *Il libro della giungla*, ill. V. Michault; Lito Editrice (Milan, 1983).

Fatica, Ottavio, *Il libro della giungla*; Einaudi (Turin, 1998).
Marrucchi, Angelica, *Il libro della giungla,* ill. Mirek (Miroslav Zahradka); Giunti 'Giunti Ragazzi Universal' (Florence, 1937/1994).
Masini, Beatrice ('translation and reduction'), *Il libro della giungla*, ill. F. Trabacchi; Bompiani-Conchiglie (Milan, 1996).
Padoan, Gianni, *I libri della giungla*, ill, G. Scarato and F. Spaliviero, with a short preface by Masolino d'Amico; appendix with a postface by the translator and with a collection of the Jungle songs/verses and Jungle Laws; Mondadori (Milan, 1987).
– *I miei animali da I libri della giungla*, ill. R. Simon; Mondadori (Verona, 1987; Éditions Gautier-Langureau 1987 for the illustrations).
Pasini, Roberto, *Il libro della giungla*, ill. A. Ripamonti; AMZ 'I Birilli' (Milan, 1989). Reprinted *Il libro della giungla*; De Agostini (Milan, 1997, 1998).
Pieroni, Piero, *Il libro della giungla*, ill. 1983 P. Mignon/H. Galeron with a preface by Roberto Denti; Edizioni E Elle (Trieste, 1991; 1983 for illustrations and 1987 for educational supplement in appendix by Éditions Gallimard).
Pittola, Umberto, first published 1903 by Mursia and republished frequently, e.g.:
– *Il 2° libro della jungla*, ill. P. Bernardini and M. Vagaggini; Mursia 'Corticelli' (Milan, 1960, 1972, 1974, 1988).
– *Storie per tutti. I libri della giungla* (containing *The Jungle books I* and *II*, *Just so stories*, the *Puck stories, and Stories and legends*, with a preface by Pietro De Logu; Mursia (Milan, no date in book but catalogued 1965).
– *Il libro della giungla* and *Il secondo libro della giungla* in *Rudyard Kipling*, with an introduction by Vittorio Beonio-Brocchieri; Utet (Turin, 1965).
– *Rudyard Kipling*, collection of Kipling's works including *The Jungle books I* and *II* and *Kim* in a series on writers of the world, with an introduction by Vittorio Beonio-Brocchieri; Club degli Editori (Milan, 1965).
– *I capolavori di Kipling,* contains *The Jungle books I* and *II*, *Kim*, and a collection of short stories and poetry; includes '*In the rukh*'; and preface by Bottalla; Mursia (Milan, 1966).
– *I libri della giungla*; Mursia (Milan, 1984).
Pozzo Galeazzi, Giuliana, *Il libro della giungla*; Rizzoli (Milan, 1951, republished 1995 Milan, Opportunity Book).
– *Il secondo libro della giungla*, unillustrated edition with a postface by Antonio Faeti; cover illustration by G Mauri and indicated 'from 10 years', includes the non-Mowgli stories; Libri & Grandi Opere (Milan, 1950, 1951, 1995). Republished in 2003 by Fabbri in the series 'I Delfini'.
– *Il libro della giungla*, ill. V. Vinci; Fabbri (Milan, 2005).

Bowdlerization as translation: dual readership and the translation of children's literature

Emer Delaney

INTRODUCTION

The term 'freedom', applied to translation, suggests a paradox: freedom in translation can (though need not always) function as a tool of censorship, limiting the author's freedom of expression and the reader's freedom of knowledge. Where children's literature is concerned, this pattern may be especially facilitated by the genre's peripheral status,[1] its strong emphasis on didactic and pedagogical norms,[2] and a relatively low number of target readers likely to have access to both original and translated versions of a text.

This last point, however, recalls the fact that all children's books can be said to have a dual readership, within which exists a power imbalance of sorts. Adults write, edit, publish, purchase and critique the books, thus determining the available content of the genre and its canon; children read what survives this filtering process.[3] Translation, then, can function as one more link strengthening an already 'extensive chain of adult authorities'.[4]

This scenario may be disrupted, however, in the case of 'crossover' texts, defined by Sandra L. Beckett as 'fiction that crosses from child to adult or adult to child audiences'.[5] On the one hand, the apparently adult-oriented elements

1 See Zohar Shavit, 'Translation of children's literature as a function of its position in the literary polysystem', *Poetics Today,* 2:4 (Summer–Autumn 1981), 171–9 at 171. **2** For a fuller discussion of the interplay of norms in translated children's literature, see Isabelle Desmidt, 'A prototypical approach within descriptive translation studies? Colliding norms in translated children's literature' in J. Van Coillie & W.P. Verschueren (eds), *Children's literature in translation: challenges and strategies* (Manchester, 2006), pp 79–94 at pp 86–7. **3** Gillian Lathey, 'Introduction' in G. Lathey (ed.), *The translation of children's literature: a reader* (Clevedon, 2006), pp 1–12 at pp 4–5. **4** Angelika Nikolowski-Bogomoloff, 'More than a childhood revisited? Ideological dimensions in the American and British translations of Astrid Lindgren's *Madicken*' in E. Ní Chuilleanáin, C. Ó Cuilleanáin & D. Parris (eds), *Translation and censorship* (Dublin, 2009), pp 173–83 at p. 174. **5** Sandra L. Beckett, *Crossover fiction: global and historical perspectives* (New York, 2009), p. 4. Nuancing this definition, Beckett acknowledges that 'in its purest form, one could perhaps argue that a true crossover title is the rare book [...] that is written, published, and marketed for readers of all ages, but this is not the case for the vast majority of crossovers. They may initially have been published for a particular audience and subsequently appropriated by another, in a process that could be called "cross-read-

of a source text may pose particular challenges to generical and cultural norms of children's literature in the target language. On the other hand, the use of free translation to preserve such norms may be constrained by the presence of an interested adult readership that values adequacy over acceptability, in Gideon Toury's terms;[6] has more access than its child counterpart to the source language, culture and text; and wields more direct consumer power.

Critics have proposed various subdivisions of cross-writing. Barbara Wall, for instance, distinguishes between 'dual address', in which child and adult readers are addressed on equal if not identical terms, and 'double address', in which adult readers are entertained while, and sometimes because, child readers are left in the dark.[7] However, Wall acknowledges that true 'dual address', according to this definition, is rarely found.[8] Moreover, it is clear that the individual variation of readers' knowledge and comprehension levels problematizes stark borders between the categories of child and adult. Sandra L. Beckett, exploring cross-writing as a means of blurring these very borders, stresses that some cross-written texts may not address a dual or double readership at all; they may rather 'target a single audience of hybrid adult-child readers'.[9]

This last possibility is of particular interest as regards Richmal Crompton's *William* stories, which form the subject of the first part of this study. *William* cannot easily be located in relation to a dual/double address dichotomy. Peter Hunt's verdict on the series is that 'the text, very knowingly, operates [...] "double narrative" [...]; that is, addressing two audiences simultaneously but separately, and the adult audience primarily'[10] – and certainly, in the early books especially, Crompton made few if any concessions to the supposed inability of children to grasp arcane vocabulary, sophisticated syntax, allusiveness or political satire. However, Ralph Stewart also makes a valid point when he states that 'most readers, *including most children*, are often in a position to condescend to William' [my italics].[11] I would extend this argument to suggest that they are

ing". [...] Thus crossover books may find an audience of both children and adults with or without authorial and/or editorial intention.' (p. 7). **6** Toury sees the choice between adequacy and acceptability as an initial norm: 'A translator may subject him-/herself either to the original text, with the norms it has realized, or to the norms active in the target culture [...] Whereas adherence to source norms determines a translation's adequacy as compared to the source text, subscription to norms originating in the target culture determines its acceptability.' Gideon Toury, 'The nature and role of norms in translation' in *Descriptive translation studies – and beyond* (Amsterdam, 1995), pp 53–69; repr. in L. Venuti (ed.), *The translation studies reader*, 2nd edition (New York, 2000), pp 205–18 at p. 208. **7** Barbara Wall, *The narrator's voice: the dilemma of children's fiction* (New York, 1991), p. 9. **8** Ibid., p. 35. **9** S.L. Beckett, *Crossover fiction*, p. 3. **10** Peter Hunt, *Children's literature* (Oxford, 2001), p. 54. **11** Ralph Stewart, 'William Brown's world', *Children's Literature Association Quarterly*, 13:4 (Winter 1988), 181–5 at 182.

simultaneously in a position to mock the 'civilized' adult world, exposed in all its artifice through the carnivalesque chaos of William's activities. Crompton's refusal to 'write down' to children,[12] then, exposes how contextually contingent is the concept of duality in readership; the authorial voice may position readers in a relation to the text and its characters that is independent of their age (albeit still dependent on their interpretative strategies). I proceed from an overview of *William*'s origins and intralingual metamorphoses to a descriptive analysis of the only available version of *William* stories in Italian, with particular attention to the fate of dual, double or 'hybrid' address in translation.

The second part of this paper deals with an excerpt from *Harry Potter and the deathly hallows*, the final book in J.K. Rowling's septology. Rowling's consciousness of her adult readers is less obvious than Crompton's, but as the series progresses there is an increase both in darkening themes and in humorous double entendres (perhaps functioning as 'double address' where some young children are concerned, but probably clear enough to many who have reached double figures).[13] In this sense, *Deathly hallows* is markedly more adult than any of its predecessors. Such a shift is to be expected; while *William* made his original 'crossing' from predominantly adult market to child market, *Harry* developed in the opposite direction, with the series initially being aimed at children and acquiring an enthusiastic adult following (and, ultimately, separate adult editions of the books) along the way. In this, Rowling's work broke with precedent, 'set in motion an extraordinary child-to-adult crossover craze' and ultimately helped redefine crossover fiction in popular parlance as referring exclusively to this uni-directional process.[14] Moreover, devotees of all ages have taken full advantage of the possibilities offered by the internet, creating a worldwide, web-literate fan base within which theories and commentaries can be exchanged internationally and – significantly – interlingually. In this light, I

12 For Crompton's own statement to this effect, see Kay Williams, *Just – Richmal: the life and work of Richmal Crompton Lamburn* (Guildford, 1986), pp 146–7. Williams also comments that 'Richmal's inadvertent discovery that children are in fact very well served by humour "deliberately keyed to adults", and her subsequent decision not to alter the style of the stories, may well account for her prodigious success' (p. 147). **13** Questioned by a fan about Aberforth Dumbledore, '"prosecuted for practicing inappropriate charms on a goat"' (*Harry Potter and the goblet of fire* (London, 2000), p. 394), Rowling asked the fan's age. On hearing, 'Eight', she acknowledged double address with the reply, 'I think that he was trying to make a goat that would be easy to keep clean, curly horns. That's a joke that works on a couple of levels. I really like Aberforth and his goats [...] So that is my answer to YOU.' (The transcript of this interview, 'J.K. Rowling at Carnegie Hall', may be found on the fansite The Leaky Cauldron, retrieved from www.the-leaky-cauldron.org/2007/10/20/j-k-rowling-at-carnegie-hall-reveals-dumbledore-is-gay-neville-marries-hannah-abbott-and-scores-more, accessed 10 Oct. 2010). **14** S.L. Beckett, *Crossover fiction*, pp 4, 17.

examine five translations (into Spanish, French, Polish, Italian and German) of a single controversial passage from *Harry Potter and the deathly hallows*.

My disparate methods of approaching Crompton's *William* and Rowling's *Harry* preclude attempts at direct comparison. Rather, I appose the two case studies, with the observation that that of *William* involves the interplay of norms and dual readership in a translation, made in a pre-Internet age, of a moderately successful series, while that of *Harry* sees pressure to uphold generical norms clashing with pressure from a largely adult, international, technologically powerful community to maintain accuracy in translation. Reading between the results of the studies, I hope to suggest some potential benefits of exploring the intersections between crossover texts and translations, both disciplines of 'crossing over'.

WILLIAM: ORIGINS AND INTRALINGUAL HISTORY

Richmal Crompton exemplifies the group of cross-writers that David Galef terms 'polygraphic authors':[15] her prolific output includes adult novels and short story collections as well as thirty-eight William books, which she apparently viewed as mere potboilers.[16] As has been noted, the publishing history of crossover texts can be key to understanding their accrual of and attraction for a dual readership;[17] an overview of William's intralingual development will shed light on this aspect of the series and provide a backdrop against which to consider his Italian incarnation.

The first stories were initially published in *Home Magazine*, which catered primarily for female adult readers; in 1922, they began to appear instead in the *Happy Mag*, aimed at the whole family. It was in this same year that William's appeal for children was realized, resulting in the gathering of twenty-six existing stories into two books, *Just – William* and *More William*. Only after the demise of the *Happy Mag* in 1940 were the stories written for immediate publication in children's books; Crompton's biographer opines that from this point on, the stories' 'content and construction became less intricate, and, although still highly entertaining, [they] moved a step away from satire towards slapstick'.[18]

In the wake of Crompton's death in 1969, William and his middle-class milieu fell out of both favour and print.[19] Nevertheless, a television series in

15 David Galef, 'Crossing over: authors who write both children's and adult's fiction', *Children's Literature Association Quarterly*, 20:1 (1995), 29–35. **16** Mary Cadogan, *Richmal Crompton: the woman behind Just William* (Stroud, 2003), p. xv. **17** S.L. Beckett, 'Introduction' in S.L. Beckett (ed.), *Transcending boundaries: writing for a dual audience of children and adults* (New York and London, 1999), pp xi–xx at p. xv. **18** Cadogan, *Richmal Crompton*, p. 69. See also Hunt, *Children's literature*, pp 54–6. **19** Indeed, in *Children's read-*

1977 revived his popularity,[20] and in 1983 Macmillan began reprinting the entire book series. The few alterations made are noteworthy ones: two stories were omitted entirely, both from *William the detective*, the first involving a plot by William and his Outlaws to become 'Nasties' and drive out the Jewish owner of the local sweetshop[21] and the second including a scene in which William, 'purple with excitement', cheers on his dog in a vicious rat-hunt.[22] Other material to which objections have sometimes been raised has been left intact, including a reference to a villain's 'Jewish nose',[23] an equation of obesity with obnoxiousness in child characters,[24] and the occasional birds'-nesting expedition – although, in the case of this latter, footnotes have been added stating that the collecting of birds' eggs is now illegal in Britain.[25] The omitted stories and the concerns raised about aspects left intact suggest that the perceived target market for the *William* books has become younger in the years of the cheerful Macmillan editions, while also hinting at an adult ideal of children's literature as a genre without grey areas. Meanwhile, William's literary afterlife includes the novel *Good omens*, collaboratively written by Terry Pratchett and Neil Gaiman, a darkly funny fantasy story aimed at teenagers and adults, in which the young antihero (who also happens to be the Antichrist) speaks in William's idiom and roams the countryside leading a band of friends of whom the second-in-command is not a boy called Ginger but a girl called Pepper.[26]

The *William* books have never done well in America; Crompton suggested that this was because American youth 'leaps straight from the cradle to the petting party'[27] and thus skips William's phase of childhood. Betty Greenway has

ing interests, a national report published in 1975, Crompton was blacklisted as 'non-quality' along with eleven other authors including Enid Blyton, W.E. Johns and Anthony Buckeridge (cited in Emrys Evans, '"Quality" and "Non-quality": some new criteria', *English in Education*, 21:3 (1987), 36–43 at 36). **20** *Just William*, dir. John Davies (London Weekend Television, 1977–8). **21** Richmal Crompton, 'William and the nasties' in *William the detective* (London, 1935). **22** Richmal Crompton, 'William and the league of perfect love' in *William the detective* (London, 1935). **23** Richmal Crompton, 'William gets his own back' in *William and the evacuees* (London, 1940). **24** E.g. William's cousin Francis/'Fatty' ('The cure' in *William again* (London, 1923)), and William's perennial foe Hubert Lane (introduced in 'William the matchmaker' in *Still – William* (London, 1925)). **25** Macmillan's relaunch of 20 William books with facsimile jackets to celebrate the 80th anniversary of the first story's publication sparked protests especially from campaigners for animal rights and against bullying. The RSPCA, referring to a story in which William paints a dog blue, expressed its concern 'especially as young children will have access to paint. We need to teach them that animals do deserve respect and are sentient beings'. A director of an anti-bullying campaign stated that 'People have got to realize that William's anti-social behaviour is not to be tolerated. To terrorize and distress someone is not the way to go'. (Quoted in Rory Carroll, 'Campaigners try to outlaw William', *Guardian*, 4 May 1999). **26** Terry Pratchett & Neil Gaiman, *Good omens* (London, 1990). **27** See Cadogan, *Richmal Crompton: the woman behind*

argued that a further reason may be that the realism of the stories was tempered by the almost idyllic security of the English village atmosphere (not to mention remarkably high instances of serendipity), rendering *William* unsuitable for a post-*Catcher in the rye* canon; attempting to explain the American success of other British children's writers, she remarks, 'Perhaps fantasy translates, but the social structure of English life doesn't'.[28] *William* has, however, been translated to greater or lesser degrees into some seventeen European languages.[29] At the more prolific end of the scale, the Swedish versions of twenty-four of the books appeared just a few years after the English originals, and 'Bill' remains popular in this incarnation. In Spanish, the books had an interesting passage through the Franco years, with casualties of translation including even the most innocuous of kisses, as well as derogatory references to missionaries and, predictably, the entire book *William the dictator*.[30] At the less prolific end, the Italian translation to be examined here was the only *William* book produced in Italy.

JUST WILLIAM IN ITALY

Le birichinate di William Brown amalgamates selections from the first two books of the series, *Just – William* and *More William*, which, as noted earlier, comprise stories originally written for adult-geared publications.[31] Translated by Lidia Sacchi Nicoli, *Le birichinate* was published in 1954 by the Catholic publishing house Edizioni Paoline. The back cover of the Italian book provides some initial clues as to the norms informing the selection of stories and the translation strategies used. The most immediately startling aspect of this cover is the sketch of an august and bearded figure intended to represent Crompton; at the time of publication, the author was apparently 'un saggio *gentleman* in pensione'. It seems likely that this misunderstanding arose more from the rarity of the name 'Richmal' than from a deliberate marketing decision, especially considering that other biographical details given – including Crompton's studies at Royal Holloway, which admitted only women until 1965 – are correct.[32] The impli-

Just William, p. 82. **28** Betty Greenway, 'William forever: Richmal Crompton's unusual achievement', *The Lion and the Unicorn*, 26 (2002), 98–111 at 101. **29** Ibid., 100. **30** See Marisa Fernández López, 'Translation studies in contemporary children's literature: A comparison of intercultural ideological factors' in *The translation of children's literature: a reader*, ed. Gillian Lathey (Clevedon, 2006), pp 41–53 at pp 43–5. **31** Source texts: Richmal Crompton, *Just – William* (London, 1922; repr. 1983); Richmal Crompton, *More William* (London, 1922, repr. 1983). Target text: Richmal Crompton, *Le birichinate di William Brown*, trans. Lidia Sacchi Nicoli (Rome, 1954; repr. 1969). *Just – William* is referred to as ST 1; *More William* is referred to as ST 2; *Le birichinate di William Brown* is referred to as TT. **32** However, Crompton's

cation for an analysis of the translation, however, is that there was little close communication between Crompton and either Sacchi Nicoli or the publisher.

Further down the cover, William's character is described in the following terms:

> Who is William Brown if not an innocent little boy, guilty only of excessive enterprise? His perennial scrapes [...] are not the fruit of badness or lack of discipline, but only of a lively imagination and a good heart. There are wise ideas even in his scattered little head, indeed William knows how to learn from his mistakes, and this should prove a pleasant lesson in prudence for everyone. Thus, a lively English boy, who personifies Professor Crompton's best memories, has something to teach his young Italian friends as well. [My translation.][33]

To those familiar with the original William Brown, the idea that lessons of prudence might be imparted in his name is, at the least, perplexing. The final sentence, in particular, confirms that although the didactic tone of the whole may be intended to appeal to adult buyers, the books' content seems primarily aimed at child readers, William's 'giovani amici italiani' – a significant divergence from the initial target market of the same stories in Britain. The emphasis on William's Englishness suggests that, counter to the tradition of domestication in translated children's literature, this translation is marked as originally foreign. One gleans an overall impression that rather than being domesticated to Italian culture, however, William is being domesticated to an international culture of appropriateness in children's literature.

Is this impression borne out within the translation? Certainly, the qualities ascribed to William in the blurb are more concentrated in the eleven stories selected than in the twenty-six from which these were chosen. Included are stories in which William displays loyalty to his friends, his dog and the little girl next door respectively, albeit with disastrous consequences; excluded are stories in which, with less noble motives, William throws a wild party and bombards the servants with missiles from the larder, turns a temperance society meeting into a

school, to which she later returned as a teacher, metamorphoses from St. Elphin's to St. Gilphin's, suggesting that the information may have been gleaned from oral or perhaps handwritten sources. **33** 'Chi è infatti William Brown se non un innocente *little boy*, colpevole solo di eccessiva intraprendenza? Le sue perenni birichinate [...] non sono frutto di cattiveria né di indisciplina, ma solo di fervida fantasia e di buon cuore [...] Anche nella sua testolina sventata albergano idee sagge, infatti William sa trarre frutto dagli errori commessi, e questo dovrebbe costituire per tutti una simpatica lezione di prudenza. Così un vivace ragazzo inglese, che personifica i ricordi più belli del professor Crompton, ha qualcosa da insegnare anche ai suoi giovani amici italiani.'

brawl and plays an April Fool's joke on his elderly neighbour, Miss Gregoria Mush. Perhaps more significantly, the stories chosen for translation are re-ordered in such a way that there appears to be a perceptible moral progression in William's character. He is at his worst in the first story, in which he exploits his aunt's snoring for financial gain; he then makes well-meaning if chaotic efforts to help out ghost-seeking Cousin Mildred and lovesick Mr Moss; he routs the unfortunate Cuthbert with motives befitting a *delitto passionale*; and, in the final story, spurred by impulsive if misplaced generosity, he removes a feast from his own home so that a poor child in the neighbourhood will have her faith in Father Christmas restored. Positioned thus, the stories make it plausible that William is indeed motivated by a 'good heart' and that he 'knows how to learn from his mistakes'. (It is perhaps fortunate that the translator did not have to contend with the thirty-six successive books, as no amount of selection or re-ordering could have disguised the fact that William, almost fifty years later, had yet to display evidence of having internalized any noticeable moral lessons.)

Pedagogical as well as didactic norms are in strongly in evidence, particularly when William's 'dreaded eloquence' is rendered in Italian. Crompton characterizes her protagonist's speech with non-standard pronunciation, grammatical slips and ellipses and a consistent blunt vigour. Sacchi Nicoli translates his orations using standard Italian. Thus William's critical appraisal of his aunt's wall-hanging, for instance ('It might be true wot it says, but I don't like the flowers messin' about all over it' – ST 2, p. 9)[34] is translated complete with correct use of the subjunctive: 'Può darsi che sia vero quello che c'è scritto, anche se non mi piacciono tutti quei fiori che ci hanno mescolato insieme' (TT, p. 74). The only exception is on an occasion when William's poor grammar has been explicitly flagged by the author:

> – E chi è l'incaricato? –
> – Me – replicò William, disdegnando la grammatica.

The atrocities of the original William's written communication put his verbal idiosyncrasies in the shade. In Italian, however, a story of his composition is presented complete with the authorial aside that 'la sua ortografia era la disperazione dei suoi maestri' (TT, p. 106), yet is devoid of spelling mistakes (the original contains such gems as 'In less time than wot it takes to rite this he was srounded by pleesemen' (ST 2, p. 155)). Although it is impossible to ascertain whether these translation choices were due to the difficulty of finding equivalent spoken registers and written errors in Italian, or to a fear of setting a poor example to child readers, it is probable that both factors came into play.

34 See note 31.

A final point concerns Crompton's most drastic deviation from the norms of children's literature: namely, her refusal to sentimentalize childhood (and her often ungentle mockery of those who did).[35] As augured by the cover blurb, several choices in the Italian version tend to undo this effect. When a visiting baby is introduced, William's mother's response to it – hilarious to the reader when filtered through the ears of the nauseated William – is rendered in standard Italian: thus, 'The *duck*! Well, den, how's 'oo, den? Go – o – oo,' becomes the far more lucid, 'Come va, piccolo, oh, caro, caro!' (ST 1, p. 130; TT, p. 26). Moreover, Sacchi Nicoli twice applies the term 'piccoli amici' to William and a female acquaintance, where there is no mention of either size or friendship in the English text. By simultaneously diminishing the force of Crompton's mimicry of baby-talk and adding diminutive references to child characters, the translator alters the perceived authorial attitude to childhood.[36] A boundary is redrawn and thickly underlined; Italian child readers are implicitly inscribed within a segregated community of 'piccoli amici'. As such, they are not expected to laugh, through the text, at both William's antics and the adult niceties they disrupt; the 'hybrid', borderland position available to readers of the original is no longer an easily accessible option.

Morally and linguistically, then, the translational shifts that have taken place limit humorous elements in order to render the text 'suitable' for children. This results in the elimination of many of the subtleties that lend the books their adult appeal in English. Crompton's composite, sophisticated child-adult addressee is sacrificed, it seems, as part of a domestication towards norms of acceptability, perhaps more genre-related than cultural.

HARRY POTTER: TRANSLATIONS OF A WITCH-FIGHT

Several aspects of *Harry Potter and the deathly hallows*[37] suggest that, as the final book of Rowling's phenomenally popular series, it was written with fewer normative constraints than its predecessors. Aside from the light relief of an occa-

35 Cuthbert, who becomes 'Cutberto' in Sacchi Nicoli's translation, is the first in a parade of lisping, curly-haired representatives of sentimentalized boyhood that meet their downfall at William's hands throughout the series; Crompton takes particular relish in depicting one 'Anthony Martin', whose doting mother composes poems about him that strongly recall the Christopher Robin of A.A. Milne's 'Vespers' (Richmal Crompton, 'Aunt Arabelle in charge' in *William the pirate* (London, 1932)). **36** For an account of a very similar process in some translations of the works of Astrid Lindgren, see Birgit Stolt, 'How Emil becomes Michel: on the translation of children's books' in Göte Klingberg et al. (eds), *Children's books in translation* (Stockholm, 1978), pp 130–46. **37** J.K. Rowling, *Harry Potter and the deathly hallows* (London, 2007).

sional joke about wizards' preoccupation with wand size, the canvas darkens in *Deathly hallows* to include background genocide, explicit depictions of torture and one implied threat of rape. There are also some striking moments of strong (for the genre) language. The most notable of these occurs in the penultimate chapter, during the final moments of the battle for Hogwarts: when the wicked Bellatrix Lestrange tries to kill 16-year-old Ginny Weasley, Ginny's mother Molly launches herself into the fray with a roar of 'NOT MY DAUGHTER, YOU BITCH!'.[38]

The words and scenario are strongly reminiscent of a scene in the 1986 film *Aliens*, in which the character of Ellen Ripley snarls, 'Get away from her, you bitch!' at the Alien Queen, who is threatening a small girl to whom Ripley is a mother figure.[39] In *Harry Potter*, ostensibly for children where *Aliens* is not,[40] Molly's use of 'bitch' is set apart not only by its visually arresting capitalization and direct address to its object, but also by the shock value that it gains in being spoken by the archetypal mother of the series, a woman normally quite ready to chastise her offspring for vulgar use of language. Within the context of the battle, in which one of Molly's sons has already died, her choice of words functions not only to reinforce her characterization as a fierce protector of her children, but to signal that her ferocity is moving to a new plane: for, just as the direct use of 'bitch' goes beyond what has previously been deemed linguistically acceptable, so Molly's subsequent action in killing Bellatrix is a unique one among the female characters on the 'good' side – indeed, taking into account its intentionality and explicit description in the text, it is unique among all the 'good' characters.

In Riitta Oittinen's terms, 'if we change any tiny detail in a text […], such as a picture or a word, the whole situation of understanding becomes new'.[41] This is particularly true in the case of a word so semantically laden as 'bitch'. Directed specifically at females (or, if directed at males, generally implying effeminacy), 'bitch' may impute various undesirable qualities to its object; historically, it signified 'a lewd or sensual woman', but today it is more often understood in modern contexts as 'a malicious or treacherous woman'.[42] As var-

38 J.K. Rowling, *Deathly hallows,* p. 589. The word 'bitch' occurs once before in the series, spoken by the obnoxious Marge Dursley, with reference to a dog but with an implied insult offered to Harry's mother (J.K. Rowling, *Harry Potter and the prisoner of Azkaban* (London, 1999), p. 24). In *Harry Potter and the deathly hallows,* groundbreaking instances of namecalling prior to Molly's 'bitch' include Aberforth Dumbledore's description of the boys that attacked his sister as 'bastards', and Ron Weasley's application of the same epithet to Draco Malfoy (pp 455, 518). **39** James Cameron (dir.), *Aliens* (Twentieth Century Fox, 1986). **40** *Aliens* holds an R [Restricted] rating in the US and an 18 certificate in Britain and Ireland. **41** Riitta Oittinen, 'No innocent act: on the ethics of translating for children' in J. van Coillie & W.P. Verschueren, *Children's literature in translation* (2006), pp 35–45 at p. 37. **42** See the

ious feminists have pointed out, it is a word that, besides demeaning its object by ascribing to her a bestial, perhaps sub-human nature, is frequently used to condemn toughness and ambition in women, when the same qualities, in men, might elicit admiration.[43] These considerations heighten the interest and implications of the Molly–Bellatrix exchange. Rowling has commented that she deliberately pitted Molly's maternal love against Bellatrix' passion for Voldemort, which is effectively an obsession with dark power and genocidal dictatorship.[44] The use of 'bitch' as a descriptor underlines this gulf between the women, perhaps implying that Bellatrix' impassioned sadism becomes still more perverse when her gender is taken into account.[45]

Translators working into the five European languages included in this study have approached this passage in varied ways.[46] At the more bowdlerized end of the scale, the Spanish version ('¡¡Mi hija no, mala bruja!!') eschews capitalization and, rather than choosing a potentially sexual insult based on an animal comparison, such as 'perra' or 'zorra', transforms 'bitch' to *mala bruja*, literally 'bad witch'. Even allowing for the qualifying adjective, it seems improbable that this would be an insult of choice within magical society. The French translation ('PAS MA FILLE, ESPÈCE DE GARCE!') is somewhat stronger, and preserves, perhaps even heightens, the associations of transgressive female behaviour inherent in 'bitch', since *garce* is the feminine of the non-offensive *gars/garçon*. Even preceded by 'espèce de', however, the word is a little less startling on Molly's lips than is its English original. Polish ('NIE W MOJ CÓRKE, SUKO!') offers quite a precise equivalent, with *suko* signifying both a female dog and an unpleasant woman. At first

online *Oxford English dictionary* entry for 'bitch' (retrieved from www.dictionary.oed.com, accessed 24 Aug. 2009). **43** See for instance Beverly Gross, 'Bitch' in *Salamagundi,* 103 (Summer 1994), 146–56 at 151: 'The metamorphosis of bitch from the context of sexuality (a carnal woman, a promiscuous woman) to temperament (an angry woman, a malicious woman) to power (a domineering woman, a competitive woman) is a touchstone to the changing position of women through this century [...] Judging by the contemporary colorations of the word bitch, what men primarily fear and despise in women is power'. See also Sherryl Kleinman et al., 'Reclaiming critical analysis: the social harms of "bitch"' in *Sociological Analysis,* 3:1 (Spring 2009), 47–68, for an argument rejecting feminist attempts to 'reclaim' the term (such as that made by the editors of *Bitch: Feminist Responses to Pop Culture*, a US magazine launched in 1996). **44** *The Leaky Cauldron*, retrieved online as in note 13. **45** It is also notable that Bellatrix, the anti-mother of a series in which maternal love (of Lily Potter, Molly Weasley and Narcissa Malfoy) is repeatedly pivotal, is singled out for uncompromising destruction in a way that her male Death Eater colleagues are not; even Voldemort himself, unlike Bellatrix, is offered a final chance of redemption. **46** Target texts: Spanish: J.K. Rowling, *Harry Potter y las reliquias de la muerte*, trans. Gemma Rovira Ortega (Barcelona, 2008). French: *Harry Potter et les reliques de la mort*, trans. Jean-François Ménard (Paris, 2007). Polish: *Harry Potter i insygnia śmierci*, trans. Andrzej Polkowski (Poznań, 2008). Italian: *Harry Potter e i doni della morte*, trans. Beatrice Masini (Milan, 2008). German: *Harry Potter und die Heiligtümer des Todes*, trans. Klaus Fritz (Hamburg, 2007).

glance, Italian ('MIA FIGLIA NO, CAGNA!') appears to do likewise, but although *cagna* refers to a female dog, the word is comparatively rarely used as an insult, and when it is thus used it carries a prominent connotation of sexual promiscuity. A more obvious translation might have been the popular insult *stronza*, but it is possible that the literal origin of this word (excrement) caused it to be considered still more taboo than the sexualized *cagna*. Finally, the German version ('NICHT MEINE TOCHTER, DU SCHLAMPE!') avoids animal imagery but uses *Schlampe*, a word which, much like the English 'slut', historically connoted dirtiness and sloth but today possesses explicitly sexual connotations.

If the inclusion of 'bitch' in the original text owes something to Rowling's awareness of her growing adult readership, and if, as seems probable, its survival in the published version is a tribute to the unusual degree of editorial control that her success has brought her, how is the diversity of European translations to be explained? Each language offers a unique and finite set of intersections between universal spectrums of insult; with the most faithful will in the world, the translator may not be able to find an expression that performs a precisely equivalent textual function. However, this problem may be compounded by stipulations of 'appropriateness' laid down by the publisher (or, more broadly, by the target culture). It seems clear that the approach of the Spanish translator, for instance, stands with the long tradition of bowdlerization in translated children's books. More surprising is the relative mildness of attenuation in French, the fidelity of the Polish version, and, above all, the sexual nuance gained in translation in Italian and German.

A factor worth considering is the varying extent to which adult readership of the series is present, or rather perceived by the publishers as present, in the different countries. As the series and its popularity grew, so did the numbers of fans – predominantly adults and older children – with the potential to read both a translation and the original, to spot inconsistencies and to post irate threads about their discoveries on the many Harry Potter web forums. The relative anonymity of internet discussion, indeed, could be argued to have assisted in breaking down the construct of age-based readership duality. By the time *Deathly hallows* was published, it seems ridiculous to suggest that any publisher remained in ignorance as to the size and vociferous nature of this fan-base; however, some had certainly adapted more speedily and effectively than others. The Spanish publisher employed four translators between the seven books, perhaps indicating an uncertainty as to optimum translation strategies. The Italian publisher employed two translators, and has issued revised editions of earlier books to limit the damage of hasty translation decisions made before 'Pottermania' took off – for instance, Ravenclaw House, associated with intellect, was initially translated into Italian as 'Pecoranera' (black sheep), but subsequently amended to 'Corvonero' (black crow/black raven), since the crest of Hogwarts portrayed the symbol of Ravenclaw as a bird of prey and the ultimate significance of this was 'difficile prevedere' (difficult to predict).[47] (The influence of Warner Bros., owners of the film rights, increased as the series has progressed, and prior instructions issued by them limited the potential for inconsistencies of this kind.) The German publisher, however, has retained a single translator for all the books, and from the beginning has used a forceful marketing strategy that suggests a strong awareness of the books' dual readership.[48]

The inevitable clash of norms in translation, then, is amplified by conflicts between sectors of the readership. Before the views of children themselves are taken into account, translators of *Harry Potter*, and in particular of the final book, perform a delicate balancing act: that of pleasing those adult readers who are sticklers for accuracy, and pleasing those adult readers whose ideals of appropriate reading material for (their) children may be threatened by such accuracy. Readers in all camps, however, have the technological facility to express their (dis)satisfaction to a wide network of potential fellow consumers. The present study is limited both by the artificiality of its focus on a single phrase and by the Eurocentric selection of languages included. However, the *Harry* books, with their huge and diverse readership and their many translations, most of which have emerged hot on the heels of the original texts, provide a rare opportunity for a broader cross-cultural exploration of the dynamics at work between dual readership, albeit subject to the (dissolvent?) influence of readers' Internet empowerment, and translation.

CONCLUSIONS

It has been suggested that cross-writing can be claimed 'as an unlocker of doors that have shut off and devalued [the field of children's literature] [...] More than a simple key, however, cross-writing offers the versatility of a critical Swiss Army knife'.[49] Crompton's *William* and Rowling's *Harry* occupy very different

47 Serena Daniele, 'Nota alla traduzione italiana' in J.K. Rowling, *Harry Potter e il calice di fuoco*, trans. Beatrice Masini (Milan, 2001). Daniele's note on translation also appears in the Italian versions of the three subsequent Harry Potter books, despite the fact that all of these were translated by Masini. It is also available online at www.salani.it/harry_potter.php (accessed 22 Mar. 2013). **48** For further analysis of the German marketing strategy, see Nancy K. Jentsch, 'Harry Potter and the tower of Babel: translating the magic' in Lathey (ed.), *The translation of children's literature* (2006), pp 190–207 at pp 205–6. The article draws comparisons between the German, French and Spanish versions of Rowling's first three books. **49** U.C. Knoepflmacher & Mitzi Myer, 'From the editors: "cross-writing" and the reconceptualizing of children's literary studies', *Children's Literature*, 25 (1997), vii–xvii at xv.

loci along the 'elusive borderland between children's and adult books',[50] and a consideration of their respective positions on this boundary helps shed some light on their fates in translation.

Intralingually, it seems that *William*'s latter-day demotion to 'children's' fiction, in the Macmillan reprints, has facilitated omissions and fostered complaints about the example set (to children) in the books. In the Italian translation *Le birichinate di William Brown*, the selection and ordering of stories, the subduing of the protagonist's linguistic eccentricities and the subtle re-introduction of sentimentality to the concept of childhood all contribute to a systemic domestication of *William* toward the (adult-dependent) norms of children's literature, and, hence, to a systemic purge of those elements that most appeal to adult – or hybrid child-adult – readers. The contrasting case of *Harry*, although focused on multiple translations of a single phrase, suggests that the situation is quite different when a text's popularity has generated a technologically united, international, interlingual fan base of adults – and, once again, of readers who resist binary categorization.[51] I have suggested that editors and translators, if aware of the communicative power of these readers, may tend to exempt the text from generical norms as a result.

If cross-written texts can help to illuminate aspects of the interplay of norms in the translation process, the converse is also true: comparative translation studies may offer some paradigms through which to explore the mechanisms of cross-writing. I have mentioned that crossover works can reveal the hazy, culturally dependent nature of the boundaries between childhood and adulthood, but to understand the extent to which the notion of duality is legitimate at all, further concentration on reader response, that is, the mechanisms of 'cross-reading', would be desirable. Aside from the possibility of comparing the reactions of readers in several languages to versions of a text that have been differently nuanced in translation – for instance, the *Harry Potter* passage discussed above – an understanding of reader reactions might usefully be formulated in language borrowed from translation theory. Peter Hollindale's argument that too much stress is placed on the content of what children read and too little on how they read it is still pertinent today,[52] and need not only apply to children; 'how one reads' a text, of course, implies an individual process of comprehension analagous to an act of translation. Do readers of different ages, with different cultural backgrounds and areas of expertise, 'translate' cross-written texts

50 Hunt, *Children's literature*, p. 54. **51** Emerson Spartz, the founder of one of the most popular Harry Potter fan sites, www.mugglenet.com, accessed 1 May 2012, exemplifies this kind of 'hybrid' reader; he was twelve when he first set up the site in 1999, although it has been used since its inception by fans of all ages. **52** Peter Hollindale, 'Ideology and the children's book', *Signal*, 55 (1988), 3–22.

according to particular sets of internalized norms or expectations? Could children sometimes be said to 'domesticate' double addressed text to the bounds of their own worldviews, while adults use their additional knowledge to 'foreignize' the text by admitting its additional, subtextual or intertextual possibilities? The discipline of translation studies, with its focus on literature that 'crosses over' in a different sense, may provide a forum in which to investigate how readers of different ages, presented with cross-written texts, carry out the final, least traceable act of translation – the conversion of written words to interpreted thought.

Reading *Murder on the Orient Express* in Italian: some (missing) translator's notes

Jane Dunnett

An imported genre, crime fiction started to arrive in Italy in the late nineteenth century. It was not until the 1930s, however, that Italian writers began to generate their own *gialli*, modelled largely on the Anglo-American detective novels with which they and the general public had become so familiar in recent years.[1] Crime fiction from abroad made up the bulk of the books on offer in the interwar years, and amongst these most were translated from the English. While the works of Simenon enjoyed a certain success, sales never reached the level of detective novels from Britain and the US.[2] Such is their popularity that books by Anna Katherine Green, Margery Allingham, Agatha Christie, S.S. Van Dine, Rex Stout and Edgar Wallace continue to circulate even now, often in the same translations that were made during the 1930s.[3]

Christie, in particular, is an author whose novels have never been out of print since they were first published in Italy. It is therefore of more than incidental interest to note that many contemporary Italian editions of her pre-war production are reprints of the translations from this period.[4] Thus, when modern-day readers purchase a copy of a book by Christie translated under Fascism, they would be justified in thinking that they were taking home the same text as Italian readers some seventy or so years earlier. But are they? Typically, the name of the original translator is given on the title page and, opposite, the date of first publi-

1 On the history and pre-history of the detective-story genre in Italy, see Loris Rambelli, *Storia del 'giallo' italiano* (Milan, 1979); Maurizio Pistelli, *Un secolo in giallo: storia del poliziesco italiano (1860–1960)* (Rome, 2006); Jane Dunnett, 'The emergence of a new literary genre in interwar Italy' in Giuliana Pieri (ed.), *Crime fiction in Italian: an introduction* (Cardiff, 2011), pp 6–26. **2** See, among others, Stephen Knight, 'The golden age' in *The Cambridge companion to crime fiction*, ed. Martin Priestman (Cambridge, 2003), pp 77–94. **3** This vast corpus constitutes the basis for a much wider investigation I am carrying out, mapping the translations of English-language detective novels into Italian first published under Fascism. **4** In the last few years, fresh translations of Christie have started to appear, some very recently indeed, e.g. *L'uomo vestito di marrone* [*The man in the brown suit*], trans. Stefano Benvenuti (Milan, 2008). First translated by Giuseppina Taddei (Milan, 1933), this novel was reprinted by Hachette (2002; 2004), using Taddei's version. There is also a new translation of *Pericolo senza nome* [*Peril at end house*] by Maria Luisa Vesentini Ottolenghi (Milan, 2009). The novel was first translated into Italian by Laura Garsin for Mondadori in 1933, with subsequent reprints. In both cases, then, two competing translations now circulate.

cation in Italy appears. So it is reasonable for readers to expect that the original translation has merely been reproduced in the more recent edition they have acquired. Of course, only a detailed survey of Christie's novels translated into Italian before 1940 could establish with certainty whether individual target texts had indeed remained the same when they were reprinted or whether they had been subjected to subsequent interventions by editors.[5]

If, for the sake of argument, we assume that the texts in print today *are* identical to, or at least substantially the same as, the ones published in the interwar era, a number of questions present themselves. What, for instance, is the precise status of these translations, given the political climate in which they were made? As we know, *all* books published under Fascism (translations as well as non-translations) had to comply with the restrictions imposed on them by the censorship authorities, which included a ban on references to suicide, abortion, incest, rape, and anything else that might offend what official documents refer to as 'Fascist morality', a category that, on the whole, coincided with Catholic morality.[6] Novelists were also strongly discouraged from portraying Italians as criminals, which impacted significantly on the way in which detective novels were translated, given that it was not uncommon for British and American writers to feature a villain who was foreign, often from Italy. To get round this, Italian translators and editors freely intervened in their target texts; they would frequently change the nationality of the fictional perpetrators of crime, thereby protecting the presumed patriotic sensibilities of their audiences. So the resulting translations were bound to be, at least in part, ideologically compromised.

TRANSLATOR'S NOTES

The remainder of this essay focuses on the Italian translation of *Murder on the Orient Express*, examining two editions of the book that came out at a distance

5 Although it is possible that over time some changes may have been introduced into Christie's original English-language texts themselves, either by her or by her editors, there are no differences between subsequent editions of the pre-war novel which is the subject of discussion here, although it was published under two different titles, one for the British market and the other for the American market (as also happened with a number of other books by Christie). Both editions appeared the same year, 1934, with the titles of *Murder on the Orient Express* (Collins) and *Murder in the Calais coach* (Dodd, Mead and Company), respectively. This alteration was intended to prevent potential confusion with another book that had appeared in the US the previous year under the title *Orient Express* (New York: Doubleday), Graham Greene's *Stamboul train* (London, 1932). 6 On the structure of the various censorial bodies as they evolved in the course of the twenty-year dictatorship, and their impact on translated texts in particular, see Jane Dunnett, 'Foreign literature in Fascist Italy: circulation and censorship', *TTR (Traduction terminologie rédaction, études sur le texte et ses transformations)*, 15:2 (2002), 97–123.

of thirty-five years.[7] The first was published in 1935 and entitled simply *Orient Express*, possibly in order to avoid drawing attention to the alleged sensationalism of detective novels denounced by the regime.[8] Moreover, and most strikingly, in accordance with the constraints of censorship outlined above, the translator Alfredo Pitta changed the nationality of a couple of characters in Christie's novel, as we shall see shortly. The second edition, published in 1970, is the one currently available to readers and it has therefore gone through numerous reprints. In restoring the source-text title – *Assassinio sull'Orient Express* – it promises to deliver a version that is closer to the original.[9] Indeed, Oreste del Buono, the editor of the volume, states that 'this new Italian edition finally sets the record straight and does away with the many censored and self-censored passages from the Fascist period' ['questa nuova edizione italiana [...] fa finalmente giustizia di tante censure e autocensure del tempo fascista'].[10] For example, in the source-text passage where Poirot reveals that the man found murdered in his compartment on the Simplon Orient Express train, a certain Ratchett, is really called Cassetti – himself responsible for the brutal murder of a child, Daisy Armstrong – Pitta replaces the Italian surname with an Irish one, O'Hara.[11] He does so systematically throughout the novel, in an operation that del Buono defines as 'anodyne'.[12] This might have been true from the point of view of the Fascist censors, but the choice of Irish nationality for the child murderer is surely not an innocent one: Pitta has merely substituted one stereotype for another. Italian surnames were readily associated with the notion of organized crime in the popular Anglo-Saxon imagination whereas in Italy an Irish name also had potentially violent associations, linked to the struggle for independence in Ireland in previous decades. Del Buono, true to his stated intention to 'undo' Fascist censorship, puts back the original name Cassetti.

7 Agatha Christie, *Murder on the Orient Express* (Glasgow, 1934). See n. 5. **8** Agatha Christie, *Orient Express*, trans. Alfredo Pitta (Milan, 1935). **9** Agatha Christie, *Assassinio sull'Orient Express*, trans. Alfredo Pitta, Preface and Postface by Oreste del Buono (Milan, 2011 [1970]). The 1970 edition of the translation was published by Mondadori in its 'I Classici del giallo' series, and is the sole edition currently in print. **10** Ibid., p. x. While del Buono gives no information as to which English edition of Christie's novel he employed for his revision of Pitta's translation, there is nothing to suggest that subsequent editions of *Murder on the Orient Express* differed from the 1934 one evidently used by Pitta. When examining interventions by del Buono, comparisons were also made with the Fontana edition of the novel, first published in 1959. For the purpose of this article, the source text referred to is that of the original edition. **11** *Orient Express*, p. 73. **12** In the Postface to the translation Oreste del Buono observes that 'L'assassinato, Samuel Edward Ratchett, è un milionario americano, anche se in successive indagini risulterà essere un rapitore e assassino di bambini d'origine italiana e chiamarsi Cassetti (nella revisione cautelativa della traduzione italiana del 1935, tempo fascista, ribattezzato anodinamente "un certo O'Hara")'. *Assassinio sull'Orient Express*, 2011, p. 222.

Not surprisingly, he amends all occurrences of 'voi' – the polite version of 'tu' which Mussolini's regime introduced in the 1930s to replace the use of 'Lei' – and reinstates the pre-Fascist form of address: for instance, 'Avrete la bontà [...] farete in modo [...]' becomes 'Abbia la bontà [...] faccia in modo'.[13] Del Buono also replaces the personal pronoun found in 'Ella si alzò' with the standard female pronoun that is used nowadays: 'lei si alzò'; on another occasion, he even changes the word order of a sentence to avoid using this pronoun: 'Ella ora parlava al cameriere' becomes 'Poirot la udì parlare al cameriere'.[14]

In addition, del Buono rightly restores the frequent French phrases and exclamations that Christie uses as part of her characterization of Poirot, as well as of other French-speakers such as M. Bouc (the Belgian director of the Compagnie Internationale des Wagons Lits) and Michel (the Wagon Lit conductor); these were all excised by Pitta (or an editor at Mondadori), presumably to respect the all but official ban on foreign words imposed under Fascism. Compare the following:

> 'Che infame!', esclamò profondamente disgustato, 'Proprio non mi dispiace che sia stato ucciso, no davvero.'[15]
>
> '*Ah! Quel animal*!' esclamò Bouc, profondamente disgustato. 'Proprio non mi dispiace che sia stato ucciso, no davvero.'[16]

The sole exception to this act of (self-)censorship is the French word 'chauffeur', which Pitta does employ; it was current in pre-war Italy, only to be supplanted by 'autista' in the postwar period; in del Buono 'chauffeur' is replaced accordingly.[17] As with the nationality of the murderer and the use of 'voi', we are dealing here with a straightforward substitution which is self-explanatory. However, other changes are less so and it would therefore have been helpful, and also philologically appropriate, had del Buono outlined his strategies for cleansing the target text of its 'ideological' overlay. Regrettably, he does not explain what criteria he adopted in revising Pitta's translation nor does he tell us which words or sentences he has 'restored' in the text.

Consequently, researchers are left with two complications. Not only is Pitta's translation suspect – done as it was under particular conditions, at a time when censorship prevailed – but it has been post-edited by del Buono. This new edition still credits Pitta as the translator; indeed, del Buono does not claim to have done a *re*-translation. Certainly, at first blush, it seems that his interpolations are fairly minimal – except, that is, in a few conspicuous cases. A line-

13 Christie, 1935, p. 31; Christie, 2011, p. 22. **14** Ibid. **15** Christie, 1935, p. 75. **16** Christie, 2011, pp 58–9. **17** Christie, 1935, p. 238; Christie, 2011, p. 195.

by-line analysis of the revised text is therefore necessary to allow us to say with exactitude what changes have been made to the second, revised target text.

By and large, del Buono has sought to modernize the language of the translation, and does this in various ways. For example, he uses the *passato prossimo* in preference to the *passato remoto*, which was employed (correctly) by Pitta but which may not have sounded natural to del Buono; by the late 1960s, the *passato prossimo* had become the default past tense for Italian speakers in the north of the country, and this had a strong influence on written Italian.[18] In the same vein, del Buono tends to replace the subjunctive with the indicative, whenever there is a choice between the two tenses. Thus, Poirot's assertion, in Chapter 7, '"*I know the dead man's real name. I know why he had to leave America.*"' is rendered by Pitta as '"so quale sia il vero nome dell'ucciso, e so anche perchè abbia dovuto lasciare l'America"' whereas del Buono has '"so qual è il vero nome dell'ucciso, e so anche perchè ha dovuto lasciare l'America"'.[19] The difference between the 1935 translation and the 1970 version is also a stylistic one, given that even today the subjunctive could have been used here. Presumably, del Buono did so in the belief that this would make the text easier to read.

Allied to this is a tendency to remove the words he considers too literary, words such as 'sicchè', 'dirimpetto', 'badare' and 'quieto'. Thus, 'Il pezzo di carta era piccolo, *sicchè* non si potevano leggere' becomes 'il frammento era piccolo, non si potevano leggere'; 'Al tavolino *dirimpetto al suo*' is changed to 'al tavolino *di fronte* al suo'; and 'non vi badavo più che tanto' is replaced by 'non ci ho prestato particolare attenzione';[20] clearly, the choice of 'ci' as opposed to 'vi' is also less literary, and confirms del Buono's decision to render the TT more colloquial. However, del Buono is not always consistent in his revisions, and on the same page when the verb 'badare' is employed again, he omits to change it: '"È difficile dire. Veda, io non badavo a chi potesse passare."' is modified only very slightly (presumably an oversight): '"È difficile vede [sic]. Io non badavo a chi potesse passare."'; 'Sempre quieto, Poirot chiamò il cameriere del vagone-ristorante' is replaced by 'Sempre con tono calmo, Poirot chiamò il cameriere del vagone-ristorante.'[21]

Elsewhere, del Buono changes word order to make a phrase sound more natural to modern ears, while again restoring the original Italian nationality of a

18 E.g. '"E non si accorse se qualcuno passasse nel corridoio?" "Passarono parecchie persone [...]"' (Christie, 1935, p. 130) is updated to '"E non si è accorto se qualcuno passava nel corridoio?" "Sono passate parecchie persone."' (Christie, 2011, p. 106); '"a che ora fu effettivamente commesso il delitto?"' (Christie, 1935, p. 253) becomes '"a che ora è stato effettivamente commesso il delitto"' (Christie, 2011, pp 207–8). **19** Christie, 1934, p. 70; Christie, 1935, p. 71; Christie, 1970, p. 55. **20** Christie, 1935, p. 71; Christie, 2011, p. 55; Christie, 1935, p. 31; Christie, 2011, p. 21; Christie, 1935, p. 130; Christie, 2011, p. 106. **21** Christie, 1935, p. 130; Christie, 2011, p. 106; Christie, 1935, p. 239; Christie, 2011, p. 196.

minor character, Foscarelli. 'Uno di essi era un grosso abbronzato brasiliano' is rearranged to produce 'uno di essi era un grosso italiano abbronzato'.[22]

In the spirit of modernizing the style of the target text, del Buono makes other, apparently minor adjustments, both lexical and grammatical. The following sentence is typical of his approach: 'Al tavolino *dirimpetto al suo* erano tre uomini, molto probabilmente viaggiatori isolati che il sicuro apprezzamento dei camerieri aveva *riuniti* insieme' is amended to 'al tavolino *di fronte* c'erano tre uomini, molto probabilmente viaggiatori isolati che il sicuro apprezzamento dei camerieri aveva *riunito* insieme'.[23] A short extract from the same scene may serve further to illustrate the kind of modifications del Buono chooses to make to the target text in the process of revision:

> A un tavolino per due era sola, tenendosi molto eretta della persona, una delle più brutte signore che egli avesse mai visto; ma era una bruttezza di distinzione, quella, e affascinava anziché ripugnare. Al collo la dama aveva un filo di grosse perle, e perle autentiche, per inverosimile che la cosa potesse sembrare [...].
>
> A un tavolino per due, sola, tenendosi molto eretta *nella* persona, *faceva spicco* una delle più brutte *donne* che avesse mai visto: era una bruttezza *distinta, aristocratica*, e affascinava anziché ripugnare. La signora portava al collo un filo di grosse perle, *naturalmente autentiche* [...].[24]

As can be seen, 'molto eretta della persona' is modernized by changing the preposition ('molto eretta *nella* persona'), a process that also occurs elsewhere.[25] A different form of updating takes place with 'una bruttezza di distinzione'; in del Buono's revised text, this becomes 'una bruttezza *distinta*', to which he adds the explanatory adjective 'aristocratica', an addition prompted perhaps by the desire to be more explicit. It also compensates for the loss of an equivalent to

22 Christie, 1935, p. 31; Christie, 2011, p. 21. **23** Ibid., emphasis added. This passage is taken from the scene in the 'luncheon-car' at the beginning of Chapter III: 'At the table opposite them were three men. They were, he guessed, single travellers graded and placed there by the unerring judgment of the restaurant attendants' (Christie, 1934, p. 30). **24** Ibid., emphasis added. 'At a small table, sitting very upright, was one of the ugliest old ladies he had ever seen. It was an ugliness of distinction – it fascinated rather than repelled. She sat very upright. Round her neck was a collar of very large pearls which, improbable though it seemed, were real.' (Christie, 1934, p. 31). **25** The contraction 'pel' in the following sentences is removed as it was already demoded by the postwar period: 'Ma pareva che Poirot non intendesse pel momento aggiungere altro' (Christie, 1935, p. 31) becomes 'per il momento' (Christie, 2011, p. 55); 'rimasto sveglio pel mal di denti' (Christie, 1935, p. 112) becomes 'rimasto sveglio per il mal di denti' (Christie, 2011, p. 90), and so on.

'dama' (which was itself an addition on the part of Pitta) in his version where 'signore' and 'dama' are each replaced by a correspondingly more informal term ('donne' and 'signore'). Equally, the expression 'faceva spicco' gives the passage a more modern feel. (Both target texts omit, presumably to avoid repetition, considered poor style in Italian, the sentence 'She sat very upright', a reiteration of the concept enunciated previously.) Finally, del Buono alters slightly Christie's comment regarding the fact that the Princess Dragomiroff's pearls are genuine, with the effect that it becomes somewhat mundane, whereas in Pitta's version the authenticity of the pearls is announced in a more suggestive fashion.

Aside from countless changes of this nature, there are, as noted, several key editorial interventions. In the space permitted here, I shall delineate some significant changes detected. Among the suspects in Christie's novel there is an Italian-American businessman by the name of Antonio Foscarelli who turns out to be one of the twelve co-murderers responsible for the crime discovered on the Orient Express train. His name would almost certainly have been an obstacle to publication in 1930s Italy, bearing in mind the censorial constraints referred to earlier. Although in the source text Foscarelli is presented as a naturalized American, in manner he is most definitely marked by his Italian background – another reason, presumably, why Pitta chose to alter the character's name and nationality: in the 1935 target text Foscarelli becomes a Brazilian called Manuel Pereira. In the 1970 text, as we have seen, he reverts to his Italian name.

If we turn to the chapter entitled 'The evidence of the Italian', we can find one of many examples of Christie's use of cliché to define foreigners: 'His face beamed. It was a typical Italian face, sunny looking and swarthy.' The first short sentence, excised by Pitta, is also absent from del Buono (it is difficult to say whether by design, or simply because he was in 'revising' rather than 'translating mode' and therefore did not notice this cut which he does *not* restore). Similarly, the description of Foscarelli as 'swarthy', here and elsewhere, is each time rendered as 'abbronzato' in del Buono's version, thereby retaining Pitta's translation: 'Era di schietto tipo latino, abbronzato e comunicativo.' What is especially interesting to note, however, is that del Buono has transformed the generalizition about Italian joviality into a more positive character trait, namely sociability; the term 'comunicativo' is itself something of a cliché in contemporary Italian culture. More glaring still is the use of the expression 'schietto tipo latino' which updates Pitta's translation: 'Era di tipo schiettamente sud-americano, abbronzato e sorridente'.[26] The adverb 'schiettamente' was common in interwar Italy; del Buono's use of 'schietto' combined with 'tipo latino' is curiously resonant of Fascist discourse, surely not an outcome he intended. He

26 Christie, 1934, p. 138; Christie, 2011, p. 116; Christie, 1935, p. 141.

could easily have phrased this sentence differently: 'tipicamente latino/mediterraneo', for example, would have been more usual.

As has emerged, the choices made by del Buono affect overall the lexis, syntax and even the grammar of the translation produced by Pitta in 1935. These decisions often go well beyond his declared aim of removing the 'ideological dimension' of the target text. Furthermore, there are many words or sentences that del Buono has cut. Some of these omissions are not easy to interpret since we do not know whether he was constrained by the need to shorten the book for commercial considerations, or whether such excisions were part of a strategy to make the translation as straightforward as possible, emphasizing the plot and removing anything deemed superfluous to that goal. In the presentation of Foscarelli, for instance, del Buono censors details of Christie's characterization that he found unpalatable, thereby making it less of a caricature – arguably a defensible position but one that should nonetheless have been explained. Other revisions seem subjective, motivated by stylistic preferences.

Inevitably, language becomes dated, and it is natural that for subsequent editions of a translated text publishers will want to make the necessary adjustments to ensure a book can be understood by the modern reader, and at the same time avoid offending their sensibility. But we might also reasonably expect editors who intervene in translations to leave a written trace of these changes, to provide as it were 'Translator's Notes', explaining why they have modified a text in a particular way. Without the benefit of potentially valuable contextual information that is now lost, many of del Buono's interventions can be explained in a number of ways, which means that any analysis of them can at best be speculative. As such, the status of the 1970 target text remains uncertain, the product of substantial text-editing rather than retranslation. Inconsistency, together with disregard for the source text, has generated a hybrid awkwardly straddling two periods.

'A good metaphor for all we do?' – fictional translators as criminals and detectives: some examples

Sabine Strümper-Krobb

Translator and interpreter figures and the theme of translation have become an increasingly popular feature in literary texts and films, and often serve to address some of the main concerns of contemporary fiction, such as issues of identity, image construction, intercultural encounter and debates about authenticity and originality.[1] The literary treatment of translation appears particularly frequently in the genre of detective or crime fiction, or in works in which crimes and their investigation are at least an element of the plot. Here, translators and interpreters can take on the role of both criminal and of detective and are thus instrumental in the investigations of right and wrong, or of 'moral and factual truth' which, according to Peter Newmark, all translation is concerned with, and which any work of crime fiction revolves around.[2]

There are a number of parallels between translation and crime detection. Translators are expected first to identify the function and meaning of particular elements of a text in order to reconstruct them as truthfully as possible in a different language, so that the reader is able to understand them appropriately. Similarly, a detective needs to collect evidence in a criminal case before he or she is able to reconstruct the crime in such a way that the reconstructed version corresponds to the actual course of events. This parallel between the role of the translator and that of the detective is hinted at in works such as the *Torrey Tunet mystery* series, *The Irish cottage murder*, *The Irish manor house murder* and *The Irish cairn murder* by the American writer Dicey Deere, in which the interpreter and translator Torrey Tunet becomes involuntarily involved in criminal cases which she solves, not least, by using her professional capacity as a disguise.[3] In another American crime series the link between the translation and the detective work

1 Two recent studies analyse this phenomenon in films and in literature respectively: Michael Cronin, *Translation goes to the movies* (London, 2009); and Sabine Strümper-Krobb, *Zwischen den Welten: die Sichtbarkeit des Übersetzers in der Literatur* (Berlin, 2009). 2 Peter Newmark, *About translation* (Clevedon, 1991), p. 1. 3 Dicey Deere, *The Irish cottage murder* (New York, 1998); Dicey Deere, *The Irish manor house murder* (New York, 2000), and Dicey Deere, *The Irish cairn murder* (New York, 2002).

of the main protagonist is shown even more strongly: the customs and immigration interpreter Margit Andersson in Tiina Nunnally's novels *Fate of ravens* and *Runemaker*,[4] uses actual translation work, such as the deciphering of old documents, coin inscriptions and notebooks, in her investigation of the crimes she tries to solve.

However, the translator's privileged role as the one who is expected to find equivalences, and so, ultimately, communicate truths, sets him or her up for two quite contradictory roles: he or she can manipulate a message and is able to conceal truth as well as revealing it. This ambivalence is played out, for example, in Bernhard Schlink's criminal novel *Die gordische Schleife* (1988),[5] whose main protagonist, through his translation job, becomes unwillingly involved in industrial espionage and then starts to investigate the forces that are behind the crimes. What he reveals is a play and counterplay of intrigues and double espionage which eventually makes him doubt the truthfulness of language in general.

What makes translators and interpreters so interesting as literary figures is the fact that they can not only drive forward a plot involving mystery and suspense, but also often contribute significantly to a discourse about the possibility of unambiguous truths, of clear distinctions between original and copy, reality and fiction. It is thus not surprising that the writers of crime fiction have taken such an interest in translator figures and in the theme of translation. For a long time detective and crime novels have been seen as rather formulaic, following a set pattern of character constellation and plot in which 'specially skilled people discover the cause of a crime, restore order and bring the criminal to account',[6] and which can be illustrated by looking, in particular, at works from the British Golden Age of crime fiction. However, in more recent decades, crime and detective novels have undergone what Stefano Tani calls a 'postmodern mutation of the genre'.[7] Rather than ultimately confirming the possibility to bring order to a 'disorderly and dangerous world',[8] the detective novel serves as a platform to show ambiguities and to blur boundaries, both on the fictional level of the plot and on the level of characterization, structure and genre. In the introduction to their collection of essays on detective narratives in European culture since 1945, Anne Mullen and Eimer O'Beirne emphasize the scope the genre has shown for thematic and formal innovation: 'The old patterns of reassurance,

4 Tiina Nunnally, *Fate of ravens* (Seattle, 1998) and *Runemaker* (Seattle, 1996). **5** Bernhard Schlink, *Die gordische Schleife* (Zürich, 1988). **6** Stephen Knight, *Form and ideology in crime fiction* (London and Basingstoke, 1980), p. 8. For conventional features attributed to the genre, especially in up to the second half of the twentieth century see Dennis Porter, *The pursuit of crime* (New Haven, 1981). **7** Stefano Tani, *The doomed detective: the contribution of the detective novel to postmodern American and Italian fiction* (Carbondale and Edwardsville, 1984), p. xiii. **8** Tani, *The doomed detective*, p. xi.

with the inevitable triumph of the intellect and restoration of a supposedly rational, ordered, and secure world, repeatedly give way in the face of a contemporary need to foreground the complexities, ambiguities, and uncertainties of the self and of society.'[9] Detective fiction does not just become 'a vehicle for lucid protest against a prevailing social situation', but can also interrogate literary structures and the construction of meaning, directing attention, in particular, to the role of the reader or critic.[10] This is, again, where a parallel can be drawn between the role of the detective and that of the translator: both are critical 'readers' of signs to which they give meaning and can thus also be seen to construct a text. At the same time, conventional notions of originality and authorship can be questioned, not least by exploring and possibly inverting the idea of the translator as a perpetrator of crimes against the (original) text and its author. Thus, fictional characters combining the function of detective and translator (or, in fact, perpetrator and translator) have a particular potential to become a major voice in the meta-fictional discourse within literary texts.

While the theme is a more frequent feature of texts from the second half of the twentieth and the beginning of the twenty-first century, earlier writers, too, exploit the literary treatment of translation in order to contribute to meta-fictional discourse in works of crime fiction.[11] In the short story 'The kleptomaniac translator' (1933) by the Hungarian author Deszö Kosztolányi, the very title identifies the main protagonist as both a translator and a thief: After spending two years in prison for theft, the former author Gallus is no longer able to publish under his own name. To make ends meet, he changes career and becomes a translator, but in his new profession he continues his criminal activities, albeit now transferred into the world of the texts that he translates. In the story, a comparison of Gallus' translation of an English detective novel with the original shows that the translator has deprived the fictional characters of valuable possessions mentioned in the source text. Items are left out or substituted with less expensive objects, stately homes are changed into more modest abodes, and sums of money are reduced by the thieving translator. An inventory of the stolen goods reveals

> that during his translation from the English original, our confused author friend had, in an improper and unacceptable manner, misappropriated

9 Anne Mullen & Emer O'Beirne, 'Introduction' in Anne Mullen & Emer O'Beirne (eds), *Crime scenes: detective narratives in European culture since 1945* (Amsterdam, 2000), pp i–ii. **10** Mullen & O'Beirne, 'Introduction', p. ii. **11** It may be questionable if all works discussed here should be categorized as 'crime' or 'detective fiction', as the crime and its investigation is not usually the only or even the main element of the plot. The difficulty in genre categorization may be precisely a result of the tendency of writers to 'take advantage of detective fiction conventions to write something quite different from detective fiction' (Tani, *The doomed detective*, p. xiii).

> 1,579,251 pounds sterling, and, also, 177 gold rings, 947 pearl necklaces, 181 pocket watches, 309 pairs of ear-rings, 435 suitcases, not to mention the entire fortunes, the forests and fields, the castles of dukes and barons, alongside other bits and bobs such as handkerchiefs, toothpicks and bells, the detailed listing of which would be tedious and presumably superfluous.[12]

By diagnosing the crimes as a manifestation of the protagonist's kleptomaniac condition, this short story seems to represent the powerlessness rather than the power of the translator. His disappearance at the end of the story can be seen as an ultimate marginalization, or even as punishment for his transgression of the boundaries of his profession. However, read on a meta-fictional level, the transfer of the crime of theft, which is, after all, a crime against the right of possession, from the real world to the world of the text, could be interpreted as a questioning of the very concept of authorship. Kosztolányi's short story certainly plays with the traditional concept of a hierarchy between original and translation that automatically attributes values like creativity and originality to the original and sees the translation as inferior, as a mere copy and a shadow of a superior source text. Kosztolányi lets the narrator ponder the poetic quality of the translation, which he calls 'artistically ambitious', and praises as a definite improvement of the original: 'It [the translation] was full of lucid sentences, meaningful phrases, inspired linguistic ideas of which this pulp magazine was not worthy.'[13] Inspired ideas are, of course, features of originality, which are attributed to the translation here that is thus identified as surpassing the source. The conventional hierarchy between original and translation is inverted, the asymmetrical relationship between original and translation at the very least questioned.

The relationship between original and translation takes centre stage in Italo Calvino's novel *Se una notte d'inverno un viaggiatore* (1979; translated into English as *If on a winter's night a traveller* [1981]). The novel deals with the writing and with the reading, dissemination and reception of literature and is typical of what Gregory Lucente has identified as the 'literary self-consciousness' in Calvino's work, a narrative mode which draws attention to itself and emphasizes both the fictional status of the text and the narrative techniques used in the text.[14] According to Lucente, the intentional mystification of the reader, the launching

12 This analysis is based on the German translation of the Hungarian text: Deszö Kosztolanyi, 'Der kleptomanische bersetzer' in Deszö Kosztolanyi, *Der kleptomanische Übersetzer und andere Geschichten*, aus dem Ungarischen von Jörg Buschmann (Nördlingen, 1988), pp 4–49 at p. 5. Translation into English by Sabine Strümper-Krobb. Further references are given in the text. **13** Ibid., pp 7–8. **14** Gregory Lucente, *Beautiful fables: self-consciousness in Italian narrative from Manzoni to Calvino* (Baltimore and London, 1986), p. 19.

of doubts and ambiguities play an important role here. In *Se una notte d'inverno*, the motif of translation and the translator figure contribute in a particular way to this kind of mystification. Translation is not just an element of the plot and part of the characterization, but it becomes an integral part of the text's structure, both on the macro-level of the narrative frame and on the micro-level of the different episodes within this frame. The novel consists of the opening chapters of ten alleged novel translations each of which has been left unfinished and is preceded by an introduction. The introductions make up the narrative frame in which a male and a female reader are brought together through the mystery of the textual fragments which they, almost like detective figures, attempt to solve. The puzzle is aggravated by the fact that the incomplete texts have been given titles that do not actually belong to them. The question if the texts really are translations, if complete versions exist and which, if any, were the original sources, remains initially open. On the level of the plot, the fictional translator Ermes Marana, who is the one who initiated the flooding of the book market with fragmented pseudo-translations, takes on the role of a criminal figure.[15] He deliberately deceives, initially to take revenge on his former lover, the female reader Ludmilla whose notion of literature he is trying to destroy: she prefers novels that represent a world in which everything is precise, concrete and exactly defined but Maranas' intrigue presents her exactly with the opposite. On a meta-fictional level, Calvino's translator figure Ermes Marana represents what Helga Schwelm calls an intrigue against literary authorship and the originality of the literary text,[16] as his manipulatory translation activity ultimately destroys not just the expectations of the fictional reader Ludmilla but also the expectations of the actual reader of Calvino's novel – for whom the satisfaction of a complete story, the fiction of a coherence that creates meaning remains elusive.

While Italo Calvino's novel uses a deceitful and manipulative translator figure and inscribes into the structure of its narrative the idea of fake translations in order to undermine notions of authorship and originality, the works of American crime fiction writer Barbara Wilson are linked by the figure of a lesbian translator and amateur detective who contributes to an entertaining play with ideas of translation and authorship, fiction and reality. In the story 'An expatriate death',[17] for example, this translator finds her pseudonym Cassandra

15 For a more detailed analysis of Calvino's novel in the context of the post-modern detective novel see Stefano Tani, *The doomed detective*, esp. pp 114–34. **16** Helga Schwelm, 'Moderne und Postmoderne: zum Problem epochaler Klassifikationen im Kontext der Moderne' in Joachim Piechotta, Ralph-Rainer Wuthenow and Sabine Rothemann (eds), *Die literarische Moderne in Europa*, iii: *Aspekte der Moderne in der Literatur bis zur Gegenwart* (Opladen, 1994), pp 355–69. **17** Barbara Wilson, 'An expatriate death' in Barbara Wilson,

Reilly as the name of a victim in a criminal novel; with other words, she sees herself changed into a fictional figure. In 'Mi novelista', [18] Cassandra Reilly leaves her role as amateur detective and commits a crime by forging a translation (similar to Calvino's Ernesto Marana, albeit less damaging to her readers and not with any sinister intentions). In this narrative it is not, as in 'An expatriate death', the translator who becomes part of the fictional plot, but the fictional author who becomes part of reality when the name Cassandra Reilly invented as that of the original writer of the text she allegedly translated is taken on by a real translator who then profits from the very real and commercial success of the work. At the beginning of Wilson's novel *Gaudi afternoon* the translator-detective Cassandra Reilly is introduced in a passage that suggests that she is difficult to pin down as a person, both in terms of gender and of location. The novel opens with the sentence 'My name is Cassandra Reilly and I don't live anywhere', and at a later point in the novel she answers the question 'Please what are you? Woman or man?' by pointing to her profession 'Neither [...] I'm a translator'.[19] Her unreliability (her visits are always, as a colleague complains, unpredictable and she cannot be counted on) and her restlessness (she constantly moves around between different residences) further undermine the model of the detective who is trying to establish a stable truth in order to restore an unambiguous order. It is precisely her double identity of translator and detective that makes Wilson's protagonist question the very possibility of such an unambiguous order and reality.

Not all of the mentioned works would fit comfortably into the genre of crime or detective novel. However, all of them play, to some extent at least, with the expectations that are part and parcel of narratives which deal with crime and crime detection: that crime tries to conceal and manipulate the truth but that clever investigation will reveal an unambiguous truth.

A final example for this is the novel *La caverna de las ideas* (2000; translated into English as *The Athenian murders* [2002]), by the Cuban author José Carlos Somoza. The name of one of the main protagonists, Heracles Pontor, places this work quite explicitly in the tradition of the crime or detective novel through the allusion to Agatha Christie's Hercule Poirot, one of the most well-known literary detectives of all time. The title of the English translation, *The Athenian murders,* embeds the novel even more firmly in this genre tradition, a signal that has been picked up by some of the reviews quoted on the back cover and in the inside of the edition where Somoza's novel is characterized as a 'murder mystery', 'whodunnit' and

The death of a much-travelled woman and other adventures with Cassandra Reilly (Chicago, 1998), pp 89–110. **18** Barbara Wilson, 'Mi novelista' in Barbara Wilson, *The death of a much-travelled woman and other adventures with Cassandra Reilly* (Chicago, 1998), pp 195–215. **19** Barbara Wilson, *Gaudi afternoon* (Seattle, 1990), pp 3, 74.

'mix of ancient crime and modern detection' and where the detective figure is compared with the well-known TV detective Chief Inspector Morse.[20]

However, *La caverna de las ideas* is not just, and not even primarily, about the investigation of a series of mysterious deaths in ancient Athens. In fact, from the start, the novels subverts the rather clichéd conventions of the genre which the author so deliberately evokes with the name of his protagonist. This is indicated already by the title of the original that cites Plato's allegory of the cave. Somoza uses the narrative of the detection of a crime as a springboard for philosophical and semiotic ruminations about the attempt to gain pure knowledge and truth, and also for a meta-fictional discourse on the process of writing.

Translator figures and the theme and motif of translation serve these concerns on various levels. On the very first page, the novel is introduced as the modern Spanish version of an anonymously written ancient original. Even before the actual story begins, a fictional translator makes his appearance in a footnote attached to the chapter titled simply 'I'. He refers both to an absent original and to a character called Montola, allegedly the editor of the version that serves as the only source for his translation.[21] This immediately raises questions about the authenticity of the narrative: for it remains unclear to what extent this story of a search for truth actually corresponds to the original source. Questions of mediation and translation, language and reality, fiction and truth are also addressed by a number of further translator figures who have an active part in the plot itself. One of them is Hercule Poirot's namesake Heracles Pontor who is requested to investigate the suspicious death of Tramachos, a student in Plato's academy. Pontor carries the nickname 'Decipherer of Enigmas' (in the Spanish original: 'El descifrador de enigmas'), he tries to solve mysteries through the decoding of visible signs, a sort of ancient detective whose work is classified by the people of Athens as translation. They believe:

> That a Decipherer of Enigmas can read the faces of men and the look of things as if they were papyri. That he knows the language of appearances and can translate it.[22]

20 José Carlos Somoza, *The Athenian murders,* translated by Sonia Soto (London, 2002). **21** Ibid., p. 1. By presenting the main text as a translation of an uncertain source and thus questioning its authenticity, Somoza inscribes his novel in a tradition that reaches back to Cervantes' *Don Quixote* in which the author presents a large part of the text as a translation of coincidentally discovered old notebooks and documents written in Arabic. Not only is the language of the original inaccessible to him but he also mistrusts the truthfulness of the account given about the history of Don Quixote. See Miguel de Cervantes, *Don Quixote,* translated by Edith Grossman (New York, 2003), pp 67–8. In modern literature, a similar strategy of what appears as a meta-fictional translator discourse is used in Umberto Eco's *Il Nome della rosa* (1980). **22** Somoza, *The Athenian murders*, p. 20.

Heracles reads the visible world around him as a text whose language he has to translate into a narrative that explains the crimes and hence leads to the culprit. He only relies on what he himself can perceive and he is convinced that this reveals a truth that can objectively be proven. However, the question of whether there is such an unambiguous truth is constantly posited in conversations between the figures in the novel, and also by the translator's voice in the footnotes. While Heracles represents the belief that signs and what they mean are equivalent to one another, his old friend Crantor and Menaechmus, a poet, sculptor and opponent of Plato's academy, reject such a notion, as is illustrated by one of Menaechmus' sculptures, which is called *The translator* and which takes the shape of a man who unsuccessfully looks for an eternal truth:

> The man who tries to decipher the mystery of a text written in a foreign language, not realising that words simply lead to other words, and thought to other thought while the Truth remains unattainable. Is it not a good metaphor for all we do?[23]

In the sculpture and in its interpretation by its creator, translation is characterized as an ultimately futile exercise, because it is based on the notion of a correspondence between sign and signified. Taking a deconstructionist approach, Menaechmus disputes the existence of any concrete, physical reality behind the linguistic and subjective realities of thought, every sign simply points to another sign in an endless spiral of referring and deferring, there is no original source, no stable meaning, no truth.[24]

As regards the actual detection of a crime, Heracles Pontor's theory of a translation of concrete evidence into a convincing narrative reconstructing the crime – and thus exactly the theory that provides the basis for the classical detective novel with which Somoza plays – is successful. Listening and observing precisely and deducing intelligently, he finally discovers the truth: what was taken to be a series of murders turns out to be the result of the rituals of a secret sect. Parallel to this conventional detective story there is an ever more elaborate

23 Ibid., p. 159. **24** Here, a parallel can again be drawn to Umberto Eco's famous novel which is discussed at length in Stefano Tani's study under the chapter title 'The metafictional anti-detective novel'. See Tani, *The doomed detective*, pp 114–34. On Eco in this context see also Pierre Bayard, *How to talk about books you haven't read,* translated from the French by Jeffrey Mehlman (London, 2008), pp 32–46. The problems of accessing a physical reality through the signs of language are also alluded to by choosing to make Menaechmus a protagonist in the novel. While historically Menaechmus is the name of a mathematician and friend of Plato's, it also refers to the twin protagonists of a play by Plautus (254BC–184BC), both named Menaechmus whose resemblance and identical name confuse others. I would like to thank Eiléan Ní Chuilleanáin for alerting me to this allusion.

plot developing in the footnotes, which is not set in ancient Athens but in the present of the modern translator figure who was introduced in the very first footnote of the novel. The footnotes and the increasing meshing of the two historically distant plots ultimately deconstruct the idea of a comprehensible reality and a reconstructable order, represented in the seemingly satisfactory crime detection, in the most radical way.

The modern translator and apparent author of the footnotes is designed by Somoza as translator and detective in equal measure. Just like Heracles Pontor, he is in search of truth. While within the novel the metaphor of translation is used to describe Heracles' detective efforts, the work of the modern translator can be seen as detective work: he assumes that the text is a sign that contains a secret message. In order to decode this message, he collects evidence (the constant repetition of certain words in the text referring to so-called 'eidetic images'), questions colleagues who are experts in this literary technique, and draws his conclusions. In a gesture of authority, as explicator of the meaning that is contained in the eidetic images, the translator initially upholds the theory of a universally valid, attainable and translatable truth. His colleagues criticize this claim, they argue that each reader could interpret such images in a different way and that, in an endless chain of images, the reader might never find the ultimate meaning: 'any written thing can refer the reader to an image which, in turn, can refer him to another, and another [...] It would make reading impossible'.[25]

In the course of the novel, the boundaries between the three versions of the text, namely the (absent) original, the (absent) modern edition and the translation become blurred, as the plot in the footnotes invades the plot in the main text and vice versa. Eventually however, both the figures of ancient Athens, and the modern translator are shown to be nothing but fictions in a literary text, written, as the epilogue reveals, by a contemporary of Plato who invented both the figure of Heracles Pontor and the unnamed translator of the footnotes 'who lives in an imaginary future'.[26] At the end of the main narrative the modern translator disappears. He has lost his function – deciphering an ultimate meaning beyond words – as the existence of such a meaning is revealed as an illusion: 'The space allocated to my words shrinks. I become as marginal as my footnotes. The author decides to end me here'.[27]

In a commentary on his novel, the author Somoza reported how the idea to include the fictional translator in the footnotes had followed the actual completion of the novel and how this additional character had then developed into a central figure, thus making a new approach to the novel necessary. The story, a conventional criminal story, a simple 'novel of suspense', set in ancient Athens,

25 Somoza, *The Athenian murders*, p. 35. **26** Ibid., p. 313. **27** Ibid., p. 312.

'changed radically and became something different.'[28] The theme of translation transforms Somoza's novel from a simple crime story into a debate on philosophical and semiotic issues, thus blurring the boundaries between 'low' and 'high' literature. Through the motif of translation, Somoza questions the referentiality of language and the existence of a reality outside the text, showing that translation has been discovered as the perfect stage for these concerns, the translator figures indeed serve as 'a good metaphor for all we do'.

As all the examples have shown, translation, as an element of plot or structure, has become a popular feature in literary works that deal with crimes or their detection. One of the reasons for this is the parallel that can be drawn between the process of translation and the detection of a crime – both are based on the reading of signs and the attempt to attribute meaning to these signs. Both are trying to reconstruct a version of reality which matches the 'original', the real course of events or the source text. Both, however, also have the power to manipulate or shape this version in such a way that the original is questioned. The literary treatment of translation in crime and detective fiction therefore directs attention towards debates about authenticity and originality. In fact, it is often the theme of translation or the inclusion of a translator figure that moves a text beyond the narrow conventional boundaries of classic crime fiction and exemplifies the 'postmodern mutation' of the genre.

28 José Carlos Somoza, 'A character in search of an author', translated by Peter J. Hearn, *The Guardian*, 14 Dec. 2002. books.guardian.co.uk/review/story/0,21084,858808,00.html, accessed 26 Oct. 2007.

Adding translation to insult

Bart Defrancq

INTRODUCTION

Until recently, conversational pragmatics was mainly concerned with describing how speakers attempt to avoid conflict in linguistic interaction. Concepts such as conversational maxims,[1] politeness and face,[2] intersubjectivity,[3] all relate to the idea of harmonious human interaction. Conflicting linguistic interaction has long been believed to be a rather marginal phenomenon.[4]

This has led to what some have called a 'conceptual bias' in politeness studies.[5] Only in recent years has the topic of impoliteness as a necessary complement to politeness gained some support in the research community.[6]

Theoretically, the use of 'dirty language', cursing and insulting, is part and parcel of the broad area of conflictive linguistic interaction. In practice, however, these topics have mostly been dealt with from a historical and lexicographic point of view[7] and not from a pragmatic one.

In translation studies, finally, the topic has been touched upon mainly in the area of audiovisual translation.[8] In more traditional written translation genres, there is one study on insults by José Mateo and Francisco Yus[9] and a number of studies on taboo words.[10] Mateo and Yus' paper takes a relevance-theoretic

1 H. Grice, 'Logic and conversation' in P. Cole & J. Morgan (eds), *Syntax and semantics 3: speech acts* (New York, 1975), pp 41–58. **2** P. Brown & S. Levinson, *Politeness: some universals in language usage* (Cambridge, 1987). **3** P. White, 'Dialogue and inter-subjectivity: reinterpreting the semantics of modality and hedging' in M. Coulthard et al. (eds), *Working with dialogue* (Tübingen, 2000), pp 67–80. **4** T. Jay, *Cursing in America* (Amsterdam, 1992); G. Leech, *The principles of pragmatics* (London, 1983). **5** G. Eelen, *A critique of politeness theories* (Manchester, 2001). **6** D. Bousfield, *Impoliteness in interaction* (Amsterdam, 2008); D. Bousfield and M. Locher, *Impoliteness in language* (Berlin, 2008). **7** T. Jay, *Why we curse: a neuro-psycho-social theory of speech* (Amsterdam, 1999). **8** M. Pavesi & A.L. Malinverno, 'Usi del turpiloquio nella traduzione filmica' in C. Taylor (ed.), *Atti del convengo 'Tradurre il cinema'* (Trieste, 2000), pp 75–89; M. Pavesi, *La traduzione filmica: aspetti del parlato doppiato dall'inglese all'italiano* (Rome, 2005). **9** J. Mateo & F. Yus, 'Insults: a relevance-theoretic approach to their translation', *International Journal of Translation*, 12:1–2 (2000), 97–130. **10** J. Varney, 'Taboo and the translator: a survey of translators' notes in Italian translations of Anglo-American fiction, 1945–2005' in *New research in translation and interpreting studies* (Tarragona, 2005), pp 47–57. See also R. Isbuga-Erel, 'A CDA approach to the translations of taboos in literary texts within the historical and socio-political Turkish context' in M. Khosravinik & A. Polyzou (eds), *Papers from the Lancaster University postgraduate conference in linguistics and lan-*

approach to the translation of insults. Its aim is to propose a typology of insults based on parameters that are likely to be relevant for the description of cross-linguistic variation in insults and should, therefore, be taken into account by translators. The perspective is normative: Mateo and Yus criticize several Spanish translations of English insults occurring in fictional texts.

The perspective adopted in this essay differs from Mateo and Yus' approach in two respects: it is purely descriptive and it focuses on the translation of a few attested, real-life cases of insults. The aim of this study is to determine how translators deal with the complex task of translating insults. As most scholars have pointed out, insults involve a wide range of pragmatic factors which are sometimes difficult to render in translation. Moreover, translators are themselves constrained by the pragmatic conditions of their translation utterances. Translations of insults will therefore greatly depend on the factors translators choose to privilege. As these factors are manifold, translations can vary considerably.

The data that constitute the empirical basis of this study are drawn from the web. They are translations of two instances of English *cunt* and French *con*:

CUNT

On 9 November 2006, Lindsay Lohan (US) insults Paris Hilton indirectly;[11] on 30 October 2008, Mary Gaitskill (US) insults Sarah Palin indirectly in an interview with a French radio network.[12]

It should be noted that Palin's opponents in the 2008 Presidential campaign had a habit of referring to Sarah Palin as a 'cunt'. The insult was even printed on t-shirts. Translations of these occurrences are also included in the data for this study.

CON

On 22 December 2007, André Flahaut (B) insults Pieter De Crem, Belgian Defence Minister, indirectly in a Parliamentary committee;[13] on 23 February 2008, Nicolas Sarkozy (F) insults a bystander directly at a farming fair in Paris.[14]

Even though *cunt* and *con* have the same anatomical meaning and can both be used as insults, their meaning and offensiveness as insults is different: while in French *con* is a relatively mild insult referring mainly to stupid men, its English

guage teaching (Lancaster, 2008), ii, pp 58–77. **11** www.youtube.com/watch?v=P9aafvHfa4s, accessed 3 Oct. 2008. **12** www.wikio.fr/culture/litterature/auteurs/mary_gaitskill#news 76862683, accessed 5 Jan. 2009. **13** www.youtube.com/watch?v=NdDyuFSA5Pc, accessed 3 Feb. 2008. **14** www.youtube.com/watch?v=axDyUNWyuw8, accessed 25 Feb. 2008.

counterpart is still felt to be one of the most offensive insults in some English-speaking countries, notably the United States, where it is one of the legendary seven words one cannot use on television.[15] Despite its etymology, *con* is only used for men, but it also forms the morphological basis for a derived feminine form *conne*, used for females, and for a number of other derived forms with stronger meanings, such as *connard, connasse*. English 'cunt' can be used for both genders.

TRANSLATIONS

Three of the four incidents were covered by national or international media, giving rise to a variety of translations both in the media and on internet forums and weblogs. In total, 41 translations were found of the above-mentioned insults. Their distribution is illustrated in Table 1.

Table 1. Translations of insults

	French	*English*	*Dutch*
Lohan	3	–	4
Gaitskill et al.	3	–	–
Sarkozy	–	13	11
Flahaut	–	–	7

Mary Gaitskill's insult is probably the only insult considered here that is translated by a professional translator. All other instances are translated by journalists and bloggers.

TRANSLATIONS OF CUNT

In French half of the occurrences of 'cunt' are left untranslated, as in the following cases:[16]

(1) Pendant ce temps à Hollywood la très jolie Lindsay Lohan (bourrée) traite Paris Hilton de ***cunt*** dans une vidéo totalement inutile donc forcement indispensable, so chic.[17]

15 S. Pinker, *The seven words you can't say on television* (London, 2008). **16** Note that web examples have been copied as they are, including spelling and other errors. I have omitted the use of <sic> in order not to reduce reading comfort too much. **17** neimad.blogspot.

(2) Sarah Palin en prend pour son grade, plus tard dans la soiree un mec affichera Sarah Palin is a **cunt** sur son tee shirt, on voit le degres de sympathie qu'il lui porte.[18]

(3) Mais en effet, je ne m'abaisserais pas au niveau des militants d'Obama qui vont jusqu'à traiter Palin de **Cunt** et placarder ça sur leurs t-shirts.[19]

In two more cases, the word is left untranslated in the relevant context, but a translation is proposed in the broader context:

(4) parce qu'elle [Hillary Clinton] est pas assez **pute/** parce que Sarah Palin **ne fait pas de doute.**[20]

(5) Lindsay Lohan a traité Paris Hilton de '***cunt***' (**littéralement**: '**chatte**').[21]

Only one author translates the insult directly

(6) Lyndsay Lohan appelle Paris Hilton **chatte.**[22]

The translation strategies differ: the professional translator in (4) adopts a pragmatic strategy, translating the English insult with a French one that has a similar degree of offensiveness. In (5) and (6), authors adopt a denotational strategy: the proposed translation *chatte* refers to the female genitals, but is not an insult in French.

In Dutch, the tendency to leave the insult untranslated is even stronger than in French: in two cases the English word is quoted:

(7) Lohan noemt Hilton een **'cunt'** wanneer haar gevraagd wordt of ze eerder ruzie had met Paris Hilton.[23]

(8) Parijs en Lilo zijn weer BFF, dus kan het bitchslappen weer beginnen. Lilo trapt af door Paris een **cunt** te noemen.[24]

In the third case, the author uses two paraphrases one of which refers to formal properties ('a four-letter word') of the word and the other to its anatomical meaning ('a vulgar expression for the female genitals'):

com/2006_11_01_archive.html, accessed 3 Oct. 2008. **18** juinphilly.blogspot.com/feeds/posts/default, accessed 3 Oct. 2008. **19** extremecentre.org/2008/10/16/presidentielle-americaine-qu%E2%80%99est-ce-qui-arrive-a-time-why-should-you-be-penalised-for-being-successful, accessed 3 Oct. 2008. **20** www.wikio.fr/culture/litterature/auteurs/mary_gaitskill#news76862683, accessed 9 Jan. 2009. **21** www.celebrityspace.fr/index.php?2006/11/p6, accessed 3 Oct. 2008. **22** absolutevoid.com/2007/09/22/paris-is-a-cunt-lindsay-lohan/fr/, accessed 3 Oct. 2008. **23** www.nieuwsblad.be/Article/Detail.aspx?articleID=dmf12112006_010, accessed 6 Oct. 2008. **24** www.bloglog.nl/NL/2006/november/10/1.php, accessed 6 Oct. 2008.

(9) Actrice en feestbeest Lindsay Lohan heeft een **vierletterwoord** naar het hoofd van zangeres en feestbeest Paris Hilton geslingerd. Op een filmpje op internet is te zien hoe Lohan, gevraagd of ze eerder ruzie had met Paris, een **platte uitdrukking** voor het **vrouwelijk geslachtsdeel** gebruikt.[25]

Finally, there is also one instance in which the author simply censors the insult:

(10) Lindsay Lohan noemt Paris Hilton een [...][26]

Example (10) is certainly the most patent case of auto-censorship, but some kind of censorship seems to be involved in most other cases as well: as most readers are not expected to be familiar with the English insult, quoting the English term, as in examples (1)–(3) and (7)–(8), is a way of avoiding the use of an insult in the target language. Referring to the denotational meaning or other properties of the English term, as in (5)–(6) and (9) probably serves the same purpose.

TRANSLATIONS OF *CON*

As shown in Table 1, thirteen English translations have been found of Sarkozy's outburst. In all, these thirteen sources use seven different terms. The frequency of each term is given in Table 2:

Table 2. English translations of *con*

Translations	#
ass	3
jerk	3
bastard	2
arsehole	1
cretin	1
idiot	1
sod	1
b*****	1

With the exception of 'arsehole' and one occurrence of 'jerk', all English insults are reinforced by an adjective, as is the case in Sarkozy's original insult

25 www.radio.nl/2003/home/q.entertainment/2006/11/113277.html, accessed 6 Oct. 2008.
26 westoek.be/?cat=11&paged=8, accessed 6 Oct. 2008.

pauvre con, which is a habitual collocation. These adjectives mostly denote stupidity ('stupid', 'dumb', 'silly') or the lower end of a scale ('poor', 'little'). Some adjectives obviously form a collocation with their noun: 'dumb' and 'ass' are always used in combination.

As French *con* is less offensive than its English equivalent, auto-censorship is less likely to occur when French is the source language. Indeed, in English target texts, Nicolas Sarkozy's insult is rendered by an English insult in all cases but one. The censored case is from a British source (*Times online*):

(11) Mr Sarkozy tells the man: "Casse-toi, pauvre con" – which can roughly be translated as 'P*** off, stupid sod', or 'Get lost, silly b*****'.[27]

Note that censorship occurs in a quality newspaper here. British tabloids like the *Sun* do not refrain from translating insults plainly:

(12) Mr Sarkozy is seen moving through the crowd at an agricultrual [sic] show on Saturday when the man tells him: 'Oh no, don't touch me.' The president, still smiling, responds: 'Get lost, then.' 'You disgust me'[28] the man says. 'Get lost, you stupid bastard,' Sarkozy fires back.[29]

Even though censorship is not common, two of the proposed translations are said to be less offensive than the original, pointing to a tendency of downtoning insults in the translation process:

(13) The climax comes when Sarkozy is shaking hands with the crowd and one man pulls back, 'Ah, no, don't touch me.' Sarko, his fixed smile unwavering says, 'Get lost, then.' To which the man responds, 'You got me dirty.' To which Sarko responds (this is a polite way of putting it), 'Get lost, you jerk.'[30]

Interestingly, English translations reflect regional differences to some extent: American sources unanimously propose 'jerk' to translate *con*, whereas most British sources opt for 'bastard'.

A regional difference is also observable in Dutch target texts. Table 3 shows the different proposed translations of Sarkozy's insult in Dutch and in Belgian newspapers:

27 www.timesonline.co.uk/tol/news/world/europe/article3426814.ece, accessed 21 Oct. 2008. **28** In the original version, the man says 'tu me salis' (you make me dirty), which sounds probably worse than the translation. **29** www.thesun.co.uk/sol/homepage/news/article848603.ece, accessed 21 Oct. 2008. **30** blog.newsweek.com/blogs/ov/archive/2008/02/28/france-to-sarkozy-get-lost-you-jerk.aspx, accessed 21 Oct. 2008.

Table 3. Dutch translations of N. Sarkozy's *con* in Dutch and Belgian newspapers

Translation	*NL*[31] #	*B*[32] #
klootzak	4	1
sukkelaar	0	2
sukkel	0	1
onnozelaar	0	1
lul	1	0
klojo	1	0

The differences are surprising in two respects: on the one hand, all items in Table 3 are known to and used by both Dutch and Belgian speakers and there are no noticeable differences between the two regions with regard to the offensiveness of the items. On the other hand, Dutch newspapers consistently use more offensive items than Belgian newspapers. The items found in Belgian newspapers refer to a stupid (*onnozelaar*) and to an unsuccessful or cowardly (*sukkelaar*, *sukkel*) person, while Dutch newspapers use items referring to an annoying and deceitful (*klootzak*, *lul*) or to a socially inept (*klojo*) person. With regard to the original insult, the items found in Dutch newspapers are more offensive and not entirely accurate in semantic terms, as the original insult usually refers to stupid people. Strengthening the offensiveness of an insult is uncommon. As pointed out earlier, insults tend not to be translated, or they are censored or downtoned. A possible explanation for the unusual translation strategy could be that the Dutch items belong to the same denotational domain as the original insult, as they too refer to genitalia, albeit to male genitalia (*klootzak* = scrotum; *lul* = penis; *klo*(*ot*) = testicle).

With the exception of one occurrence of *klootzak*, the items used in Belgian newspapers are less offensive than the original insult: *sukkel* and *sukkelaar*, for instance, can be used without the intention to insult. In semantic terms, only *onnozelaar* is an accurate translation of the original insult.

Surprisingly, Belgian newspapers use completely different items when translating the other occurrence of *con*. Table 4 shows the items used to translate the

31 *De Volkskrant*, 24 Feb. 2008; *Het Parool*, 24 Feb. 2008 (2 proposals); NRC, 24 Feb. 2008; *Trouw*, 25 Feb. 2008; *NRC*, 26 Feb. 2008. **32** *De Morgen*, 24 Feb. 2008; *De Standaard*, 24 Feb. 2008; *Gazet van Antwerpen*, 24 Feb. 2008; *Het Laatste Nieuws*, 24 Feb. 2008; *Knack*, 25 Feb. 2008.

occurrence of *con* produced by André Flahaut, a Belgian MP commenting on the Belgian Defence Minister's policy:

Table 4. Translations of A. Flahaut's *con* in Belgian newspapers[33]

Translation	#
klootzak	5
onnozelaar	1

In this particular case, the translations are much more in line with the translations proposed by Dutch newspapers of Sarkozy's insult. As pointed out, *klootzak* is more offensive than the original and semantically inaccurate, although it belongs to the same semantic domain as *con*. This discrepancy raises an interesting question: considering that, with the exception of one, the newspapers are the same in both cases, how come the items used to translate one and the same insult differ so radically?

Several hypotheses can be put forward to explain the discrepancy. First of all, both insults are not strictly identical: in Sarkozy's case, *con* is reinforced by *pauvre*, whereas Flahaut's insult stands on its own. If, however, this were the underlying reason for the differences between translations, one would expect Sarkozy's insult to be translated by more offensive items and not by less offensive ones, as is the case. The difference could also be explained by the different speech act status of both insults: Sarkozy's insult is directly addressed at the insultee as a reaction to an insult produced by his interlocutor ('you got me dirty'), whereas Flahaut produces his in the absence of the insultee, as a reaction against a proposal made earlier on by the minister. However, in this case as well one would expect Sarkozy's insult to be felt more strongly, which is not what the translations suggest. Third, it could be that cultural differences exist between France and Belgium with regard to the offensiveness of particular items. Translators could take into account these cultural differences by using more offensive items in one case (Flahaut, Belgium) and less offensive ones in the other (Sarkozy, France). However, none of the informants[34] who were consulted on this issue confirmed that this was the case. Finally and most plausibly, the different tendencies in translating insults are due to different stereotypes which exist about the insulters. André Flahaut is a French-speaking Belgian ex-

33 *De Morgen*, 23 Feb. 2008; *De Standaard*, 23 Dec. 2007; *Gazet van Antwerpen*, 23 Feb. 2008; *Het Laatste Nieuws*, 23 Feb. 2008; *Het Nieuwsblad*, 23 Dec. 2007; *Knack*, 23 Dec. 2007. **34** S. Kleinen; P. Hambye; G. Rooryck.

minister with a very bad record in the Dutch-speaking Belgian press. He is generally depicted as a rude, corrupt and incompetent politician, which probably accounts for the fact that the insult he produces is translated by strongly offensive items. Nicolas Sarkozy, on the other hand, is depicted, as in most European newspapers, as hyperactive, womanizing and showing off his own wealth and that of his select circle of friends. It is hardly surprising that the items used to translate Sarkozy's insult refer to poverty and cowardice. In other words, Belgian newspapers seem to promote a particular image of the insulter through the items used to translate the insults he or she produces. Whether this is or is not the case in Dutch newspapers remains to be checked. In any case, Dutch newspapers do not seem to promote the same kind of image of Nicolas Sarkozy as Belgian newspapers.

CONCLUSIONS

Although relatively scarce, the data presented in this paper allow us to draw some prudent conclusions. First of all, strong insults tend not to be translated. Authors either censor their own translations or quote the original items. These strategies can be viewed as part of a target-oriented strategy: translators are aware that the probability of readers taking offence is higher when insults are translated accurately than when they are not translated.

On the other hand, less offensive insults tend to be translated, but results vary from overstating to understating the insult. In both cases, target-orientation seems plausible: some authors indicate that the translation is (even) less offensive than the original ('polite'), which is completely in line with strategies deployed for offensive items. In other cases, translation strategies seem to reflect and probably reinforce stereotypes that already exist among the readership.

Taboo and translation in audiovisual works

Ilaria Parini

TABOO LANGUAGE

Even though taboo language presents several interesting elements from a linguistic perspective, it remains an object of study investigated by a relatively small number of scholars. The scholars who have dealt with this topic, however, seem to agree that obscene language represents a constant element in most cultures, and agree in delineating some general features regardless of the languages and the cultures they belong to.[1]

The origin of linguistic taboos in a society is clearly explained by Edgar Radtke in an essay on euphemism. He argues that every culture has its own taboos, that is, realities that are somehow refused by the members of that society. The process of linguistic tabooization originates from the attitudinal tabooization of such realities, that is to say the intentional refusal to name tabooed facts and circumstances. However, the contradictory necessity to name something which is unnameable gives rise to two linguistic phenomena in opposition, that is, euphemism and dysphemism.[2]

As far as euphemism is concerned, in his essay Radtke reports the definition proposed by Widłak:

> Euphemism is a linguistic action, more or less conscious, whose purpose is to replace a socially forbidden syllable, word, or group of words with an indirect form, formally attenuating, which veils and masks their inconvenient content in a given psycho-social situation.[3]

1 See A. Montagu, *The anatomy of swearing* (London, 1968); B. Risch, 'Women's derogatory terms for men: that's right, "dirty" words', *Language in Society*, 16 (1987), 353–8; D. Garrioch, 'Verbal insults in eighteenth century Paris' in P. Burke & R. Porter (eds), *The social history of language* (Cambridge, 1987), pp 104–19; G. Hughes, *Swearing* (Oxford, 1991); D. Hayley, 'What makes bad language bad?', *Language and Communication*, 9:1 (1989), 1–9; V. De Klerk, 'How taboo are taboo words for girls?', *Language in Society*, 21 (1992), 277–89; K. Allan & K. Burridge, *Euphemism and dysphemism: language used as shield and weapon* (Oxford, 1991). **2** E. Radtke, 'Eufemismo e norma sociale', *Atti dei convegni della società linguistica italiana*, 21 (1983), 387–95 at 387–94. **3** S. Widłak, *Alcuni aspetti strutturali del funzionamento dell'eufemismo. Antonimia, sinonimia, omonimia e polisemia* (Wroclaw, 1972), p. 6 quoted in Radtke, 390; my translation.

Through the device of euphemism, therefore, it is possible to attenuate the taboo of the word or expression, by replacing it with a less direct and harsh form, making a given reality pronounceable and diminishing the awareness of its forbidden quality.[4]

What is more interesting for the purposes of taboo language analysis, however, is the opposite phenomenon, that is dysphemism. This has in common with euphemism 'the tendency to replace the "normal" part, which does not happen to obey principles of decency'; dysphemism, on the contrary, 'is inclined towards a worsening which makes the original idea more pejorative, more obscene, or more vulgar. Both processes deprive the base notion of its neutrality'.[5] What is denoted 'obscene language', therefore, originates from a process of dysphemization of tabooed standard language. For example: the term *prostitute* in English represents the base lexeme (or orthophemism) of a tabooed sphere; the expression *lady of the evening* is one of the many euphemisms used to replace it, and the term *bitch* can be one of its many dysphemisms.

As far as the characteristics of taboo language are concerned, first of all it has to be noted that it occurs mainly in oral production (diamesic dimension). Even though it is certainly possible to find examples of dysphemisms in written production, it is much more common to observe them in spontaneous spoken language. This is linked to the different nature of the two modes of expression: written language is permanent, oral language is ephemeral.[6] In language, 'taboo is associated with things that are *not* said, and in particular with words and expressions which are *not* used'.[7] Consequently, it is understandable how such words and expressions can be perceived as even more strong and powerful when written down, and are therefore used more cautiously in written production: words and expressions which are uttered last a little lapse of time, while when written down they may last forever, and their strength is reinforced by this condition of permanence. As Peter Trudgill reports, '(n)ot so long ago, the use in print of words such as *fuck* and *cunt* could lead to prosecution and even imprisonment, and they are still not widely used in most newspapers'.[8] This is why the examples of written works which present high occurrences of taboo language usually tend to reproduce spoken language (such as certain series of comics, especially those targeted at adults, and exchanges of dialogues in novels) or belong to genres which are expected to deal with tabooed spheres, especially sex (erotic literature and some popular literature).

4 For an exhaustive study of euphemism see N. Galli de' Paratesi, *Le brutte parole: semantica dell'eufemismo* (Turin, 1964) and Allan & Burridge, *Euphemism and dysphemism*. **5** Widłak, quoted by Radtke, my translation. **6** Of course oral production can become permanent, through the use of recordings of various kinds, but in this context I am referring to ordinary circumstances of spontaneous conversation. **7** P. Trudgill, *Sociolinguistics. An introduction to language and society*, 4th ed. (London, 2000), p. 18, emphasis in original. **8** Ibid., p. 19.

What is more interesting to investigate, however, are the diastratic and diaphasic dimensions. Scholars seem to agree that the use of this peculiar language is to be related to social factors and contextual variables. As far as the diastratic variable is concerned, the studies conducted by Radtke show that vulgar language prevails in the production of low level social classes.[9] Radtke claims that this is due to the fact that low social classes usually display an antithetic attitude towards social norms, which is reflected in their linguistic production, as dysphemisms evidence a verbal aggression meant to overcome the taboo. The use of euphemisms, on the contrary, denotes an attitude of respect of social needs and constraints and indicates a regressive verbal use towards the taboo, which is more typical of high social classes. Euphemisms and dysphemisms, therefore, have a function of social markers in the sociolinguistic stratification (ibid.). This point of view seems to be shared also by Keith Allan and Kate Burridge, who maintain that:

> It is surely relevant that behavior which offends against the middle-class politeness criterion is often referred to as *coarse behaviour*; and language which offends the middle-class politeness criterion is *coarse language*. The adjective *coarse* is used in its primary sense of 'ordinary, common, mean (in the depreciatory sense of these epithets); base; of inferior quality or value; of little account' to quote the *OED*, which later adds 'unrefined; rough, rude, uncivil, vulgar […] gross, indelicate […] indecent, obscene'. Thus *coarse language* is, by association, that of the vulgar classes, untrammeled by the middle-class politeness criterion.

They also argue that according to the middle-class polite criterion, '[i]n order to be polite to a casual acquaintance of the opposite sex, in a formal situation, in a middle-class environment, one would normally be expected to use the euphemism or orthophemism rather than the dispreferred counterpart [the dysphemism]'.[10] Similarly, David Singleton observes:

> It seems to be quite widely assumed that [vulgar] language is mostly to be found on the lips of people at the lower end of the social scale. Indeed, the very word *vulgar* comes from a Latin word, *vulgus*, which means 'the common people', and there has been a longstanding tendency to associate the use of 'bad' language with stigmatized social categories.[11]

9 Radtke, p. 391. **10** K. Allan & K. Burridge, *Forbidden words: taboo and the censoring of language* (Cambridge, 2006), p. 37 (emphasis in original); p. 35. **11** D. Singleton, 'Unspeakable words: the taboo fringe of the lexicon' in M. Dynel (ed.), *Advances in discourse approaches* (Newcastle upon Tyne, 2009), pp 130–46 at p. 135.

However, Allan and Burridge also claim that the notion of a middle-class environment implied in the middle-class politeness criterion is used to exclude both those so uneducated, poor and deprived that they are unaware of, or cannot afford to observe, the niceties of social conventions observed by the mass of the community, but also those so rich and/or so powerful that they can disregard such conventions, thus indicating that also the members of the upper class are prone to using taboo language.[12] The fact that such language is used exclusively by the vulgar classes is questioned also by Singleton, as he observes that, 'oaths, curses, profanities and obscenities have also been a royal and an aristocratic prerogative' and 'the traditionally choice language of nobility is reflected in the expression *to swear like a lord*'. Such statements are also supported by Hughes, who affirms that 'within the English class system, both the upper and the working classes, preferring directness to euphemism in most things, maintain traditions of fairly heavy swearing, so that most of the "four-letter" words thrive in these socially separated circles.' He concludes by stating that it is the middle class who seems to be the least inclined to using taboo language, as 'the bourgeoisie maintains strict taboos against any such utterance'.[13]

As far as the diaphasic variable is concerned, scholars also agree in claiming that the situational context plays a fundamental role in making the speakers choose whether to use taboo expressions or not. Indeed, it is much more common to observe the use of obscene linguistic forms in very informal situational contexts, whereas in formal situations they are usually avoided. This is confirmed by the fact that the middle-class politeness criterion invoked above indicates a 'formal situation' as a context where people are usually expected to use euphemisms or orthophemisms rather than dysphemisms.

Besides the social and contextual variables, indeed, other determining factors, such as the gender, age, tone, and intentions of the speakers, may play a role. In some cases taboo expressions and insults can be used among the members of the same social group with purely expressive purposes, losing their offensive potentiality and gaining an affective connotation.[14] Moreover, as Trudgill notes, 'for those who use taboo words "breaking the rules" may have connotations of strength or freedom which they find desirable'.[15]

12 Allan & Burridge, *Forbidden words*, p. 35. **13** Singleton, 'Unspeakable words', pp 135–6; Hughes, *Swearing*, p. 251. **14** See W. Labov, *Language in the inner city: studies in the Black English vernacular* (Philadelphia, 1972), for studies of ritual insults among Afro-Americans (a ritual known as 'sounding' or 'playing the dozens') conducted by Labov. **15** Trudgill, *Sociolinguistics*, p. 18.

TABOOS IN SOCIETIES

As has been observed, taboo language presents a series of recurrent peculiarities which seem to be constant in various cultures. However, this does not mean that taboo languages are similar in all cultures. Indeed, taboo language is a tool through which people try to overcome a limit imposed by social conventions, by breaking a taboo. Consequently, the differences within taboo language among various cultures originate from the basic fact out of which the language proceeds, from the tabooed social sphere. Indeed, the tabooization of given realities in some cultures gives rise to a series of linguistic expressions considered as obscene which refer to those tabooed realities. However, the same realities might not be considered as taboo in other cultures, or in any case not at an equal level. Therefore, if the tabooed spheres turn out to be different in two – or more – cultures, the taboo language of those cultures will also have different referents. In Trudgill's words 'the type of word that is tabooed in a particular language will be a good reflection of at least part of the system of values and beliefs of the society in question'.[16]

The studies conducted on the subject have shown that in Western cultures there exists a certain correspondence in the areas tabooed by social conventions. Such areas would cover sex, religion, excretion, body parts, people's intellectual abilities, and death. However, very often there exist specific differences concerning the way the speakers of the various cultures relate to such realities. For example, as far as sex is concerned, in Italian taboo language there are no expressions related to the topic of incest. This is not because it is not considered as a taboo field, but quite the opposite, because the subject is tabooed to such an extent that the language refuses it *a priori*, avoiding to even dysphemize it. On the contrary, the American English term *motherfucker* and its derivatives refer directly to an incestuous activity. Another example of the differences between English and Italian is represented by blasphemy. Italian taboo language presents a wide range of insults addressed to religious figures. This presupposes a very strong reaction against a topic which is highly tabooed for a traditionally Catholic society such as the Italian one, where even the act of naming God in vain is considered as a sin. In the Anglo-American language the range of insults addressed to divinities turns out to be much more limited compared to Italian, and this might be determined by a less relevant role played by religion in English and American society, or also, possibly, by a different attitude of Protestants, who might disapprove even more strongly of irreverent use of the name of God.

16 Ibid., p. 18.

TABOO LANGUAGE AND TRANSLATION IN DUBBING

Since the dialogues of audiovisual works are written with the purpose of representing spontaneous spoken language, it is not surprising that taboo language is one of the features, together with slang and non-standard forms, which characterize many contemporary works, especially films. Indeed, such elements contribute to characterizing the variety both at the diamesic, and at the diaphasic and diastratic levels. As Pavesi and Malinverno observe, these features have become even more common in a recent stream of American films, such as spy, mafia and gangster films, films starring drug addicts and dealers, prostitutes, homeless people, soldiers, convicts, warders, and policemen. Moreover, obscene language is more likely to be used by young characters, and by men rather than women.[17]

Taboo words in films may play several roles, just as happens in authentic dialogues. Their function can be expletive (typically swearing, such as exclamations, which are non-reciprocal and have no particular addressee), or abusive (typically insulting). Nevertheless, it ought to be noted that some words are used as mere fillers, as they have become more or less desemanticized, and are used simply to make the language more expressive and informal.[18]

As far as Italian dubbing is concerned, the studies conducted reveal a general tendency to attenuate the level of obscene expressions present in the original films.[19] Sometimes this is due to the differences in the levels of tabooization of certain fields between the two cultures. As previously seen, one such context is represented by the religious taboo. Indeed, offensive expressions referring to the Holy Family are forbidden in the Italian media. Therefore, while in American films it is possible to find cursing which invokes them (for example, in *Reservoir dogs* the character of Mr Orange says 'I swear to fuckin' God'), in Italian dubbed films such occurrences are not tolerated.

On other occasions taboo expressions are not translated because of a lack of semantic and functional correspondence between English and Italian. This happens, for example, with the taboo term *fucking*, which is polyfunctional, and whose functions cannot always find a correspondence with its many Italian

17 M. Pavesi & A.L. Malinverno, 'Usi del turpiloquio nella traduzione filmica' in C. Taylor (ed.), *Tradurre il cinema* (Trieste, 2000), pp 75–89, at pp 76, 78. **18** G. Azzaro, *Four-letter films* (Rome, 2005), pp 4–6 and 9; Pavesi & Malinverno, 'Turpiloquio', p. 75; A. Spadafora, *InterMedia: la mediazione linguistica negli audiovisivi* (Viterbo, 2007), p. 89. **19** I. Parini, 'Quentin Tarantino in italiano' in T.G. Giordano et al. (eds), *Quaderni di doppiaggio* (Finale Ligure, 1998), pp 160–222, at pp 208–9; Pavesi & Malinverno, 'Turpiloquio', pp 77, 82; Delia Chiaro, 'The British will use tag questions, won't they? The case of *Four weddings and a funeral*' in Taylor (ed.), *Tradurre il cinema,* pp 27–40 at p. 29; M. Pavesi, *La traduzione filmica: aspetti del parlato doppiato dall'inglese all'italiano* (Rome, 2005), p. 47.

equivalents.[20] For example, in Italian there are no intensifiers pre-modifying verbs or non-gradable adjectives. Nevertheless, a shift in the grammatical class of the word modified by *fucking* may allow the translation to maintain the general level of expressiveness and informality given by the taboo expression. Sometimes translators actually opt for inserting a modifier external to the original utterance, such as an exclamation (mainly *cazzo*), succeeding in characterizing the line at the level of obscenity. However, in many cases they simply decide to omit the taboo expression, without compensating in other ways.

Some other times, however, the mitigation of taboo language in Italian dubbing is not ascribable to formal constraints, but is rather due to policies of censorship or self-censorship. Indeed, attenuating the level of vulgarity of the language of American films is quite the norm in Italian dubbing. Gianni G. Galassi, a well-known Italian dubbing professional, claims that translators are required to exercise on their own initiative a heavy form of preemptive censorship on the works they dub in Italian, because they know that the person who will check the dubbed product will ask them to modify it. To give an example, in the original version of the film *Pulp fiction* there are 389 occurrences of taboo words, while in the Italian dubbed version they amount to 272.[21]

TABOO CONTENT AND TRANSLATION IN DUBBING. A CASE STUDY: SEXUAL REFERENCES IN QUENTIN TARANTINO'S FILMS

As shown in the previous section, Italian dubbed films undergo a frequent process of censorship as far as taboo language is concerned. Moreover, quite often censorship is operated not only at the level of the single words, but rather of content. This means that sometimes the original lines uttered by the characters are purged of the references to subjects which might be considered as taboo. As mentioned before, sex is one of the areas that are considered as taboo in Western countries. Sexual references in films, therefore, sometimes represent a topic that undergoes a process of mitigation in Italian dubbing, consistently with the translational behaviour of self-imposed censorship mentioned above.

Explicit sexual references are present in most of the screenplays written by Quentin Tarantino, as taboo references (as well as taboo language) are one of the elements that characterize his films.[22] However, analysis of the Italian

20 See Pavesi & Malinverno, 'Turpiloquio', pp 83–8. **21** G.G. Galassi, 'Panni da risciacquare: candeggio, lavaggio, ammorbidente' in S. Patou–Patucchi (ed.), *L'italiano del doppiaggio: I convegno per la ricerca 'l'influenza del linguaggio cinematografico sulla lingua italiana parlata'* (Rome, 1999), pp 70–8 at p. 76; Pavesi & Malinverno, 'Turpiloquio', p. 82. **22** Parini, 'Quentin Tarantino'; I. Parini, 'Pulp dubbing: doppiaggio da rapina?' in R.M. Bollettieri

dubbed versions of three of these films, *Reservoir dogs* (1992), *True romance* (1993) and *Pulp fiction* (1994), reveals a lack of homogeneity in the translation strategies adopted. In some cases the translators have opted for censoring the text by omitting the sexual references. In other cases, on the contrary, the references have been maintained, as the original lines have been translated almost literally. Interestingly, though, this lack of homogeneity in translational behaviour is observable within the very same films.

From *True romance*

Example 1 (Lee and Elliot are talking on the phone about a guy called Dick. The viewer sees Elliot but cannot hear what Lee says):

ELLIOT: (utterly bewildered)
You want me to suck his dick?
(relieved, repeats what Lee has just told him)
Ah, 'who the fuck is Dick?'!

Dubbed Version:
ELLIOT: Sei incazzato con Dick?
Ah, 'chi cazzo è Dick?'!

Back Translation:
ELLIOT: Are you pissed off with Dick?
Ah, 'who the fuck is Dick?'!

As we see, in this case the translator has omitted the reference to oral sex, therefore operating a form of censorship on the dialogue and attenuating the level of vulgarity of the text. It is true that by translating the line literally the pun between *dick* as a taboo word, and *Dick* as a proper noun, would not work in Italian. However, Elliot's reaction is not really realistic, as he is far too shocked by what he thinks he has just been told.

Example 2:

BIG D: What the fuck are you talkin' about?
DREXL: Floyd say he don't be eatin' pussy.
BIG D: Shit, any nigger say he don't be eatin' pussy is lyin' his ass off.
MARTY: I heard that
FLOYD: Hold on a second, Big D. You sayin' you eat pussy?

Bosinelli et al. (eds), *La traduzione multimediale: quale traduzione per quale testo?* (Bologna, 2000), pp 243–59.

BIG D: Nigger, I eat everything. I eat the pussy. I eat the butt. I eat every motherfuckin' thing.
FLOYD: Looky here. If I did eat some pussy – I would never eat any pussy – but, if I did eat some pussy, I sure as hell wouldn't tell no goddamn body. I'd be ashamed as a motherfucker.

DV:
BIG D: Di che state parlando figli di troia?
DREXL: Floyd dice che non gli piace leccare la passera.
BIG D: Drexl, qualunque negro che dice che non gli piace la passera è un bugiardo.
MARTY: Ha ragione.
FLOYD: Vuoi dire che a te piace leccarla?
BIG D: Sì, testa di cazzo. A me piace fare tutto, hai capito?
FLOYD: Io, ammesso che lo facessi, non andrei certo a raccontarlo a nessuno. Me ne vergognerei come uno stronzo.

BT:
BIG D: What are you talking about, you sons of bitches?
DREXL: Floyd says he doesn't like eating pussy.
BIG D: Drexl, any nigger that says he doesn't like pussy is a liar.
MARTY: He's right.
FLOYD: Do you mean you like eating it?
BIG D: Yes, dickhead. I like doing everything, do you understand?
FLOYD: If I did it I surely wouldn't tell anybody. I'd be ashamed as shit.

In this extract, some of the references to oral sex have been maintained, while some others have been censored. In the line uttered by Drexl, the reference to the practice of cunnilingus has been maintained and translated (almost) literally. However, in the second line uttered by Big D the action is generalized, as it does not refer to the practice of cunnilingus, but simply to the female genitalia. In the first line uttered by Floyd, however, the practice related to oral sex is once again mentioned. Interestingly, in the third line uttered by Big D once again the text is generalized. Not only is the reference to cunnilingus deleted, but also the reference to anilingus has been omitted. Moreover, also in the second line uttered by Floyd the direct reference to oral sex is avoided and generalized.

From *Reservoir dogs*

Example 3:
MR BLUE: Our girl was nice.
MR PINK: Our girl was okay. She didn't do anything special.

MR BLUE: What's something special? Take you in the kitchen and suck your dick?

DV:
MR BLUE: Sì, ma questa è stata gentile.
MR PINK: Sì, d'accordo. Ma che ha fatto di speciale?
MR BLUE: E che doveva fare? Succhiarti l'uccello sotto al tavolo?

BT:
MR BLUE: Yes, but this one was nice.
MR PINK: Yes, sure. But did she do anything special?
MR BLUE: What was she supposed to do? Suck your dick under the table?

In this case the reference to oral sex has been maintained. Interestingly, in the translation the setting of the action referred to is no more the kitchen, but the table, which somehow intensifies the effect (the scene takes place in a café, a public place, where the action could be witnessed by all the customers).

Example 4:
EDDIE: Now, ain't that a sad sight, daddy? Walks into jail a white man, walks out talkin' like a nigger. It's all that black semen been shootin' up his butt. It's backed up into his brain and comes out of his mouth.

DV:
EDDIE: E' una vera tristezza papà. Uno entra in galera da bianco ed esce che parla come uno sporco negro. Sai una cosa Vic? Mi sa che a stare in cella con quei negracci bastardi quel cazzo di cervellino che avevi ti è andato in acqua e adesso dici solo stronzate.

BT:
EDDIE: It's really sad, daddy. One man walks into jail as a white man and walks out talkin' like a dirty nigger. You know something, Vic? I think that living in the same cell with those nigger bastards has made that fuckin' brain of yours turn into water and now you can only talk bullshit.

In the Italian translation Eddie implies that Vic 'talks bullshit' because he has spent too much time in jail with people of colour, whose company has made him unable to think properly ('his brain has turned into water') and has influenced his way of speaking. The original line is actually much more crude and vulgar, as Eddie refers to anal intercourse. Besides, it is interesting to note that while the text has been censored in its sexual references, it is much more derogatory in the way it refers to people of colour. Whereas in the original version we can observe one single occurrence of the derogatory term *nigger*, and one of the more neutral term *black*, in the dubbed version the first occurrence has been transposed with the noun *negro* (which is offensive in itself), pre-modified by the adjective *sporco* (dirty), and the second term with the noun *negracci* (a derived form of *negro*, obtained through the addition of the pejorative suffix *acci*), and further modified by *bastardi* (bastards).

From *Pulp fiction*

Example 5:
VINCENT: It's laying hands on Marsellus Wallace's new wife in a familiar way. Is it as bad as eatin' her pussy out? No, but you're in the same fuckin' ballpark.
JULES: Whoa, whoa, whoa, stop right there. Eatin' a bitch out and givin' a bitch a foot massage ain't even the same fuckin' thing.

DV:
VINCENT: E' mettere le mani in modo intimo sulla nuova moglie di Marsellus Wallace. Voglio dire, è così grave come se gliel'avesse leccata? No, ma è lo stesso fottuto campo da gioco.
JULES: Oh, aspetta, fermo lì. Leccargliela a una troia e farle un massaggio ai piedi non è esattamente la stessa cosa.

BT:
VINCENT: It's laying hands in an intimate way on Marsellus Wallace's new wife. I mean, is it as bad as if he had eaten her out? No, but it's the same fuckin' ballpark.
JULES: Oh, wait, stop there. Eatin' a bitch out and givin' her a foot massage is not exactly the same thing.

In this case, both the references to oral sex which are present in the source text have been maintained.

Example 6:
FABIENNE: Butch? Will you give me oral pleasure?
BUTCH: Will you kiss it?
FABIENNE: But you first.

DV:
FABIENNE: Voglio che mi baci come hai fatto l'altro giorno.

BUTCH: Fallo prima tu.
FABIENNE: Sì, ma prima tu.

BT:
FABIENNE: I want you to kiss me as you did the other day.
BUTCH: You do it first.
FABIENNE: Yes, but you first.

In this case we can observe a clear example of censorship of the sexual reference. The reference to oral sex has been generalized, and even though the Italian public can infer what Fabienne is referring to (as within few seconds Butch goes down with his head and the reason why he does is clear), the dubbed version turns out to be deprived of the reference, at least at the verbal level.

CONCLUSIONS

As is clear from the examples analysed, the translators of the films have not revealed a consistent translational behaviour as far as the references to explicit sexual activities are concerned. Sometimes they have maintained them, some other times they have attenuated the level of vulgarity through the use of different strategies, and some other times they have omitted them. The practice of censorship does not come as an utter surprise, considering the common practice of levelling out the level of taboo language in Italian dubbing. The lack of homogeneity in the strategies adopted is actually consistent with the translational behaviour displayed as far as taboo expressions are concerned. In Italian dubbing taboo language is usually mitigated, though not completely eliminated. Likewise, the references to the taboo area of sex have been attenuated, though not completely censored. The censoring attitude observed, however, does not seem to be ascribable to different ideologies on the part of the translators, or on policies imposed by the commissioners. This is proved by the fact that the different behaviours are observable in the very same films. The same translators have sometimes omitted the sexual references in some parts of the film, while in others they have maintained them, showing therefore a basic inconsistency in their translational behaviour.

From this analysis one might deduce that Italian dubbing professionals seem to believe that Italian public is probably too chaste and demure to tolerate an excessive exposure to the topic of sex, and they have identified a tolerance threshold which should not be passed. However, where this threshold exactly lies is indeed a matter of personal perception. Studies conducted on the perception of taboo language apparently have shown that Italian spectators perceive the level of language obscenity in foreign dubbed films as very high, despite the common practice of levelling out mentioned in this paper.[23] Similar investigation focusing on the perception of sexual references might possibly give an answer, and would provide an interesting object of study.

However, it ought to be noted that in Italy films are classified into three main groups, according to their suitability for audiences in terms of issues such as sex, violence, substance abuse, profanity, explicit language, or other types of mature content. Films can be rated T (suitable for all ages), VM14 (only people over 14 years of age are allowed into cinemas or advised to watch the DVD versions), or VM18 (for people over 18 years of age only). It is a fact that Tarantino's movies are usually targeted at an adult public. Indeed, *Reservoir dogs* and *Pulp fiction* have been rated VM18, while *True romance* has not received any restrictive rating, in spite of the violent scenes displayed and the themes treated.[24] In the case of VM18 films, the kind of censorship in translation that has been observed in this essay is clearly not necessary: spectators are grown up people, who are presumably able to decide whether they can tolerate exposure to some topics or not. The choice should be theirs, not somebody else's.

As Galassi claims, dubbing professionals usually translate/adapt film dialogues keeping in mind the ideal spectator of the specific film: in Tarantino's case, surely an adult person. He also maintains that their aim is 'to induce in the ideal spectator of the dubbed film the same emotions and to communicate the same information that, according to [their] analysis, the film induced and communicated to the ideal spectator of the source culture'.[25] However, if dubbing omits or manipulates some peculiar features of the original versions of the films, it is an indubitable fact that in most cases such a result turns out to be very difficult – if not impossible – to achieve.

23 See Pavesi & Malinverno, 'Turpiloquio', p. 82. **24** In fact, *True romance* has been rated R (barred to under-18s unless accompanied) in the United States. **25** G.G. Galassi, 'Fottiti, amico' in C. Taylor (ed.), *Tradurre il cinema* (Trieste, 2000), pp 3–8 at p. 8 (my translation).

PART 2

HISTORY AND POLITICS OF TRANSLATION

> Cast as an act of love, and as an act of disruption, translation becomes a means of repositioning the subject in the world and in history, a means of rendering self-knowledge foreign to itself; a way of denaturalizing citizens, taking them out of the comfort zone of national space, daily ritual, and pregiven domestic arrangements.
>
> Emily Apter, *The translation zone* (2006)

Judging the translator: Ortega y Gasset's characterization of the translator

Pilar Ordóñez López

Despite the consolidation of translation studies as a *sui generis* discipline and the cultural turn experienced therein, translators occupy a subsidiary position, especially from a socio-professional point of view, as stated by Lawrence Venuti, Susan Bassnett and Wendy Leech.[1] In contemporary translation studies little attention seems to be paid to the figure of the translator. Given this situation, it is especially relevant to review Ortega y Gasset's portrait of the translator, contained in his essay 'The misery and the splendour of translation' (1937),[2] which has given rise to a notable degree of controversy within contemporary translation theory.

Even though translators play an indispensable role in our increasingly globalized society, their importance does not seem to be fully acknowledged. In recent studies scholars such as Bassnett and Venuti have highlighted the issue of the position held by translators in society, making reference to their low status. The lack of acknowledgment of the work and role of translators leads to a series of social and professional attitudes such as the spread of misconceptions about what being a translator implies.

Furthermore, the scarcity of literature thoroughly targeting the analysis of translators from a socio-professional perspective reinforces their invisibility. Research and analysis of the socio-professional profile of translators are needed to tackle this situation. This contribution aims to analyze Ortega y Gasset's perceptions of the translator in order to reveal the anticipatory and audacious nature of his work.

1 Lawrence Venuti, *The translator's invisibility: a history of translation* (London, 1995); L. Venuti, *The scandals of translation. Towards an ethic of difference* (London, 1998); Susan Bassnett, *Translation studies* (London, 1980); S. Bassnett, 'The meek or the mighty: reappraising the role of the translator' in R. Alvárez, and C.A.Vidal (eds), *Translation, power, subversion* (Clevedon, 1996), pp 10–25; Wendy Leech, *The translator's visibility: an investigation into public perceptions of the translator and how to raise the translator's status in society* (2005), isg.urv.es/library/papers/leech_translator_visibility.pdf, accessed 10 Feb. 2009. **2** All quotations in English from Ortega's 'The misery and the splendor of translation' are to the translation by Elizabeth Gamble Miller in R. Schulte & J. Biguenet (eds), *Theories of translation: an anthology of essays from Dryden to Derrida* (Chicago, 1992), pp 93–112.

In 'The misery and the splendour of translation' Ortega presents his views on the role and character of the translator. First, it is important to note that the essay was published prior to the consolidation of translation studies as a discipline. Notwithstanding this, translators occupy a notable position in Ortega's thought on translation.

ORTEGA'S VIEWS ON TRANSLATION

Ortega's vision of translation[3] is clearly influenced by his ideas about language,[4] which he understands as a social phenomenon, intrinsically linked to a society; a language is a secret belonging to the people from the same country:

> Who without being stupid can believe that he really knows a foreign language? Only he who has lived almost his entire life in that foreign country could hope to know it, but in that case, if he has lived there all or almost all his life, where is this person really from?[5]

This implies that, according to Ortega, 'languages have their borders with customs',[6] by which he means that when transferring one's thoughts from one language to the other, certain components are 'confiscated', that is, they cannot be expressed in the target language. Part of the reason for this is that language has a strong influence on its speakers' patterns of thinking: 'not only do we speak in a specific language, but we also think in a way that follows pre-established pathways imposed by our linguistic destiny'.[7] Furthermore, 'every language imposes a specific framework of categories, of mental pathways'[8] on its speakers.

Ortega's approach to translation is rooted in nineteenth-century German hermeneutics and is characterized by a theoretical and philosophical perspective. His vision of translation is expressed in two antagonistic terms: 'the misery' and 'the splendour'. The misery is, essentially, due to the lack of exact correspondence between different languages. A typical example of this is Ortega's obser-

3 For a detailed account of the influence of German nineteenth century tradition on Ortega's views on translation see Pilar Ordóñez López, 'Revisión del pensamiento de Ortega sobre la traducción a la luz de la tradición hermenéutica', *Sendebar*, 17 (2006), 49–60. **4** For an in-depth analysis of Ortega's ideas about language see Pilar Ordóñez López, *Miseria y esplendor de la traducción. La influencia de Ortega en la traductología* (Castellón de la Plana, 2009), pp 41–91, in which the philosophical and hermeneutic aspects of his ideas on language are examined. **5** My translation. José Ortega y Gasset, *Obras completas* (Madrid, 1983) [12 vols.] viii, p. 417. **6** My translation. Ibid., p. 267. **7** My translation. Ortega, 1983, v, p. 447. **8** Ibid., p. 448.

vation that some languages tend to suppress what other languages tend to express:

> each language is a different equation of statements and silences. All peoples silence some things in order to be able to say others [...] From this we deduce the enormous difficulty of translation: in it one tries to say in a language precisely what that language tends to silence.[9]

Language and, inevitably, silence, are considered crucial obstacles to translation but, at the same time, they become the means to attain the possible 'splendour' of translation:

> one glimpses a possible marvellous aspect of the enterprise of translating: the revelation of the mutual secrets that peoples and epochs keep to themselves [...] in short – an audacious integration of Humanity.[10]

In order to attain this audacious integration of humanity, Ortega claims, there is only one procedure translators must follow: 'it is only when we force the reader from his native linguistic habits and oblige him to move within those of the author that there is actually translation'.[11] Ortega's categorical advocacy of foreignizing translation has clear consequences for translators, which will be analyzed in the next section. In addition, his concept of translation itself also contributes to his characterization of the figure of the translator:

> Translation is not a duplicate of the original text [...] The simple fact is that the translation is not the work, but a path toward the work [...] the translation is no more than an apparatus, a technical device that brings us closer to the work without ever trying to repeat or replace it.[12]

THE SHY TRANSLATOR

Ortega's portrait of translators contains some of the most wide-spread commonplaces about translation:

> To write well is to employ a certain radical courage. Fine, but the translator is usually a shy character. Because of his humility, he has chosen such an insignificant occupation.

9 Schulte & Biguenet, *Theories of translation*, p. 104. **10** Ibid., p. 104. **11** Ibid., p. 108. **12** Ibid., p. 109.

> [...] What will he do with the rebellious text? Isn't it too much to ask that he also be rebellious, particularly since the text is someone else's? He will be ruled by cowardice
>
> [...] he will place the translated author in the prison of normal expression; that is, he will betray him. *Traduttore, traditore.*[13]

First, the description of translators as 'shy[14] characters' is perhaps one step further in the common image of translators as isolated professionals, hidden behind the curtain of authorship. Works like Venuti's and Rabassa's provide solid arguments to substantiate the claim that the shadowy and hidden position traditionally occupied by translators is not always a voluntary choice but is frequently motivated by translators' legal status and rights regarding their work.[15]

Another important issue raised by Ortega in the above quotation is the consideration of translation as an 'insignificant occupation'. This is, undoubtedly, a sort of paradox: how can translation be considered an insignificant occupation if, as stated in the essay, there is a need 'to restore the prestige [of translation] and value it as an intellectual work of the first order'?[16] There is probably a hidden intention on the part of Ortega to provoke the reaction of translators, as well as a certain degree of irony in his words.

Furthermore, Ortega's use of the proverb *Traduttore, traditore* is noteworthy. According to Ortega, treason is the result of the translator's cowardice; it should be interesting to determine to what extent this cowardice is a result of the alleged shyness of translators or simply a consequence of a lack of professional and legal recognition throughout history.

Finally, concerning the pessimistic tone of his words, Ortega's declared intention of emphasizing the miseries in order to attain the splendour should be borne in mind. This relates to his distinction between the 'good' and the 'bad utopian', the latter being convinced that because translation is '*desirable,* it is possible':

> With such an attitude, he won't give much thought to the question of how one must translate, and without further ado, he will begin the task. This is the reason why almost all translations done until now are bad ones.[17]

13 Ibid., p. 94. **14** In the original Spanish text the adjective translated as 'shy' is '*apocado*', which has a wide range of meanings. Elizabeth Gamble Miller's translation as 'shy' appears appropriate in the context of Ortega's essay (p. 93 in Schulte & Biguenet); the primary meaning of 'apocado' is 'timid' (see *Diccionario Español-Inglés Inglés-Español*, Glasgow, 2009, p. 71), a near synonym of 'shy'. **15** Lawrence Venuti, *The scandals of translation: towards an ethics of difference* (London, 1998); Gregory Rabassa, *If this be treason: translation and its dyscontent: a memoir* (New York, 2005). **16** Schulte & Biguenet, pp 111–12. **17** Ibid., p. 98.

The good utopian, on the other hand, is fully aware of the difficulty and the misery which are inherent to translation:

> [he] thinks that, *because* it would be desirable to free men from the divisions imposed by languages, there is little probability that it can be attained; therefore it can only be achieved to an approximate measure. But this approximation can be greater or lesser, to an infinite degree, and the efforts at execution are not limited, for there always exists the possibility of bettering, refining, perfecting: 'progress', in short.[18]

It may thus be claimed that the inclusion in his essay of some of the most widespread misconceptions about translation is due to Ortega's decision to admit the difficulties translators must face, to make them aware of the challenges they have to overcome, and to encourage them to become 'good utopians'. In this vein, Ortega's explicit defence of foreignizing translation implies, on the one hand, a high degree of visibility of the translator, who should allow 'the ways of speaking appropriate to the translated author'[19] to cross into the target language. This requires active participation by the translator, who should make the translation 'clear' by adding any necessary explanations.[20] On the other hand, foreignizing translation demands courage from the translator, it requires a translator who is willing to step out and abandon the shadows.

THE SHY TRANSLATOR WITHIN CONTEMPORARY TRANSLATION STUDIES

Ortega's portrait of the translator has given rise to a certain degree of controversy within contemporary translation studies. Controversy is mainly found within the Spanish-speaking translation context; nevertheless, a number of other European scholars have also discussed Ortega's views.[21]

Christian Schmitt regards Ortega's portrait of the translator as one of the most prestigious descriptions of translators. According to him, Ortega's acknowledgment of the heavy constraints translators must face constitutes a valuable intent to enhance their status:

18 Ibid., pp 98–9. **19** Ibid., p. 112. **20** Ibid., p. 111. **21** For an in-depth study of the reactions to Ortega's views on the translator within contemporary translation studies, see Pilar Ordoñez-López, 'Ugly translations: Ortega y Gasset's ideas on translation within contemporary translation theories', *Cadernos de tradução*, 21 (2008), 41–66 at 50–61; Ordónez-López, *Miseria y esplendor*, pp 161–253; Pilar Ordóñez-López, 'The Misery and splendour of translation: a classic in translation studies', *Skase Journal of Translation and Interpretation*, 4:1 (2009), 53–78.

> Par contre, en sens contraire, l'éloge d'une profession peut-elle être plus grande, plus prestigieuse que celle qu'a prononcée en faveur des traducteurs le philosophe espagnol Ortega y Gasset qui estime la traduction comme un travail intellectuel de tout premier rang, qui voit cette activité comme une des pierres fondamentales de la philologie et souligne que le combat entre l'impossible confère au traducteur la plus grande noblesse.[22]
>
> [Whereas, on the other hand, can anything stronger be said in praise of a profession than the words of the Spanish philosopher Ortega y Gasset, who considers translation to be intellectual work of the first order and views this activity as one of the cornerstones of philology, emphasizing that the battle with impossibility confers the highest nobility on the translator?]

Valentín García-Yebra makes reference to the low status of translation and translators, corroborating Ortega's views:

> En España [...] han sido relativamente pocos los grandes escritores que han traducido. Y algunos, al hacerlo, se han ocultado tras el pseudónimo, como si temieran que esa ocupación tan modesta [...] pudiera manchar su nombre.[23]
>
> [In Spain [...] there have been relatively few writers who have translated. And some of them, while doing so, have hidden behind a pseudonym, as if they were afraid that such a modest activity [...] could blemish their name].

Katharina Reiß claims that Ortega's portrait of the translator no longer reflects the perception that current translators have of themselves. In her opinion, translators have overcome their inferiority and position themselves at an equal level to authors:

> Und der Übersetzer literarischer Kunstwerke läßt sich nicht mehr von Ortega y Gassets Urteil beeindrucken, daß der Übersetzer meist ein sehr zaghafter Mensch sei, daß er aus Schüchternheit diese, die geringste aller geistigen Betätigungen, gewählt habe. [...] Er fühlt sich heute eher als

22 My translation. Christian Schmitt, 'Traduction et linguistique', *Babel*, 27:33 (1991), 150–65 at 151–2. **23** My translation. Valentín García-Yebra, *En torno a la traducción* (Madrid, 1983), p. 329.

„Double", als „Komplize" des Autors, wie es der soeben mit einem Übersetzerpreis ausgezeichnete Rudolf Wittkopt einmal ausdrückte.[24]

[And the translator of literary works of art can no longer be impressed by Ortega y Gasset's judgement that the translator tends to be a shy person, that he has chosen this activity, the lowest of all, out of shyness. [...] Nowadays, he feels more like the author's "body double", his "accomplice", as Rudolf Wittkopf, who recently received a translation prize, once said].

Julio César Santoyo expresses his disagreement with Ortega's description of translators as shy characters, supporting his argument with a wide range of well-known translators, known for their strong personality and determination, such as Martin Luther, Saint Jerome, King Alfred the Great, Octavio Paz, and others:

Si atendemos a su opinión, apocados habrían sido Lutero, san Jerónimo, Unamuno y Quevedo, los cuatro bien notorios por su genio, notorios incluso por su mal genio [...] los dos Machado [...] Juan Ramón Jiménez, el rey Alfredo de Inglaterra y Alfonso X el Sabio en España [...] Octavio Paz y Agustín García Calvo [...] por sólo citar un pequeño ramillete de personalidades 'apocadas', todas ellas bien conocidas por sus traducciones.[25]

[In his opinion, Luther, St Jerome, Unamuno and Quevedo, all four of them well-known for their temperament, well-known even for their bad temper [...] both Manuel and Antonio Machado [...] Juan Ramón Jiménez, Alfred the Great of England and Alfonso X of Spain [...] Octavio Paz and Agustín García Calvo [...] are just a few of the 'shy' personalities, all of them well-known for their translation].

According to Rexina R. Vega, Ortega has not been forgiven for having written that translators are shy characters, not courageous enough to behave as freely and bravely as authors. However, Vega understands Ortega's words as an invitation for translators to be subversive:

No se le perdona que haya escrito [...] que el traductor es un 'ser apocado' que no se atreve a ascender al monte de la autoría [...] lo que

24 My translation. Katharina Reiß, 'Der Text und der Übersetzer' in R. Arntz (ed.), *Textlinguistik und Fachsprache: AILA symposium* (Zurich, 1988), pp 67–75 at p. 67. **25** My translation. Julio César Santoyo, 'En torno a Ortega y Gasset: miseria y esplendor de la reflexión traductora' in J.C. Santoyo, *Historia de la traducción: quince apuntes* (León, 1999), pp 237–50 at p. 247.

> muchos consideran un agravio, un desprecio del noble ejercicio de la versión, no es más que una invitación a la rebelión del traductor.[26]
>
> [He has not been forgiven for having written [...] that translators are 'shy people' who dare not climb the mountain of authorship [...] which by many is considered an insult, showing disdain for the noble practice of translation, but which is nothing more than an invitation for the translator to be rebellious].

CONCLUSION

Ortega's views on translation are formulated from a philosophical perspective and thus his portrait of the translator should be interpreted within this perspective. It is also necessary to take into account that Ortega refers to a specific type of translation, that is, philological or erudite translations, which are to be used as a 'path' or a 'guide' to the work and should never replace it.

Bearing in mind the previous considerations, Ortega's portrait of the translator is certainly praiseworthy for its time, especially taking into account that, until relatively recently, little attention has been paid to the figure of the translator within translation studies.

Regarding the controversy his views have given rise to, it can be assumed that, taking into account Ortega's thoughts on translation, his portrait of translators should be understood as an attempt to make them aware of the challenges that have to be overcome in this profession, in order to encourage them to progress towards producing better translations and to enhance their status, allowing them to step out of the shadows.

26 My translation. Rexina R. Vega, *Ortega y el traductor* (2000), www.cvc.cervantes.es/trujaman/anteriores/abril_00/19042000.htm, accessed 2 Mar. 2009.

Muchay – worshipping God and the *huacas*: the complex usage of a Quechua word in the colonial Andes

Sabine Dedenbach-Salazar Sáenz

INTRODUCTION: TRANSLATION IN A COLONIAL CONTEXT

Drawing on Spain's colonial history in South America, this essay will show how, when translating a key concept from another culture, the translation may appear absolutely 'right' on linguistic, cultural and religious grounds, and yet can sometimes produce results quite different from those envisaged by the colonial translator – the crucial point being that the indigenous population may have had their own understanding of Christian religion.

There is of course no single way of translating correctly or incorrectly a word, a text or a situation. Not only does the content of the translation depend on the translator; it is also conditioned by the whole of the communicative act. In this sense it is useful to formulate the 'right or wrong' question in the following way: what do the authors/translators wish to convey when rendering an idea in another language? In order to know this, we have to take into consideration their intellectual and cultural background as well as their familiarity with the situational context itself, and their motive for translating at all. This background knowledge conditions our understanding of the translation.

In a colonial context in particular, the language as well as the relationship of the representatives of the colonial power with the indigenous subjects are important elements which influence the translation itself. Although translation has to be seen as a communicative *process* or event, it is impossible to do this when studying seventeenth-century sources. Here we only have the *results*, and by taking into consideration the participants' background, the re-constructed context, and the knowledge of the languages in question (also re-constructed), we may be able to answer the question why an author would have chosen, for example, a certain term or phrase as the 'right' translation for his purpose. It is also necessary to examine how the message might have been understood by the potential recipients.

COMMUNICATION BETWEEN HUMAN BEINGS AND DEITIES

Prayers, often part of rituals (such as offerings), were (and are) used in Andean[1] and Christian religion to address supernatural beings that shape and influence humans' lives and wellbeing.

In what follows I will examine the word *muchay*, from the Peruvian Quechua language, also known as the language of the Incas. The word may best be rendered as 'to worship'. In order to capture and analyse this complex concept, the meanings it had in the native and then christianized Andes, and the translation and interpretation it was subjected to, colonial dictionaries as well as samples of Christian and indigenous religious texts will be studied.

When the Spaniards conquered Peru in 1532, the Quechua language had been used for several centuries as a *lingua franca* in large parts of the Andes. The Christian missionaries decided very early on that it would be good to use the most widespread native languages to christianize the population, because this was widely felt to be the only way to explain Christianity to them (although this opinion was not shared by everyone in the Church). Thus, using the Spanish alphabet, linguistic studies of indigenous languages and texts written in Quechua were produced and printed in the second half of the seventeenth century.[2] Indigenous Quechua texts, on the other hand, are few and have only survived as manuscripts.[3]

THE ANDEAN MEANING OF 'MUCHAY'

The earliest documentation of the word *muchay* as an indigenous concept goes back to an anonymous manuscript which consists of 33 chapters of myths and rituals told in Quechua, most probably by more than one narrator, at the beginning

1 For informed presentations of religion in the Inca era see María Rostworowski de Diez Canseco and Craig Morris, 'The fourfold domain: Inka power and its social functions' in Frank Salomon & Stuart B. Schwartz (eds), *The Cambridge history of the native peoples of the Americas* (Cambridge, 1999), vol. III, *South America, Part I*, pp 769–863 at pp 791–8; for the colonial period see Kenneth Mills, 'The naturalization of Andean Christianities' in R. Po-Chia Hsia (ed.), *The Cambridge history of Christianity* (Cambridge, 2007), *vol. 6: Reform and expansion 1500–1660*, pp 504–35; for contemporary religion in the Andes see Manuel M. Marzal, 'The religion of the Andean Quechua in Southern Peru' in Manuel M. Marzal et al., *The Indian face of God in Latin America* (Maryknoll, NY, 1996), pp 67–118 and Xavier Albó, 'The Aymara religious experience' in Marzal et al., *The Indian face of God*, pp 119–67. **2** For a comprehensive study of pastoral Quechua see Alan Durston, *Pastoral Quechua: the history of Christian translation in colonial Peru, 1550–1650* (Notre Dame, IN, 2007). **3** These texts use the Latin alphabet and Spanish orthography; the Incas did not have a writing system.

of the seventeenth century.[4] These so-called *Huarochirí Traditions (Tradiciones de Huarochirí)* contain the word *muchay*[5] and derivations of the verb in many chapters, as might be expected from the religious framework of the texts.

When reading the texts, different motives, occasions and purposes of offerings and worship become evident. The addressee of the act of worship is always a supernatural being, called *huaca*, with whom people communicate directly or through a specialist, in the form of words as well as offerings.[6] I will here render *huaca* as 'deity' for want of a more adequate English term.

In chapter 1 the narrator quotes a prayer to Cuniraya Viracocha and introduces this as follows:

4 *Tradiciones de Huarochirí. Runa yndio ñiscap machoncuna ñaupa pacha* [...] MS 3169, fol. 64–114. Madrid: Biblioteca Nacional. As the manuscript originated in the environment of the Christian priest and extirpator of idolatry Francisco de Avila, we have to acknowledge that it does not represent 'pure' Andean usage (for a concise presentation of the manuscript, its text and context see Frank Salomon, 'Introductory essay: the Huarochirí manuscript' in *The Huarochirí manuscript. A testament of ancient and colonial Andean religion*, translation from the Quechua by Frank Salomon & George L. Urioste, annotations and introductory essay by Frank Salomon, transcription by George L. Urioste (Austin, TX, 1991), pp 1–38). Nevertheless, it was possibly meant as a kind of indigenous 'bible': cf. Frank Salomon, 'La textualización de la memoria en la América andina: una perspectiva etnográfica comparada', *América Indígena*, 54:4 (1994), 229–60 at 240–50. The narrators tell the myths and describe the rituals from the point of view of the peoples in Huarochirí (a region in the highlands east of Lima). These peoples differentiate themselves from and – through their deities – even fight against the Yunga peoples who live in the lower mountain valleys. The mythical stories are about beings who were at the time of the writing of the manuscript still worshipped as deities, but in the remote past which the myths talk about, these *huacas* behaved like human beings: they walked about, had loving and hateful relationships etc., and their behaviour reflected people's lives, in a personal way, but above all through the identification of certain villages with certain deities. Pariacaca and Cuniraya Viracocha, for example, were the deities of the Huarochirí peoples, whereas Huallallo Caruincho and Tamtañamca those of the Yunga peoples. **5** *-y* is a nominalization commonly used to represent the infinitive. The verb stem is *mucha-*. **6** A *huaca* can be any element or feature found in nature and considered to have particular force and power. *Huaca* refers to both, the physical manifestation of the supernatural force (e.g. a mountain peak, a stone), or to the force or being itself, either as an abstract concept of a numinous being located in these features of nature, or a man-made object representing it (e.g., a statue). All the acting 'persons' in the Huarochirí traditions are *huacas*, and certain astronomical constellations were also considered *huaca*. This explains another important characteristic of the Andean conceptualization of 'deities', i.e. they can transform themselves into human beings, animals, stones etc. However, the *huacas'* power is not permanent (although they hardly ever die or disappear completely): it can increase or diminish over time, especially as a *huaca* is closely related to a community or region, and the prosperity or decline of the *huaca* and the community are closely related. Some *huacas* were important oracles.

Table 1. *Tradiciones de Huarochirí* (*c.*1608, ch. 1, fol. 64v)

Quechua text[7]	*Translation*
Runacuna ña **mucha**spapas: 'coniraya viracocha, runacamac, pachacamac, yma aycuyuc cammi canqui: campam chacraiqui, campac runayqui', ñispa **mucha**c carcan.	**Worship**ping him and saying: 'Cuniraya Viracocha, [you] who infuse [us] with life, who infuse the world with life, you are the one who owns everything: yours are the fields, yours are the people', [in this way] people used to **worship** him.
Yma ayca saça ruranacta callarijpacpas, paitaracmi machocuna cocanta pachaman vischuspa: 'cayta yuyachiuai, amutachiuay, cuniraya viracocha' ñispa; mana viracuchactaca ricuspatac, ancha ñaupa rimac **mucha**c carcanco	And in order to begin to work on something difficult, the ancients would throw coca leaves[8] to the ground for him, saying: 'Let me remember this, let me find out [how it works], Cuniraya Viracocha'; although they could not see Viracocha, they would speak to him, **worship** him above all [others].

Another *huaca*, Tamtañamca, an ancient, powerful deity and the competitor of the Huarochirí peoples' deities, is said to have been honoured and worshipped by many. Here the act of reverence reflects his social as well as his religious status (Table 2/1). However, he is very ill (which would probably mean that his power was fading). Huatyacuri, a Huarochirí deity, finds the cause, promises to cure him and requests that afterwards he should adore Huatyacuri's father, Pariacaca (Table 2/2) – this shows that power is not permanent, but can shift, and the relationship between powerful and weaker deities reflects that

7 These passages are transcriptions from the original manuscript (*Tradiciones de Huarochirí*, *c.*1608), made by SD [Sabine Dedenbach; this abbreviation is used throughout], indicating chapter and folio(s); the punctuation has been added. The translations, also by SD, are kept close to the original Quechua text; brackets are used to adapt the text to English structure. A good critical edition and English translation is that of Salomon and Urioste (*The Huarochirí manuscript*, 1991). **8** For the complex role coca leaves still play nowadays in divination, see Emanuele Amodio, 'Cocacha mamacha. Prácticas adivinatorias y mitología de la coca entre los quechuas del Perú' in *Bulletin, société suisse des américanistes/ Schweizerische Amerikanisten-Gesellschaft*, 57–8 (1993–4), 123–37.

between human beings. Moreover, the deity's influence reflects the power constellation of the communities who worship them.

Table 2. *Tradiciones de Huarochirí* (*c*.1608, ch. 5, fol. 67r)

	Quechua text[7]	*Translation*
1	Chaysi cay runacta chica alli causascanta ricuspa, tucoy hinantin llactacunamanta hamuspa yupaicharcan **mucha**rcã.	Then, when they saw that this man lived really well, they honoured and **worship**ped him, coming from all the villages.
2	Chaymantam ña alliyaspã tucoy hima aycacta yallispa ñocap yayaita **mucha**nqui.	Then, when you will have become well [again], you will **worship** my father who excels everything else.

An example of *muchay* in the context of a complex ritual is the cleaning of the irrigation canal in honour of the female deity Chuquisuso:

Table 3. *Tradiciones de Huarochirí* (*c*.1608, ch. 7, fol. 71v)

Quechua text[7]	*Translation*
Mayo quellapi canancamapas chay pacham tucoy hinantin runacuna chay chuquisuso ñisca huarmip tiascanhuã-man rircancu, assuanhuan tictinhuan cuynhuan llamanhuan, chaypi chay supay huarmicta **mucha**ypac. Chaymi ña chayta **mucha**spari, pihca ponchaosi chaypi quishuaruan quenchaspa runacunactapas. Mana purichispa chaypi tiapayarcã.	In the month of May, and until now, in that time all the people came to the place where that woman called Chuquisuso lived, with their maize beer, with their *ticti* drink, with their guinea pigs and with their llamas, in order to worship that Devil[9] woman. Then, when they had begun to **worship** her, they made an enclosure with *quishuar*-wood for five days. Not allowing [anyone] to walk out, they stayed there.

9 Here the narrator uses the Andean word *supay* – which originally referred to an ambiguous being, related to the dead and ancestors – with the new, colonial meaning it acquired soon after the conquest, namely that of the Devil. See Gerald Taylor, 'Supay', *Amerindia,* 5 (1980), 47–64,

Muchay was also used to refer to sacrifices, as the following passage shows: in this case it is about the ritual slaughter of a llama and the divination in its entrails, performed by the Inca to worship Pariacaca, the highest Huarochirí deity.

Table 4. *Tradiciones de Huarochirí* (*c.*1608, ch. 18, fol. 83r)

Quechua text[7]	*Translation*
Chaysi huc punchaoca huc llamaãhuan yaurihuanaca sutioc llamahuan **mucha**rcancu …	Then, one day, he **worship**ped him [Pariacaca] with one of his llamas, with a llama called Yaurihuanaca … [In the text that follows, the narrator goes on to describe how they examined the heart and entrails.]

From the usage in this document it becomes clear that *muchay* has a number of semantic components: to worship the most powerful deities, using words, that is prayers, as well as rituals, such as offerings and divination. *Muchay* means 'to worship, to adore', by praying, by making offerings, by dancing etc. (see Guaman Poma de Ayala's illustrations [*c.*1615][10] which give us a visual impression of what *muchay* activities might have been like: see Illustrations 1 and 2).

COLONIAL MISSIONARY ADAPTATIONS: DICTIONARIES

The first Quechua dictionary and grammar were published in 1560, and during the 1580s, at the initiative of the Third Lima Council, an obligatory Christian doctrine, a confessionary and a sermonary were produced, in Spanish, with translations into Quechua and Aymara.[11] The most comprehensive dictionary up to the

and Lindsey Crickmay, 'Outward change, inner continuity: the Andean concept of "Devil"', in Iris Gareis (ed.), *Entidades maléficas y conceptos del mal en las religiones latinoamericanas / Evil entities and concepts of evil in Latin American religions* (Aachen, 2008), pp 24–40. **10** Felipe Guaman Poma de Ayala was an indigenous author who wrote, in Spanish, his 'New chronicle and good government' in order to give an account of the history of Peru and the living conditions in the Andes and suggestions as to how to remedy the situation which he conceived of as difficult and unjust for the indigenous population. His manuscript comprises more than 1,000 pages and many illustrations. A digitized version may be consulted at www.kb.dk/permalink/2006/poma/info/en/frontpage.htm, accessed 8 Jan. 2013. See Rolena Adorno, 'Guaman Poma and his illustrated chronicle from colonial Peru: from a century of scholarship to a new era of reading. An introduction to the web publication of the *Nueva corónica y buen gobierno*', 2002: www.kb.dk/permalink/2006/poma/info/en/project/project.htm, accessed 8 Jan. 2013. **11** Aymara was (and is) another widely spoken language of the Andes. For further reading on the colonial works see

The Inca says:

Uaca bilcacona – pim camcunamanta
ama parachun – cazachun runtochun
ñinqui/ rimari/ chaylla
'*Huacas* and *vilcas*: Who of you has said
"It shall not rain, it shall freeze, it shall hail"?
Speak! Go ahead!'

manam nocacunaca ynca
'It was not us.'

con todas las uacas habla el ynga
The Inca speaks with all the *huacas*.

Fig. 1. Worshipping Andean deities: 'vaca billca' (source: The Guaman Poma Website, p. 261 [263]; Copenhagen Royal Library MS GKS 2232 4°: Guaman Poma, *Nueva corónica y buen gobierno* (1615), by kind permission of Det Kongelige Bibliotek, Copenhagen)

Fig. 2. Offering of a llama to a *huaca* (source: Guaman Poma [*c*.1615], p. 270 [272])

present day was published by the Jesuit missionary and linguist Diego González Holguín in 1608 (Text sample 1). All colonial Christian texts and dictionaries were explicitly written for missionary usage. González Holguín mentions that he had support from native consultants, and he did not limit himself to terms relevant for his missionary work.[12] His dictionary covers all aspects of life, and is very detailed as far as different forms and derivations of individual words are concerned.[13]

Text sample 1. González Holguín ([1608] 1989: 246–7): *muchay* entries

Muchhani, muchhaycuni. o vpaycuni. Adorar, rogar, reuerenciar, honrar, venerar, o bessar las manos.
Muchaycuni, muchaycuscayquim ñipuni. Agradecer, o dar gracias de palabra, yupaychani, de obra.
Allichaquenta muchaycuk, o vpaycuk o muchaycuscayqui ñipuk. El agradecido de palabra.
Allichaquenta yupaychak. El que haze caso y estima al bien hechor.
Allichaquenta mana vpaycuc, o, mana vpaycuscayqui ñipuk. El desagradecido aun de palabras.
Allichaquenta mana yupaychak. El desagradecido que no haze caso de su bienhechor, ni lo estima.
Allichaquen muchaycuy, o, yupaychacuy. El agradecimiento.
Muchaycuni, o, muchani. Bessar a alguno honestamente con reuerencia, o, hazer cortesía, o, bessar la mano.
Muchallini. Bessar en la boca, o cara torpemente, o dar bessos con amor deshonesto, y no es para cosa honesta.
Muchallicuy. El besso torpe.
Muchallinacuni. Darse bessos vno a otro, aun los casados. Y a los niños, muchallini.
Muchallipayani, o muchallichacuni. Dar mil bessos, o demasiados.
Muchallircarini, o muchallircayani. Bessar assi a muchas.
Muchapayani, vpapayani. Importunar rogando, o rogar mucho.

Sabine Dedenbach-Salazar Sáenz, 'Dictionaries, vocabularies, and grammars in Andean indigenous languages' in Joanne Pillsbury (ed.), *Guide to documentary sources for Andean studies, 1530–1900* (Norman, OK, 2008), i, pp 235–64; Regina Harrison, 'Doctrinal works' in Pillsbury (ed.), *Guide to documentary sources*, i, pp 217–34; and Marie Timberlake, 'Provincial councils of Lima' in Pillsbury (ed.), *Guide to documentary sources*, i, pp 197–208. **12** González Holguín, *Vocabvlario de la lengva general de todo el Perv llamada lengua qquichua o del Inca* [Ciudad de los Reyes, 1608] (Lima, 1989), p. 8 ('Al christiano lector'). **13** When using the missionaries' linguistic works and catechetical texts for this kind of analysis, we have to be aware that they were written by clerics for other clerics, and that, as manuals, they did not necessarily reflect the actual usage of Christian terminology in practice; rather they were models to be followed.

Muchapayay Diosta. Pide a Dios con grande ahinco o instancia.
Muchapuni. Interceder por otro, o tornar otra vez a rogar.
Muchaycupuni, o vpaycupuni. Tornarse a sujetar, a dar la obediencia el reñido o alçado, o, pedir perdon al mayor, o reconciliarse con su mayor, o con Dios.
Muchascca. Adorado, reuerenciado, bessado en cosas sagradas.
Muchachicuni. Dexar, o hazer adorar, reuerenciar, o bessar, o hazer dar obediencia.

The dictionary's entries show that the basic meanings of *muchay* are 'to kiss', also given with the additional component of 'reverently', and 'to adore, plead, revere, honour, venerate'.[14] There are several more semantic elements which *muchay* can have (depending on the verb-modifying suffixes it receives): one is 'to request'; another one is, according to González Holguín, 'showing obedience, asking for pardon', thus indicating an asymmetric relationship with the addressee of the utterance. This is supported by the Dominican linguist Domingo de Santo Tomás' entry which includes the component that the word is used in addressing senior persons, and implies a usage in the social as well the religious sphere.[15]

Table 5. Meanings of *muchay*

Meanings for muchay and its derivatives according to the dictionaries prepared by González Holguín and Santo Tomás

- to kiss
- to worship, revere, adore
- to request
- to show obedience, ask for pardon

— the meanings always imply a social hierarchy, with the speaker below and the addressee above

---

As a whole, the meanings (including those which do not make explicit reference to Christian religion) which González Holguín and other authors present seem in Andean culture to reflect very much the same attitude as that of a person adoring God in Christianity.

14 González Holguín, p. 246. **15** Domingo de Santo Tomás, [1560] 1951. *Lexicon, o vocabulario de la lengua general del Perú* (Lima, 1951), p. 323 [Facsimile of 1560 edition, Valladolid]; Sabine Dedenbach-Salazar Sáenz, 'Terminología de parentesco y trato social andino: datos lingüístico-etnohistóricos de Huarochirí' in Denise Y. Arnold (comp.), *Gente de carne y hueso. Las tramas de parentesco en los Andes* (La Paz, 1998), pp 167–85 at pp 172–7.

Text sample 2. *Doctrina christiana*, 1584, fol. 2r, showing Quechua and Aymara versions of the 'Hail Mary'[16]

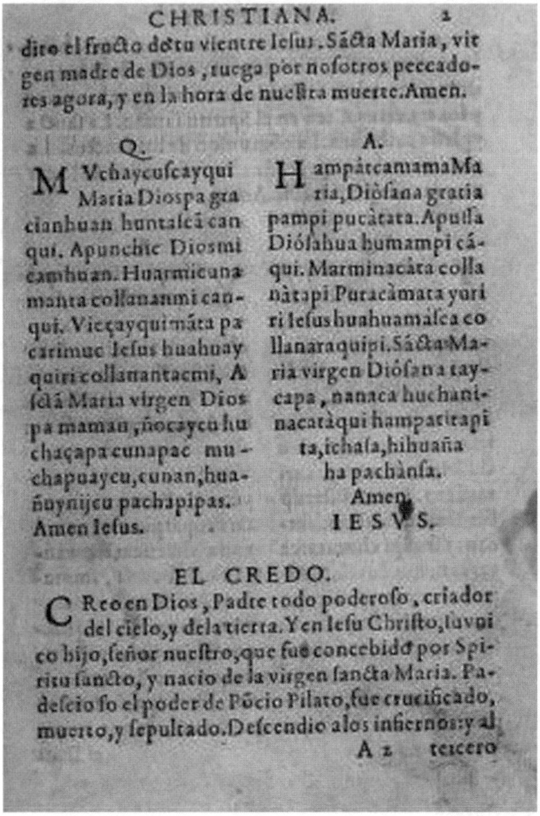

CHRISTIANA. 2

dito el fructo de tu vientre Iesus. Sācta Maria, virgen madre de Dios, ruega por nosotros peccadores agora, y en la hora de nuestra muerte. Amen.

Q.

MVchaycuscayqui Maria Diospa graciankuan huntascā canqui. Apunchic Diosmi camhuan. Huarmicunamanta collananmi canqui. Vicçayquimāta paccarimuc Iesus huahuayquiri collanantacmi, A sctā Maria virgen Diospa maman, ñocaycu huchaçapa cunapac muchapuaycu, cunan, huañuynijcu pachapipas. Amen Iesus.

A.

Hampàtcamama Maria, Diòsana gratia pampi pucàtata. Apusa Diósahua humampi cáqui. Marminacāta collanàtapi Puracàmata yuri ri Iesus huahuamalca co llanaraquipi. Sācta Maria virgen Diósana taycapa, nanaca huchaninacatàqui hampatitapita, ichala, hihuaña ha pachànsa. Amen.

IESVS.

EL CREDO.

CReo en Dios, Padre todo poderoso, criador del cielo, y dela tierra. Y en Iesu Christo, su vnico hijo, señor nuestro, que fue concebido por Spiritu sancto, y nacio de la virgen sancta Maria. Padescio so el poder de Pōcio Pilato, fue crucificado, muerto, y sepultado. Descendio alos infiernos: y al

A 2 tercero

CHRISTIAN DOCTRINAL TEXTS

On the decision of the Third Lima Council, which was held in 1582–83, it was decided to produce a catechism ('Doctrina christiana'), a confessionary ('Confessionario') and a volume of sermons ('Tercero cathecismo'), in Spanish, Quechua and Aymara, to be used by parish priests in their missionary work.[17]

16 See www.openlibrary.org/books/OL24440872M/Doctrina_christiana_y_catecismo_para_instruccion_de_los_indios_y_de_las_de_mas_personas_que_han_de_s, accessed 8 Jan. 2013; http://openlibrary.org/works/OL15480197W/Confessionario_para_los_curas_de_indios, accessed 8 Jan. 2013; http://openlibrary.org/works/OL15435929W/Tercero_cathecismo_y_exposicion_de_la_doctrina_christiana_por_sermones, accessed 8 Jan. 2013. **17** *Doctrina christiana, y catecismo para instrvccion de los Indios …* (Lima, 1984). For more information see Sabine Dedenbach-Salazar Sáenz and Frederike Meyer, 'Die "Ayuda a bien morir" der *Doctrina christiana y catecismo* (Lima 1585): Übersetzung, Analyse und Kontextualisierung eines kolo-

Table 6. *Doctrina christiana*, 1985

Prayer	Spanish	English translation from Spanish[18]	Quechua translation in *Doctrina christiana*	English translation from Quechua
Catecismo **mayor** (fol. 59v, p. 138)	los christianos … **adoran** a Iesu Christo	the Christians … **adore** Jesus Christ	quiquin IESV CHRISTOCTAM **muchanchic**	**we worship** Jesus Christ himself[19]
Pater Noster (fol. 1r–2v, pp 22–23)	**sanctificado** sea el tu nombre	**sanctified** be your name	sutijqui **muchasca** cachun	your name shall be **worshipped**
Ave María (Text sample 2) (fol. 1v–2r, pp 22–23)	Dios **te salue** Maria	**may** God **greet you**, Mary	**mvchaycuscayqui** Maria	**I worship you affectionately**, Mary (literal translation); may God greet you, Mary (according to the authors/translators)[20]
Salve fol. 3r–3v, pp 25–26)	**Ruega por nos** sancta madre de Dios	**pray for us** holy Mother of God	sancta Diospa maman **ñocaycupac muchapuaycu**	Holy Mother of God, **intercede for us**[21]
Catecismo mayor (fol. 57v, p. 134)	**Sanctificar** las fiestas	**sanctify** the holy-days	domingocunapi, fiestacunapipas çamacunqui, Diosta **muchancapac**	you will rest on Sundays and also on holy-days, **in order to worship** God

nialzeitlichen spanischen und Quechua-Textes aus Peru', *Anthropos*, 100:2 (2005), 473–93. **18** The translations from Spanish and from Quechua into English are by SD. **19** Whilst the orig-

The doctrinal texts use *muchay* to translate a variety of Spanish words in several prayers and in the catechism. As can be seen in Table 6, the same Quechua word, *muchay*, is used for different Spanish expressions – in addition to the meaning 'to worship'.

Thus – in a very similar manner to the dictionary entries – the Quechua translations used in the texts are 'to worship', and, including the suffix *-pu* ('to do something in favour of oneself or someone else'), 'to intercede, request in favour of someone'.

The translation of 'worship' and related terms as *muchay* and its derivatives in Christian doctrinal texts reflects the effort made by the Church to find a unified Quechua vocabulary, and it may not be coincidence that different words in Spanish are all translated by *muchay* in Quechua. The people responsible for the translation[22] might have thought it would be better for comprehension and transmission to introduce *one* Quechua word for all the closely related Spanish words, rather than translating each with a different term. This might not only have been thought to avoid confusion among the indigenous addressees, but it might also have been conceived of as a help for the parish priests so as not to get lost themselves in a labyrinth of words.

'MUCHAY' IN THE DISCOURSE OF THE EXTIRPATION OF IDOLATRY AND THE POSSIBLE CONSEQUENCES

It is remarkable that in their Quechua translations the Christian missionaries used the same word they had appropriated for the worship of *their* God also for the indigenous worship of the *huacas*, as can be seen, for example, in sermon 19 of the 1585 sermonary:

inal Spanish text creates a distance between the speaker and the listener by using the third person plural indicating 'the Christians', the translators opted for the inclusive 'we' in Quechua: 'we (you and I/we) worship Jesus Christ himself'. **20** The *Doctrina christiana* authors say explicitly that 'Dios te salue' is the translation although the suffix '-yqui' means 'I (to) you' (fol. 75v, p. 170), so that the literal translation would be: 'I greet/adore/honour you, Mary'. This latter is the meaning Quechua speakers would automatically infer from the form used here. (See also Durston, *Pastoral Quechua*, 2007, p. 209.) The fact that *muchay* was normally employed for the worship of Andean deities may have contributed to the deity-like status Mary received (cf. below). **21** 'mucha–pu–uaycu' means literally 'adore–in favour of–2nd person sg. subject-1st person pl. excl. object'. Cf. Celia L. Cussen, 'The search for idols and Saints in colonial Peru: linking extirpation and beatification', *Hispanic American Historical Review*, 85:3 (2005), 417–48, for the emphasis Christian teaching laid on the Saints as intercessors. **22** The eminent Jesuit scholar José de Acosta was responsible for the work as a whole, and there were a number of, mostly *mestizo*, translators (for a summary see Dedenbach-Salazar Sáenz and Meyer, 'Die "Ayuda a bien morir" der *Doctrina christiana*').

Table 7. *Tercero cathecismo* [1585], 1985, sermón XIX, fol. 113r, p. 573[23]

Spanish	*English translation from Spanish*	*Quechua translation in Tercero Cathecismo*	*English translation from Quechua*
No aueys de **adorar** las guacas …	You must not **worship** the *huacas* …	Ama huacacta **mucha**nquichi[c]chu …	You must not **worship** the *huacas* …

PATRES
Cermon del padre cura
euangeliota sagrada escritura uillascayque churicona – /
uaca uilcataca manam sermoyquicho/
chaytaca naupa machoyquichic yacharca/
camca bautisa[s]ccanam canqui churi

FATHERS
Sermon of the father priest
I will tell you about the Gospel, the Holy Scripture, my children/
I will not preach about the *huacas* and *vilcas*
[the indigenous deities]/
your ancestors from before knew about them/
now you are baptised, my child

Fig. 3. A parish priest preaching
(source: Guaman Poma [*c.*1615], p. 609 [623])

Already in the sixteenth century the Quechua word *muchay* was integrated into Spanish as *mochar*, a loan that only referred to the worship of indigenous deities and became established by the extirpators of idolatries. One of these extirpators, José de Arriaga, for example, wrote in 1621: 'They also worship and

23 Cf. *Doctrina christiana*, fol. 58r, p. 135.

mochan high mountains and hills and some very big stones [...]'.[24] It may have found its way into Spanish through the *visitas*, ecclesiastic inspection tours, possibly through the interpreters. The meaning it received in Spanish was clearly negative as it only occurred with Andean deities viewed as 'false gods' or 'idols'.[25]

We can hypothesize that the indigenous population would by then have made the transposition of *muchay* from Andean to Christian deities and back, because in Quechua the missionaries liberally equated Andean and Christian expressions of worship, thereby giving, as they must have believed, the indigenous population an understanding of the Christian practice. But at the same time they also opened up for the Andean people a legitimate way of integrating the Christian deity into the Andean pantheon, or at least of equating both.[26] For example, the fact that *muchay* was equally used for the Virgin Mary (and probably also other Saints) explains the ease with which the Virgin could become part of the indigenous Mother Earth, Pachamama.[27]

Table 8. Colonial usage of *muchay*

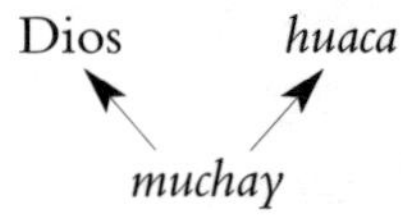

24 'A cerros altos y montes y algunas piedras muy grandes también adoran y mochan [...]' (Pablo José de Arriaga, [1621], 'Extirpación de la idolatría del Pirú' in Francisco Esteve Barba (ed.), *Crónicas peruanas de interés indígena* (Madrid, 1968), pp 193–277 (cap. II, p. 201). Cf. a later publication from 1560/61: Agustinos, *Relación de la religión y ritos del Perú hecha por los padres agustinos, edición, estudio preliminar y notas de Lucila Castro de Trelles* (Lima, 1992), fol. 2v, p. 10 and fol. 3v, p. 12 respectively: 'mochavan', 'Hazen mocha'. **25** It is interesting to observe that in Spanish different words were used for worshipping the 'good' Christian God (*adorar* etc.) and the ancient, 'pagan' deities of the indigenous people (*mochar*). In Quechua, however, the same verb, *muchay*, was employed for both. Again, this may have contributed to a mutual integration of both religions rather than the extirpation of Andean belief. **26** It has been argued that it was exactly the translation which made it easier to integrate indigenous religion into Christian faith (César Itier, 'La littérature quechua d'évangélisation (XVIe et XVIIe siècles) comme source ethnolinguistique', *Amerindia* 19/20 (1994–5), 321–31 at 326. My analysis of the data suggests the contrary: using the native language of the conquered peoples at worst led to confusion and at best to the opportunity to integrate Christian beliefs into the Andean system. This question can, of course, never be answered conclusively because we lack sources of explicit indigenous response to the imposition of Christianity and in particular the language related to it (as stated by Durston, *Pastoral Quechua*, p. 210). **27** This is reflected in a 20th century observation by a Quechua speaker from Southern Peru: 'Kay pacha paqarinmantan kay Pachamamaqa nisqa: "Ñuqan kani Santa Tirra, Uywaq, ñuñuq, ñuqan kani. Pacha Tirra, Pacha Ñusta, Pacha *Virgen* ñuqa kani," niq kasqa.' – 'Since

THE PROBLEM OF TRANSLATION RECOGNIZED?

Kissing the Cross is mentioned in the *Tercero cathecismo* [1585] 1985, sermón XXVIII, fol. 182v, p. 712) – 'besando la cruz', 'cruzta muchaycunquichic', 'you kiss/adore the cross reverently' – and kissing the cross or the statues of saints is a common expression of worship in the Hispanic world, and it seems that both cultures may have very similar concepts in this area, if we suppose that the Andean people also kissed the representations of their deities. This is supported by the fact that the authors of the sermons which form the *Tercero cathecismo* apparently feel the necessity to call the indigenous population's attention to the difference in the worship of the Andean deities and that of the Christian Saints. They explain that, when Christians kiss the Virgin's and Saints' images, they do not worship the material they are made of, but the deity or Saints themselves, who dwell in heaven. Thereby they imply that the indigenous people worshipped the image or object itself.[28] However, the same Quechua word is used for both, and in order to explain the difference the translators use the locative suffix *-pi*, 'in', 'on', 'at', versus the locative adverb *ucu-pi*, 'inside (a body, the earth etc.)', although in this context the latter may just be considered an emphatic form of the former. Different verbs are used to mark that the Saints actually live in heaven: *causa-*, which is 'to live' in the sense of existence and being, whereas *tiya-* is used to affirm that they do not live in the image: *tiya-* means 'to live', in the sense of 'reside, live in a place, sit' (see Table 9).

Besides these linguistic finesses, the problem was, of course (even if this sermon message ever reached the indigenous people) that the Andean population did not believe that their deities were literally located in the images and statues; in Andean belief they were just as well conceived of as abstract concepts, maybe even more so than the Christian God living in heaven.[29] As indigenous deities were essentially non-physical, one might also ask what the difference would have been for the indigenous people to conceive of a deity as dwelling in an image or in heaven.

the birth of the world Pachamama [World Mother] has said: "I am the Holy Earth, the Nurturer, the Breastfeeder am I. I am World Earth, World Inca Princess, World *Virgin*."' See Bernabé Condori and Rosalind Gow, *Kay Pacha, tradición oral andina* (Cuzco, 1976): 'Pachamama', pp 9–12 (translated by SD). **28** As Mills, 'The naturalization of Andean Christianities' points out (p. 528), a mid-seventeenth century priest, Estanislao de Vega Bazán, 'questions a distinction between Catholic veneration of sacred images and native Andean "idolatry" that has long been a plank in the refutation of the native Andean religious system'. **29** See Table 1: the indigenous people worship a deity they cannot see. Also, according to the *Tradiciones de Huarochirí* (ch. 20, fol. 84v), when cultivating her field, a woman finds 'cay huaca ricurimantapas', 'this *huaca*'s appearance', or, as suggested by Salomon and Urioste (ibid., p. 101, paragraph 236), 'this *huaca*'s visible form' – which is then, by an Andean priest, made to talk to people.

Table 9. *Tercero cathecismo* [1585] 1985, sermon XIX, fol. 115r, p. 577[30]

Spanish	*English translation from Spanish*	*Quechua translation in Tercero Cathecismo*	*English translation from Quechua*
Hijos mios muy differente cosa es lo que hazen los Christianos, y lo que hazeys vosotros.	My children, it is a very different thing what the Christians do and what you do	Ricuychic churi Christianocunap rurascanca huc hamum camcunap rurascayquichicpas huc hamutacmi	See children, what the Christians do is one way, and what you do is another way.
Los Christianos no **adora**n, ni besan las ymagenes, por lo que son, ni **adora**n aquel palo o metal, o pintura,	The Christians do no **worship** or kiss the images for what they are, nor do they **worship** that stick or piece of metal or painting	Christianocunaca manam ymagencunacta chay caynioc cascanmantachu **mucha**ncu, manam cullumanta, antamanta ymamantapas yachachisca cascanmantachu **mucha**ncu	The Christians do not **worship** the images because they possess something [themselves]; they do not **worship** what is made of wood, of metal, or from whatever it has been made of.
mas **adora**n a Iesu Christo en la ymagen del Crucifijo, a la madre de Dios nuestra señora la virgen Maria en su ymagen, y a los sanctos tambien en sus ymagenes	rather they **worship** Jesus Christ in the image of the crucifix, the Mother of God, Our Lady the Virgin Mary in her image, and the Saints also in their images,	ychaca. IESV CHRISTOCTAM cruznimpi **mucha**ncu, Virgen sancta Mariap ymagenñimpim pay quiquinta **mucha**ncu, Santocunap ymagenñimpipas paycunatatacmi **mucha**ncu	Rather they **worship** Jesus Christ on his cross, they **worship** the Virgin Saint Mary herself in her image, they **worship** the Saints them[selves] in their images.
y bien saben los Christianos que Iesu Christo y nuestra Señora y los sanctos estan en el Cielo viuos y gloriosos	and the Christians know well that Jesus Christ and Our Lady and the Saints are in Heaven, alive and glorious	Christianocunaca allim ari yachaycu IESV CHRISTOCA, NVESTRA SEÑORA sancta Mariaca, Santocunaca, hanac pachapim ari cancu viñaypac cauçaspa, ancha cussicuspa,	Thus we, the Christians (and not you) know well that Jesus Christ, Our Lady Saint Mary, the Saints are, of course, in Heaven [lit. the upper world], living forever, being very happy,
y no estan en aquellos bultos o ymagines sino solamente pintados, …	and they are not in those bundles or images, but only painted, …	manam chay ymagen vcupichu, paycunaca tiancu, ychaca paycunap ricchaynillanmi chaypi tian, …	they do not dwell inside that image, rather therein only dwells their figure/appearance ….

We can see that the Christian authors thought that the problem was one of a crucial distinction of object-centred indigenous worship and content-centred Christian worship. Yet they used the same verb for both, and therefore they tried to clarify the difference they saw through complex explanations. Not only did they see differences which one might find discussable, but they also do not seem to have recognized that the simple transposition of a verb and its indigenous meaning into Christian discourse might have neutralized the differences they considered to be so important.[31]

SUMMARY AND CONCLUSIONS

The meaning of *muchay* in the early colonial era, in relation with both Andean and Christian deities, can be summarized as follows:

Table 10. The meaning of *muchay* in the colonial era

Quechua verb forms	*English translation (SD on basis of colonial sources)*
mucha- *muchayku-*	to kiss, adore, revere, worship – asymmetrical, respectful interaction, social and religious context (Andean Quechua applies to: general usage, words, rituals; Christian Quechua to: general usage, words)
muchapu-	to intercede, request in favour of someone

The Christian colonial interpretation of Andean deities was a negative one and the authors thus necessarily interpreted the verbs applied to Andean practices as such. However, at the same time, the Christian missionaries started using these words to refer to their own deity and thereby ran the risk that the Andean people might not become aware of the difference the priests understood: if the indigenous people used a verb to refer to an action related to their deities and

30 This sermon takes up the First Commandment (cf. *Doctrina christiana*, fol. 59r–60r, pp 137–9. **31** There were other solutions the linguist missionaries tried to implement, e.g. with the term and concept of 'offering', equally present in both languages. But even where different terms were chosen, a consistent application to one and the other sphere was not carried through (see Sabine Dedenbach-Salazar Sáenz, 'Andine traditionelle Kulturen und das Christentum' in Joachim G. Piepke (ed.), *Kultur und Religion in der Begegnung mit dem Fremden* (Nettetal, 2007), pp 113–78: pp 160–2 for this example; see Itier, 'La littérature quechua d'évangélisation' for further translation strategies, with a different interpretation from mine).

were taught to use the same word for a Christian deity, the effect was – in hindsight – obvious: Andean and Christian deities became equated and fused. What the Spaniards had hoped for was that, on the contrary, the belief in indigenous deities would disappear and consequently a shift from worshipping them to worshipping the Christian deity would occur and any 'con/fusion' would be impossible, as there were no Andean deities any more (they were, after all, not real gods but only fictions the Devil had created for those peoples who were not yet Christians).

Looking at the colonial missionary enterprise of translating the Christian doctrine into indigenous languages, in this case the translation which seemed to have been 'right' for the author/translator because of a certain conceptual convergence, in a way turned out to be the 'wrong' choice: it allowed the addressees/recipients not only to understand the Christian meaning of the term and its concept, but it also enabled them to connect the new belief forms and practices to their own ones and thus make sense within their own system of this 'interference' the Christians brought. This implies that the idea of christianizing in indigenous languages might have been the 'wrong' approach for the Church, but it turned out to be not entirely negative for the affected population because it enabled them to create an acceptable fusion of both religions for themselves. As time passed, Christianity spread and gained its own roots in the Andes: Andean Christianity has integrated the Christian God and Saints into its own pantheon and worldview, supported by a well established and reconfirmed application of the basic words to the now fused concepts.

Table 11. *Muchay*/worship – desired outcome vs. real outcome

Christian author/ translator:	*worship God and Saints*	*desired outcome:*
		eradicate *huacas*
→ the 'right' translation turns out to be the 'wrong' one for the Church		
Indigenous recipient:	*worship huacas, God, Saints*	*real outcome:*
		fusion of Christian and Andean deities
→ it turns out to be a productive translation for the Andean people		

The rights and wrongs of translating Patrick Pearse

Anne Markey

With the adoption, if not quite the imposition, of English as the vernacular of the majority of the population, language has played a crucial role in Irish cultural politics over the last two centuries. Translation, too, has made a significant, and at times contested, contribution to the development of both Irish literature and national identity. This essay explores how Patrick Pearse (1879–1916), the executed leader of the abortive Easter Rising of 1916, helped foster the development of Irish-language, prose literature. Attention then turns to a consideration of the ethics of translating into English a number of Irish-language stories written by Pearse, who trenchantly opposed efforts to produce a distinctively Irish form of writing in the English language. A consideration of the strategies adopted by Joseph Campbell (1879–1944) in his translations of Pearse's stories reveals an ethical compromise between the author's original intentions and the translator's desire to make the work accessible to a wider readership.

The final decades of the nineteenth century witnessed the emergence of two distinct movements that aimed to raise the status of Irish culture. The Gaelic League, founded by Douglas Hyde (1860–1949) in 1893, promoted the restoration of Irish as the *lingua franca* of the island. By contrast, the Irish literary revival, associated with writers including W.B. Yeats (1865–1939), Lady Gregory (1852–1932) and John Millington Synge (1871–1909), aimed to create a distinctively Irish national literature in the English language. Despite their shared desire to cultivate a sense of pride in Ireland's heritage, these two movements differed on the language through which this ambitious project should be conducted. Patrick Pearse, an active member of the Gaelic League, regarded the development of Irish literature in English with deep hostility, declaring: 'Literature which is in Irish is Irish literature; literature which is not in Irish is not Irish literature'.[1]

Convinced that the short story was the form 'in which the renascent prose literature of Ireland is likely to achieve its chief successes', Pearse set about writing short stories in the Irish language.[2] *Íosagán agus sgéalta eile*, a collection of

1 Patrick Pearse, 'Irish Literature', *An Claidheamh Soluis*, 13 Apr. 1907. 2 Patrick Pearse, 'Recent Booklets', *An Claidheamh Soluis*, 7 Oct. 1905.

four of these stories published by the Gaelic League in 1907, met with a generally positive critical reaction from fellow language enthusiasts. Alongside his increasing political activism, Pearse continued to contribute to the development of modern Irish-language literature, as Dundalgan Press published *An mháthair agus sgéalta eile*, containing a further six stories, in January 1916. All ten stories, set in Connemara, were designed to demonstrate the literary potential of the vernacular Irish spoken in that district.

Following the Rising and Pearse's subsequent execution, Dundalgan Press published *The mother and other tales*, containing translations by Revd T.A. Fitzgerald (1862–1921) of five of the stories that made up Pearse's second collection of short fiction. This volume also contained a foreword written by Helena Concannon (1878–1952), an Irish-language scholar and historian who taught in St Enda's, the bilingual school for boys founded by Pearse in 1908. In 1917, the Dublin firm of Maunsell, which had obtained the rights to Pearse's literary estate, published Joseph Campbell's translations of all ten of Pearse's short stories, as part of the *Collected works of Pádraic H. Pearse*, in the volume entitled *Plays, stories, poems*. Both sets of translations brought the work of a man who was increasingly seen as an heroic figure to a wider, English-speaking audience who had no access to the stories in their original form. Nevertheless, these English-language versions undermined Pearse's attempt to create a modern prose literature in the Irish language, so raising questions about the ethical and political dimensions of translation.

Significant differences between their translations reveal that Campbell, more than Fitzgerald, adopted strategies that enabled him to remain true in spirit to the tone of Pearse's original stories. Because language is connotational as well as denotational, no translation is ever an exact replica of the original and no two translations are ever exactly the same. T.A. Fitzgerald, a Franciscan priest who spent several years in Rome and Australia after his ordination in 1879, learned the Irish language and authored several collections of humorous Irish sketches in English on his return to Ireland in the early years of the twentieth century.[3] Joseph Campbell, who joined the Gaelic League in 1895, later moved to London and published several volumes of English-language poetry, which attracted the admiration of Ezra Pound among others. On his return to Ireland, he joined the staff of St Enda's and, with Pearse, was a founding member of the Irish Volunteers. Notwithstanding his resignation on health grounds, he continued to allow the Volunteers and James Connolly's Irish Citizen Army to drill on the lawn of his home during the period leading up to the 1916 Rising. Although he

3 Stephen J.M. Brown, *Ireland in fiction: a guide to Irish novels, tales, romances, and folk-lore* (New York, 1970), p. 107.

did not take part in the planning or the insurrection itself, he was friendly with, and supportive of, many of its organizers.[4] These two translators, with divergent political affiliations and literary talents, produced quantitatively and qualitatively different versions of Pearse's stories. For a start, while Campbell translated all of Pearse's short fiction, Fitzgerald translated only five of the stories contained in *An mháthair agus sgéalta eile*. He omitted 'An Dearg-Daol' ['The black beetle'], the story Pearse himself regarded as his 'best and grimmest', which features an authoritarian cleric who condemns a sinful woman from the altar.[5] In her Foreword, Concannon described how Pearse '"went forth" like Mary's Son "to die, amidst the scorn of men – for whom he died"'.[6] As the volume was intended as homage to the Christlike Pearse, it is telling that Fitzgerald, the Franciscan, chose not to translate a story that presents Catholicism in an unflattering light.[7]

The following example, taken from 'An bhean chaointe' ['The keening woman'], demonstrates that Fitzgerald censored Pearse on political as well as religious grounds. The young narrator's father tells how Muirne, the lamenting woman of the title, lost her reason when her beloved only son died as a result of wrongful imprisonment on the word of a police informer, during the land war of the late-nineteenth century. At the end of the tragic tale, the narrator's little brother vows that when he grows up, he will kill the spy.

> Leag m'athair a lámh ar chloigeann Sheánín.
> 'B'fhéidir, a mhaicín', ar seisean, 'go mbeadh muid uilig ag baint teailaí hó as an arm dubh sula rachas cré orainn' [original][8]
>
> My father laid his hand on Shawneen's head. 'Perhaps, my little son', said he, 'the whole of us may be better off before the clay goes over us' [Fitzgerald's translation].[9]
>
> My father laid his hand on Seaneen's head.
> 'Maybe, little son', says he, 'we'll all be taking tally-ho out of the black soldiers before the clay will come on us' [Campbell's translation].[10]

While Campbell retained the force and threat of the original, Fitzgerald, in the immediate aftermath of the failed insurrection of 1916, substituted a mean-

4 Anne Markey (ed.), *Patrick Pearse: short stories*, trans. by Joseph Campbell (Dublin, 2008), p. xvi. 5 Desmond Ryan, *Remembering Sion, a chronicle of storm and quiet* (London, 1934), p. 187. 6 T.A. Fitzgerald (trans.), *The mother and other tales* (Dundalk, 1916), p. ix. 7 For a discussion of how translation of Irish texts into English favoured works which conformed to a revivalist image of the nation as noble and sacred, see Louis de Paor, 'Cumhacht an aistriúcháin' in R. Ní Frighil & C. Dillon (eds), *Aistriú Éireann* (Belfast, 2008), pp 1–15. 8 Cathal Ó Háinle (ed.), *Gearrscéalta an Phiarsaigh* (Dublin, 1999), p. 105. 9 Fitzgerald, *The mother*, p. 88. 10 Markey (ed.), *Patrick Pearse: short stories*, p. 102.

ingless platitude for Pearse's ominous prediction of ongoing violence. The political nature of translation could hardly be clearer.

Although the opening sentences of these extracts proceed in almost identical fashion, the two English versions reveal telling differences at the level of lexical choice. Not only does Fitzgerald's use of 'Shawneen' smack of anglicizition, but the formality of '"Perhaps, my little son", said he' contrasts with Campbell's more casual and idiomatic '"Maybe, little son", says he'. In another passage, Campbell's evocative and allusive rendition of Muirne's description of her son similarly conveys a fluidity that is lacking in Fitzgerald's more prosaic version:

> You'd know him easily. He's the heartiest boy in the neighbourhood, an active, well-knit young fellow. He has a fair head, like you and grey eyes [...] like his father. He is wearing homespuns [Fitzgerald's translation].[11]

> You'd know him easy. He's the playboy of the people. A young, active lad, and he well set-up. He has a white head on him, like is on yourself, and grey eyes...like his father had. Bawneens he's wearing [Campbell's translation].[12]

Although Fitzgerald's 'heartiest boy in the neighbourhood' is lexically closer to Pearse's 'an buachaill is scafánta ar an bpobal',[13] Campbell's deliberate reference to Synge's famous play enriches his translation. Similarly, the retention of Gaelic syntax and vocabulary in 'Bawneens he's wearing' succeeds in replicating at least some elements of Pearse's vernacular Irish.

The opening stanzas of his translation of Muirne's lament for her dead son exemplify Campbell's efforts to retain the tone of the Irish-language original:

> Brón ar an mbás, 'sé dhubh mo chroíse,
> d'fhuadaigh mo ghrá is d'fhág mé cloíte,
> gan caraid gan compánach faoi dhíon mo thíse,
> ach an léan seo im' lár, is mé ag caoineadh.
>
> Ag gabháil an tsléibhe dhom tráthnóna
> do labhair an éanlaith liom go brónach,
> do labhair an naosc binn is an crotach glórach
> ag faisnéis dom gur éag mo stórach.[14]

11 Fitzgerald, *The mother*, p. 63. **12** Markey (ed.), *Patrick Pearse: short stories*, p. 86. **13** Ó Háinle (ed.), *Gearrscéalta an Phiarsaigh*, p. 131. **14** Ó Háinle (ed.), *Gearrscéalta an Phiarsaigh*, p. 133

Sorrow on death, it is it that blackened my heart,
That carried off my love and that left me ruined,
Without friend, without companion under the roof of my house
But this sorrow in my middle, and I lamenting.

Going the mountain one evening,
The birds spoke to me sorrowfully,
The melodious snipe and the voiceful curlew,
Telling me that my treasure was dead.[15]

Here, the almost literal translation eschews rhyme in favour of retaining, even enhancing, the disturbing imagery and disconsolate melancholy of Pearse's original, thereby resulting in lines of unequal length and variable metre. Compare this with Helena Concannon's version in Fitzgerald's collection, where even the numbering of stanzas conveys a sense of conventional rigidity that has little in common with Pearse's idiomatic Irish.

I
My grief on Death! From my roof-tree lonely
He has stolen my dear one, and left me woe!
He has stolen my child, and there sits now only
The Changeling, Grief, by my heart-flame low.

II
I crossed the mountain when eve was falling;
The birds' loud *caoine* rang in my ear;
I heard the snipe and the curlew calling
That he was dead whom I loved so dear.[16]

The inclusion of the italicized '*caoine*', the recourse to a strained ABAB rhyming scheme and regular metre, the repeated exclamations, and the personification of death as a changeling render this version affected and lifeless. It might seem that here and elsewhere Campbell adopts what Lawrence Venuti describes as a 'foreignising method' that draws attention to the strangeness of his English translations of Irish material, while Fitzgerald and Concannon adopt a 'domesticating method' that elides the differences between the source context and language and those of the translations.[17] However, given that the volumes

15 Markey (ed.), *Patrick Pearse: short stories*, p. 85. **16** Fitzgerald (trans.), *The mother*, p. 86. **17** Laurence Venuti, *The translator's invisibility* (London, 1995), pp 19–20.

containing these very different translations were published in Ireland and intended primarily for an Irish, but not Irish-speaking, readership, the situation is more complex than it first appears. Unlike Concannon's version, which imposes a conventionally poetic, English-language idiom on the Irish original, Campbell's translation retains a Gaelic feel, and so more effectively bridges the differences between source and target contexts, readerships and languages.

Campbell, of course, was not the first to produce a literary English idiom that reflected the syntax and lexical patterns of the Irish language. Patronizing portrayals of native Irish characters with funny accents appeared in the work of several nineteenth-century novelists.[18] The publication of Douglas Hyde's colloquial translations of the traditional *Love songs of Connaught* in 1893, though, revealed the rich literary potential of Hiberno-English, and inspired both Lady Gregory and John Millington Synge to develop their own distinctive Irish idioms. While opinions vary on the authenticity of both Gregory's Kiltartanese and her young associate's lyrical Synge-song, their work highlights the way in which translation provided a bridge between traditional Gaelic culture and the emergence of a distinctively Irish literature in English. Campbell's idiomatic translation of Pearse's stories develops the attempts of his Anglo-Irish predecessors, including Hyde, Synge, and Gregory, to recreate in literary form the speech patterns of Irish country people.

Successive drafts of Campbell's versions of Pearse's stories show translation to be the tool that enabled him to produce an idiom that differed from the literary dialect of those predecessors, as he continually strove to replicate the syntax, straightforward style, and simple language of the Irish-language originals. The manuscripts of these drafts illustrate how Campbell frequently crossed out complicated or stilted words and phrases, and inserted simpler, more idiomatic substitutes.[19] Retention in the published versions of words and phrases such as 'a chuisle' [darling], 'mar 'eadh' [as if] and 'muise' [indeed] signal that the stories emanate from, and resonate with, a Gaelic culture that cannot be seamlessly transposed into English. This effect of linguistic and cultural estrangement is most obvious in Campbell's decision not to translate the title of either 'Iosagán' or 'The Dearg-Daol'. Again, the retention of Gaelic words signals that these translations are opaque reflections of their source texts, wherein original elements commingle with new features. Hovering between Irish and English,

18 See, for example, the reported speech of the men who converse with Lord Colambre's postillion in Chapter X of Maria Edgeworth's *The absentee* (1812); of Captain O'Mealy in Lady Morgan's *The O'Briens and the O'Flahertys* (1827); of Lowry Lubie in Gerald Griffin's *The collegians* (1829); of the title character in Samuel Lover's *Handy Andy* (1842); of Cornelius Delany in Samuel Lever's *Jack Hinton* (1842); and of most of the inhabitants of Charles Kickham's *Knocknagow* (1879). **19** TCD Manuscripts 10185/3–9.

Campbell's translations simultaneously bridge the gap between the two languages, while drawing attention to the cultural chasm between them.

In terms of form, content and style, Pearse's stories were groundbreaking, as he attempted to describe life in Connemara in the language spoken by the people who lived there. Yet, as Pearse was not from that region and because Irish was his second language, the stories, even in their original form, involved a degree of ventriloquism that left their author open to charges of unethical inauthenticity.[20] By translating the stories into English, Campbell was undermining Pearse's attempt to create a modern prose literature in the Irish language while simultaneously promoting and endorsing Pearse's vision of Irish national identity as essentially Gaelic. This dilemma was partially resolved by Campbell's choice of an idiom that reflected Pearse's pioneering use of vernacular Irish as much as it resembled the type of Hiberno-English associated with the Anglo-Irish renaissance. Standing at the nexus of Gaelic and Anglo-Irish revivalists' disparate efforts to develop Irish literature, then, Campbell's translations of Pearse's stories represent an ethical compromise between the competing cultural claims that characterized their particular historical context.

20 See, for example, Richard Henebry's criticisms of 'Iosagán' in 'Revival Irish', *The Leader*, 6 Feb. 1909.

Editing Germany's Nazi past in German translations of Anne Frank's *Het Achterhuis* and Daniel Jonah Goldhagen's *Hitler's willing executioners*

Simone Schroth

At first sight, the choice of source texts for this chapter might seem arbitrary, as Anne Frank's writings about life in hiding and Daniel Jonah Goldhagen's analysis of potential motives behind the atrocities committed by Germans under the Nazi regime belong to different periods as well as different genres. However, both texts have been the subject of controversial debates in Germany and elsewhere,[1] and in both cases their translations into German have been part of these debates. There has been criticism of mollifying changes made when translating Anne Frank's *Het Achterhuis* in the immediate post-war years, and Goldhagen's book nearly half a century later. This chapter will present a commentary on some of the existing examinations of this question as well as adding a few findings from my own comparison of the source and target texts. At the outset, we should note a fundamental difference between the conditions under which the target texts were produced. Whereas the first German translation of *Het Achterhuis* may be described as the result of a co-operation between Anne Frank's father Otto Frank and former journalist Anneliese Schütz, a family friend and Holocaust survivor, the choice of Klaus Kochmann as the translator of Goldhagen's book was part of a publishing procedure decided by the publishers, Wolf Jobst Siedler Verlag.[2]

1 See David Barnouw, 'Anne Frank and academia' in Harry Paape, Gerrold van der Stroom et al. (eds), *The diary of Anne Frank: the revised critical edition* (New York, 2003), pp 103–8. See www.diss-duisburg.de/Internetbibliothek/Buecher/Goldhagen.htm, accessed on 27 Aug. 2009, and Robert R. Shandley (ed.), *Unwilling Germans? The Goldhagen debate* (Minneapolis, 1998). **2** See Gerrold van der Stroom, 'The diaries, *Het Achterhuis* and the translations' in Harry Paape, Gerrold van der Stroom et al. (eds), *The diary of Anne Frank: the revised critical edition* (New York, 2003), hereafter cited as van der Stroom, *Revised edition*, pp 59–77 and Simone Schroth, *Das Tagebuch/The diary/Le journal: Anne Franks 'Het Achterhuis' als Gegenstand eines kritischen Übersetzungsvergleichs* (Münster, 2006); hereafter Schroth, *Tagebuch/Diary/Journal*, pp 123–4. See also Susanne Lauscher, 'Translatqualität – ein Konsens' in Larisa Schippel (ed.), *Übersetzungsqualität: Kritik – Kriterien – Bewertungshandeln* (Berlin,

ANNELIESE SCHÜTZ'S VERSION OF ANNE FRANK (1950)

Since its first publication in 1950, Anneliese Schütz's translation of Anne Frank's *Het Achterhuis* has repeatedly been criticized for 'toning down' or omitting anti-German comments and for changing the text accordingly.[3] One of the central examples in this respect is a passage from the diary entry that appears under the date of 9 November 1943. After describing the suffering caused by the occupation of the Netherlands and the deportation of Jews, Anne Frank states that she is not German any more and that there are no greater enemies in the world than Germans and Jews. In the 1950 German edition, this reads: 'Und eine größere Feindschaft als zwischen *diesen* Deutschen und den Juden gibt es nicht auf der Welt!'[4] The implied differentiation between 'good' and 'bad' Germans, which cannot be found in the original, was added; through a later comment from Otto Frank we know that this was done intentionally.[5] Similarly, in the entry dated 17 November 1942, the remark that the people hiding in the secret annex had to speak in low voices all the time and to use the language of civilized people, thus no German, was changed to 'Alle Kultursprachen [...] aber leise!',[6] so the necessity of avoiding any noise is stressed, while the evaluation of Anne Frank's mother tongue as uncivilized is eliminated. In some cases, the term 'Germans' is replaced by 'the occupying force' or 'oppression'.[7] Also, the derogatory term 'moffen', which Anne Frank uses several times to refer to the Germans, is put into inverted commas.[8] In one of her two public comments on her work, Anneliese Schütz expressed concern about the negative effect that too many anti-German remarks might have had on the reception of her 1950 German-language version, *Tagebuch der Anne Frank*.[9]

Nevertheless, it needs to be said that the euphemistic representation of Germans and Nazis in the 1950 translation of *Het Achterhuis* is not as straight-

2006); hereafter Lauscher, 'Translatqualität', pp 55–73. **3** See Alvin H. Rosenfeld, 'Popularization and memory: the case of Anne Frank' in Peter Hayes (ed.), *Lessons and legacies: the meaning of the Holocaust in a changing world* (Evanston, 1991), pp 243–78. See also André Lefevere, 'On the construction of different Anne Franks' in André Lefevere, *Translation, rewriting, and the manipulation of literary fame* (London & New York, 1992), pp 59–72, and others. **4** See Anne Frank, *Das Tagebuch der Anne Frank*, trans. Anneliese Schütz (Heidelberg, 1950), hereafter Schütz, *Tagebuch*, p. 40; emphasis in the original. The Dutch original will not be given here for lack of space; as dates for the diary entries will always be provided, it will be possible to find the passages in question in corresponding editions. The paraphrasing of quotations is done on the basis of the latest *Het Achterhuis* translation into English: *The diary of a young girl. The definitive edition*, trans. Susan Massotty (London, 1995). **5** See van der Stroom, *Revised edition*, p. 85. **6** See Schütz, *Tagebuch*, p. 52. **7** See Rosenfeld, 'Popularization and memory', pp 267–8. **8** See Schütz, *Tagebuch*, pp 147, 258. **9** See Anonymous, 'Was schrieb das Kind?', *Der Spiegel*, 14 (1 April 1959, pp 51–5, at p. 55).

forward or radical as has sometimes been stated.[10] For instance, Anne Frank concludes her D-Day entry by expressing her hopes to be liberated soon from those awful Germans that have oppressed and threatened the occupied countries for so long. Although one might have expected some mollifying strategy here, none comes up in Schütz's translation.[11] In the entry for 9 October 1942, from which the first quote (about the Germans and Jews as enemies) was taken, the translator seems to follow a strategy opposed to the one that became apparent in my first few examples. Voicing her anxiety about the ongoing deportations, Anne Frank refers to BBC reports about gassings and comments that this might be the quickest way to die.[12] The German translation reads: 'Das englische Radio berichtet von Gaskammern, aber vielleicht ist das noch die schnellste Vernichtungsmethode'.[13] This means that Schütz not only made the horror of the reports more concrete by using the German equivalent of 'gas chambers' but also declared them 'the quickest method of annihilation'. The threat posed by the Nazis is thus not made more vague (as was the case in the examples given above) but more concrete: the term 'gas chambers' conveys a more detailed picture of the killing method employed, and the victims not only die but are annihilated, which indicates that their death is purposefully induced and that this happens on a widespread scale.

The fact that two quotations from the same entry can be used to indicate opposing strategies – 'toning down' with regard to the enmity between Germans and Jews, 'toning up' with regard to the fate of the deported – can be seen as characteristic of Schütz's translation as a whole: an extensive analysis of the target text[14] has shown that this is not only true for passages referring to Germans or Nazis: omissions, additions and rephrasings can be found throughout the 1950 German translation, and it is not always possible to spot a consistent motivation or strategy. This means that Schütz's way of representing anti-German remarks needs to be partly re-evaluated as well as put into the context of the translation in its entirety. To describe it only as 'toning down' is not sufficient.

10 See for example the texts of Rosenfeld and Lefevere mentioned in footnote no. 3. **11** See Schütz, *Tagebuch*, p. 250. **12** It is with a certain unease that examples such as the above and those following from Goldhagen's book are used in this article, as their content makes it appear inappropriate to discuss them and their translations from a linguistic or evaluating perspective. At the same time, it can be said that the reception of both texts in translation contributes to the commemoration of those murdered in the Holocaust, which makes their examination an important task. **13** Schütz, *Tagebuch*, p. 39. **14** See Schroth, *Tagebuch/Diary/Journal*, pp 121–83.

DANIEL JONAH GOLDHAGEN TRANSLATED BY KLAUS KOCHMANN (1996)

'[T]he fact remains that there is a whole pattern of differences, that is, there is converging evidence for the hypothesis that the German translation is systematically toned down in many specifiable instances and on different linguistic levels.' Although I have tried to show in the previous section that there can be limits to the consistency of patterns when it comes to translation strategies, the second part of this statement could easily be assumed to be an extract from a description of Anneliese Schütz's *Het Achterhuis* translation. It is taken, in fact, from the chapter on Daniel Jonah Goldhagen's *Hitler's willing executioners* that forms part of Juliane House's sample translation analyses in her book *Translation quality assessment: a model revisited,*[15] which makes House the first – and, to my knowledge, the only – scholar to provide an extended commentary on Klaus Kochmann's translation work very soon after the publication of *Hitlers willige Vollstrecker* in the summer of 1996. The fact that House's remark could have been applied, unchanged, to both of the books under consideration here is interesting: both Klaus Kochmann and the Siedler editor responsible for the Goldhagen translation project felt considerable pressure, due to the fact that the target text would be exposed to the scrutiny of both the author himself – who had set numerous rules for the translation in his contract with the German publisher – and the reading public.[16] This makes their situation different from the working conditions of Anneliese Schütz and Otto Frank, who had not yet found a publisher for a Dutch or German edition of *Het Achterhuis* when taking up their task, and who had no reason to foresee that both books would become bestsellers. In fact, one would assume that the criticism of 'toning down' on behalf of the target group was one of the aspects the Siedler team had been most aware of. At any rate, this is implied in the fact that Goldhagen paid special attention to the German readership by providing a preface for the Siedler edition[17] and stressing in his acknowledgment that his co-operation with Siedler resulted in a faithful rendering of the original in German.[18] The term 'wortgetreu' is used here.[19] This indicates that the author felt the wish, as well as the need, to express his approval of a translation he knew readers would look at

15 Juliane House, *Translation quality assessment: a model revisited* (Tübingen, 1997); hereafter House, *Translation quality assessment*, pp 147–57 at p. 156. **16** See Lauscher, 'Translatqualität', p. 65. **17** Daniel Jonah Goldhagen, 'Vorwort zur deutschen Ausgabe' in Daniel Jonah Goldhagen, *Hitlers willige Vollstrecker: Ganz gewöhnliche Deutsche und der Holocaust*, trans. Klaus Kochmann (Munich, 2000 [Berlin, 1996]); hereafter Kochmann, *Hitlers willige Vollstrecker*, pp 5–13. **18** Daniel Jonah Goldhagen, 'Dank' in Kochmann, *Hitlers willige Vollstrecker*, pp 551–3 at p. 552. **19** See also Lauscher, 'Translatqualität', p. 68.

carefully as well as critically; by doing so, he shows that the prospective readers' interest in the 'faithfulness' of the target text had been taken into consideration.[20]

Despite this assurance by the author, my own conclusions, which come from an analysis similar in scale to House's, correspond to her critical findings. One example of this concerns an omission: the sentence 'All of these [guiding principles of state policy] characterized not just the Nazi leadership but the vast majority of the German people, who were aware of what their government and their countrymen were doing to Jews, assented to the measures, and, when the opportunity presented itself, lent their active support to them' does not appear in the German translation.[21] As the question to what extent the majority of the population of Hitler's Germany were aware of what happened in the occupied countries and the concentration camps can be seen as one of the central elements of the Holocaust discourse, it is striking that it should be missing here. This could be interpreted as 'toning down'. Of course, a more extensive analysis of the frequency of potential omissions would be necessary here.

At the same time, I have found passages that show that Kochmann does not always seem to follow the same strategy. Two examples will suffice here. In chapter 4, Goldhagen states that '[t]he move to gassing […] – contrary to the widely accepted belief – was prompted not by considerations of efficiency, but by the search for a method that would ease the psychological burden of killing for the Germans.'[22] In Kochmann's translation, this reads: 'Der Übergang zu Vergasungen […] erfolgte – anders als weithin angenommen – nicht aus Gründen der Effizienz, sondern weil man den Vollstreckern den Völkermord psychisch erleichtern wollte.'[23] This short excerpt provides us with two points of interest. First, two opposing tendencies become obvious in the choice of words: whereas 'die Vollstrecker' is used to represent the whole population of 'the Germans' (that is, a 'toning down'), 'Völkermord' – 'genocide' – appears as a synonym of 'killing' (that is, 'toning up').[24] Second, the translation of the

20 As Lauscher (see pp 68 f.) points out, the concept of 'faithfulness' would need some further specification in this context. **21** See Daniel Jonah Goldhagen, *Hitler's willing executioners, ordinary Germans and the Holocaust* (New York, 1996); hereafter Goldhagen, *Hitler's willing executioners*, p. 90. See also Kochmann, *Hitlers willige Vollstrecker*, p. 118. **22** See Daniel Jonah Goldhagen, *Hitler's willing executioners*, p. 157. **23** Kochmann, *Hitlers willige Vollstrecker*, p. 193. **24** To get a better idea of how Kochmann represents the word 'German' in his translation, pp 152–63 (pp 188–200 in the German edition), i.e., the last 12 pages of 'The Nazis' assault on the Jews: its character and evolution', were examined. In the original, the terms 'German' or 'the Germans' appear 45 times. In Kochmann's target text, the German equivalents, 'deutsch' and '[die] Deutsch[en]' can be found in 33 of the cases. At the same time, there are 12 cases where the adjective has been omitted or the reference to 'Hitler's willing executioners' in terms of their nationality has been replaced by a synonym. For example, Goldhagen's 'other German camps' and 'from the Germans' shots' (pp 160, 161) become 'in

insertion 'contrary to widely accepted belief' is of interest. In German, 'annehmen' can mean both 'to accept' and 'to assume'. The fact that the German executioners were apparently in need of something to ease the psychological burden of killing is somehow in opposition to Goldhagen's core thesis that the Germans were 'willing executioners' – were they really that 'willing' after all if such measures had to be taken? Nevertheless, Goldhagen does not leave out that point. He even draws more attention to it by pointing out that the concept of the Nazis as coldblooded killers focused on fulfilling their task is based on a 'widely accepted belief'. One would expect that the translator, thinking of his German readers and the reservations they might have with regard to Goldhagen's core thesis, would want to convey the sentence in question as faithfully as possible. Kochmann, however, reduces the emphasis Goldhagen puts on the discrepancy between the Nazis' assumed and actual motives by dropping the element of 'belief' and choosing an ambiguous expression for 'accept'.

CONCLUSION

My last example in the previous section could be used as the basis for my concluding remarks: House's statement on Klaus Kochmann's translation can safely be supported, as can Lauscher's (presumably) rhetorical question as to whether the discussion of Kochmann's work would have evolved differently if the translator had provided a detailed commentary.[25] Whereas the criticism of 'toning down' has, in my opinion, been proved sufficiently, other aspects like the frequency of omissions and a pattern that might arise from listing more of them – if they exist – would have to be examined in further detail. In the case of Schütz's *Het Achterhuis* translation, this has been done, although, as outlined above, it is not always possible to identify a consistent translation strategy.

In my comparative approach on two translations of texts dealing with Germany's Nazi past it has become apparent that certain changes made with regard to a German reading public were considered necessary in the immediate

anderen Lagern' and 'durch Schüssse' (pp 196 and 197). In Kochmann's translation, 'the Germans' are for instance represented by 'Täter[n]', ('those responsible'), 'man' ('one') or 'die anderen beteiligten Einheiten' ('the other units involved'; see Goldhagen pp 157, 156, 157 and Kochmann, p. 193 for all three examples). Although the use of omissions and synonyms might be, at least partly, explained by German rules of style that classify repetitions as something to be avoided, it could be argued that in a case as this, where the avoiding strategy could be interpreted as 'toning down', it would be appropriate to prioritize the close rendition of the original over prescriptions of style. At any rate, the amount of omissions and replacements seems quite striking here. **25** See Lauscher, 'Translatqualität', p. 69.

post-war period as well as in the late nineties of the past century. Since then, *Het Achterhuis* has been retranslated.[26] It remains to be seen whether future editions of *Hitler's willing executioners* will include changes to the translation and/or a translator's commentary.

26 See *Tagebuch*, trans. Mirjam Pressler (Frankfurt am Main, 1991). See also Schroth, *Tagebuch/Diary/Journal*, pp 146–55.

PART 3

TRANSLATION NOW

Translation is the paradigm, the exemplar of all writing. It is translation that demonstrates most vividly the yearning for transformation that underlies every act involving speech, that supremely human gift.

Harry Mathews, *The human country* (2002)

The right to translation and advertising in English in France

Kathleen Shields

My intention in this essay is to examine one of the places where the ideology behind the symbolic values of a language connects with language legislation. How does one piece of legislation (the 1994 law on the use of the French language) manifest itself in the practice of translations, in this case the translation of advertisements into French?[1] In other words I intend to look at a particular instance of where the arbitrary (the symbolic value of a language) meets the non-arbitrary (language planning) in examples of translations.[2] The example of translation in advertising shows us one of the places where, to borrow an expression of Louis-Jean Calvet, *in vitro* planning comes up against *in vivo* language use.[3]

These translations can be set against a broader background since the issue of English in advertising is part of the more slowly unfolding debate about English as a world language and how French situates itself in relation to it. Much language policy comes about not as a result of overt legislation or planning but rather as a result of *bricolage* or ad hoc arrangements deriving from unspoken assumptions about language and nation.[4] Some of these assumptions can flicker into view in language debates at moments of crisis or change.

La loi relative à l'emploi de la langue française or as it has come to be known the Loi Toubon (which came into effect in January 1995) stipulates that a French version must be provided of documents relating to goods and services and to advertising on the territory of France. It also covers internet sales and advertising. I will touch on this later. In addition, it legislates for the use of French in work and other contracts, teaching establishments, and conferences.[5] The use of

1 'Relative à l'emploi de la langue française', *LOI. Journal officiel de la République française*, 94:665 (2 Aug. 1994), 11240–2. **2** Jan Blommaert, 'Language planning as a discourse on language and society', *Language Problems and Language Planning*, 20:3 (1996), 199–222 at 199. **3** Louis-Jean Calvet, *La guerre des langues et les politiques linguistiques* (Paris, 1987), p. 11. **4** Blommaert, 'Language planning', 206. **5** For commentary on the Loi Toubon, see, for example, Claude Truchot, 'The spread of English: from France to a more general perspective', *World Englishes* 16:1 (1997), 65–76, at 74–5; Rodney Ball, *The French-speaking world: a practical introduction to sociolinguistic issues* (London, 1997), pp 210–4; Marie-Josée de Saint Robert, *La politique de la langue française* (Paris, 2000), ch. 4; Marie Landick, 'French courts

English in the workplace is not covered by the law and while information to consumers must be provided in French this does not exclude the parallel use of other languages.

At the time in the second half of 1994 and before it came into force at the beginning of 1995, the most controversial part of the law was the obligation to use terms coined by ministerial terminology committees because this was considered to be an unconstitutional infringement on individual liberties. The law was referred to the *Conseil Constitutionnel* mainly by socialist opposition deputies but also by some centre-right Balladur government deputies of the UPF. The constitutional council kept this obligation for state communications but suppressed it for everyday language use. The parts of the law relating to information for consumers and to the terminology committees are the really lasting ones. In practice the terminology committees cannot keep up with the vast flow of English words coming into France.

To a person outside France it might appear that the Loi Toubon has been forgotten, having been left fairly toothless by the *saisine* or ruling of the constitutional council. However, the use of English in advertising and the workplace still generates heated debate on French blogs and in the press. The right to use French as a language of the workplace, while not covered by the 1994 law, has become a union issue and the Loi Toubon is a recurring point of reference in these debates.

It might be thought that the use of English in France today is comparable with that at the time of René Étiemble who in 1964 published his entertaining book *Parlez vous franglais?* and that current French negative attitudes and resistance to English are simply more examples of purism and chauvinism.[6] It is a fact of life that borrowing and calque have always been part of language use and that it is futile to try to impose prescriptive solutions on the march of a language. However, I believe that there is now a qualitative difference in the use of English in France due to the huge dominance of English as a world language.

Languages themselves are now commodified so that local languages can be used in a global market. Old ideologies of language and the nation-state are mutating or breaking down.[7] In the current period of what Anthony Giddens calls 'high modernity' (or what others call global capitalism) there is now a tension between monolingual nation-states and supra-national structures and processes. The old adage that you buy in your own language but you sell to the

and language legislation' in Marie Landick (ed.), *La langue française face aux institutions* (Paris, 2003), pp 111–36. **6** René Étiemble, *Parlez-vous franglais?* (Paris, 1964). **7** Anthony Giddens quoted by Monica Heller, 'Alternative ideologies of la francophonie' in Roxy Harris & Ben Rampton (eds), *The language, ethnicity and race reader* (London, 2003), pp 225–42 at p. 225.

Fig. 1. 'Travel for Real'

other person in his or her language no longer holds true since English has become the global language of transactions. In France, perhaps more than in other countries, the linguistic tension is played out in the political arena.

I propose now to look at some examples of the use of English and its translation in print advertising in France (Figs. 1–4). Foreign languages are sometimes used in advertising, either to denote origins, for example with English marmalade, Scotch whisky or French perfume, or else for their connotative power. A good example of this is the use of German in car advertisements with its connotations of engineering excellence. The use of English in advertising in France today goes far beyond connotation and origins. Products such as cars, mobile phones, jewellery, tourist destinations are systematically advertised with English slogans. Some of these products are even of French origin.

The tourism advertisement for Morocco comes from *Paris Match* so is clearly intended for French speakers (see Fig. 1).[8] The question then arises as to why

8 *Paris Match*, 3118, 19–25 Feb. 2009.

Fig. 2. 'The Irony of Swatch'

the slogan 'Travel for real' should be in English, especially as Moroccan products such as oranges are usually marketed with the country's French name, Maroc. The tiny translation in French on the left-hand side, 'voyager pour de vrai', is in deference to the Loi Toubon. The use of English in this case is similar to that in car advertisements in France where the English slogan is systematically attached to a brand name, for example, 'Honda. The power of dreams', 'Today, Tomorrow, Toyota', 'Saab. Move your Mind', 'Shift family life. Nissan', 'Volvo. For Life'. In these advertisements the French translations are in minuscule print, tucked away at the bottom or in the margins. It is worth noting an inconsistency in the application of the Loi Toubon to car advertisements. Volkswagen cars are marketed in France with the untranslated slogan 'Das Auto'. It is possible to conclude that global English or *globish* is the language specifically targeted by the Loi Toubon and not other languages.

Since the end of the Second World War English has increasingly been the other against which French defines itself. A good example of this is to be found in the popularizing writings of the linguist Henriette Walter. In her best-selling book, *Le Français dans tous les sens* (1988), she argues in her chapter titled 'Le français, bon second' that French is second to the English language.[9] Spanish

9 Henriette Walter, *Le Français dans tous les sens* (Paris, 1988), p. 198.

Fig. 3. 'shop now'

and Mandarin are not considered, neither are the other languages spoken on French territory, such as Arabic. In the case of Walter there is a denial that French is losing its place in the ranking of world languages. In other cases there is an underlying anxiety that within the territory of France there is too much subservience to English in certain areas of life.

There is no real need for English as a lingua franca within France. In this regard it is instructive to compare the current situation in France with that in neighbouring countries. In Swiss advertisements English can function as a supra language to communicate to the different language communities in that country (see Fig. 2). In regard to the Swatch advertisement with its English slogan, 'the irony of Swatch', it has been pointed out that the wordplay on 'iron' and 'irony' is perhaps elitist as it is lost on German and French speakers.[10] A greater irony is that Swatch is a portmanteau English word invented by the Swiss and that the watches are produced in Switzerland. Does it matter what language the advertisement is in so long as money is rolling into Swiss coffers? In contrast,

10 'L'anglais dans la publicité: la langue en délire' [interview with Marc Bonhomme and Michael Rinn], www.comanalysis.ch/ComAnalysis/Publication23.htm, accessed 14 Aug. 2009. **11** Truchot, 'Spread of English', 66.

what is manifest in the French advertisements for cars or tourist destinations is not the use of English as a lingua franca, or the use of English in a situation of what Claude Truchot has called 'transglossia'.[11] It is an elevation of English that borders on diglossia in certain areas of life, not just in advertising but in information technology, communications, business education, scientific research, the workplace in multinational companies. I will return to this point later.

English has become the language of fashion, shopping and consumption in France and the Armani example, taken from *Le Monde*, is just one of many (see Fig. 3).[12] The language of advertising is akin to poetry and is notoriously difficult to translate. However, the translations provided for the French consumer, besides being almost illegible, are often approximate or even meaningless. In an advertisement for jewellery the play on words 'the gift of legendary style' is translated approximately as 'un cadeau au style légendaire' but the actual meaning of the translation is not important since the function of English as a signifier is to work as an additional logo.[13]

Some of the slogans in English are for French products such as Dior perfumes, for instance, 'Dior Addict' and 'Pure Poison'. The latter example startled at least one French consumer because of its wrong agreement if it is read as French. Some advertisements for French products, for toiletries or tailoring, are written in questionable English: 'L'Oréal Men expert', 'Façonnable. The modern elegance from the French Riviera'. Again, the creativity of the English or the accuracy of its translation into French is not important.[14]

Some weblog writers comment on the lack of creativity in the way English is used in advertising. Others comment that they feel bludgeoned and even provoked by the use of English in advertisements, a case in point being the campaign by the Dutch telecoms company Orange where the advertisment consisted of the single word 'open' in English in giant orange letters, translated by '=s'ouvrir' in tiny print.

A second point that comes up in articles by language lobby groups and in blogs is the lack of parity of esteem in size of typography even though the Loi Toubon calls for legibility and equal size of characters. Here the French situation contrasts with that of Québec for example. A final point that emerges, for example in the publications of the ALF (Avenir de la Langue Française), is the tokenism of the French. Perhaps surprisingly, very little reference is made to the inaccuracy of the translations although this figures in the

12 *Le Monde*, 6 Dec. 2008. **13** Tiffany advertisement, *Le Monde*, 6 Dec. 2008. **14** www.christophecourtois.blogspot.com/2007/10/ras-le-bol-de-langlais-dans-les.html, accessed 26 Feb. 2009. Also www.richard.ying.fr/blog/ 2007/10/26/751/, accessed 14 Aug. 2009, and www.lexpress.fr/actualite/societe/l-anglais-au-bureau-no_464219.html, accessed 14 Aug. 2009.

Fig. 4. Non-translation of English: inernet sites

text of the law. It is clear that what is at stake here is the symbolic value of the two languages.

Inconsistencies in the application of the Loi Toubon become apparent in my last illustration which is an advertisement for a social networking site (see Fig. 4).[15] Code-mixing is now widespread in France in computing, electronics, communications, business and management. Is this English (or French) as we know it? There are chunks of untranslated English in this text such as 'free people network' while other parts use English (or rather Franglais) vocabulary with French syntax, as in 'leader du marketing relationnel'.

France is unusual compared to other countries in attempting to cover internet sales and advertising by legislation, in Article 3 of the Loi Toubon. As Geoffrey Nunberg says, 'few non-English-speaking nations have followed France in trying to explicitly mandate the use of the national language on websites and the like'.[16] Nunberg makes an important distinction between the internet and other media when he points to the multilingualism of its users, namely that users

15 *Le Monde*, 13 Feb. 2009. **16** Jeffrey Nunberg, 'Languages in the wired world' in Tony Judt & Denis Lacorne (eds), *Language, nation, state: identity politics in a multilingual age* (New York, 2004), pp 231–4 at pp 232, 234.

of print or audiovisual media are tied to one language whereas internet users can flick from sites in one language or another depending on the situations in which they use these languages. This may be the case for, say, Icelandic or Hispanophone users. However, it would be interesting to see how multilingual first language speakers of Anglo-American really are when they use the web. The fact remains that French speakers want to be able to use French as one of the languages of the internet, particularly when they are buying products.

The resistance to the use of English in advertisements can be linked to the campaign for the right to use French in the workplace that peaked in January 2007. The campaign was led by several unions across the political spectrum but also supported by language lobby groups such as DLF (Défense de la Langue Française) and ALF, which are in turn supported by the Académie Française.[17]

Contrary to what some French anti-American commentators say, the use of English in the workplace is a European and global phenomenon, not always imposed by American companies. Many companies that use English are originally European, such as Ericsson, Saab and Bull. Some US companies, such as IBM, favour the use of local languages. As mergers take place there is often a switch to English in the workplace, as was the case for example with AXA Tech. A good example of this is the case of Jean-Marie Messier at Vivendi, originally a French company. Messier took over an old-style corporation, the *Compagnie Générale des Eaux* and turned it into one of the biggest media and communications companies in the world after gaining control of a major Hollywood studio (Universal). Under Messier's direction Vivendi-Universal adopted English as its working language to satisfy the wish of the majority of its board of directors.[18] A comparable figure to Messier is Alain Minc, essayist and businessman, who supports the use of English in the EU, considering the English language to be 'the only contribution Britain has made to Europe'.[19]

Is the use of English necessary in the French branches of these companies, if French is the first language of 99 per cent of the employees? During the campaign for the use of French in the workplace, employees from various companies such as Alcatel-Lucent Nozay, Europ Assistance and Société Générale claimed that they were experiencing 'linguistic alienation' in the workplace due to the systematic use of English in emails and communications from management. Use of English was unnecessary and gave rise to fatigue, health and safety issues, loss of promotion prospects and fears of outsourcing.[20]

17 Malcolm Offord, 'The Role of private associations' in Marie Landick (ed.), *La langue française* (Paris, 2003), pp 95–109. **18** Denis Lacorne, 'Anti-Americanism and Americanophobia: a French perspective' in Tony Judt & Denis Lacorne (eds), *With us or against us: studies in global anti-Americanism* (New York, 2005), pp 35–8. **19** Truchot (1997), p. 73. **20** www.voxlatina.com/ Dossiers, accessed 5 Mar. 2009.

What appears to be a matter of respective symbolic values of English and French in the domain of advertising is perhaps a manifestation of more concrete examples of linguistic dominance in other areas of French life. What we are seeing here is a clash between two varieties of linguistic nationalism. The French 'nation form', as Étienne Balibar has described it, a complex of ideas (or myths) about the French language dating back to the Revolution, locks horns with what Joshua Fishman has described as the 'banal nationalism' of US English policies of the 70s and 80s, now expanded to a world scale.[21] Both varieties are tested in their claims to universality, claims which render translation unnecessary. Translation can take place out of the language (be it world English or French) but not into it because accepting translation would mean accepting the dominance of the other language over one's own.

To claim the right to translation into French as the Loi Toubon does, is equivalent to accepting a situation of bilingualism, perhaps even diglossia. Diglossia is at work in the hierarchies of scientific research between publication in journals and discussion in the lab or on electronic networks.[22] It is increasing in the EU between formal and informal meetings.[23] It is present in the service industries, finance and computing. Here I mean diglossia in Fishman's rather than in C.A Ferguson's[24] sense: as between two different languages rather than between high and low forms in the same language.

Linguistic insecurity in the face of English, allied with the belief that French needs protection and support, is to be found right across the political spectrum in France. As the linguist Robert Chaudenson observes, when it comes to the language there are few fundamental differences between right and left, 'nationalism is a value shared by both the Communist Party and the French far right, a fact at once strange if explicable'.[25] There is a related debate about whether English is a vital communication tool that should be in the armoury of French speakers or whether English undermines the communicative power of French and is harmful to its integrative and symbolic value.

A good example of this disagreement occurred within the same political party during the Sarkozy election campaign in 2007. Sarkozy made a promise to break with the *tout-anglais* prevalent in an increasing number of companies in France, stating that he would make sure that in companies on French territory

21 Quoted in Étienne Balibar, 'The nation form: history and ideology' in Étienne Balibar & Immanuel Wallerstein (eds), *Race, nation, class* (London, 1991), pp 86–106, trans. Chris Turner. **22** Philippe Lazar, 'La hantise des laboratoires: "to be" ou ne pas être?', *Manière de voir*, 97 (2008), 66–8. **23** Claude Truchot, *L'Anglais en Europe: repères* (Strasbourg, 2002). **24** C.A. Ferguson, 'Diglossia', *Word*, 15 (1959), 325–40. **25** Robert Chaudenson, 'Geolinguistics, geopolitics, geostrategy: the case of French' in Jacques Maurais & Michael A. Morris (eds), *Languages in a globalizing world* (Cambridge, 2003), pp 291–7.

the working language would be French, where there was no economic or commercial necessity calling for the use of another language. At the same time, in a conversation with journalists, Valérie Pécresse, between 2007 and 2011 minister of Higher Education and Research, stated that she wanted courses in French universities to be delivered in English.[26]

While the situation of French in relation to English probably is no different from that of other EU countries, there is an important conceptual difference that marks out French attitudes towards the language. Republican concepts of nation, state and language are unHerderian and do not depend on race or soil. Rather, French is the one and indivisible language of the one and indivisible republic, committed to by plebiscite at the time of the revolution. The language has an important political symbolism and function that can also give rise to ambiguous and paradoxical positions, not least in relation to the minority languages within the territory.[27]

There are different strategies for resisting the authority of a dominant language. Adoption is one (as Valérie Pécresse and many advertisers choose to do). Partial adoption is another. Reclamation and counter-proclamation are two other possibilities.[28] Alain Supiot has noted that much commentary on the language oscillates between triumphant statements about its prestige and despair at the domination of global English, between what he calls 'francophone bluster and an acceptance that English now rules'.[29] Another possible way is adaptation of old ideas about the French language to the new world order.

A good example of this kind of reclamation (perhaps mutation) is to be found in the ideas of the well-known linguist Claude Hagège, for example in his book, *Le Français, histoire d'un combat*, which was an expanded version of a television series that he presented in 1996. In his concluding chapter on the future of French, Hagège reuses old concepts such as *rayonnement*, humanism and universality. He argues that French has a special mission to speak on behalf of all languages that are not English, concluding, 'le combat en faveur de la langue française est aussi, à plus d'un titre, un combat pour l'humanité'.[30] The old paradox of the universality of French reappears in a new guise: the language is uniquely equipped to speak for all of the oppressed languages of the earth.

26 'Rupture linguistique entre M. Sarkozy et Mme Pécresse', *Le Monde Diplomatique*, www.monde-diplomatique.fr/carnet/2008-03-07-Rupture-linguistique, accessed 16 Aug. 2009. **27** Alain Fenet, 'Difference rights and language in France' in Judt & Lacorne (eds), *Language, nation, state*, pp 19–61. **28** R.D. Grillo, *Dominant languages: language and hierarchy in Britain and France* (Cambridge, 1989), p. 221. **29** Alain Supiot, 'The condition of France', *London Review of Books*, 8 June 2006, 24–6. **30** Claude Hagège, *Le Français, histoire d'un combat* (Paris, 1996), pp 167–8. See also by the same author 'Que s'ouvre enfin l'ère de la deuxième francophonie!', *Le Monde*, 8 Nov. 2008.

The universality of French is not a belief shared by all, for example by Breton, Occitan or Corsican speakers who within the territory of the republic had to undergo the domination of French. Perhaps for political reasons to do with the 1994 genocide, Rwanda has recently adopted English rather than French as the language of education from primary to third level.[31] It is increasingly the case that in many African countries, English rather than French exerts a growing appeal for educated elites.

Translation is one of the ways the Loi Toubon tries to regulate the conflict between two kinds of linguistic authority. The advertisements (with their token translations) are one rather unsuccessful attempt of French linguistic nationalism to adjust to modernity. The Toubon solution is a kind of *exception culturelle* applied to the language. However, there is a general lack of understanding about these issues outside France. While some elements of French culture, such as cinema, cuisine, fashion, and film, achieve the status of *exception culturelle*, others such as popular song, cartoon strips and the language do not export themselves so well.

31 Jean-Pierre Tuquoi 'Le Rwanda élimine le français de son enseignement', *Le Monde*, 18 Oct. 2008.

In search of the right translation: sorting out translation problems when subtitling scientific documentaries: translating *Crude*

Francisca García Luque

Although during recent decades a substantial number of works concerning research on audiovisual translation have been published, mainly concentrating on dubbing and subtitling, almost all of them refer to fictional films based on actors' performances. The present contribution sets out to determine whether some of the conclusions that are generally accepted for film dialogues may also be applied to documentaries, especially where subtitling is involved.

When analysing translations of documentaries, the scholar is aware of the constraints that bind the text, because of the audiovisual context in which it is required to fulfil the communication process. The Titford term 'constrained translation'[1] reflects the idea that the translator is somehow limited by circumstances that are mainly related to technical issues.

Nevertheless, audiences in general ignore the fact that what they hear is not exactly what they will read in the subtitle. Depending on their knowledge of the original language (which can still be heard) they create some expectations that could be reasonably fulfilled with appropriate translation techniques and a good dose of imagination.

Among the constraints audiovisual translators deal with when subtitling any kind of programme, the first one that comes to mind is the need to reduce the text (in terms of characters, and sometimes even in terms of information) to the spatial limits of a standard subtitle. The 'loss' of some minimal parts of the original text is generally accepted as a *sine qua non* condition for the existence of subtitles. But when the nature of the text involved in the translation process is scientific, this 'loss' of information must be handled carefully, as such texts are terminologically and semantically much more dense than other types of audiovisual texts, such as fictional films, and their main purpose, as scientific texts, is to communicate objective information.

The present essay aims to study the different problems a translator may encounter when trying to find a proper and acceptable translation that could be

1 Christopher Titford, 'Subtitling: constrained translation', *Lebende Sprachen*, 27:3 (1982), 113–16.

potentially considered by the audience as the 'right' translation, despite the constant exercise of linguistic compression that is forced on the text. The starting point for the discussion is my personal experience of translating into Spanish an English-language documentary entitled *Crude*, on the history of oil; this film was released at the 'International Biennial of Scientific Film' on November 2008 in Ronda (Spain). After a preliminary review of different types of problems, the essay will consider some possible solutions and a global translation strategy that might be used in such cases in order to arrive at the 'right' translation.

SUBTITLING STRATEGIES

As Jorge Díaz Cintas states, 'subtitles are not, and cannot be, a complete and detailed translation of the dialogues of the original version'.[2] And there are several reasons for this. First of all, our reading speed is considerably slower than our hearing speed. That is why subtitles cannot always contain exactly the same information as oral dialogues. In addition, we must bear in mind the related point that when dealing with subtitles we are in an audiovisual context, which entails that the translation of linguistic elements must be adjusted to both sound and image. This refers to the concept of synchrony, originally introduced by Istvan Fodor, and developed later by other authors such as Rosa Agost or Frederic Chaume.[3] According to this feature of audiovisual texts, what is written in the subtitles must be adapted to the length of the oral rendition, so that both speech acts, the original one (oral) and the translated one (written), reach the audience at the same time. This is one of the conventions mentioned also by Roberto Mayoral[4] as one of the main features of the translation of audiovisual texts. Finally, we must mention some technical aspects. Depending on the screen size, there are limitations to the number of characters that a line may contain, ranging from 32 to 40.

All of these factors are responsible for the two main strategies used when translating for subtitles: condensation and elimination.[5] The first one refers to the need to paraphrase and reduce the length of the written words that appear in the subtitles in order to comply with the maximum number of characters

2 The translation is mine. The original reads: 'los subtítulos no son, ni pueden ser, una traducción completa y detallada de los diálogos de la versión original'. Jorge Díaz Cintas, *Teoría y práctica de la subtitulación, inglés-español* (London, 2003), p. 201. **3** Istvan Fodor, *Film dubbing: phonetic, semiotic, esthetic and psychological aspects* (Hamburg, 1976); Rosa Agost, *Traducción y doblaje: palabras, voces e imágenes* (Barcelona, 1999), Frederic Chaume Varela, *Cine y traducción* (Madrid, 2004). **4** Roberto Mayoral, 'Nuevas perspectivas para la traducción audiovisual', *Sendebar*, 13 (2002), 123–40. **5** Díaz Cintas, pp 201–14.

allowed by synchrony. The use of shorter synonyms, and of deixis, is highly recommended wherever necessary. The second strategy is related to the need to eliminate parts of the original dialogue when even condensation fails to adapt the text sufficiently to the time and space limits imposed by the audiovisual context. In this case, the grammatical elements affected are mainly repetitions, redundant elements, information shown in the images and proper nouns. Mayoral provides a list that also includes perfect tenses, explanations, emphatic structures, and so on.[6]

This is the context in which subtitling documentaries must be approached. These strategies or recommendations are usually presented as applying to all audiovisual products, regardless of the specific nature and content of the programme. It is clear, however, that the main category of programmes taken into account when formulating these strategies is the mainstream feature film. There is a need for empirical research on other audiovisual products, such as documentaries, in which scientific and technical contents are highly relevant; where the relationship between images and words is different; and the aim is not so much to entertain, but to instruct the audience. The purpose of the research would be to check whether the same recommendations and strategies are used, or might be used. And this is what I shall try to do in the following sections, which consider in some detail the problems involved in translating the documentary *Crude*, and the strategies adopted.

PROBLEMS

The first problem I faced when I accepted the work was that no special subtitling software was provided; nor was there a spotting list.[7] Subtitling software is the tool used by translators to create appropriate and synchronized subtitles and can be seen as an absolute necessity nowadays if one is to do the subtitling properly. But even more important is the spotting list, in which the original dialogue is divided into units, so that each unit corresponds to a subtitle with its own time code. This is the only way the subtitling software can work, once the system recognizes the extension and duration of each single subtitle, including the time code. I received time codes referring to the images in each particular

6 Roberto Mayoral, 'Procedimientos que persiguen la reducción o expansión del texto en la traducción', *Sendebar*, 14 (2003), 107–25 at 112–13. **7** Among the main elements of spotting lists we find: subtitle number for cross-referencing; duration, that is, total number of feet-and-frames the subtitle is on the screen; who-to-who notation of who is speaking. For a detailed list see 'Scripts and lists', *Cynetip Hollywood*, www.cinetyp/scripts/html, accessed 28 Feb. 2012.

scene, but not to the dialogues. I was given to understand that I just had to deliver the translation and then someone else would do the spotting and all the technical work in order to create each subtitle. Unfortunately this situation is more common than one might wish when the audiovisual product is not to be released in cinemas, and the budget is limited.

This is a problem because the translation given for each subtitle depends on the number of seconds into which each part of the sentence or the paragraph is divided; so if one does not know exactly what period every subtitle is meant to occupy it becomes very difficult to decide how many characters every sentence or paragraph should be allocated. In these circumstances one can only give an approximate translation, but can never be sure that it will respect the so-called 6 second rule. This rule refers to the fact that a subtitle may remain on screen for a maximum of 6 seconds and may contain a maximum of 32/40 characters, depending on the setting (cinema, DVD, TV, etc.). According to this premise, there is a system to calculate the maximum number of characters for each subunit of 6 seconds. The subtitling software relies on this system to calculate the number of characters that each subtitle must contain, depending on the length of time for which the original dialogue is heard. What I did was to try to reduce my text as much as possible, especially in those fragments where I could hear the characters speaking more quickly. But even then, I had problems in reading some of my subtitles quickly enough, although I knew them almost by heart.

A second problem is the mixture of spontaneous dialogue and narration. In entertainment films, 99 per cent of the text to be translated is normally represented by dialogues between the characters. However, in documentaries there is always a narrator who gives the main information, and other speakers, normally specialists in the field, who give their opinion and complete the analysis or the case study presented in the documentary. Thus, we have two different types of texts with different features to be taken into account. While the spontaneous dialogue of the specialists is similar to oral language, the narrator's interventions tend to reflect written style (longer sentences, subordinate clauses, and so on).

In relation to the difference just described, a third aspect that could be seen as problematic is the difference in speech rhythm between the narrator's contributions and those of the specialists. Among the latter, speech rhythms tend to be even quicker than those found in film dialogues, as they are not reciting a written text that tries to reproduce the features of oral language, but are really talking spontaneously, and sometimes very rapidly. As a result, the translation strategy applied to these two different types of text cannot be the same.

The fourth feature I identified as a potential translation problem is the mixture of language levels. In this documentary we find sentences including words and expressions that belong to a very familiar register – for example 'stuff', 'pretty much', 'the whole thing' – together with specific chemical, biological or geological terms such as 'anticlines', 'cap rocks', 'carbon dioxide', 'reservoir rocks', 'bottom hole pressure gauge', 'anoxic oceanic events', 'hydrogene sulphide', 'euxinic', 'mesocosm', 'sulphur bacteria' among others.

A further difficulty was the presence of a certain degree of irony in the narrator's voice-overs. As humour is well known to be difficult to translate, the transfer of ironic elements inevitably posed additional challenges. In some cases, the translation was easy, but in others it was harder to find an appropriate solution:

> Example 1:
> V.O.: As a means of capturing solar energy and storing it for later use, photosynthesis is brilliant.
> V.S. Para capturar la energía solar y guardarla para el futuro, la fotosíntesis es brillante.
>
> Example 2:
> V.O.: The waters here have a bit of a nutrient problem, courtesy of the Mississippi river.
> V.S.: Las aguas tienen un pequeño problema de nutrientes, cortesía del río Missisipi.
>
> Example 3:
> V.O.: The sludgy remains of tiny, brainless plants waiting to hold dramatic sway on the future of the most intelligent life form the planet has ever seen [...]
> V.S.: Los restos fangosos de unas minúsculas plantas sin cerebro que arrasarían el futuro de la forma de vida más inteligente que el planeta ha conocido [...]

The word 'brainless' referred both to the fact that, as microorganisms, these plants are too small to have a brain, and also to the idea that they are not intelligent, they are stupid, especially compared to humans.

As a final translation issue I would like to mention the presence of specialized terminology, which cannot be avoided in the translation process. While other parts of the sentences might be transformed or manipulated, even eliminated if necessary, verbs and specially nouns which refer to specific concepts and notions must be kept in translation and this sometimes represents a problem. First of all because the terminological density of some paragraphs is remarkable; and also because in the linguistic combination we are dealing with, the length of words is much greater in one of the two languages (in Spanish). For example, oil rig = plataforma petrolífera.

STRATEGY AND SOLUTIONS

The general strategy I adopted to address the translation problems mentioned above was to adapt the length of every sentence to the differences in speech rhythm heard in the original version. Considering the general need for minimizing many of the sentences, this reduction should be particularly noticeable in the specialists who appeared on screen being interviewed, and especially, in those who spoke more quickly.

Nevertheless, in the narrative passages, I tried to keep almost everything, wherever I could. It was easier to do so in this part of the text because there were no oral language features, such as repetition of words, grammar mistakes, introduction structures without a real semantic meaning, and so on. In addition to that, in many instances, images go together with dialogue, rendering translation easier in those cases where some part of the text would have to be sacrificed in order to respect the subtitle length.

As far as solutions are concerned, I will divide this section into 'Condensation' and 'Elimination', according to the general strategies mentioned earlier. Each of these subdivisions contains different categories that I will review briefly by giving some examples. Most of them belong to the spontaneous oral utterances of specialists who talk about the specific matter dealt with, but some other examples are drawn from the narrative passages.

CONDENSATION

Use of shorter impersonal structures (gerund, impersonal 'se' and 'al' + infinitive)

Example 1:
V.O.: And <u>if you consider</u> all categories of oil […]
V.S.: <u>*Considerando*</u> *todos los tipos de petróleo* […]

Example 2:
V.O.: […] but en-masse, <u>you can see</u> them from space.
V.S.: […] *pero juntas* <u>*se ven*</u> *desde el espacio.*

Example 3:
V.O.: […] if <u>you cracked it open.</u>
V.S.: […] <u>*al partirlo*</u>.

Different structures with nouns into verbs

Example 1:
V.O.: [...] even the mighty Ghawar oil field is showing its age.
V.S.: [...] *incluso el enorme campo de Ghawar envejece.*

Example 2:
V.O.: With both faltering currents and overfertilised surface waters, the stage was set to push large areas of the ocean [...]
V.S.: *Las corrientes vacilantes y las aguas superficiales [...] causaron en amplias zonas del océano [...]*

Different structures with adjectives into verbs

Example 1:
V.O.: Pennsylvania was literally the leading oil producing area [...]
V.S.: *Pensilvania lideraba las áreas productoras de petróleo [...]*

Example 2:
V.O.: [...] both of the things they find essential are available.
V.S.: [...] *encuentran las dos cosas que necesitan.*

Shorter forms of verbs (continuous tense changed into simple tense, perfect tense into simple tense, passive voice into active voice, periphrasis into a single verb)

Example 1:
V.O.: We're using it up in the blink of an eye.
V.S.: *Lo gastamos en un plis plas.*

Example 2:
V.O.: But somebody, somewhere has just released our carbon atom back to the atmosphere.
V.S.: *Pero alguien, en algún lugar, devolvió nuestro átomo a la atmósfera.*

Example 3:
V.O.: The answer can be found [...]
V.S.: *Podemos hallar la respuesta* [...]

Example 4:
V.O.: We would like to be able to conclude that [...]
V.S.: *Nos gustaría afirmar que* [...]

Sentence into a noun or adjective

Example 1:
V.O.: Back then locating oil reservoirs was much easier than explaining where the precious liquid hydrocarbons had come from.
V.S.: *Localizar las reservas de petróleo era más fácil que explicar el origen de los preciosos hidrocarburos líquidos.*

Example 2:
V.O.: [...] in the ancient plants and their descendants still found growing today.
V.S.: [...] *en las antiguas plantas y sus actuales descendientes.*

Use of figures and symbols

Example 1:
V.O.: [...] which means it is now putting out something like 50 to 60 cubic kilometres of ice a year [...]
V.S.: *[...] perdiendo 50 o 60 Km² de hielo al año* [...]

Example 2:
V.O.: The more carbon dioxide in the air, the fewer pores the leaves need.
V.S.: *Cuanto más CO_2 hay en el aire, menos poros necesitan.*

ELIMINATION

Presentation or introduction structures

Example 1:
V.O.: You know, I mean, that's incredible to me how fast we've done it and how long it took to make this stuff.
V.S. *Es increíble lo rápido que se gasta y el tiempo que tardó en formarse.*

Example 2:
V.O.: I think it's one of the most important elements in modern society and civilization.
V.S.: *Es uno de los materiales más importantes en la civilización moderna.*

Repetitions

Example 1:
V.O.: Everything came together in August of 1859. There was the refining process. There was the lamp that could burn kerosene without

giving off too much smoke. There was the financiers in New York and Connecticut that had the land and the money. And there was Edwin Drake who was a retired railroad conductor who was in poor health who needed a job.
V.S.: *Todo se juntó en agosto de 1859. El proceso de refinado, la lámpara para quemar queroseno sin demasiado humo, los financieros de Nueva York y Connecticut que poseían la tierra y el dinero. Y Edwin Drake, un ex-conductor de trenes mal de salud y que necesitaba dinero.*

Emphatic structures

Example 1:
V.O.: It is crude that underpins the growth that keeps our economies solvent.
V.S.: *El crudo mantiene nuestras economías solventes.*

Example 2:
V.O.: What we know for sure is that we're doing something […]
V.S.: *Sabemos que estamos haciendo algo […]*

Cushion words

Example 1:
V.O.: […] we kind of forgot about all that other stuff.
V.S.: *[…] olvidamos lo demás.*

Adverbs and adjectives

Emphatic value

Example 1:
V.O.: Basically, oil is formed from living material, from tiny microscopic in fact plants that proliferate in the surface of the oceans.
V.S: *Básicamente el petróleo está formado por material vivo, por plantas microscópicas de la superficie de los océanos.* (Spontaneous dialogue)

Example 2:
V.O.: They are definitely the beginning of the oil history.
V.S.: *Son el principio de la historia del petróleo.* (Spontaneous dialogue)

Example 3:
V.O. Plus, of course, the unfolding effects of global warming.
V.S.: *Además de los efectos del calentamiento global.*

Information given by the image

Example 4:
V.O.: Here at Kimmeridge Bay, in Dorset, we have the so-called Kimmeridge clay.
V.S.: *En la bahía de Kimmeridge, en Dorset, tenemos la arcilla de Kimmeridge.*

Example 5:
V.O.: What happened next in this quiet green valley in Pennsylvania changed the world forever.
V.S.: *Lo que pasó después en este valle de Pensilvania cambió el mundo para siempre.*

Information deduced by context

Example 6:
V.O.: Our carbon dioxide molecule is transformed into an energy-rich sugar via the flash of a prehistoric sunbeam.
V.S.: *Nuestra molécula se transforma en un azúcar rico en energía a través de los destellos de los rayos de sol.*

Example 7:
V.O.: [...] we enter what local fishermen have dubbed 'the dead zone'.
V.S.: [...] *entramos en lo que los pescadores llaman 'la zona muerta'.*

Superfluous information

Example 8:
V.O.: Imagine for a moment a gigantic building full of oil. It's enormous.
V.S.: *Imagine un momento un edificio giganteso lleno de petróleo.*

Example 9:
V.O.: [...] we were getting completely addicted.
V.S.: *[...] nos estábamos volviendo adictos.*

Linking words (deduced by context)

Example 1:
V.O.: Then those deep waters will become anoxic.
V.S.: *Esas aguas profundas se volverán anóxicas.*

Example 2:
V.O.: So the first big thing was to modify it.
V.S.: *Lo primero era modificarla.*

Example 3:
V.O.: <u>Now</u> if you compare one of these modern leaves [...]
V.S.: *Si compara una de estas hojas modernas [...]*

Example 4:
V.O.: <u>But</u> at around 20 metres [...]
V.S.: *A los 20 metros [...]*

CONCLUSIONS

Before commenting on the findings, it must be admitted that our corpus is limited to a single example, so what follows cannot claim to be categorical.

The overall conclusion I have reached is that, from a translator's standpoint, there are similarities and differences between feature film dialogues and documentary dialogues. Among the similarities, the grammatical elements affected by transformation or elimination are the same in both cases, and the same as listed by Mayoral:[8] perfect tenses, explanations, emphatic structures, repetitions, and so on. In relation to this first idea, the presence of oral language in the dialogues found in documentaries, as well as those found in feature films, is responsible for the similarity. That is why the same elements can be systematically condensed or eliminated in both cases.

The differences, however, may be more interesting. The first one I would underline is the presence of written language, even if presented as oral language: somebody – the narrator – is pronouncing the sentences that the audience hears. The language register, the grammar and the structure of the different clauses reveal the patterns of written language, something that is systematically avoided in fictional film dialogues.

A second notable difference is the presence of real spontaneous oral language, which may render the translation process more difficult. According to Chaume, in ordinary film dialogues the language used by actors is not really spontaneous, although it seems so.[9] It is written to be performed as if it were oral, but it really is not. Also, the rhythm has to be appropriate, so that the audience can follow the conversations easily. In the case we have analysed, we can say that the people we see on screen are really talking, considering the words they use and the structure of the sentences they make. Many elements suggest that their language is really spontaneous. When people talk, especially about something of which they have a deep understanding, they tend to speak very

8 Mayoral, 'Procedimientos'. **9** Chaume, *Cine y traducción*, p. 168.

quickly, as happens in this documentary. In such cases, the translator is forced to be especially careful with the condensation or elimination of information.

A third difference worth mentioning is the possibility of using symbols and figures. While in ordinary film dialogues, translators are strongly advised against the use of symbols,[10] in this case, their presence is arguably justified at times because the audience of the documentary might be more familiar with special characters than the general public. This form of notation has to be handled carefully, but can be employed if necessary.

A fourth significant aspect is the terminological density of some sentences and paragraphs. Even in those cases where popular films or TV series display some degree of specialization, such as *ER, Grey's Anatomy* or *House*, just to cite a few in the field of medicine, the audience can generally understand enough to follow the plot. In the case we are analysing, some passages involve a density of technical or specialized meaning that exceeds the scientific knowledge that could be assumed among a general audience.

> Example 1: V.O.: Purple sulphur bacteria are photosynthetic, they need light but they also need hydrogen sulphide.

A fifth distinctive feature is the relationship of textual and visual elements within the documentary *Crude* – a relationship which needs to be considered as part of the translation process. While in film dialogues, the norm is not to transmit the same information by both images and words, we have had the opportunity to see that, in this case, the opposite applies. Most of the time, what the viewers are watching is exactly what they are being told by the narrator or by some of the specialists appearing on the screen.

A final reflection comes to mind when trying to find an answer to the question stated in the introduction: how can we offer the audience a 'right' translation despite all the transformations and eliminations involved? Four suggestions might be worth considering: (a) respecting terminology (nouns), especially in the narrator's interventions; (b) eliminating information that can be easily deduced from the images or from the context; (c) trying to omit oral language features only if necessary; (d) using symbols that might be easily understood by the target audience for this kind of audiovisual product.

10 Díaz Cintas, *Subtitulación*, p. 182.

Understanding fan-translation: pop culture and geeks too cool for translation schools?[1]

Minako O'Hagan

This article addresses fan-translation, a phenomenon particularly conspicuous in popular culture genres of Japanese origin such as anime and manga (that is, animation films and comics respectively) where fans engage in unsolicited translation. Their primary motivation is a desire to share what they think are good titles by making them accessible through translation to those who do not understand the source language. These activities were first motivated by both the over-editing applied in the early days of exported anime and also by a lack of official translation, with a large proportion of them remaining untranslated due to the sheer volume of anime and manga published in Japan. While these works were often mainly produced for the domestic market, the widespread fan-base that has developed outside Japan, especially for anime, has embraced fan-translation which often provides rapid access to the latest releases. The internet has further facilitated timely delivery of some of these materials with translations to fans and other internet users who have now come to expect faster availability of all kinds of information and content. Fan-translation of anime subtitles is known as fansubs whereas that of manga is called scanlation, a compound made up of 'scan' and 'translation' in reference to the key operations of scanning pages of comics and translating them. Although fan-translation was present in the pre-internet era it has become globally visible and widespread, particularly with more recent enhancements of internet technologies collectively known as Web 2.0, now on its way to Web 3.0. This can be thought of as a new communications infrastructure that harnesses 'participation, interactivity, collaborative learning, and social networking' of users.[2] All these characteristics were well suited to further promote fan-translation. For modern fan translators who procure source materials, collaborate on their translation and distribute their work online, the Internet has become the hub of their activities.

Focusing on fan translators as a new breed of practitioners who are increasingly empowered by such technological environments, this article challenges

1 The author wishes to acknowledge her inspiration which comes from the title of the article 'Gaming: too cool for school?' by Katie Dean which appeared in *Wired News*, 15 Jan. 2001. **2** T. Flew, *New media: an introduction* (Oxford, 2008), p. 17.

the traditional remit of translation studies. The phenomenon of fan-translation indeed calls into question the limited scope of the discipline with its focus on canonical texts[3] rather than 'less respectable' texts such as those emanating from popular culture genres and, similarly, the general tendency to ignore less mainstream practices such as translations performed by fans. That said, more recently there has been an increasing interest by translation scholars in translation as performed by those who fall outside the strictly professional group.[4] The topic of fan-translation further brings to attention the neglected dimension in translation studies of wider translation practices which are flourishing today in the new technological milieu. Furthermore this article considers the modern fan-translation phenomenon in light of the emerging model of 'translation crowdsourcing' whereby the Internet crowd carries out translation mostly on a voluntary basis, responding to an open call by the organizer. The new generation of the Internet led to the proliferation of so-called user-generated content as exemplified in YouTube and Wikipedia, providing a vehicle for user sharing and collaboration in a wholly new manner on a global scale. The resulting unprecedented encroachments by ordinary users into professional areas of activity have a significant implication for translation. Embedded in this inquiry into fan-translation are the wider questions of the rights or wrongs of translation by fans, and ethical and legal issues that underlie often unsolicited user-generated translations.

PRIOR WORK AND THE FOCUS OF THE PRESENT ARTICLE

Perhaps because of the perception of fandom as something marginal associated with a sub-culture, and thus not as a mainstream activity, fan-translation has long been neglected by translation scholars while attracting the attention of writers on cultural studies, particularly among those scholars with an interest in anime.[5] The connection of fan-translation to Japanese may have further hampered its study by translation scholars as Japanese translation phenomena remain little explored in translation studies, which have until relatively recently devel-

3 T. Hermans (ed.), *Translating others* (Manchester, 2006), p. 9. **4** See Sebnem Susam-Sarajeva & Luis Pérez-González (eds), 'Non-professionals translating and interpreting: participatory and engaged perspectives', *The Translator*, 18:2 (special issue, 2012). **5** E.g. see Sean Leonard, 'Progress against the law: anime and fandom, with the key to the globalization of culture', *International Journal of Cultural Studies*, 8:3 (2005), 281–305; Antonia Levi, 'The Americanization of anime and manga: negotiating popular culture' in Steven T. Brown (ed.), *Cinema anime* (New York, 2006), pp 43-63; Susan J. Napier, *Anime from* Akira *to* Princess Mononoke*: experiencing contemporary Japanese animation* (New York, 2000); Napier, *From impressionism to anime* (New York, 2007).

oped mainly from Western perspectives.[6] However, fan-translation is not confined to Japanese popular culture and there is now an increasing interest in fansubs especially in the context of audiovisual translation (AVT). For example, Jorge Díaz Cintas and Pablo Muñoz Sánchez[7] examined the approach and process taken by fansubbers, describing fansubs as a 'hybrid' form, diverting from standard subtitles with some similarities to subtitles for the deaf and hard of hearing (SDH) in terms of the use of colours and positioning of subtitles. They highlighted how fansubs are produced primarily for fans by fans on the basis of their own needs and illustrated their often inconsistent quality. A detailed description of fansub processes is also provided by Lewis Pérez González[8] who places fansubs as representing a unique form of media intervention within AVT and further linked them to the increasing empowerment of media consumers in the media landscape albeit outside strict legal remits.

An early contribution of particular relevance that called attention to fan-translation was an essay by the film studies scholar Abé Markus Nornes,[9] treating fansubs as 'abusive subtitles' in reference to an experimental translation strategy as explained below. In his appeal, aimed at the shortcomings of often too domesticating mainstream subtitles for Japanese films, Nornes sought inspiration from fansubs which freely break the norms of subtitles in an attempt to convey the authentic voice of the original. He links the motivation behind fansubs to the concept of 'abusive fidelity'. The latter was advocated by Philip Lewis[10] who argued against domesticating translation strategies where the translator succumbs to the 'use-values' in the target language at the expense of losing the kind of 'abuse' present in the source text. Dealing with these texts, Lewis encourages a translation strategy which is more experimental for the sake of conveying the edgy flavour of the original to the point of breaking the target language norms. In Nornes' view such an approach is embodied in subtitles produced by fans. The tendency of fansubs is often to defy norms by their placing of gloss or cultural notes, for example, in the middle of the screen, the use

6 Mona Baker & Gabriela Saldanha (eds), *Routledge encyclopedia of translation studies* (London, 2009), pp xx–xxii. Similarly Hermans brought to light in Western-centric translation studies what he calls 'translating others' by extending the Western-centric focus to non-Western contexts, stressing the 'radical difference' and 'the sheer variety' of translation phenomena. See Hermans, *Translating others,* p. 9. **7** Jorge Díaz Cintas & Pablo Muñoz Sánchez, 'Fansubs: audiovisual translation in amateur environment', *Journal of Special Translation*, 6 (2006), 37–52. **8** Lewis Pérez González, 'Fansubbing anime: insights into the "butterfly effect" of globalisation on audiovisual translation', *Perspectives*, 14:4 (2006), 260–77. **9** Abé Markus Nornes, 'For an abusive subtitling' in Lawrence Venuti (ed.), *The translation studies reader* (New York, 2004), pp 447–69. **10** E. Philip Lewis, 'The measure of translation effects' in Lawrence Venuti (ed.), *The translation studies reader* (London, 2000), pp 264–83.

of colours or leaving certain words untranslated. By comparison, mainstream subtitles, which Nornes calls 'corrupt subtitles' conform to the conventions and norms, and are seen as succumbing too readily to the constraints of time and space,[11] at the expense of the loss of 'abuse' which could be detectable in the original.[12] In this way, Nornes considers the fansub approach as legitimized and something innovative and courageous, rather than dismissing it as a dilettante gesture detrimental to the established quality standards.

Furthermore, with the advent of the internet technology promoting user-generated content and peer collaboration, the assumption that fansubs are an anomaly confined within a small group of fans and are likely to be short-lived, is increasingly being challenged.[13] With an apparent instinctive affinity between the anime fan and technology as observed over a decade ago[14] the fans seem to be leading the way, if by accident, through their own practices, and demonstrating how technology can harness translation activities. For example, a pilot study on fan-translation networks for scanlation[15] found merit in these networks in which translation practices are situated in an authentic environment, thus serving as a potentially effective translator learning and training environment in light of social constructivist framework.[16]

Prior works in translation studies[17] characterize fan-translation as translation performed by self-selected fan groups organically formed in the area of their following where their main reason for translating is to serve their own interest and that of the community of fellow fans. Whether projected in positive or negative light, the visibility of fan-translation is clearly on the rise in translation studies as evidenced in its inclusion in the second (2008) edition of Munday's widely referenced textbook *Introducing translation studies*. In making a brief reference to fansubs Munday identifies them as one of the new forms of translation that evolved as a result of a rapid development of technology. In his description, fansubs were 'originally used for the translation of mainly Japanese manga and anime cartoons and the practice has now proliferated thanks to the greater access to and afford-

11 Nornes, 'For an abusive subtitling', p. 447. Condensation is a key feature of subtitles which are expected to fit in the margin at the bottom of the screen so as not to mar the aesthetics of the film and also to be contained within the prescribed length calculated against the standard reading speed of the viewers. **12** Nornes, 'For an abusive subtitling', p. 447. **13** Pérez González, 'Fansubbing anime', 275. **14** As early as 1995 *Wired* magazine considered the anime fan community as the most wired of all fan subcultures (cited in Napier, *Anime from* Akira *to* Princess Mononoke, p. 16. **15** Minako O'Hagan, 'Fan-translation networks: an accidental translator training environment?' in John Kearns (ed.), *Translator and interpreter training: methods and debates* (London, 2008), pp 158–83. **16** See Don Kiraly, *A social constructivist approach to translator education: empowerment from theory to practice* (Manchester, 2000). **17** Díaz Cintas & Muñoz Sánchez, 'Fansubs', pp 37–52; O'Hagan, 'Fan-translation networks', pp 158–83; Pérez González, 'Fansubbing anime', 260–77.

ability of subtitling software'.[18] In this way, fan-translation has now appeared on the radar screen in translation studies as a new practice linked to changes in technological environments. It is in this wider technological context that we will next examine the significance of fan-translation practices.

TRANSLATION AND THE CONSEQUENCES OF WEB 2.0

Like many other professional practices, the field of translation has embraced the internet, which has become an indispensable part of the infrastructure for translators. Its impact has permeated the whole spectrum of translation practice from text transmission, translator-client communication and essential research tools to providing a distributed workflow mechanism. Furthermore the internet has enhanced existing forms of networks of various kinds in which professional translators have been involved. For example, Julie McDonough categorizes professional translation networks into: professional-oriented; practice-oriented; education-oriented and research-oriented according to the main purpose of interactions.[19] Professional translators circulate in and out of different types of networks and learn from others how best to perform their jobs. What has not always been made explicit and yet underlies these different networks are social networks, albeit not based on face-to-face encounters, which are beginning to have unprecedented consequences on different professional practices. For example, one of the most active social interactions on the internet, contributing to user-generated content, is by amateur photographers through 'social photography' sites such as Flickr.[20] They exchange tips and various peer feedback on their photography among fellow hobbyists, with some making their spare-time activities into business by selling their creations. It is such virtual social networking that is promoting peer collaboration and learning environments on a mass scale and blurring the boundary between the professional and the non-professional as manifest in fan-translation.

Wikipedia, YouTube, Facebook and a huge range of blogs represent successful applications of Web 2.0 promoting sharing and collaborating among peers. Each of these examples relies on contributions by users without which the whole concept ceases to exist. For example, YouTube is a collection of user-generated audiovisual material, including appropriated media material such

18 Jeremy Munday, *Introducing translation studies: theories and applications* (London, 2008), p. 190. **19** Julie McDonough, 'How do professionals organize themselves? An overview of translation networks', *Meta*, 52:4 (2007), 793–815. **20** Don Tapscott & Anthony Williams, *Wikinomics: how mass collaboration changes everything* (New York, 2006), p. 38.

as TV programmes, commercial films, etc., which is made open to free viewing with some contributions attracting mass-scale visits. Some audiovisual content such as YouTube may be subtitled by users to make it more widely available to speakers of different languages. An early best known example of mass collaboration by users is the online encyclopedia Wikipedia which solicits users to contribute to specialized entries using open source Wiki platforms allowing the users to overwrite a prior contribution for the purpose of continuously improving the existing material. Contrary to the general scepticism about the quality of Wikipedia, a comparative analysis conducted by the science journal *Nature* showed an interesting yet somewhat controversial result.[21] It randomly inspected 42 science entries from each of Wikipedia and *Encyclopedia Britannica* and found a small difference in quality between them, detecting 4 and 3 inaccuracies per entry respectively. But a significant difference was that the errors found in the former were quickly corrected, following the publication of the *Nature* article whereas *Britannica* errors remained stuck in print media. Wikipedia is also being translated by volunteer groups using the Wiki platform, turning it into a massive multilingual source of information. In this way, the internet-driven collaboration for Wikipedia has clearly challenged the area of work traditionally guarded by professional editors and lexicographers by leveraging the intelligence of the internet crowd.

In a similar way, non-professional translator networks have emerged leveraging platforms such as Wiki to facilitate collaboration between volunteers. Chief among them are those contributing to translation of open source software.[22] Youcef Bey et al. classify volunteer-based translation into so called 'mission-oriented' groups that mainly deal with technical documents, such as those associated with open source software, and 'subject-oriented' translators who may translate online messages and documents in particular topic areas, such as humanitarian causes which they support.[23] Fansub groups can be considered as 'mission-oriented' taskforces which set goals of their own to complete their translation by a set date when their work goes 'public'. Fan-translation can also be considered as 'subject-oriented', as practitioners only engage in areas of their

21 Jim Giles, 'Internet encyclopaedias go head to head', *Nature*, 438:531 (2005), 900–1. www.nature.com/news/2005/051212/full/438900a.html, accessed 5 Sept. 2009. **22** FLOSS Manuals (www.flossmanuals.net) founded in 2006 in the Netherlands is a leading example where volunteers contribute to creating free manuals and their translations for open source software applications. FLOSS stands for Free Libre Open Source Software. **23** Youcef Bey, Christian Boitet & Kyo Kageura, 'The TRANSBey prototype: An online collaborative Wikibased CAT environment for volunteer translators' in Elia Yuste Rodrigo (ed.), *Proceedings of the 3rd international workshop on language resources for translation work, research & training* (Paris, 2006), pp 49–54.

own interest, with such groups tending to specialize in certain sub-genres of anime, manga or video games. One common element between volunteer translators of open source software and fan translators is that both tend to be genre-experts even if that is by self-declaration. The original rationale for going outside professional translation with the need to translate open source software documentation was partly that professional translators lacked domain-knowledge, in this case on open source software, a view shared by Facebook[24] as discussed below. Similarly, the distinctive advantage of fansubbers and scanlators lies in their subject knowledge and often tenacity in carrying out translation, which comes from their fervent interest in, and thus devotion to a given genre. This is particularly conspicuous with fan-translation of video games by hardcore gamers who tend to have intricate knowledge of particular games as well as expert-like technical knowledge of game code and how complex localization can be performed without formal training.[25] Such expert domain knowledge may have earned them names like nerds or geeks, indicating their often extraordinarily intensive involvement in a given genre, not always seen in a positive light, but often resulting in their acquisition of a high level of knowledge. It is such in-depth knowledge that sometimes challenges the translation competence of professional translators whose work may be viewed extremely critically by certain of these fans.

Facilitated by the current technological environments on the Internet, and the widespread expectation of 'free' content and contributions, the modern era fan-translation is beginning to develop into something significant in terms of scale, to the extent that it could soon seriously impact on the professional practice of translation. In the area of video games the user contribution to modifying games, known as 'modding', is already being taken seriously by the game industry with some user creations leading to commercial production and also with user experience in modding regarded as a legitimate track-record when the game industry recruits new talent. Similarly, an official translation of anime may be commissioned from active fan translator groups who are known to produce high quality translation.[26] Relevant to this trend is the business plan announced

24 Kate Losse, 'Achieving quality in a crowd-sourced translation environment'. Keynote presentation at the *13th Localisation research conference localisation4all*, Marino Institute of Education, Dublin, 2–3 Oct. 2008. **25** See Pablo Muñoz Sánchez, 'Video game localization for fans by fans: the case of rom hacking', *The Journal of Internationalization and Localization*, 1:1 (2009), 168–85, www.lessius.eu/jial/, accessed 23 Sept. 2010; James Newman, *Playing with videogames* (New York, 2008), p. 158; Minako O'Hagan, 'Evolution of user-generated translation: fansubs, translation hacking and crowdsourcing', *The Journal of Internationalization and Localization*, 1:1 (2009), 94–121, www.lessius.eu/jial/, accessed 31 July 2011. **26** Colm Caffrey, 'Relevant abuse? Investigating the effects of an abusive subtitling procedure

by Digital Manga Publishing (DMP) to distribute legally some manga titles translated by scanlators who will be remunerated. According to Hikaru Sasahara, the CEO of DMP, the venture is motivated by 'the high up-front costs of licensing manga titles, coupled with long production time'.[27] Such a business will test how fan translation is able to cross the border to the professional arena with DMP seeking no less than quality work as Sasahara made clear: 'This is a real business and no longer a hobby or fun site so anyone who participates in it needs to be qualified'.[28] In order to appreciate this new breed of translators and their motivations an understanding of their sub-culture background and fandom seems crucial.

FAN-TRANSLATION OF ANIME AND MANGA

The study of fandom is neither a particularly new area of academic interest nor is it tied only to new technological environments, as is evident from earlier works by cultural and media studies scholars like Henry Jenkins[29] discussing media fandom triggered by popular TV series such as *Star Trek*. Borrowing Michel de Certeau's concept of 'textual poachers'[30] characterizing 'popular' reading of texts, Jenkins further developed it to explain how fans appropriate media text to their own liking by fragmenting and reassembling it to their own needs. For example, modern fan pursuits have manifested in such forms as *fanfic (fan fiction)*, where fans extend, embellish and publish a story of their own based on TV series, comics, films, video games, etc. Similarly, *cosplay* meaning costume play can be considered as another embodiment of fan engagement where fans create and don a costume to make themselves look like their favourite character from their chosen media, be it anime, comics or video games. Studies by Napier[31] on anime fandom suggest the development of a new type of spectatorship of 'committed media fan' who are deeply engaged in interaction with cultural objects. Jenkins' subsequent concept of 'participatory culture'[32] situates fan activities more explicitly in technological environments in the Internet era which further facilitate a deep media engagement by fans. Fan engagements such as fansubs exemplify passive spectatorship extended into specialized areas of professional activity such as translation.

on the perception of TV anime using eye tracker and questionnaire' (PhD, DCU, 2009). **27** See www.animenewsnetwork.co.uk/news/2010-06-17/dmp-ceo/new-venture -to-launch-1000+manga-online, accessed 14 Apr. 2012. **28** The interview with Hikaru Sasahara is available at www.ani.me/zine/manga/article/12/, accessed 14 Apr. 2012. **29** Henry Jenkins, *Textual poachers* (New York, 1992). **30** Michel de Certeau, *The practice of everyday life* (Berkeley, 1984), p. 174. **31** Napier, *Anime*, p. 242. **32** Henry Jenkins, *Fans, bloggers, and gamers: exploring participatory culture* (New York, 2006).

Compared with different kinds of volunteer translation that emerged more recently, anime fansubs have a longer history going back to the 1980s and closely related to the globalization of the genre. Anime have been distributed in the US and Europe on TV networks since the 1960s[33] and more recently released as feature films as well as on DVDs replacing VHS tapes. The TV networks remain the most common form of distribution of anime, typically airing popular anime series in dubbed form, targeting mainly young viewers. In spite of their often Japanese-specific culture-bound content, anime today has gained a worldwide popularity with a 60 per cent share of all animation titles broadcast on TV worldwide; the figure rises to 80 per cent in Europe.[34] However, according to more recent data,[35] contrary to the increasing recognition of Japanese anime internationally, the business, which draws its revenues mainly from licensing fees, has seen a downturn with such licensing revenues reduced from 20 billion Japanese yen (JPY) in 2006 to JPY 13 billion in 2010 in its largest market, the US, with the world market size estimated at around JPY 19.5 billion in 2010. While the world-wide economic recession and the rising yen are likely contributing factors to the reduced revenue, the increasing availability of anime on the Internet due to user-generated content, including fan translation, can hardly escape blame. We will return to this issue in the next section.

The fansub practice developed during the 1980s despite the lack of accessible audiovisual editing technology at the time to allow non-professional subtitling. Despite the technical and also the economic challenges of amateur subtitling, fansubs were originally prompted by the ruthless editing practices applied by Western TV networks,[36] where problematic approaches were adopted in the name of translation typically in the form of dubbing. Kusanagi chronicles how anime were extensively mutilated and transformed in order to erase their foreign origin in fear of alienating the target audience. Editing decisions taken by American TV network chiefs often resulted in drastic changes in storylines, names of characters and settings, as well as extensive cuts to shorten the length of the entire episode. Fans who became aware of this brutal treatment sought more 'authentic' text[37] and opted to produce their own translations, more faithful to the original.

33 The first Japanese TV anime to be launched in the US was 'The new adventure of Pinocchio', broadcast in 1960. See Satoshi Kusanagi, *アメリカで日本のアニメはどう見られてきたか? [How have Japanese anime been received in the USA?]* (Tokyo, 2003). Also see Tomoyuki Sugiyama, *Cool Japan: 世界が買いたがる日本 [Japan –the world keen to buy]* (Tokyo, 2006), p. 111. **34** Ichiya Nakamura and Megumi Onouchi (ed.), *日本のポップパワー [Japan's pop power]* (Tokyo, 2006), p. 30. **35** Humanmedia, www.humanmedia.co.jp/database/PDF/5-1.pdf, accessed 20 Sept. 2011. **36** Sean Leonard, 'Progress against the law', 281–305. **37** Laurie Cubbison, 'Anime fans, DVDs, and the authentic text', *The Velvet Light*

The lesser known practice of fan-translation of manga, known as scanlation, is a relatively new phenomenon.[38] The term scanlation refers to 'a streamlined manga fan-translation practice where officially published pages of manga are first scanned, setting off the subsequent electronic process'.[39] By comparison with anime, manga have so far been overshadowed by the former's international popularity, despite their primary position in the Japanese publishing industry within the domestic market in Japan. This is likely to be due to the domain-specific formats and conventions of manga, including the way panels are arranged, the prominent use of onomatopoeic expressions appearing as part of artwork as well as the page opening conventions specific to Japanese reading directions, and so on. They tended to present a higher barrier to the reader than anime does to their viewer especially when presented in dubbed form. These two popular culture genres are nevertheless closely linked as anime are mostly based on best-selling manga, although different motivations drove the fan translation for each genre. While anime typically suffered extensive editing in official translations because of the unfamiliarity at the time with this genre, and with the Japanese culture portrayed in anime, the practice of scanlation developed after anime became relatively well-known. This meant that the viewers were more exposed to aspects of Japanese culture, creating more informed markets to accept their related genre, manga, without the need for the same extent of editing. Such differences in external contexts explain why scanlation does not always display the same extent of 'abusive' tendencies as fansubs. For example, the case study[40] that compared a scanlator with a professional translator found that the former was more concerned with creating natural sounding translation rather than explicitly foreignized translation, defying the hallmark characteristics of fansubs. Also the motivation for scanlation is more strongly driven by the lack of official translation rather than as a reaction against over-editing in official translations.

While these fan-translation activities have been ongoing prior to the era of the internet, more recent widespread and enhanced Internet technologies have enabled greater online collaboration among fans across diverse geographical locations.[41] Fans themselves distinguish the post-internet fansub activities which

Trap, 56:1 (2005), 45–57. **38** Dirk Deppey, in 'Scanlation nation: amateur manga translators tell their stories', *The Comics Journal*, 269 (2005), suggests the emergence of scanlation to be in the late 1990s although Wikipedia credits the practice as starting after 2000; see www.tcj.com/269/n_scan.html, accessed 5 Sept., 2009; www.en.wikipedia.org/wiki/Scanlation, accessed 14 Apr. 2012. **39** O'Hagan, 'Fan-translation networks', p. 162. **40** Ibid. **41** Natalia Trykowska reports the active manga scanlation scene in Poland where scanlating manga starts with scanlations done in other languages rather than the original in Japanese due to the lack of a talent pool competent in Japanese. 'Manga scanlation in Poland', *Translation Ireland*, 18:1 (2009), 5–24.

wholly rely on digital technology by calling them 'digisubbing'.[42] The more recently formed scanlation in the Internet era has always utilized such environments from the scanning of the original manga pages and reworking of artwork to the re-distribution of translated manga in digital format.[43] While the official manga either in original or in translation are predominantly distributed and consumed in print scanlation adheres to electronic distribution. Fan-translation of anime is also extended to 'fandubs' where fans conduct dubbing of anime, sometimes also adding their own choice of sound track.[44] In this way, anime translation by fans in part merges with other fan activities such as music mashup and remixing where commercial music is further processed by amateur musicians and is also linked to creation of fanfic. Digisubs and scanlation in turn can be regarded as a form of user-generated content in so far as they are presented as 're-mediated' products by users adding a translation. Considerable technological savvy is part and parcel of these modern fan-translation activities as claimed by earlier studies mentioned above. This is especially applicable to the case of fan-translation known as 'romhacking' of video game localization by fans, which demands considerable technical knowledge and skills as well as tenacity to tackle a huge volume of structurally complex content.[45]

CHARACTERISTICS OF FAN-TRANSLATION PRODUCTION

A defining characteristic of the fan-translation production that distinguishes it from professional translation is the fact that the former is not financially rewarded and is an entirely self-driven exercise. Apart from these two aspects fan-translation environments parallel in many ways their professional counterparts in terms of work procedures driven by deadlines and often conducted in a team.[46] For example, fan-translators normally work in a pre-defined role and their translations are subject to review by editors before the final version is agreed on for public release. The most thorny issue surrounding fan-translation is that of legality.[47] An ironic aspect of this is the fact that the lenient, rather than hard-nosed, response by Japanese copyright holders in the early days inadvertently boosted the popularity and establishment of these genres outside of Japan.[48] Leonard argues that fansubs played a crucial role in fostering the initial demand formation when anime were a largely unknown quantity in the

42 Leonard, 'Progress against the law'. **43** O'Hagan, 'Fan-translation networks', p. 163. **44** What has come to be known as 'anime music videos' are a new art form created primarily by young adults by synchronizing anime with popular music tracks of their selection (Tapscott & Williams, *Wikinomics*), p. 53. **45** James Newman, *Playing with videogames* (New York, 2008), p. 158. **46** O'Hagan, 'Fan-translation networks'. **47** Leonard, 'Progress against the law'. **48** Ibid.

American market and elsewhere. Not dissimilar to anime, manga spread throughout the rest of the Asia from the late 1980s when 'many best-selling manga series were illegally copied and translated by foreign publishing companies based in East Asia'.[49] It was not until the late 1990s that manga publishers started to officially publish translated versions.[50] Regardless of the fact that in most cases fan-translation was condoned by Japanese copyright holders in the past and there may have been tacit agreements among fans to retrieve their translations once official versions are released, the practice breaches protected intellectual property where unsolicited translations are freely distributed in the public domain without any prior consent from the original copyright holders. More recently a focused aggressive action against scanlation was launched in 2010 by the major manga publisher coalition Japanese Digital Comic Association to crack down on 'growing and rampant' fan translation activities.[51] In particular they are targeting 'scanlation aggregator' websites that run as a business making a profit through advertising revenues using freely translated materials, thus contrary to the original spirit of some of the early fan translation groups.[52] In this light fan translation is no longer cast as innocent fan activity driven by their devotion, but as something sinister leading to illicit business opportunities. While there are undoubtedly still some innocent fans performing translation out of love, the new environments afforded by the Internet are highlighting the darker dimension of some of the user activities. This illustrates a grey area challenging the general development of user-generated content, which includes user-generated translation on copyrighted materials.

EMERGING MODEL OF CROWDSOURCING

With the rapidly developed concept of user-generated content and peer collaboration in the technological environment of Web 2.0, a new collaboration-based approach to translation sometimes called 'community translation' has emerged. It builds on the success of Wikipedia where variously qualified volunteer contributors continue to improve upon the encyclopedia entries whose quality is not far behind professionally produced counterparts as demonstrated

49 Sharon Kinsella, *Adult manga: culture and power in contemporary Japanese society* (Honolulu, 2000), p. 168. **50** It is noteworthy that the initial reason for Japanese manga publishers taking serious interest in offshore markets was partly to deal with piracy problems particularly in Asia. See Takashi Kubo, 'マンガはどこへ行く [Where are Manga heading?]', *The Tsukuru*, 39:5 (2005), 72–85. **51** Calvin Reid, 'Japanese, US manga publishers unite to fight scanlations' (2010). www.publishersweekly.com/pw/by-topic/digital/copyright/article/43437-japanese-u-s-manga-publishers-unite-to-fight-scanlations.html, accessed 24 Sept. 2011. **52** Leonard, 'Progress against the law'.

by the aforementioned random test conducted by *Nature*. These activities essentially trust and take advantage of the 'wisdom of the crowd'[53] where free contributions by self-selected volunteers can be trusted to head in the right direction. Such an approach is becoming a new distributed problem-solving mechanism by leveraging the Internet crowd whose advantage is its sheer number. This is now largely described as 'crowdsourcing', a term coined by the *Wired* magazine journalist Jeff Howe who defines the concept as: 'the act of taking a job traditionally performed by employees and outsourcing it to an undefined, generally large group of people in the form of an open call'.[54] Fan-translation can be considered to be an example of crowdsourcing in which an initiator usually calls for free contributions by self-selected volunteers on the internet. The most high-profile application of this model to translation to date is the case of Facebook that involved its users to help translate the social networking site into different language versions.[55]

Facebook developed a user-friendly technology platform[56] thus allowing any volunteers who are registered members to contribute translations relatively easily. For example, it allows 'inline translating' where the immediate context in which the translated sentence fits is shown and also prompts an available glossary so the already established terms are shown to the contributor to retain consistency in the use of terminology. In this manner Facebook has been localized into different language versions relatively rapidly, primarily by soliciting users' assistance.[57] According to Facebook,[58] one reason for deploying users as opposed to professional translators was because of the former's familiarity with the specific social networking environment of Facebook, which manifests in various site-specific concepts and terminology. Indeed translators without a certain level of familiarity with Facebook are likely to find it difficult to get the right 'feel' with their translations for certain Facebook-specific concepts. Furthermore one of the most interesting translation-related features of the Facebook translation

53 James Surowiecki, *The wisdom of crowds: why the many are smarter than the few* (London, 2004). **54** Jeff Howe, *Crowdsourcing: how the power of the crowd is driving the future of business* (London, 2008). **55** Losse, 'Achieving quality'. **56** Facebook's patent application entails embodiments of the invention which 'provide techniques for translating text in a social network' through its translation platform for crowdsourcing translation. The patent application was filed in Dec. 2008 with the US Patient & Trademark office and appears still pending at the time of writing in Sept. 2011. A full patent application is open to public for viewing: (www.appft.uspto.gov/natacgi/nph-Parser?Sect1=PTO2&Sect2=HI). **57** Following the launch of the technical platform 'Translations' to crowdsource translation, *Facebook*'s Spanish site was launched in Feb. 2008 and as of Aug. 2009 over 60 languages are covered. See Jason Kincaid, 'Faceboook wants to own idea of crowdsourced translations', www.techcrunch.com/2009/08/26/facebook-files-for-patent-on-crowdsourced-translations, accessed Sept. 2009. **58** Losse, 'Achieving quality'.

environment is its quality control mechanism that also leverages a crowdsourcing model. In order to determine the suitability of user-generated translation, or 'optimization of quality' according to Facebook,[59] it employs a user-voting system whereby asking the users which translation comes across better. Users are not only asked to vote on the quality of translations but may also contribute a better alternative. Furthermore volunteers who contributed the translations receiving the most votes are shown in the leader board. Their acknowledged status in the leader board also adds to the weight of their own votes when they cast votes assessing the quality of translations by other contributors.[60]

What has emerged from the early example of Facebook applying a crowdsourcing model to translation is that user-based translation works for them because of the alleged domain-specific knowledge by users about Facebook. Furthermore, the motivational factor seems sufficient for the volunteer translators to commit to the task based on their desire to build high quality localized Facebook sites for their own use as well as for the benefit of the whole community. The application of translator leader boards and the voting systems to determine the quality of translation appear to add to such motivational factors. Votes of confidence by other users indeed seem to boost the morale of even already enthused volunteers. The highly motivating effect of 'user assessment' by real potential readers of a particular text is acknowledged in translator training literature[61] if 'used at appropriate points in training and for well-chosen tasks'. The crowdsourcing model as applied by Facebook appears to have struck the right note. This also shows that the spirit behind such community translation is somewhat similar to what inspires fan translators of popular culture genres. The difference is that crowdsourcing is clear of copyright issues as it is the owner of intellectual property or a formally delegated party who is organizing a volunteer-based translation.

CONCLUSIONS

In the context of the technological evolution arising from internet-related applications, fan-translation, which is particularly prevalent in the popular culture genres of anime and manga, signals a significant new possibility and a challenge facing the profession of translation. Initially perceived and most likely dismissed as an isolated development within a small cluster of enthusiastic fans, fan-translation appears to be going from strength to strength, empowered by technological environments which privilege user contributions. In particular the more recent

59 Ibid. **60** Sophia Huang & Hiromi Nakajima, 'The advantages and challenges of crowdsourcing as a globalization strategy'. A presentation made at the *LISA Asia Forum*, Taipei, Taiwan, 6–9 Apr. (2009). **61** Dorothy Kelly, *A handbook for translator trainers: a guide to reflective practice* (Manchester, 2006), pp 143–4.

concept of crowdsourcing briefly introduced above is a further indicator that a collaborative translation model that solicits Internet crowds is likely to be extended to other types of translation. Given the strong and growing number of fans of different media genres increasingly empowered by new technological environments, this could indeed be seen as a serious threat to professional translators who make a living by being paid for their work. Even under the banner of assisting humanitarian causes, volunteer translators have not always been entirely welcomed by the professional community, which wishes to protect its painstakingly built profession over many years' of language learning and familiarization with different cultures. The main threat to the profession was once perceived as coming from machine translation (MT) but it is now human fan- and amateur-translators as well as the wider community of Internet users who happily volunteer to translate free of charge.

From the point of view of translation professionals, one of the key issues of crowdsourced translation especially leveraged by for-profit organizations is of an ethical nature, that is, the apparent exploitation of translators, whether qualified or not, as the business makes money based on such free donations of translations. This underlying suspicion by translators was manifested in the incident in 2009 with LinkedIn, which is a social networking site especially targeted for professionals. Its alleged user survey conducted in June 2009, asking its professional translator members about their willingness to 'translate free for fun' backfired.[62] This attempt at crowdsourcing translation through professional translators led to immediate angry reactions by the site's translator members. It also prompted an official letter of complaint[63] from the president of the American Translators' Association (ATA) which is the largest professional translator organization in North America. This incident only served to illustrate unease and volatility arising from the new concept of crowdsourcing of translation, legitimizing solicitation of professional skills as free contributions in the manner similar to free user-generated content. As such it signals deregulation of otherwise professional areas of practice. There are parallels with the open source software movement which caused serious friction with companies such as Microsoft who described the movement as a 'cancer' threatening the livelihood of those who rely on charging for software products.[64] So far their protest has not stopped the now widespread Free Libre Open Source Software (FLOSS)

62 Andrew Adam Newman, 'Translators wanted at LinkedIn. The pay? $0 an hour', *New York Times*, 28 June 2009, www.nytimes.com/2009/ 06/29/technology/start-ups/29linkedin.html?_r=1, accessed 21 Aug. 2009. **63** The letter by the ATA president Stejskal (2009) spelt out how 'crowdsourcing translation cannot work unless volunteers are competent [...] and companies lose face and money by relying on amateurs.' **64** David M. Berry, *Copy, rip, burn: the politics of copyleft and open source* (London, 2008).

movement and the open source software concept seems to be firmly here to stay and develop further. The FLOSS concept is taking root in the business community and companies such as IBM that supported the concept from its early stage are now beginning to reap the benefit through accumulated knowledge of 'community' formation and dealings with them.[65] If the professional translator group can take any lesson from the FLOSS developments, it is perhaps that in dynamically changing business and technological environments as faced by many professions today, an open attitude will help the profession to move forward. After all translators themselves are also beneficiaries of much freely available material on the internet which result from volunteer user contributions, be it encyclopaedia, book reviews or free software applications. Rather than simply barking at those who apply a new model which may go against the traditional one it will be far more productive for the professional translation community to keep an open mind and to try to understand why this new model is working in some areas and to explore a way to leverage the new technological environments which appear to be serving so successfully some of the new breed of translators, even if they are untrained in any formal sense.

As FLOSS is still grappling with legal issues surrounding the whole concept of open source, fan-translation also has an uphill battle to face before it can be considered a completely legitimate practice. The new venture by Digital Manga Publishing of turning scanlators into professional translators will be observed with great interest. The concept of Creative Commons launched in 2002 by Laurence Lessig[66] allows others to make derivative work while protecting the creator's copyright ownership, but this has yet to be ironed out to fully embrace the full implications of user-generated translation in the digital era. The fan-translation phenomenon is a timely reminder to both the discipline of translation in academia and the profession that narrow mindedness and protectionist attitudes allowing only for established ways are more likely to lead to the demise of the profession by blocking an understanding of the wider contexts that are unfolding. Translators need to be aware that they too are part of the Internet crowd and they too have inadvertently contributed to the emergence and the success of the whole new 'open' and 'free' global digital culture spawned on the Internet by merely being users themselves of free content. Understanding fan-translation will help translators and translation scholars gain insight into how to lead and develop the translation profession and research into a successful next phase. There are many thorny issues ahead, of a legal and ethical nature, which could provide a fertile field of research for translation studies scholars.

65 Berry, ibid. **66** See 'Creative commons' in www.en.wikipedia.org/wiki/ Creative_ Commons, accessed 3 Mar. 2012.

The knowledgeable audience as critic: an empirical study of folk perceptions of good and bad translations in subtitles

Annjo K. Greenall

INTRODUCTION

Film and TV audiences around the world may seem to be spending rather sizeable portions of their spare time criticizing translations in general, and subtitles in particular (the latter obviously lending themselves especially well to this kind of activity, due to the simultaneous availability of the source and target languages). This kind of informal criticism takes place in multiple arenas; face-to-face over a coffee or a beer, in blogs or other kinds of website devoted to the phenomenon,[1] in newspaper articles[2] or even in books.[3]

The kind of criticism we are talking about in no way, of course, involves a justly proportioned offering of negative and positive opinions. On the contrary, this kind of activity aims straight at where it hurts the most. The most ridiculous errors are systematically hunted down for the purpose of (maliciously) displaying them to the world. Some of these errors become classics; the following constitute a small collection of English-Norwegian subtitle howlers presented in a Norwegian blog[4] (all back translations and glosses are in square brackets):

(a) This is your father's light sabre (*Dette er din fars lette sabel* [This is your father's light (not heavy) sabre]) (*Star Wars*)
(b) When did you get this bike? It is not a bike, it's a chopper (*Det er ikke en sykkel, det er et helikopter* [It's not a bike, it's a helicopter]) (Pulp Fiction)
(c) Mommy, I want a mullet (*Mamma, jeg vil ha en multe* [Mummy, I want a cloudberry]) (*Family Guy*)

Obviously, this kind of activity – 'spotting and displaying' – has its roots in a critical attitude, but it could nevertheless be said that criticism in and of itself is not its primary function. For example, the incongruities created by such mis-

1 E.g., www.titlevision.dk/boeuf.htm, accessed 14 July 2009. 2 E.g., www.nrk.no/underholdning/1.2322, accessed 14 July 2009. 3 E.g., Charlie Croker, *Screwed up English* (2008). 4 www.espeniversen.com/?p=1409, accessed 14 July 2009.

translations generate no small amount of humour, and translation and subtitling errors could in fact be said to constitute an entire sub-genre of humorous texts (one might, for that reason, dub the whole activity 'criticism for entertainment'). A second, more tacit function of critical activity in general, and of this type of critical activity in particular, is to draw attention to the critics' knowledge and competence. And the kinds of knowledge and competence that folk criticism of subtitles is possibly intended to draw attention to, are the critics' own knowledge of the source language, and also, possibly, his or her media-savviness.

The incentive for this study was nevertheless folk criticism of subtitles *as* criticism. What exactly is it that people criticize? In (a)–(c) above, the subtitles contain breaches of a possibly very central folk perception, namely, *Thou shalt translate the meanings of words correctly!* The question is, however, whether this is the only *expectancy norm*[5] that subtitle audiences will display a sensitivity to in a given context. What, if any, additional expectancy norms do they abide by? In order to find an answer to this question, I set up an experimental situation intended to more or less mimic the situation inherent in 'criticism for entertainment', but with the aim of eliciting a set of more varied data. I did this by having a group of Norwegian respondents watch the Alan Parker film *The Commitments* (1991) with Norwegian subtitles, and asking them to evaluate transcripts of dialogue extracts and their subtitles afterwards. I then used their criticisms to identify a broader set of expectancy norms, looking in particular at which norms seem to apply in relation to the subtitling of swearing. Finally, I looked at the identified norms in connection with the two mentioned areas of supposed competence, knowledge of English and media savviness, asking the questions, to what extent are the respondents' competence in English reflected in their expectations of what subtitles should be like, and how much do they seem to know about subtitling?

PREVIOUS RESEARCH ON SUBTITLE RECEPTION

Not much research has been done in this field, a fact lamented by several researchers within translation studies.[6] The only issues that seem to have been

5 Andrew Chesterman, 'From "is" to "ought": laws, norms and strategies in translation studies', *Target*, 5:1 (1993), 1–20 at 9–11; and Andrew Chesterman, *Memes of translation: the spread of ideas in translation theory* (Amsterdam, 1997), pp 64–7. **6** E.g. Irena Kovacic, 'Reception of subtitles: the non-existent ideal viewer' in Yves Gambier, *Audiovisual communication and language transfers* (Strasbourg, 1995), pp 376–83; and Yves Gambier, 'Screen transadaptation: perception and reception', *The Translator*, 9 (2003), 171–89.

given any systematic attention are those of viewer's preferences for subtitles over dubbing or vice versa,[7] subtitle decoding,[8] and intralingual subtitling.[9] The only study with any direct relevance to the present one falls into the latter category; Gottlieb[10] studied viewers' reactions to subtitles for the deaf and hard-of-hearing; a large number of subjects were shown snippets of TV programmes and asked to press a so-called 'complaint button' when subtitles appeared which they thought were of bad quality. This method allowed Gottlieb to say something about what the respondents judged as bad subtitles; it did not, however, allow him to say much about why they thought the given subtitles were bad.

DESIGN AND AIMS OF THE STUDY

Constituting an initial attempt at establishing the viability of investigating the issue of expectancy norms among subtitle audiences by means of an elicitation-type methodology, the experiment was deliberately limited in scope. It was carried out on twelve Norwegian third and fourth-year students of English at the Norwegian University of Science and Technology (NTNU), most of them between 19 and 25 years of age, both male and female. Assumed proficiency for students of English at this point in their studies is B2/C1 (Common European Framework of Reference for Languages), although individual variation is to be expected. The subjects would all have had experience with translation as a tool for acquiring language proficiency at university, but would not have had any formal knowledge of translation (or subtitling) theory, since they were drafted as subjects just as they were about to embark on their Department's only course in translation studies.

The students were told, in very general terms, that they would be involved in judging the subtitles of a film. They were then invited to a film viewing; the film chosen for the experiment was Alan Parker's *The Commitments*, based on a novel by the Irish writer Roddy Doyle, depicting a group of Dublin youths getting together to form a soul band. This film was selected among other things

7 E.g., Olivier Goris, 'A la recherche de normes pour le doublage' (PhD thesis, Leuven 1991); Adrián Fuentes Luque, 'The reception of AV translated humour', *The Translator*, 9 (2003), 293–306; and Jun Tang, 'A cross-cultural perspective on production and reception of Disney's *Mulan* through its Chinese subtitles', *Journal of English Studies*, 12 (2008), 149–62. **8** E.g. Gery d'Ydewalle et al., 'Watching subtitled television', *Communication Research*, 18 (1991), 650–66. **9** E.g. Vera L. Santiago Araújo, 'Closed subtitling in Brazil' in P. Orero (ed.), *Topics in audiovisual translation* (2004), pp 199–212; and Jorge Díaz Cintas & Aline Remael (eds), *Audiovisual translation: subtitling* (Manchester, 2007). **10** Henrik Gottlieb, 'Establishing a framework for a typology of subtitle reading strategies: viewer reactions to deviations from subtitle standards' in Y. Gambier (ed.), *Audiovisual communication*, pp 389–409.

because of the relatively large amount of profane language in it, swearing being one of the aspects I particularly wanted to look at.

The film, with Norwegian subtitles, was shown to the group in its entirety. Beforehand, I had prepared a questionnaire which, in addition to instructions, contained a transcription of thirty-five consecutive dialogue segments and their Norwegian subtitles from a scene occurring relatively near the end of the film (a scene where the band members are arguing backstage because the manager had promised them that the soul legend Wilson Pickett would turn up at their gig, and then he never did). Before the viewing, I let the students know that they needed to pay particular attention to one particular scene, as the upcoming task would focus on it specifically. During the viewing, I alerted the subjects to the scene just before it started. After the film ended, I handed out the questionnaire and asked them to fill it in at home, and return it to me within two days.

The questionnaire asked them to underline examples of good and bad translation in the transcriptions (in blue and red ink, respectively), and – most importantly – to write down, in English or Norwegian (their choice), *why* they thought the selected elements were good or bad,[11] immediately below each dialogue segment (space was provided in the questionnaire for this). They were also instructed that there was no need to comment on all of the subtitles, only those that somehow struck them as particularly good or particularly bad. Finally, they were asked to contribute any general comments they might have on the overall quality of the subtitles; space for such general comments was provided at the end of the questionnaire.

One essential difference between a study such as that of Gottlieb[12] and the present one is, of course, that the former looks at responses to subtitles *in situ*: with full access to the entire audiovisual context, the members of the audience in Gottlieb's study are asked to display their impromptu reactions by pressing buttons. This kind of 'there-and-then' approach might, perhaps, by many, be considered the only acceptable way to study subtitle reception, since audiences, here, get to respond to the subtitles in their proper environment, among the visual and other auditory elements of the film. Placing a temporal barrier

11 The notions of 'good' and 'bad' were presented to the students as unanalysed wholes. This might obviously cause some concern considering all of the different definitional possibilities inherent in these notions. I was, however, worried about tainting their intuitions by providing detailed definitions, and providing examples of potentially good and bad subtitling would certainly have greatly limited the breadth of their contributions. What I needed was something to trigger a normative response, and 'good' and 'bad' turned out to do this job very well. And whatever the subjects felt I had 'meant' by 'good' and 'bad', or whatever they understood by 'good' and 'bad', was, moreover, reflected in the form of their responses, as anticipated. **12** Gottlieb, 'Establishing a framework', pp 389–409.

between the viewing of the film and the filling in of the questionnaire, as was done in this study, inevitably means that the significance of these other elements fades in the minds of the subjects. In addition, the dialogue – which in the film is an auditory element – appears in the questionnaire as a written text, together with the transcribed subtitles. These factors might possibly be seen to cause the subjects to relate to the subtitles less as subtitles, and more as 'ordinary' monosemiotic translation, something that might be seen to undermine the validity of a study such as this one. The view taken here, however, is that this way of looking at it narrows down the view of subtitles as something that only has a function within the transient moment, whereas the fact is that the life of a subtitle often continues well beyond this moment. Subtitles possess *durativity*. Films are watched over and over again. Videos and DVDs are paused. Samples of bad and quirky subtitles are collected and displayed on the internet for co-critics to savour at length. We may perhaps talk about the 'lingering phase' of subtitles. The representation of dialogue + subtitles in the questionnaire, then, merely adds another element to this lingering phase. Whether or not subtitles experienced at some distance from their immediate audiovisual context will seem more like ordinary translation to subjects is, of course, an issue that in and of itself merits scrutiny; the admittedly scant evidence available here suggests, as will be seen, that the subjects are quite aware that the 'decontextualized' subtitles they are presented with are precisely that, subtitles (and not ordinary translations).

When the target of the study is norms, it certainly pays to shift the attention from subjects' initial *reactions* (the object of Gottlieb's study), to a different and later phase in their reception processes, because the time lapse and the possibility for closer scrutiny quite simply give subjects better opportunity to consult their inner critic. It was my hope that by examining their submitted criticisms it would be possible to pinpoint a set of reasonably agreed-upon expectancy norms (for subtitles in their lingering phase). In contrast to so-called professional norms, which have – as their source – standard-setting actors within the translational *milieu*, expectancy norms[13] are generated by the interaction between translated texts and their audiences: '[expectancy norms] are established by the receivers of the translation, by their expectations of what a translation (of a given type) should be like, and what a native text (of a given type) in the target language should be like.'[14] Little if any empirical research has been done on the inventory and nature of these norms, thus the present study also makes a hopefully useful – albeit small – contribution in this direction, examining such norms

13 By 'general expectancy norms', I mean norms that apply across the board, not for any specific type of linguistic item, expression, or stretch of discourse. **14** Chesterman, 'From "is" to "ought"', 9.

as they apply in the context of subtitles in their lingering phase, and in the context of one particular type of audience, viz. young Norwegians.

INITIAL OBSERVATIONS

Using the method described above, I managed to collect 259 response tokens (that is, individual comments on a given dialogue-subtitle pair, henceforth 'responses'), distributed (unevenly) across the twelve participants. One initial observation was that the views on what constitutes good and bad translation in subtitles vary a lot. All thirty-five dialogue-subtitle pairs were commented on by at least three respondents, and almost all of the pairs received both a thumbs up and a thumbs down by different respondents, sometimes in terms of the same linguistic/translational aspect, other times in terms of different aspects. Secondly, not all responses were equally easily interpretable and/or easily relatable to norms. The following example and the two selected responses to it illustrate both of these phenomena:

(1)

Outspan: Jimmy! Is Wilson[15] back there?
S: Jimmy, er Wilson bak der? [Jimmy, is Wilson back there?]

Respondent 3: 'Perfect'

Respondent 5: '"Bak der" høres litt rart ut?' ['Back there' sounds a bit odd?]

Obviously, Respondent 3's comment is not sufficient to identify any norms. He or she has merely re-stated[16] that he or she think the translation is a good one, no reason why is given. Respondent 5, by contrast, thinks the translation is bad, and does give a reason why, but the formulation is quite vague and the response is phrased as a question which means that it is very difficult to tell which norm is referred to here.

THE FAITHFULNESS NORMS

The majority of the interpretable responses were, however, reasonably relatable to some norm or other:

(2)

Joey: I told you I spoke to the man. I did me best.

15 Wilson = Wilson Pickett. **16** The subtitle had also been underlined in blue ink.

> S: Jeg gjorde mitt beste [I did my best].
>
> Respondent 11: 'Her utelates også over halvparten av dialogen – ikke bra' [Here too half of the dialogue is left out – not good]

Here, the respondent is reacting negatively to the (rather commonplace) occurrence of condensation in subtitles.[17] The norm referred to in this example is, in the context of my material at least, the strongest one of all; it is the first of three *faithfulness norms* (see Table 1) identifiable on the basis of the elicited material. This is a set of norms that seem to speak to the first half of Chesterman's description of the 'generative engine' of expectancy norms (see *design and aims of the study* section), namely the audience's expectations of what a translation should be like.[18] The first of the three faithfulness norms is the completeness norm: *Subtitlers should translate all of the dialogue*,[19] and it is represented in 62 of the 259 responses. The strength of this response calls to mind Gottlieb's finding that even in the process of viewing, that is, even before having had the chance to properly consult their inner critic, 'viewers [...] react immediately when they believe they are being deprived of information'.[20] This might suggest that the completeness norm is indeed a strong norm, although it is important to bear in mind that evidence of norms and of their strength will probably always be a reflection of the material given to the respondents to evaluate. Different material displaying different translational problems and solutions might elicit other norms and other patterns of strength. All that I am purporting to prove here, is that *a* set of examples can elicit focus on *a* set of norms, such that one can begin to draw up an inventory of norms, and start looking into their nature.

Table 1. Faithfulness norms

Faithfulness norms		
The completeness norm (62 of 259 response tokens): *Subtitlers should translate all of the dialogue*	The closeness norm (33 of 259 response tokens): *Subtitlers should aim for as close a translation as possible*	The correctness norm (8 of 259 response tokens): *Subtitlers should translate the meaning of the dialogue correctly*

17 See H. Gottlieb, 'Subtitling' in Mona Baker (ed.), *Routledge encyclopedia of translation studies* (London, 1998), pp 244–8. **18** Chesterman, 'From "is" to "ought"', 9. **19** The tentative formulations of these norms are based on a synthesis of their various forms of expression in the respondents' comments. **20** Gottlieb, 'Establishing a framework', p. 398.

The second of the three faithfulness norms I have called the closeness norm: *Subtitlers should aim for as close a translation as possible.* Thirty-three responses carry formulations that suggest that this kind of norm is at work, for example:

> (3)
>
> Natalie: You don't need a new amp, Outspan
> S: Du trenger ikke ny forsterker, Outspan [You don't need a new amp, Outspan]
>
> Respondent 12: 'Good, simple and direct'
>
> Respondent 3: 'This translation is a direct translation, pretty much word-for-word and it gets the meaning across. The translator doesn't leave anything out'

Respondents who pinpoint this norm often employ descriptors such as 'direct' and 'word-for-word' in a positive context (that is, accompanied by blue underlining). Note that the closeness norm, for most respondents, is not a literalness norm; respondents only seem to accept word-for-word translations if they do not lead to unidiomatic Norwegian (although what counts as idiomatic/unidiomatic Norwegian is often a matter of debate among the respondents; see next section).

The correctness norm, which is identical to the one that I identified earlier as being the basic norm at work in 'criticism for entertainment' is not represented by very many responses in my material, only eight; this is probably because there are not very many strictly speaking incorrect translations in the transcribed excerpt. Still, one could argue that it is represented, in examples such as these:

> (4)
>
> Derek: It's not, Jimmy, is it? He will come, won't he?
> S: Han vil vel komme, Jimmy? [He will come, won't he Jimmy?]
>
> Respondent 12: 'Bad, completely wrong translation'

> (5)
>
> Bernie (to Imelda): You're probably fuckin' goin' with him, too!
> S: Du blir sikkert med ham også! [You will probably come along with him too!]

> Respondent 9: 'Her betyr vel "goin' with him" at ho har eit forhold til han, og det er ikkje det oversettinga seier' [Here, 'goin' with him' probably means that she is in a relationship with him, and this is not what the translation says]

The response to (4) cannot be seen as anything but a misunderstanding of the source text or the target text or both: something is certainly missing from the subtitles, but the translation cannot strictly speaking be said to be wrong. The response to (5), by contrast, contains a correct observation regarding incorrectness. What (4) illustrates, however, is that correct uptake is irrelevant to the task of determining which norm a given respondent is summoning, especially in cases like this, where the choice of words ('wrong') so unambiguously points towards a specific norm.

THE DOMESTICATION NORM

The final norm identifiable in my material is one that speaks to the second half of Chesterman's description of the sources of expectancy norms, namely audiences' expectations of 'what a native text (of a given type) in the target language should be like.'[21] The domestication norm – phraseable as *Subtitlers should translate into grammatical and idiomatic, contemporary Norwegian* – is the only norm that can compete with the completeness norm within the context of my material, in terms of numbers: it was alluded to in 44 of the 259 responses.

The responses that target this norm often make reference to Norwegian linguistic appropriateness, in terms of suggesting an alternative translation (one that is more idiomatic) and/or referring to a linguistic convention or grammatical rule:

> Response to (1):
>
> Respondent 4: 'Direct translation. Instead of "bak der" [back there], I think a better alternative is "hos dere/med dere [with you]"'
>
> Response to (3):
>
> Respondent 4: 'The noun "forsterker" should have an article in front of it'

In the first of these two examples the respondent proposes to replace a slightly clumsy formulation by a smoother, more idiomatic one. In placing the notion of 'direct translation' in a negative context (red underlining), Respondent 4 provides

21 Chesterman, 'From "is" to "ought"', 9.

a neat illustration of a point made earlier, regarding how word-for-word translations, which respondents normally see as praiseworthy, only seem to be accepted as long as they do not interfere with idiomatic quality in the target language (see above). The second of the responses above refers to a grammatical rule pertaining to article use – the respondent wants an article inserted in order to improve the Norwegian (whereas other respondents have not noticed anything untoward in (3); see above). As it happens, whether an article is inserted or not, the sentence is both grammatical and idiomatic, but there is perhaps a regional difference in the preference for one or the other that may explain the disagreement between the respondents. Whatever the explanation, it is certainly the case that this kind of ambiguity constitutes one possible reason for the great variety – and sometimes seemingly contradictory nature – of many of the responses given.

NORMS PERTAINING TO SWEARING

The members of the band (The Commitments) are all working class, speak Dublin Irish English, and swear a lot.[22] Only a portion of this swearing is represented in the subtitles.[23] This might be due to naturally occurring condensation: swearing (arguably) belongs to the category of pragmatic markers, members of which are typically seen by subtitlers as expendable.[24] It may also be due to the taboo of swearing that might mean that its representation in subtitles is additionally norm restricted (this facet might be strengthened by the fact that rude expressions are generally felt to be more acceptable in spoken than in written language).[25] In light of the completeness norm, the scantiness of the representation of swearing in the subtitles constitutes a potential tension area in the reception process. Thus, the responses to dialogue-subtitle pairs where at least the dialogue contains swearing (108 in all) were singled out for special scrutiny.

The first noteworthy point is that there seem to be specific swearing versions of all of the three faithfulness norms, although only the completeness norm (for swearing: *Subtitlers should translate all of the swearing in the source text*), reached a significant number. Referred to in 17 of the 108 responses, it is by far the most prevalent norm in the given selection. The following is an example:

22 See Annjo K. Greenall, 'Translating breaches of intersubjective constraints on interaction: the case of swearing in Roddy Doyle's novel *The Commitments*', *Meta*, 56:3 (2011), 336–55. **23** See Annjo K. Greenall, 'The non-translation of swearing in subtitling: loss of social implicature?' in A. Serban, A. Matamala & J-M. Lavaur (eds), *Audiovisual translation in close-up: practical and theoretical approaches* (Bern, 2011), pp 45–60. **24** See Basil Hatim & Ian Mason, 'Politeness in screen translation' in L. Venuti (ed.), *The translation studies reader* (London, 2000), p. 430. **25** Díaz Cintas & Remael, *Audiovisual translation*, p. 196.

(6)

Outspan: Thinks he's fuckin' Prince!
S: Tror han er Prince! [Thinks he's Prince]

Respondent 7: 'Rougher language'

This is a call for rougher language in a context where the swearing is not rendered at all in the subtitles. If it turns out that there is indeed a trend in the direction of a demand for more swearing in subtitles this is interesting for many reasons. *The Commitments* is a film from 1991, probably subtitled into Norwegian shortly afterwards. According to Jan Emil Tveit, Norwegian television has traditionally 'handled four-letter words with caution' because of what he describes as Norway's deeply-rooted 'puritan traditions',[26] and there is reason to believe that the same has been the case when it comes to film subtitling. At the present moment, Díaz Cintas and Remael observe some movement towards a greater inclusion of swearwords in subtitles, at least in Europe.[27] The results of the present study as regards the completeness norm for swearing might perhaps suggest that Norwegian audiences are now catching up with this trend.

The closeness norm and the correctness norm for swearing were not identifiable in very many of the responses (one and six, respectively). The first of the following three responses targets the former, the second and third the latter:

(7)

Imelda: What d'yeh mean 'Wilson'! You didn't know who the fuck Wilson Pickett was a month ago, you stupid fuckin' cow!

S: 'Wilson'! Du visste ikke hvem Wilson Pickett var for en måned siden, dust! [Back translation: 'Wilson'! You didn't know who Wilson Pickett was a month ago, idiot]

Respondent 5: 'Hva mener du med "Wilson"?! Du visste ikke [...] (Din jævla ku)' [What do you mean 'Wilson'?! You didn't know [...] (You devilish cow)]

Respondent 2: '"Fuckin' cow" and "dust" [idiot, silly person] don't correspond well. Okay, so both of them are insulting, but, in Norway, who over the age of 10 years old uses it?'

Respondent 6: 'Ikke sterkt nok uttrykk: Hva med "Din stygge ku!"' [Not a strong enough expression: What about "You ugly cow"!]

26 Jan Emil Tveit, *Translating for television: a handbook in screen translation* (Bergen, 2004), p. 112. **27** Díaz Cintas & Remael, *Audiovisual translation*, p. 197.

The closeness norm for swearing could be phrased as *Subtitlers should translate the swearing as closely as possible to the original.* The first of these three responses targets the closeness norm by way of suggesting an alternative, literal translation of the original. Note that this example may be seen to provide an exception to what I said earlier about how literal translations are only accepted insofar as they produce idiomatic Norwegian, since the direct transfer of 'you [...] fuckin' cow' creates a neologism in Norwegian (and every neologism is, strictly speaking, unidiomatic, at least until it has become established). However, the fact that most of the respondents are students of English in their early to mid-twenties might mean that English – their strongest foreign language and a ubiquitous presence in Norwegian society – and Norwegian language become occasionally hybridized in their minds so that (some) anglicisms will just slip by unnoticed. Alternatively, it may simply be the case that unidiomaticity in the form of grammatical 'incorrectness' (as in (3)) is more frowned upon than 'foreign-sounding' expressions that are, after all, grammatically correct.

The second of the responses targets the correctness norm for swearing, which, at least in the context of the present study, reflects a consideration of how *Subtitlers should translate the swearing to the correct level of strength.*[28] According to Respondent 2, the strength of the swearing expression has not been calibrated correctly in the Norwegian version. 'Dust' is seen as a weak swear word in Norwegian, one commonly used by children, and hence without the requisite impact. The third response targets this norm even more explicitly ('Not a strong enough expression'), and the suggested translational alternative to 'dust' ('Din stygge ku' [You ugly cow]) represents, like the response of Respondent 5, direct translation, arguably with a certain measure of domestication thrown in (insofar as 'jævla' is a swearword like 'fucking', while 'stygge' introduces a new semantic element which moves the expression closer to what we might consider idiomatic Norwegian).

The domestication norm, which, as we saw, was very strong in the material as a whole, is actually not very prevalent in the responses to dialogue-subtitle pairs containing swearing. Only three of the 108 responses were found to target the domestication norm for swearing: *Subtitlers should translate the swearing into idiomatic Norwegian.* Again, this may be due to incidental factors, such as, for example, a possible, general domesticating approach to the translations of most of the swearwords in the given sample. The following response targets this norm:

(8)

Mikah: Where the fuck is he, then?

28 See Greenall, 'Translating breaches'.

S: Hvor i helvete er han? [Back translation: Where the hell is he?]

Respondent 1: 'I find the translated version of "fuck" very good since it would not mean the same thing if it was translated into the Norwegian definition of the word'

Here, the respondent commends the translator for choosing the non-literal, idiomatic translation 'hell' instead of a more direct translation of 'fuck'. In English, the semantic domain of sexuality is the most common generator of swearwords, whereas in Norwegian, this role has traditionally been played by the domain of religion,[29] and hence most of our established swearwords come from that domain, although this situation may be changing. For example, 'fuck' is sometimes, nowadays, used in untranslated form in Norwegian, but this use is still not fully established. A direct translation of 'fuck' in the above example would probably have been recognizable as a swearword by a Norwegian audience, but it would nevertheless have constituted a very foreign element, and, as the respondent points out, it would not have 'meant' quite the same as the original (despite being denotatively equivalent to it).[30]

Interestingly, no response unambiguously targeted a norm addressing the taboo aspect of swearing (that is, *Subtitlers should not translate (much of) the swearing (since swearing constitutes bad language)*). Possible reasons for the lack of evidence for such a norm might be that the norm has basically lost its hold once and for all, at least for the kind of audience represented in this study.[31] Or alternatively, we could again be looking at patterns that are due to the makeup of the material. As I said earlier, far from all of the swearing was translated; if all of the swearing had been translated, this might have triggered the norm in question.

CONCLUDING REMARKS

At the outset I asked two questions related to the two competence areas implicitly claimed in people's involvement with entertainment criticism. I asked, to what extent is the respondents' (awareness of their) proficiency in English reflected in their expectations of what subtitles should be like? And, how much do they really know about subtitling?

As far as the first question is concerned, it is interesting to note that despite their background in English studies and the generally relatively high level of

29 See Tor Erik Jenstad, 'Banning' in M. Ljung (ed.), *Banning i norsk, svensk og 18 andre språk* (Oslo, 1987), pp 40–4. **30** Werner Koller, 'Equivalence in translation theory' in Andrew Chesterman (ed.), *Readings in translation theory* (Helsinki, 1989), pp 99–104 at p. 101. **31** Cf. Díaz Cintas & Remael, *Audiovisual translation*, pp 195–200.

proficiency of Norwegian speakers of English in this particular age group, the overwhelming majority of responses that reflect norms in this material, demand translation of more of the dialogue. This holds both across the board and when swearing is singled out. Elsewhere, I have argued that subtitlers into Norwegian could, in choosing not to translate some or a lot of the swearing, be seen to be allowing themselves to rely on the audience's proficiency in English, since such salient elements ought to be easily retrievable, for a proficient audience, from the audiovisual channel.[32] Hence it is quite surprising that none of the responses to the lack of swearing expressed any opinions to the effect that the swearing does not need to be translated because we can hear it and understand it as we watch the film. This fact might suggest any of a number of things: an actually insufficient proficiency (not likely), or a lack of trust in this proficiency; a lack of insight into subtitling and/or an understanding of how it works in unison with the visual and auditory tracks at the actual moment of viewing, or, alternatively, the potential lack of perceived relevance of such insight at the moment of carrying out the task, since the task, despite the advance film viewing, is (deliberately) relatively decontextualized.

As regards the possible lack of insight into or awareness of how subtitling functions at the moment of carrying out the task, I mentioned earlier that the respondents were asked to add general comments at the end of the questionnaire. This general-comment field allowed the respondents to take a bird's eye perspective on what they had done, and what emerged was that whereas very few of their item-by-item evaluations commented on the special form of translation that subtitling is, some of the *general* comments introduced this element if not explicitly, then at least implicitly:

> Respondent 11: 'Generelt sett vil alle som leser undertekstene på denne filmen få med seg hovedinnholdet av det som blir sagt, men noe som er gjennomgående er utelatelse av ting i konversasjonen som ikke er veldig viktige for å forstå sammenhengen. Dette kan jo gå bra, men den som ser filmen og bare kan norsk vil da ikke får den fulle forståelsen av den. Til tider er det likevel veldig god oversettelse synes jeg, med gode valg av fraser som egentlig kan være vanskelige å oversette til forståelig norsk.' [Generally, everyone who reads the subtitles of this film will get the gist of what is being said, but one thing that occurs over and over again is the omission of things in the conversation that are not important in order to

32 See Greenall, 'The non-translation of swearing', and Niels Brunse, 'Litterær oversættelse' in V.H. Pedersen & N. Krogh-Hansen (eds), *Oversættelseshåndbogen* (Copenhagen, 1994), pp 91–2.

understand how the plot hangs together. This could work well, but those who see the film and only know Norwegian will of course not get a full understanding of it. Still, sometimes the translation is very good, I think, with a good choice of phrases that really can be difficult to translate into understandable Norwegian]

Respondent 5: 'Generelt synes jeg at oversetteren har vært for "fri" i sine oversettelser. Det mangler litt banning, slang og vulgæriteter i oversettelsene. Jeg synes at man skal forholde seg til karakterene, som tydelig ikke var redde for å banne og slenge dritt. [Nytt avsnitt] Jeg kan se at lengre setninger har blitt noe forkortet. Dette kan selvfølgelig være en fordel når dialogen/samtalen går fort, samt for å spare plass i bildet.' [Generally I think that the translator has been too "free" in his/her translations. The translations lack swearing, slang and vulgarities. I think that one should take the characters as a point of departure, they were obviously not afraid of swearing and trash talking. [New paragraph] I notice that longer sentences have become somewhat abbreviated. This could of course be an advantage when the dialogue/conversation is fast, in addition to the fact that this saves space on the screen]

The second of these two examples, in particular, signals both a knowledge and an awareness of the nature and function of subtitles *in situ*, and an awareness of the difference between reflecting on the quality of something, on the one hand, and using subtitles as a support in the viewing situation, on the other. Thus, the durative versus the more instantaneous aspects and functions of subtitles are reflected in the dual nature of some of the material, with norms being obviously active and operative in the process of evaluation, but their governing import downplayed when respondents reflect on the overall function of subtitling. Furthermore, this dualism supports the methodological choice made in this study of trying to (somehow) replicate an arena for folk criticism, because it is, then, quite obvious that it is in this reflective phase that norms come into play most vigorously and most strongly, whether this phase occurs spontaneously, as in the case of folk criticism (or 'criticism for entertainment'), or whether it is prompted, like in the experiment presented in this paper. When retrospectively considering the function of subtitles at the moment of viewing, the subjects tend to be less harsh.

Judging translation: the use of anchor phenomena in plagiarism attribution in English–Spanish literary translations

Alberto Fuertes Puerta

This contribution sets out to explore the suitability of using data from descriptive studies on anchor phenomena (grammatical resources that appear to be cross-linguistically equivalent but in fact convey partially divergent meanings, for example, progressive forms in English and Spanish) for the detection of plagiarism between translations. Studies conducted in Spain show that contemporary Spanish translators have often resorted to previous translations of a given source text in English as a way of 'rendering' their texts. To date little has been published on the subject, although more and more attention is being paid to this phenomenon in the fields of translation studies and forensic linguistics. This growing interest is leading to the development of a number of tools which can help linguists determine whether or not a given translation has been produced as a result of plagiarism. This paper provides an outline of plagiarism detection in English-Spanish translations, and shows how identities in the choice of translation solutions for the rendering of cross-linguistically problematic areas can be used to illustrate evidence of plagiarism.

While there may be several reasons why translation could be put on trial, I focus on one issue: translation as infringement of the Spanish Intellectual Property Law. However, my concern here is not with the interests of the author of the source text but with those of translators. Since, as far as the Intellectual Property Law is concerned, translators are considered owners of the wording and syntax of their versions,[1] translations, just like authorial works, can be subject to theft. So, I deal with translation which results from a process of intralinguistic copying of a previous translation where the plagiarist credits the author of the source text but claims the linguistic authorship of the target text.

In Spain, scholars consider plagiarism to have been one of the most common strategies when translating literary texts from English into Spanish in the twentieth century.[2] Some interesting findings have been made within the

1 J.M. Rodríguez Tapia, 'Traduttore, traditore: plagio y originalidad de una traducción. Comentario a la sentencia del Tribunal Supremo (sala 1ª) de 29 de diciembre de 1993', *Revista general de derecho*, 604–5 (1995), 771–9 at 774. 2 J.C. Santoyo, 'El plagio en las tra-

field of Descriptive Translation Studies, plagiarism having been found to be a recurrent strategy in drama translation during the second half of the twentieth century.[3] However, none of the referred works go into the quality of the alleged plagiarisms in any depth; the authors simply make a statement based on their expert opinion and juxtapose the plagiarized text and the plagiarist's text to provide evidence to sustain their thesis. This has been the usual approach to plagiarism in literary translation, one that takes plagiarism for granted without further considerations or questions about its nature and/or peculiarities with respect to other types of plagiarism.

THE FORENSIC LINGUISTICS APPROACH

The first scholar to study the nature of plagiarism in literary translation was Professor María Teresa Turell in an article published in 2004.[4] Working in the field of forensic linguistics, Turell uses the case *Pujante v. Montalbán*[5] to exemplify her proposal for translation plagiarism detection. She proposes a linguistic analysis based on the use of both qualitative and quantitative evidence. While qualitative evidence focuses on the lack of originality of the wording and syntax of a given translation with respect to others, quantitative evidence accounts for the extent of the alleged plagiarism. These two types of evidence are essential for an expert witness to successfully sustain his or her thesis in a court of justice.

Turell's proposal for qualitative evidence is based on the idea of idiolect, which refers to the extension of lexicon stored in the brain of a given individual and the particular selection that this individual tends to make from that lexicon when he or she is to produce spoken or written language. This means that different language users are expected to produce different utterances even when they are talking about the same topic. Plagiarism detection in literary translation presents some difficulties of its own, as translations tend to reflect the content

ducciones inglés-español', *Atlantis*, 2:1 (1981), 60–4 at 60. **3** R. Merino, 'La traducción del teatro inglés en España: cuarenta años de plagios', *Perspectivas de la traducción inglés/español*, 3 (1995), 75–88 at 75–6. **4** M.T. Turell, 'Textual kidnapping revisited: the case of plagiarism in literary translation', *The International Journal of Speech, Language and the Law*, 11:1 (2004): 1–26; 'El plagio en la traducción literaria' in M.T. Turell (ed.), *Lingüística forense, lengua y derecho: conceptos, métodos y aplicaciones* (Barcelona, 2005), pp 275–97. **5** In 1993, Manuel Vázquez Montalbán was declared guilty of plagiarism of Pujante's translation of Shakespeare's *Julius Caesar* (1987) by the Spanish High Court of Justice. According to the expert witness that took part in the trial, there was a significant amount of plagiarism throughout Vázquez Montalbán's version (1988). He was sentenced to pay 15% of the translation's authorial rights to Pujante. This was the first time someone was charged with plagiarism of a translation in Spain.

and expression of the source text[6] making it likely for the different translators of a given source text to choose the same translation solutions and therefore produce similar translations. However, there is always a margin for originality. If the fragment of the source text that is to be translated creates interlinguistic problems of communication, the likelihood of two translators selecting the same translation solution is lower, as translators are language users that make their own linguistic choices when faced with the same translation problem.

Drawing on the expert witness report used in *Pujante v. Montalbán*, Turell proposes a selection of interlinguistically problematic fragments made by the expert witness, juxtaposed with the translation solutions adopted by the different translators, so as to show deviation from the source text, similarity between the plagiarized and plagiarist's text, and differences of these two with respect to other translations, if any. Yet, according to Turell, the likelihood of two translators adopting the same wording for a given translation solution, however original or unexpected this is, should be checked against target language use. For that purpose, she uses monitor corpora, performing searches on the phrases or sentences that translators have used to see whether they are frequently used in the language or not. If they are not, and systematic coincidence is reported in two different translations, the chances of one of them having plagiarized the other are higher.

For quantitative evidence, she proposes the use of an analytic tool called CopyCatch, which retrieves and highlights matching sentences between texts and makes calculations on the number of examples of hapax legomena and dislegomena which are shared. According to previous research, the threshold of expected similarity for texts on the same topic ranges from thirty per cent to fifty per cent of shared vocabulary.[7] Any figures above fifty per cent would be indicative of plagiarism. Taking into account the nature of translations as works that tend to reflect the content and expression of the source text, Turell proposes a much higher threshold of similarity for translations of the same source text, one of seventy per cent of shared vocabulary. In the case *Pujante v. Montalbán*, the level of similarity reported by Turell in her article reached eighty two per cent of shared vocabulary. However, she does not limit quantitative data to raw shared vocabulary; she also looks for coincident phrases of a minimum of three words per phrase, as this is an even more informative indicator of textual similarity than the coincidence of independent words.[8]

However, the main problem with this kind of analysis is that qualitative and quantitative evidence are not interdependent, that is, quantitative data do not really quantify the extent of plagiarism shown by qualitative data, they simply

6 Turell, 'El plagio en la traducción literaria', p. 275. **7** Ibid., p. 281. **8** Ibid., p. 284.

record shared vocabulary and phrases without taking into account whether the source text favours similarity between translations or not. Furthermore, the use of raw corpus data, to determine whether a given structure is frequently used in the language or not, is also problematic for the same reason; most of the time it is the source text which first determines the likelihood or not of two translators choosing the same solution. The most obvious evidence of this is the occurrence of additions and suppressions as they can only be observed if target text and source text are juxtaposed. Translation errors, materialized in a lexical chain whose meaning does not correspond to that of their counterpart in the source text, are also observed in relation to that source text, independently from their being frequently used in the language or not. All these facts could be used by the opposing party in a trial as a counterargument, thereby compromising the validity of the expert witness report.

ANCHOR PHENOMENA AND TRANSLATION PLAGIARISM DETECTION

One way of unifying qualitative and quantitative data is to identify frequently occurring expressive resources in the source language that pose problems of interlinguistic transfer to translators, therefore allowing the expert witness to quickly locate them in the source text, check what the translation solutions in the different translations are and whether there is systematic coincidence or not.

The answer seems to lie in anchor phenomena, which are defined as 'grammatical resources that are perceived as being cross-linguistically equivalent but that tend to and/or do convey partially divergent meanings, such as the future in English and French or progressive forms in English and in Spanish'.[9] An anchor phenomenon consists of a given grammatical resource in one language and the corresponding similarly perceived equivalent in another language. The meanings these resources carry in their respective languages can be partially similar and partially divergent. The areas of similarity are conveyed by the similarly perceived resources in both languages, but there may be other resources carrying the same or similar meanings. The areas of divergence or interlinguistic gaps represent meanings that are not conveyed by the similarly perceived expressive resources in the two languages. All these dissimilarities in the ways grammatical meanings are conveyed are 'a constant source of cross-linguistic problems affect-

9 R. Rabadán, 'Refining the idea of applied extensions' in M. Shlesinger, D. Simeón & A. Pym (eds), *Beyond descriptive translation studies: in homage to Gideon Toury* (Amsterdam, 2008), pp 103–18 at p. 107.

ing both text processing and production',[10] which may cause translators to make wrong choices based on wrong form-meaning associations or force them to look for other formal resources to fill in the interlinguistic gaps. This combination of factors ultimately prompts a large paradigm of right and wrong translation solutions in the target language for a single grammatical resource in the source language.

Several English-Spanish cross-linguistic analyses on a number of these anchor phenomena have been conducted by the ACTRES research group at the University of León (Spain), including the English simple past into Spanish,[11] *-ly* adverbs of degree,[12] or modal verbs such as *must*[13] among others. Working in the field of descriptive translation studies, their final aim is to supply translation solutions for interlinguistic gaps which are not obviously corresponding, by using a unidirectional parallel corpus. The importance of these studies for us lies in the fact that they provide descriptive evidence of the problems of interlinguistic transfer that certain grammatical resources pose to English-Spanish translators. In other words, these studies show that, when faced with these expressive resources, different translators tend to choose different and varying translation solutions for the meanings they have to convey. This means that, although two different translators may choose the same solution for the same resource in the source text, a systematic coincidence is not to be expected and therefore could be indicative of some kind of derivative relationship between two translations. On top of that, their representativeness as indicators of plagiarism is ensured by their frequency of occurrence in the source language.

A CASE-STUDY ON DICKENS' DAVID COPPERFIELD

The following is a case-study on four different translations into Spanish of *David Copperfield*,[14] those of Lafuerza (TT_1),[15] Bourquet (TT_2),[16] Luaces (TT_3)[17] and Méndez Herrera (TT_4).[18] Systematic coincidence in the choice of translation

10 Ibid. **11** R. Rabadán, 'The applicability of description: empirical research and translation tools', *Revista canaria de estudios ingleses*, 51 (2005), 51–7. **12** N. Ramón & B. Labrador, 'Translations of "-ly" adverbs of degree in an English-Spanish parallel corpus', *Target*, 20:2 (2008), 275–96. **13** R. Rabadán, 'Divisions, descriptions and applications: the interface between DTS, corpus-based research and contrastive analysis' in M. Shlesinger & R. Stolze (eds), *Translation studies: doubts and directions* (Amsterdam, 2007), pp 237–52. **14** C. Dickens, *David Copperfield* (London, 1996). **15** C. Dickens, *David Copperfield*, trans. Gregorio Lafuerza, 3 vols. (Buenos Aires, 1916). **16** C. Dickens, *David Copperfield*, trans. María Nelida Bourquet (Buenos Aires, 1940). **17** C. Dickens, *Historia y vicisitudes del joven David Copperfield*, trans. Juan G. Luaces (Barcelona, 1943). **18** C. Dickens, *David Copperfield*, trans. José Méndez Herrera (Madrid, 1950).

Fig. 1. Shared vocabulary per chapter for each translation pair

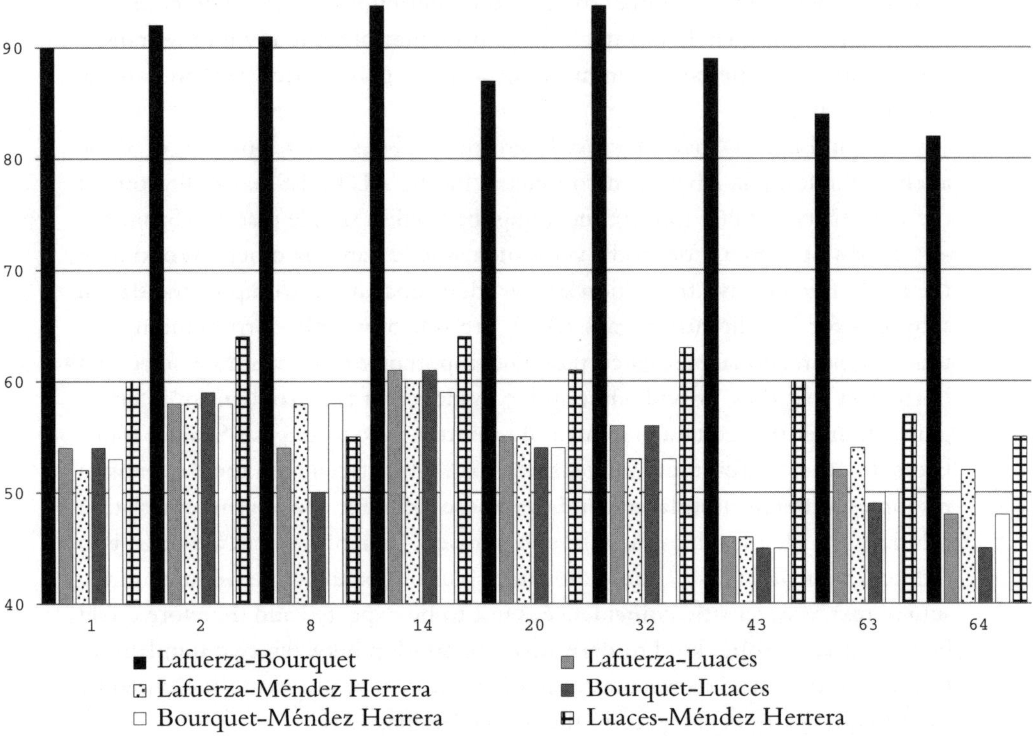

solutions for the modal verb *must* – which, according to Rabadán's data,[19] is a source of interlinguistic problems for English-Spanish translators – will be used to illustrate evidence of plagiarism in Bourquet's text. The directionality of plagiarism is based on the date of publication, and the translations of Luaces and Méndez Herrera will serve as a control group against which to contrast the similarities observed between plagiarized and plagiarist's texts.

For the purpose of this study, I have just chosen nine chapters randomly out of the total of sixty-four that comprise Dickens' work of fiction. The chapters are 1, 2, 8, 14, 20, 32, 43, 63 and 64, and token/type counts in the source text using JVocalyse v 2.05 amount to 43,319 instances of 5,020 distinct words. A total 28,362 tokens include function words as well as recurrent names and surnames of 332 types, whereas the remaining 14,957 tokens correspond to 4,688 types of lexical words. The total number of tokens of *must* in the source text is 51, which is not much when compared with average type-token ratios for func-

19 Rabadán, 'Divisions, descriptions and applications', p. 246.

tion words. However, even though *must* is regarded as a function word in that it conveys grammatical meanings, it is comparable to lexical words from the point of view of interlinguistic transfer, as its rendering is not as straightforward as that of function words such as *and* or *the*. In that light, 51 instances of *must* is not as narrow a number as it may seem at first but it is still not sufficient to reach a conclusive judgement over the originality or lack of originality of a translation.

However, the anchor-phenomena data can be complemented by resorting to data on the extent of raw lexical overlapping between two different texts. Using CopyCatch for data retrieval we get the table shown on the next page.

Shared vocabulary refers to the mean of the total number of tokens of lexical hapax legomena and dislegomena present in two texts relative to the total amount of tokens of lexical words in each text separately. Fig. 1 reports a high degree of lexical coincidence for Lafuerza-Bourquet, well above Turell's threshold of seventy per cent shared vocabulary. Other comparisons involving either Lafuerza or Bourquet show similarly low amounts of textual overlapping for all the pair combinations whereas figures for Luaces-Méndez Herrera reveal a slightly closer relationship in terms of shared vocabulary.

Having located all 51 instances of *must* in the source text we look for their corresponding translation solutions in all four target texts and organize them according to the semantic labels proposed by Rabadán.[20] In the process, one of the occurrences of *must* is excluded from the analysis since, being part of a question tag, it is devoid of semantic meaning.

Table 1 shows a rich paradigm of translation solutions for the different meanings of *must*, as previous research had already revealed.[21] The ones appearing on a dark background are wrong because they do not really convey the meaning *must* carries in the source text, but that is part of the potential for diversity of the translation of *must* into Spanish. Notice that TT_3 and TT_4 show some original solutions of their own which they do not share with the rest of translations. The next step is to contrast the different translations with one another so as to see whether translation solutions for each occurrence of *must* in the source text are coincident or not.

Table 2 reveals a high degree of similarity in the choice of translation solutions for the pair Lafuerza-Bourquet, as they share a total ninety-six per cent, thus pointing towards a correlation between these data and those reported for shared vocabulary. Similarly, the rest of the textual pairs present low numbers parallel to those detailed in Fig. 1. However, it is worth noting that the pair Luaces-Méndez Herrera shows lower amounts of textual overlapping with respect to the rest of translation pairs than those reported for raw shared vocabulary.

20 Ibid., p. 243. **21** Ibid., p. 246.

Table 1. Meaning-form distribution of translation solutions for *must*

Meaning	*ST*	*Translation Solutions*	TT_1	TT_2	TT_3	TT_4
Obligation	22	*Deber+inf* (similarly perceived equivalent for *must*)	6	6	3	6
		Futuro ('simple future')	7	7	4	1
		Tener que+inf (have to)			5	8
		Ser preciso/necesario+inf (need/be necessary)	1	1	3	5
		Modulation/Transposition	3	3	2	
		Omission	3	3		
		Verb in corresponding tense			4	1
		haber que+inf (have to)	1	1	1	
		Tener derecho a+inf (to have the right to)	1	1		
		Haber de+inf (have to)				1
Passive Obligation	5	*Poder+inf* (can/be able to)	2	2	1	1
		Imperativo (Imperative)	1	1	1	
		Modulation/Transposition			2	1
		Omission	1	1		
		Deber+inf (similarly perceived equivalent for *must*)				2
		Haber de+inf (have to)			1	1
		Ser preciso/necesario+inf (need/be necessary)	1	1		
Confident Inference	23	*Deber+inf* (similarly perceived equivalent for *must*)	4	5	6	1
		Futuro (simple future)	4	4	2	1
		Verb in corresponding tense	2	2	3	3
		Omission	3	3	2	1
		Modulation/Transposition	3	3	1	2
		Deber de+inf (must)	1		1	6
		Conditional (conditional tense)	2	2	2	2
		Compression	2	2	2	
		Seguramente que/Seguro que (To be very likely to)			1	4
		Tener que+inf (have to)	1	1		2
		Ser evidente que (to be evident that)	1	1		
		Sin duda que (No doubt)			1	
		Ir a+inf (to be going to)			1	
		Subjunctive			1	
		Haber de+inf (have to)				1

Table 2. Percentage of shared translation solutions for each translation pair

	Lafuerza	*Bourquet*	*Luaces*	*Méndez Herrera*
Lafuerza	1	0.96	0.34	0.18
Bourquet		1	0.36	0.18
Luaces			1	0.28
Méndez Herrera				1

Fig. 2. Shared translation solutions for each pair of texts

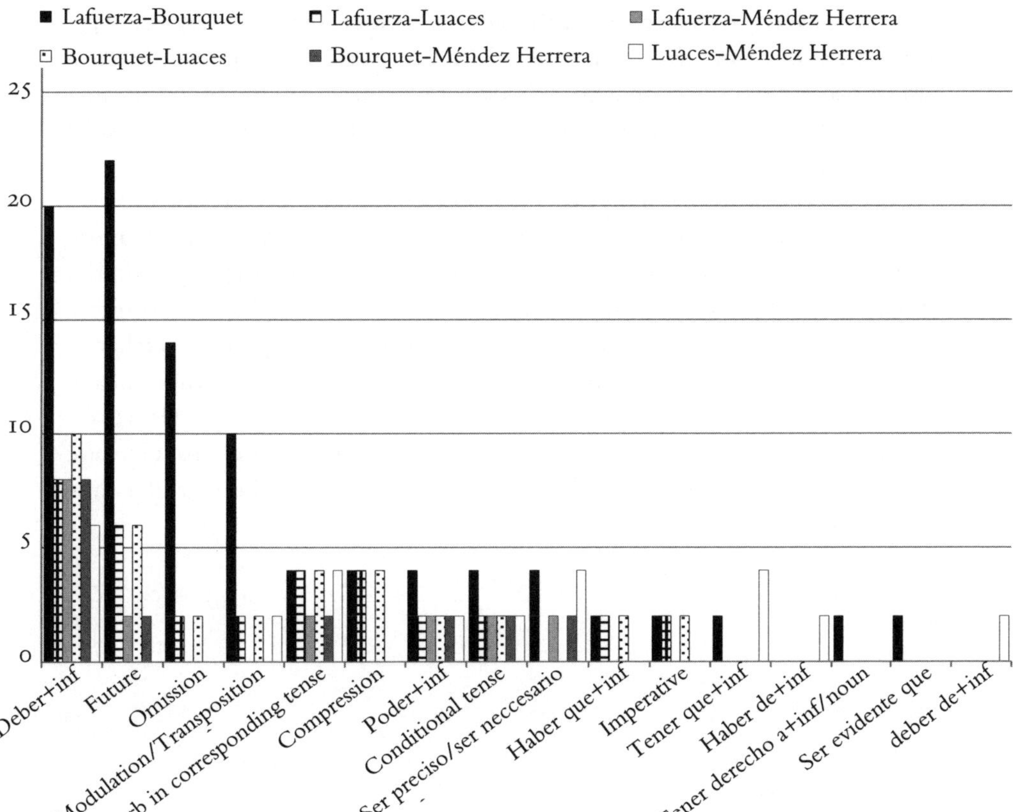

Although these data speak clearly of the intertextual relationship between Lafuerza and Bourquet, typically shared translation solutions are not accounted for. In looking for originality, it must be taken into account that less favoured translation solutions tend to be marginally shared between texts, which means that any two independent translators are expected to show a much lower degree of overlapping for those solutions than for those favoured by language pair associations.

Fig. 2 details shared translation solutions for each of the translation pairs. Since there is a large paradigm of possible renderings of *must* into Spanish, it is quite suspicious that Lafuerza and Bourquet made the same choices for the translation of most of the occurrences of *must* in the source text. *Future tense*, *omission* and *modulation/transposition* are preferred translation solutions by Lafuerza which are not particularly favoured by the source text,[22] yet being systematically mimicked by Bourquet. This highly contrasts with the low amounts of similarity reported in the rest of pairs for the same target language resources. Furthermore, resources such as *deber de+inf* or *haber de+inf* are marginally shared by Luaces-Méndez Herrera, even though the former is favoured by language pair associations[23] and the latter implies literal translation. As for *tener derecho a* and *ser evidente que*, these are used only once by Lafuerza-Bourquet in the same contexts, which is not to be expected since they do not convey the modal meanings *must* carries.

It is important to highlight that the approach outlined here is not an alternative to the analysis proposed by Turell but rather a complement to add more evidence to the expert witness hypothesis while minimizing the opportunities of the opposing party's for counter-argumentation. Anchor phenomena introduce a quantitative dimension to qualitative evidence allowing the researcher to see whether the use of the same translation solutions for cross-linguistically problematic areas is systematic or not in two different translations. However, further research is needed as to the number of cross-linguistically problematic resources that should be used to ensure representativeness and the greater suitability of one over another.

22 Rabadán, p. 247. **23** Ibid.

Contributors

JOSEPHINE BALMER's latest book of poems, *The word for sorrow*, appeared from Salt in 2009. Earlier books include *Chasing Catullus: poems, translations and transgressions*, *Catullus: poems of love and hate*, *Classical women poets* and *Sappho: poems & fragments*, all Bloodaxe. She has just completed a study of classical translation and poetry for Oxford University Press' 'Classical Presences' series.

SUSANA BAYÓ BELENGUER is an assistant professor of Spanish at Trinity College Dublin. Her research interests include the literature of the Spanish civil war; literary and genre theory, translation theory and practice. Among her publications is *Theory, genre, and memory in the 'Carvalho' series of Manuel Vázquez Montalbán*.

SABINE DEDENBACH-SALAZAR SÁENZ is a senior lecturer at the University of Stirling. Her research interests focus on Andean indigenous languages; prehispanic, colonial and modern ethnohistory of the Andean peoples; methods in ethnohistory; microhistory; and the language of christianization.

BART DEFRANCQ is a lecturer at University College Ghent. Trained as a linguist, he obtained his PhD in French linguistics at Ghent University and teaches French interpreting and translation. He is also visiting professor at the College of Europe and Ghent University. His research interests are in corpus based contrastive linguistics, translation and interpreting studies.

EMER DELANEY is an IRCHSS Government of Ireland Scholar at Trinity College Dublin, where she is completing her doctoral research, in Italian and Gender Studies, on language and gender in the Italian women's suffrage movement, 1900–22.

JANE DUNNETT is a lecturer in Italian at Swansea University, an associate editor of *Romance Studies*, and Research Fellow in Translation Studies at the University of South Africa (UNISA). Her research fosuses on 20th-century Italy – theatre, publishing, Fascist censorship, popular literature and crime fiction, including translation/adaptation. She is completing an AHRC-funded monograph on Italian detective novels from the interwar years.

ALBERTO FUERTES PUERTA has a PhD in translation and interpreting from the University of León. He is the author of a thesis on plagiarism as a translation strategy and he is also a freelance translator of youth literature and specialized texts.

FRANCISCA GARCÍA LUQUE is currently working at the University of Málaga. Her main research focus is on audiovisual translation since 2002, when she obtained her PhD degree based on research into intersemiotic translation. Since then, she has published several articles about film adaptation, subtitling and dubbing.

ANNJO KLUNGERVIK GREENALL is an associate professor of English language at the Department of Modern Foreign Languages at the Norwegian University of Science and Technology. She holds a PhD in pragmatics, and has published a number of articles within the field of translation studies.

VIRGINIA JEWISS is a lecturer in the Humanities at Yale University and director of the Yale Humanities in Rome program. Her translations from Italian to English include Melania Mazzucco's novel *Vita*, Roberto Saviano's *Gomorrah*, and the screenplay for Paolo Sorrentino's *This must be the place.*

CARMEN MANGIRON is a lecturer and researcher at the Universitat Autònoma de Barcelona. She is a member of the research group TransMedia Catalonia, part of the Centre for Ambient Intelligence and Accessibility in Catalunya. Her research interests include literary translation, translation of cultural references, ideology and translation, translation techniques, explication in translation, game localizition and game accessibility.

ANNE MARKEY teaches in the School of English at Trinity College Dublin. She has written widely on Irish literature, with particular emphasis on the intersection between Gaelic traditions and Irish writing in English. Her edition, *Patrick Pearse: short stories*, was published in 2009, an edited volume of *Children's fiction, 1765–1808* appeared in 2011, and *Oscar Wilde's fairy tales: origins and contacts* was published in 2012.

EILÉAN NÍ CHUILLEANÁIN is an emeritus professor of English at Trinity College Dublin. She has published translations from Irish, Italian and Romanian, and numerous articles on renaissance literature.

CORMAC Ó CUILLEANÁIN is a professor of Italian at Trinity College Dublin. A founder member of the Irish translators' and interpreters' association, his research interests include issues in translation and aspects of medieval Italian literature.

MINAKO O'HAGAN is a senior lecturer at Dublin City University. She has been involved in interdisciplinary research with a main interest in translation and technology. Her recent work includes an edited volume on internet user participation in translation.

PILAR ORDÓÑEZ LÓPEZ lectures in translation studies at the Universitat Jaume I in Castellón. Her research interests include history of translation, translation theory and corpus-based translation studies, and she has published widely in these areas.

ILARIA PARINI is a contract lecturer in English at the University of Milan. She graduated in translation from the University of Bologna at Forlí and holds a PhD in English linguistics and translation from the University of Milan. She has published several articles on audiovisual translation in Italy.

METTE RUDVIN holds a PhD in translation studies and is a researcher at the University of Bologna. Her research interests include translation theory, children's literature, Anglo-Indian literature and community interpreting, on which she recently published (with Elena Tomassini) *Interpreting in the community and workplace: a practical teaching guide* (2011).

SIMONE SCHROTH has taught in the German Departments at University College Dublin and Newcastle University. Among her research interests are the Second World War and translation quality assessment. Her Dr. Phil. thesis on translations of Anne Frank's *Het Achterhuis* was published in 2006 (Waxmann, Münster).

KATHLEEN SHIELDS is a lecturer in French at the National University of Ireland Maynooth. She has published in lexicography, translation studies and on French language issues, and as editor of the *Oxford-Hachette dictionary*. *Gained in translation: language, poetry and identity in twentieth-century Ireland* appeared in 2000. She co-edited with Michael Clarke *Translating emotion: studies in transformation and renewal between languages* (2011).

SABINE STRÜMPER-KROBB is a lecturer in German in the School of Languages and Literatures at University College Dublin. She received a PhD from the University of Göttingen, Germany, and has published books and articles in the area of German-Scandinavian literary relations and translation studies.

MICHELLE WOODS is assistant professor of English at SUNY New Paltz. She is the author of *Translating Milan Kundera* (2006) and *Censoring translation: censorship, theatre and the politics of translation* (2012).

GIULIA ZUODAR is a PhD student at Trinity College Dublin and a translator. Her research interests include translation and ideology, translation of culture-specific references and translation of post-colonial literature, with a special focus on the Australian, New-Zealand and West-Indian contexts. She has taught computerized translation and Italian language at Trinity College Dublin.

Bibliography

PRINT SOURCES

Agard, John, *The young inferno* (London, 2008).

Agost, Rosa, *Traducción y doblaje: palabras, voces e imágenes* (Barcelona, 1999).

Albó, Xavier, 'The Aymara religious experience' in Marzal et al. (eds), *The Indian face of God*, pp 119–67.

Allan, Keith, & Kate Burridge, *Euphemism and dysphemism: language used as shield and weapon* (Oxford, 1991).

Álvarez, R., & M.C. Vidal, *Translation, power, subversion* (Philadelphia, 1996).

Amodio, Emanuele, 'Cocacha mamacha. Prácticas adivinatorias y mitología de la coca entre los quechuas del Perú', *Bulletin, Société Suisse des Américanistes/ Schweizerische Amerikanisten-Gesellschaft*, 57–8 (1993–4), 123–37.

Anonymous, *Was schrieb das Kind? Der Spiegel*, 1 Apr. 1959.

——, *Doctrina christiana. [1584]. Doctrina christiana, y catecismo para instrvccion de los Indios* (Lima, 1984).

——, *Doctrina christiana. [1584/85]. Doctrina christiana y catecismo para instrvccion de indios; Confessionario para los cvras de indios; Tercero cathecismo*, vol. 26–2 (Madrid, 1985).

——, *The Huarochirí manuscript [c.1608]. A testament of ancient and colonial Andean religion. Translation from the Quechua by Frank Salomon and George L. Urioste. Annotations and introductory essay by Frank Salomon. Transcription by George L. Urioste* (Austin, 1991).

Arrojo, Rosemary, 'Fidelity and gendered translation', *TTR*, 7:2 (1994), 147–63.

Azzaro, Gabriele, *Four-letter films: taboo language in movies* (Rome, 2005).

Bailey, Jonathan, 'The problem with detecting translation plagiarism', *Plagiarism today*, 24 Feb. 2011.

——, 'Translation plagiarism', *Plagiarism Today*, 13 Aug. 2005.

Baker, Mona, 'Linguistics and cultural studies: complementary or competing paradigms in translation' in Angelika Lauer, Heidrun Gerzymisch-Arbogast, Johann Haller & Erich Steiner (eds), *Übersersetzungswissenschaft im Umbruch: Festschrift für Wolfram Wilss* (Tübingen, 1996).

——, 'Towards a methodology for investigating the style of a literary translator', *Target*, 12:2 (2002), 241–66.

Baker, Mona, & Gabriela Saldanha (eds), *Routledge encyclopedia of translation studies*, 2nd ed. (London, 2009).

Balibar, Étienne, 'The nation form: history and ideology' in Étienne Balibar & Immanuel Wallerstein (eds), *Race, nation, class: ambiguous identities* (London, 1991), pp 86–106.

Ball, Rodney, *The French-speaking world: a practical introduction to sociolinguistic issues* (London, 1997).

Balmer, Josephine, 'Jumping their bones: translating, transgressing and creating' in S. Harrison (ed.), *Living Classics*, pp 43–64.

——, 'Forget Homer: salute the translator,' *New Statesman*, 21 Feb. 1997.

——, *Chasing Catullus: poems, translations & transgressions* (Tarset, Northumberland, 2004).

——, 'Subverting the national: the classical model', *In Other Words*, 22 (2004), 37–42.

——, 'What comes next: reconstructing the classics' in Susan Bassnett & Peter Bush (eds), *The translator as writer* (London, 2006), pp 184–95.

——, *The word for sorrow* (Cambridge, 2009).

Barnouw, David, 'Anne Frank and academia' in Paape et al. (eds), *The diary of Anne Frank* (New York, 2003), pp 103–8.

Bassnett, Susan, 'The meek or the mighty: reappraising the role of the translator' in Alvárez & Vidal (eds), *Translation, power, subversion*, pp 10–25.

——, *Translation studies* (London, 1980).

Bayard, Pierre, *How to talk about books you haven't read* (London, 2008).

——, *Le plagiat par anticipation* (Paris, 2009).

Beckett, Sandra L., 'Introduction' in Sandra L. Beckett (ed.), *Transcending boundaries: writing for a dual audience of children and adults* (London, 1999), pp xi–xx.

——, *Crossover fiction: global and historical perspectives* (New York, 2009).

Berry, David M., *Copy, rip, burn: the politics of copyleft and open source* (London, 2008).

Bey, Youcef, Christian Boitet & Kyo Kageura, 'The TRANSBey prototype: An online collaborative Wikibased CAT environment for volunteer translators', in Elia Yuste Rodrigo (ed.), *Proceedings of the 3rd international workshop on language resources for translation work, research & training* (Paris, 2006).

Beye, Charles, 'A response' in Hallet & Van Nortwick (eds), *Compromising traditions*, pp 153–67.

Biau Gil, José Ramón & Anthony Pym, 'Technology and translation (a pedagogical overview)' in A. Pym, A. Perekrestenko & B. Starink (eds), *Translation technology and its teaching* (Tarragona, 2006).

Blommaert, Jan, 'Language planning as a discourse on language and society', *Language Problems and Language Planning* 20 (1996), 199–222.

Boa, Elizabeth, *Kafka: gender, class and race in the letters and fictions* (Oxford, 1996).

Bogic, Anna, 'Rehabilitating Howard M. Parshley: a socio-historical study of the English translation of Beauvoir's *Le deuxième sexe*, with Latour and Bourdieu' (MA, Ottawa, 2009).

Böhme, Hartmut, 'Mother Milena: on Kafka's narcissism' in Angel Flores (ed.), *The Kafka debate* (New York, 1977), pp 80–99.

Bosinelli Bollettieri, Rosa Maria, C. Heiss, M. Soffritti & S. Bernardini (eds), *Atti del convegno Internazionale La traduzione multimediale: Quale traduzione per quale testo? Multimedia translation: which translation for which text?, Forlì, 2–4 aprile 1998* (Bologna, 2000).

Bousfield, Derek, *Impoliteness in interaction* (Amsterdam, 2008).

——, *Impoliteness in language: studies on its interplay with power in theory and practice* (Berlin, 2008).

Brondeel, H., 'Teaching subtitling routines', *Meta*, 39 (1994), 26–33.

Brown, Penelope, & Stephen C. Levinson, *Politeness: some universals in language usage* (Cambridge, 1987).

Brown, Stephen J. M., *Ireland in fiction: a guide to Irish novels, tales, romances, and folk-lore* (New York, 1970).

Brunse, Niels, 'Litteraer oversættelse' in V.H. Pedersen & N. Krogh-Hansen (eds), *Oversættelseshåndbogen* (Copenhagen, 1994), pp 79–92.

Buber-Neumann, Margarete, *Kafkas Freundin Milena* (Munich, 1963).

Burke, Peter, & Roy Porter (eds), *The social history of language* (Cambridge, 1987).

Butrica, J.L., 'History and transmission of the text' in M. Skinner (ed.), *A companion to Catullus* (London, 2007), pp 13–34.

Černa, Jana, *Kafka's Milena*, trans. Gerald Turner (London, 1988).

Cadogan, Mary, *Richmal Crompton: the woman behind Just William* (Stroud, 2003).

Caffrey, Colm, 'Relevant abuse? Investigating the effects of an abusive subtitling procedure on the perception of TV anime using eye tracker and questionnaire' (PhD, DCU, 2009).

Calvet, Louis-Jean, *La Guerre des langues et les politiques linguistiques*, Langages et sociétés (Paris, 1987).

Calzada Pérez, María, *El espejo traductológico* (Barcelona, 2007).

Carne-Ross, Donald, 'A mistaken ambition of exactness', *Delos*, 2 (1) (968), 171–97.

Carpenter, William Boyd, *The spiritual message of Dante*, William Belden Noble lectures (London, 1914).

Carroll, Rory, 'Campaigners try to outlaw William', *Guardian*, 4 May 1999.

Carson, Anne, *Men in the off hours* (New York, 2000).

Castro de Trelles, Lucila (ed.), *Relación de la religión y ritos del Perú hecha por los padres agustinos* (Lima, 1992).

Catullus, Gaius Valerius, *The shorter poems*, trans. John Godwin (Warminster, England, 1999).

——, *Poems of love and hate*, trans. Josephine Balmer (Tarset, Northumberland, 2004).

——, *The poems of Catullus*, trans. Peter Green, Bilingual ed. (London, 2005).

Catullus, Gaius Valerius, ed. G.P. Goold, *Catullus*, Duckworth classical, medieval, and renaissance editions (London, 1983).

Cerna, Jana, *Adresat Milena Jesenska* (Prague, 1991).

Cervantes Saavedra, Miguel de, *Don Quixote*, trans. Edith Grossman (New York, 2003).

Chamberlain, Lori, 'Gender and the metaphorics of translation' in Venuti (ed.), *Rethinking translation*, pp 57–74.

Chaudenson, Robert, 'Geolinguistics, geopolitics, geostrategy: the case of French' in Jacques Maurais & Michael A. Morris (eds), *Languages in a globalising world* (Cambridge, 2003), pp 291–7.

Chaume Varela, Frederic, *Cine y traducción* (Madrid, 2004).

Chen, Irene, 'Translating rape', *Translation Journal*, 13:2 (2009).

Chesterman, Andrew, 'From "is" to "ought": laws, norms and strategies in translation studies', *Target*, 5 (1993), 1–20.

——, *Memes of translation: the spread of ideas in translation theory* (Amsterdam, 1997).

Chiaro, Delia, 'The British will use tag questions, won't they? The case of *Four weddings and a funeral*' in C. Taylor (ed.), *Tradurre il cinema* (2000), pp 27–40.

Christie, Agatha, *Il pericolo senza nome*, trans. Laura Garsin (Milan, 1933).

——, *L'uomo vestito di marrone*, trans. Giuseppina Taddei (Milan, 1933).

——, *Murder in the Calais coach* (New York, 1934).

——, *Murder on the Orient Express* (London, 1934).

——, *Orient Express*, trans. Alfredo Pitta (Milan, 1935).

——, *Assassinio sull'Orient Express*, trans. revised with a preface and postface by Oreste del Buono Alfredo Pitta, I classici del giallo (Milan, 1970, 2011).

——, *L'uomo vestito di marrone*, trans. Stefano Benvenuti (Milan, 2008).

——, *Pericolo senza nome*, trans. Maria Luisa Vesentini Ottolenghi (Milan, 2009).

Crickmay, Lindsey, 'Outward change, inner continuity: the Andean concept of "devil"' in Iris Gareis (ed.), *Entidades maléficas y conceptos del mal en las religiones latinoamericanas/ Evil entities and concepts of evil in Latin American religions*, vol. 45, Bonner Amerikanistische Studien/ Bonn Americanist Studies (Aachen, 2008), pp 24–40.

Croker, Charlie, *Screwed up English* (Avon, MA, 2008).

Crompton, Richmal, *Just – William* (London, 1922).

——, *More William* (London, 1922).

——, *William again* (London, 1923).

——, *Still – William* (London, 1925).

——, *William the pirate* (London, 1932).

——, *William the detective* (London, 1935).

——, *William and the evacuees* (London, 1940).

——, *Le birichinate di William Brown*, trans. Lidia Sacchi Nicoli (Rome, 1954).

Cronin, Michael, *Across the lines: travel, language, translation* (Cork, 2000).

——, *Translation goes to the movies* (London, 2009).

——, 'Review of Bella Brodzki, *Can these bones live? Translation, survival, and cultural memory*', *Comparative Literature*, 62:2 (2010), 189.

Cubbison, Laurie, 'Anime fans, DVDs, and the authentic text', *The Velvet Light Trap*, 56:1 (2005), 45–57.

Cunningham, Hugh, *The invention of childhood* (London, 2006).

Cussen, Celia L., 'The search for idols and saints in colonial Peru: linking extirpation and beatification', *Hispanic American Historical Review*, 85:3 (2005), 417–48.

Daniele, Serena, 'Nota alla traduzione italiana' in J.K. Rowling, *Harry Potter e il calice di fuoco* (Milan, 2001).

Davies, Mark, 'Creating useful historical corpora: a comparison of CORDE, the corpus del español, and the corpus do português' in Andrés Enrique-Arias (ed.), *Diacronía de las lenguas iberorromances: nuevas perspectivas desde la linguistic de corpus* (Frankfurt, 2010), pp 139–68.

Dávila-Montes, José, *La traducción de la persuasión publicitaria* (Lewiston, 2008).

De Arriaga, Pablo José, 'Extirpación de la idolatría del Pirú' in Francisco Esteve Barba (ed.), *Crónicas peruanas de interés indígena* (Madrid, 1968), pp 193–277.

De Beauvoir, Simone, *The Second Sex*, trans. H.M. Parshley (London, 1953).

——, *The Second Sex*, trans. Constance Borde & Sheila Malovany-Chevallier (New York, 2010).

Dedenbach-Salazar Sáenz, Sabine, 'Dictionaries, vocabularies, and grammars in Andean indigenous languages' in Pillsbury (ed.), *Documentary sources*, pp 235–64.

——, 'Terminología de parentesco y trato social andino: datos lingüístico-etnohistóricos de Huarochirí' in Denise Y. Arnold (ed.), *Gente de carne y hueso: las tramas de parentesco en los Andes*, vol. 2 (La Paz, 1998), pp 167–85.

——, 'Andine traditionelle Kulturen und das Christentum' in Joachim G. Piepke (ed.), *Kultur und Religion in der Begegnung mit dem Fremden* (Nettetal, 2007), pp 113–78.

Dedenbach-Salazar Sáenz, Sabine, & Frederike Meyer, 'Die "Ayuda a bien morir" der Doctrina Christiana y Catecismo (Lima 1585): Übersetzung, Analyse und Kontextualisierung eines kolonialzeitlichen spanischen und Quechua-Textes aus Peru', *Anthropos*, 100:2 (2005), 473–93.

De Certeau, Michel, *The practice of everyday life* (Berkeley, CA, 1984).

Deere, Dicey, *The Irish cottage murder* (New York, 1999).

——, *The Irish manor house murder* (New York, 2000).

——, *The Irish village murder* (New York, 2004).

De Klerk, V., 'How taboo are taboo words for girls?', *Language in Society*, 21 (1992), 277–89.

De Mooij, Marieke, 'Translating advertising', *The Translator*, 10:2 (2004), 179–98.

De Paor, Louis, 'Cumhacht an aistriúcháin' in Charlie Dillon & Ríona Ní Fhrighil (eds), *Aistriú Éireann* (Belfast, 2008), pp 1–15.

Deppey, Dirk, 'Scanlation nation: amateur manga translators tell their stories', *The Comics Journal*, 269 (2005).

De Saint Robert, Marie-Josée, *La politique de la langue française* (Paris, 2000).

De Santo Tomás, Domingo, *Lexicon, o vocabulario de la lengua general del Perú [Valladolid 1560]. (Facsimile.)* (Lima, 1951).

Desmidt, Isabelle, 'A prototypical approach within descriptive translation studies? Colliding norms in translated children's literature' in Van Coillie & Verschueren (eds), *Children's literature in translation*, pp 79–94.

Díaz Cintas, Jorge, *Teoría y práctica de la subtitulación, inglés-español* (London, 2003).

Díaz Cintas, Jorge, Anna Matamala & Josélia Neves (eds), *New insights into audiovisual translation and media accessibility* (Amsterdam, 2010).

Díaz Cintas, Jorge, & Pablo Muñoz Sánchez, 'Fansubs: Audiovisual translation in amateur environment', *Journal of Special Translation*, 6 (2006), 37–52.

Díaz-Cintas, Jorge, & Aline Remael, *Audiovisual translation: subtitling* (Manchester, 2007).

Dickens, Charles, *David Copperfield*, trans. Gregorio Lafuerza (Buenos Aires, 1916).

——, *David Copperfield*, trans. María Nelida Bourquet (Buenos Aires, 1940).

——, *Historia y vicisitudes del joven David Copperfield*, trans. Juan G. Luaces (Barcelona, 1943).

——, *David Copperfield*, trans. José Méndez Herrera (Madrid, 1950).

——, *David Copperfield* (London, 1996).

Dickinson, Peter, *The lizard in the cup* (London, 1972).

Dunnett, Jane, 'The Emergence of a new literary genre in interwar Italy' in Giuliana Pieri (ed.), *Crime fiction in Italian: an introduction* (Cardiff, 2011), pp 6–26.

Durston, Alan, *Pastoral Quechua. The history of Christian translation in colonial Peru, 1550–1650* (Notre Dame, IN, 2007).

D'Ydewalle, Gery, Caroline Praet, Karl Verfaillie & Johan Van Rensbergen, 'Watching subtitled television', *Communication Research*, 18 (1991), 650–66.

Eagleton, Terry, 'Faking it: the art of literary forgery,' *The Guardian*, 6 June 2002.

Eelen, Gino, *A critique of politeness theories* (Manchester, 2001).

Espasa, E., 'Myths about documentary translation' in P. Orero (ed.), *Topics on audiovisual translation* (Amsterdam, 2004), pp 183–97.

Étiemble, René, *Parlez-vous franglais?* ([Paris], 1964).

Evans, Emrys, '"Quality" and "non-quality": some new criteria', *English in Education*, 21:3 (1987), 36–43.

Even-Zohar, Itamar, 'The position of translated literature within the literary polysystem' in James S. Holmes, José Lambert & R. van den Brook (eds), *Literature and translation* (Leuven, 1978), pp 117–27.

Fenet, Alain, 'Difference rights and language in France' in Judt & Lacorne (eds), *Language, nation, state*, pp 19–61.

Ferguson, C.A., 'Diglossia', *Word*, 15 (1959), 325–40.

Fernández López, Marisa, 'Translation studies in contemporary children's literature: a comparison of intercultural ideological factors' in Lathey (ed.), *The translation of children's literature*, pp 41–53.

Flew, Terry, *New media: an introduction*, 3rd ed. (Oxford, 2008).

Flotow, Luise von, 'This time "the translation is beautiful, smooth, and true": theorizing retranslation with the help of Beauvoir', *FLS*, 36 (2009), 35–49.

Fodor, István, *Film dubbing: phonetic, semiotic, esthetic and psychological aspects* (Hamburg, 1976).

Fowler, Edward, 'Rendering words, traversing cultures: on the art and politics of translating modern Japanese fiction', *Journal of Japanese Studies*, 18 (1992), 1–44.

Franco, E., 'Documentary film translation. A specific practice?' in A. Chesterman, N. Gallardo & Y. Gambier (eds), *Translation in context* (Amsterdam, 2000), pp 233–42.

Frank, Anne, *Het achterhuis: dagboekbrieven van 12 Juni 1942–1 Augustus 1944* (Amsterdam, 1947).

——, *Das Tagebuch der Anne Frank: 14. Juni 1942–1. August 1944*, trans. Anneliese Schütz (Heidelberg, 1950).

——, *Tagebuch*, trans. Mirjam Pressler (Frankfurt am Main, 1991).

——, *The diary of a young girl*, trans. Susan Massotty, Definitive ed. (London, 1995).

Frank, Anne, ed. Abraham Harry Paape, Gerrold van der Stroom & David Barnouw, *De dagboeken van Anne Frank* (Amsterdam, 1986).

Frank, Anne, ed. Gerrold Van der Stroom, Harry Paape & David Barnouw, *The diary of Anne Frank: the revised critical edition* (New York, 2003).

Fuentes Luque, Adrián, 'An empirical approach to the reception of AV translated humour', *The Translator*, 9 (2003), 293–306.

Fulquet, Joan Pla, 'La detecció de plagi en traducció literària. Anàlisi de tres versions de *El Barón Rampante* de Italo Calvino a l'espanyol' (MA, Universitat Pompeu Fabra, Barcelona.

Fundación José Ortega y Gasset, *Desde Occidente: 70 años de 'Revista de Occidente'* (Madrid, 1993).

Gaffney, Phyllis, '"The achieve of, the mastery of the thing!": Pierre Leyris's verse translations of Gerard Manley Hopkins' in Jean Boase-Beier & Michael Holman (eds), *The practices of literary translation: constraints and creativity* (Manchester, St Jerome, 1999), pp 45–58.

Gaisser, Julia Haig, *Catullus in English*, Penguin classics (London, 2001).

Galassi, G.G., 'Panni da risciacquare: candeggio, lavaggio, ammorbidente' in S. Patou-Patucchi (ed.), *L'italiano del doppiaggio* (Rome, 1999), pp 70–8.

Galef, David, 'Crossing over: authors who write both children's and adult's fiction', *Children's Literature Association Quarterly*, 20:1 (1995), 29–35.

Gambier, Yves (ed.), *Audiovisual communication and language transfers* (Strasbourg, 1995).

——, 'Screen transadaptation: perception and reception', *The Translator*, 9 (2003), 171–89.

García-Yebra, Valentín, *En torno a la traducción* (Madrid, 1983).

Gargatagli, Ana, & Juan Gabriel López Guix, 'Ficciones y teorías de la traducción: Jorge Luis Borges', *Livius: Revista de Estudios de Traducción*, 1 (1992).

Garrioch, D., 'Verbal insults in eighteenth century Paris' in Peter Burke & Roy Porter (eds), *The social history of language* (Cambridge, 1987), pp 104–19.

Gentzler, Edwin, *Contemporary translation theories*, 2nd ed. (Clevedon, 2000).

Gibbons, John, & M. Teresa Turell (eds), *Dimensions of forensic linguistics* (Amsterdam, 2008).

Goldhagen, Daniel Jonah, *Hitlers willige Vollstrecker: ganz gewöhnliche Deutsche und der Holocaust*, trans. Klaus Kochmann (Munich, 1996).

——, *Hitler's willing executioners: ordinary Germans and the Holocaust* (New York, 1996).

González Holguín, Diego, *Vocabulario de la lengua general de todo el Peru llamada lengua qquichua o del Inca. [1608]* (Lima, 1989).

Goold, G.P., *Interpreting Catullus* (London, 1974).

Goris, O., 'A la recherche du normes pour le doublage. Etat de la question et propositions pour une analyse descriptive' (PhD, 1991).

Gottlieb, Henrik, 'Subtitling' in Baker & Saldanha (eds), *Routledge encyclopedia of translation studies.*

——, 'Establishing a framework for a typology of subtitle viewing strategies: viewer reactions to deviations from subtitle standards', *Audiovisual Communication and Language Transfer, Translatio – FIT Newsletter*, 14 (1995), 389–409.

Gow, Rosalind, & Bernabé Condori, *Kay Pacha: tradición oral andina* (Cuzco, 1976).

Gray, Francine du Plessix, 'Review of *The second sex*,' *New York Times Sunday Book Review*, 27 May 2010.

Greenall, Annjo K., 'The non-translation of swearing in subtitling: loss of social implicature?' in A. Serban, A. Matamala & J-M. Lavaur (eds), *Audiovisual translation in close-up* (Bern, 2011), pp 45–60.

——, 'Translating breaches of intersubjective constraints on interaction: the case of swearing in Roddy Doyle's novel *The Commitments*', *Meta*, 56:3 (2011), 336–55.

Greene, Ellen, 'Re-figuring the feminine voice: Catullus translating Sappho', *Arethusa*, 32:1 (Winter 1999), 1–18.

Greenway, Betty, 'William forever: Richmal Crompton's unusual achievement', *The Lion and the Unicorn*, 26 (2002), 98–111.

Grice, H., 'Logic and conversation' in P. Cole & J. Morgan (eds), *Syntax and semantics 3: speech acts* (New York, 1975), pp 41–58.

Grillo, R. D., *Dominant languages: language and hierarchy in Britain and France* (Cambridge, 1989).

Gross, Beverly, 'Bitch', *Salamagundi*, 103 (1994), 146–56.

Guaman Poma de Ayala, Felipe, *Nueva corónica y buen gobierno (Codex péruvien illustré) [c. 1615]*, vol. 23 (Paris, 1936).

Gutbrodt, Fritz, *Joint ventures: authorship, translation, plagiarism* (Bern, 2003).

Hagège, Claude, *Le Français, histoire d'un combat* (Paris, 1996).
——, 'Que s'ouvre enfin l'ère de la deuxième francophonie!,' *Le Monde 8 November*, 2008.
Hallett, Judith P., & Thomas Van Nortwick (eds), *Compromising traditions: the personal voice in classical scholarship* (London, 1997).
Hannay, Margaret P., *Silent but for the word: Tudor women as patrons, translators, and writers of religious works* (Kent, OH, 1985).
Hardie, Philip R. (ed.), *The Cambridge companion to Ovid* (Cambridge, 2002).
Harrison, Elizabeth, *The vision of Dante: a story for little children and a talk to their mothers* (Chicago, 1892).
Harrison, Regina, 'Doctrinal works' in Pillsbury (ed.), *Documentary sources*, pp 217–234.
Harrison, S.J. (ed.), *Living classics: Greece and Rome in contemporary poetry in English* (Oxford, 2009).
Hatim, Basil, & Ian Mason, 'Politeness in screen translation' in Venuti (ed.), *The translation studies reader*, pp 430–45.
Hayley, D., 'What makes bad language bad?', *Language and Communication*, 9:1 (1989), 1–9.
Hearn, Peter J., 'A character in search of an author', *The Guardian*, 14 Dec. 2002.
Heller, Monica, 'Alternative ideologies of *la francophonie*' in Roxy Harris & Ben Rampton (eds), *The language, ethnicity and race reader* (London, 2003).
Henebry, Richard, 'Revival Irish', *The Leader*, 6 Feb. 1909.
Hermans, Theo, 'Paradoxes and aporias in translation and translation studies' in Alessandra Riccardi (ed.), *Translation studies: perspectives on an emerging discipline* (Cambridge, 2002), pp 10–23.
——, *Translating others*, 2 vols (Manchester, 2006).
Hockaday, Mary, *Kafka, love and courage: the life of Milena Jesenska* (London, 1995).
Hollindale, Peter, 'Ideology and the children's book', *Signal*, 55 (1988), 3–22.
Holmes, James, 'The name and nature of translation studies' in Gideon Toury (ed.), *Translation across cultures* (New Delhi, 1998), pp 10–25.
Holmes, James S., 'The name and nature of translation studies' (1972), in Holmes (ed.), *Translated! Papers on literary translation and translation studies* (Amsterdam, 1988).
Honig, Edwin, *The poet's other voice: conversations on literary translation* (Amherst, 1985).
Horace, trans. Emily Gowers, *Satires. Book 1*, Cambridge Greek and Latin classics (Cambridge, 2012).
House, Juliane, *Translation quality assessment: a model revisited* (T bingen, 1997).
Howard, R., & A. Robillard (eds), *Pluralizing plagiarism, identities, contexts, pedagogies* (Portsmouth, 2008).
Howe, Jeff, *Crowdsourcing: why the power of the crowd is driving the future of business* (New York, 2008).
Huang, Sophia, & Hiromi Nakajima, *The advantages and challenges of crowdsourcing as a globalization strategy*, LISA Asia Forum (Taipei, Taiwan, 2009).
Hughes, Geoffrey, *Swearing: a social history of foul language, oaths and profanity in English* (Oxford, 1991).
Hunt, Peter, *Criticism, theory and children's literature* (Oxford, 1991).
——, *Children's literature* (Oxford, 2001).

Isbuga-Erel, R., 'A CDA approach to the translations of taboos in literary texts within the historical and socio-political Turkish context' in M. Khosravinik & A. Polyzou (eds), *Papers from the Lancaster university postgraduate conference in linguistics & language teaching* (Lancaster, 2008), ii, pp 58–77.

Itier, César, 'La littérature quechua d'évangélisation (XVIe et XVIIe siècles) comme source ethnolinguistique' in *Amerindia (Actes: La 'découverte' des langues et des écritures d'Amérique)*, vol. 19/20 (Paris, 1994–95), pp 321–31.

Ivarsson, Jan, *Subtitling* (Shimrishamn, 1992).

Janairo, Michael, '"Botchan" only improves in translation,' *Times-Union*, 16 Oct. 2005.

Jay, Timothy, *Cursing in America* (Amsterdam, 1992).

——, *Why we curse: a neuro-psycho-social theory of speech* (Amsterdam, 2000).

Jenkins, Henry, *Textual poachers: television fans & participatory culture* (New York, 1992).

——, *Fans, bloggers, and gamers: exploring participatory culture* (New York, 2006).

Jenstad, Tor Erik, 'Banning' in M. Ljung (ed.), *Banning i norsk, svensk og 18 andre språk* (Oslo, 1987), pp 40–4.

Jentsch, Nancy K., 'Harry Potter and the Tower of Babel: translating the magic' in Lathey (ed.), *The translation of children's literature*, pp 190–207.

Jewiss, Virginia, *Dante's journey: an infernal adventure* (Florence, 2009).

Kafka, Franz, *Letters to Milena* (New York, 1990).

Kapuściński, Ryszard, *Travels woth Herodotus* (London, 2007).

Kaufmann, F., 'Le sous-titrage des documentaires: Défis et enjeux de l'établissement du texte de "départ"' in A. Serban & J.M. Lavau (eds), *La traduction audiovisuelle. Approche interdisciplinaire du sous-titrage* (Brussels, 2008), pp 69–83.

Kelly, Dorothy, *A handbook for translator trainers: a guide to reflective practice* (Manchester, 2005).

Kinsella, Sharon, *Adult manga: culture and power in contemporary Japanese society* (Honolulu, 2000).

Kipling, Rudyard, *Il secondo libro della giungla*, trans. Giuliana Pozzo Galeazzi (Milan, 1950).

——, *Il libro della giungla*, trans. Giuliana Pozzo Galeazzi (Milan, 1951).

——, *Il 2° libro della jungla*, trans. Umberto Pittola (Milan, 1960).

——, *Il libro della giungla* and *Il secondo libro della giungla* in *Rudyard Kipling*, trans. Umberto Pittola (Turin, 1965).

——, *Il libro della giungla* and *Il secondo libro della giungla* in *Rudyard Kipling*, trans. Umberto Pittola (Milan, 1965).

——, *Storie per tutti. I libri della giungla*, trans. Umberto Pittola (Milan, 1965).

——, *I capolavori di Kipling*, trans. Umberto Pittola (Milan, 1966).

——, *Il libro della giungla*, trans. Fausto Catani (Milan, 1971).

——, *Il libro della giungla*, trans. Maria Paola De Benedetti (Milan, 1983).

——, *I libri della giungla*, trans. Umberto Pittola (Milan, 1984).

——, *I libri della giungla,* trans. Gianni Padoan (Milan, 1987).

——, *Il libro della giungla*, trans. Roberto Pasini (Milan, 1989).

——, *ll libro della giungla*, trans. Piero Pieroni (Trieste, 1991).

——, *Romanzi*, trans. Lidia Conetti (Milan, 1993).

——, *Il libro della giungla*, trans. Angelica Marrucchi (Florence, 1994).

——, *Il libro della giungla*, trans. Giovanni Arduino (Casale Monferrato, 1996).

——, *Il libro della giungla*, trans. Beatrice Masini (Milan, 1996).

——, *Il libro della giungla*, trans. Ottavio Fatica (Turin, 1998).

——, *The Jungle books* (London, 2000).

——, *Il libro della giungla*, trans. Giuliana Pozzo Galeazzi (Milan, 2005).

——, *The Jungle book*, introduction Christopher Paolini (London, 2009).

Kiraly, Donald C., *A social constructivist approach to translator education: empowerment from theory to practice* (Manchester, 2000).

Kleinman, Sherryl, Matthew B. Ezzell & A. Corey Frost, 'Reclaiming critical analysis: the social harms of "bitch"', *Sociological Analysis*, 3:1 (2009), 47–68.

Knight, Stephen, *Form and ideology in crime fiction* (London, 1980).

——, 'The golden age' in Martin Priestman (ed.), *The Cambridge companion to crime fiction* (Cambridge, 2003), pp 77–94.

Knoepflmacher, U.C., & Mitzi Myer, 'From the editors: "cross-writing" and the reconceptualizing of children's literary studies', *Children's Literature*, 25 (1997), vii–xvii.

Koller, Werner, 'Equivalence in translation theory' in Andrew Chesterman (ed.), *Readings in translation theory* (Helsinki, 1989), pp 99–104.

Kosztolányi, Dezsö, *Der kleptomanische Übersetzer und andere Geschichten*, trans. Jörg Buschmann (Nördlingen, 1988).

Kovacic, Irena, 'Reception of subtitles: the non-existent ideal viewer' in Gambier (ed.), *Audiovisual communication*, pp 376–83.

Krontiris, Tina, *Oppositional voices: women as writers and translators of literature in the English Renaisssance* (London, 1992).

Kubo, Takashi, 'マンガはどこへ行く [Where are Manga heading?]', *The Tsukuru*, 39:5 (2005), 72–85.

Kundera, Milan, *Testaments betrayed*, trans. Linda Asher (London, 1995).

Kusanagi, Satoshi, アメリカで日本のアニメはどう見られてきたか？ [How have Japanese anime been received in the USA?] (Tokyo, 2003).

Labov, William, *Language in the inner city: studies in the Black English vernacular* (Philadelphia, 1972).

Lacorne, Denis, 'Anti-Americanism and Americanophobia: a French perspective' in Tony Judt & Denis Lacorne (eds), *With us or against us: studies in global anti-Americanism* (New York, 2005), pp 35–8.

Landers, Clifford E., *Literary translation: a practical guide* (Clevedon, 2001).

Landick, Marie, 'French courts and language legislation' in Landick (ed.), *La langue française*, pp 111–36.

—— (ed.), *La Langue française face aux institutions* (Paris, 2003).

Lathey, Gillian, 'Introduction' in Lathey (ed.), *The translation of children's literature*, pp 1–12.

—— (ed.), *The translation of children's literature: a reader* (Clevedon, 2006).

Lauscher, Susanne, 'Translatqualität – ein Konsens' in Larisa Schippel (ed.), *Übersetzungsqualität: Kritik – Kriterien – Bewertungshandeln* (Berlin, 2006), pp 55–73.

Lazar, Philippe, 'La hantise des laboratoires: to be ou ne pas être?', *Manière de voir*, 97 (2008), 66–8.

Leech, Geoffrey, *Principles of pragmatics* (London, 1983).

Leech, Wendy, 'The translator's visibility: an investigation into public perceptions of the translator and how to raise the translator's status in society' (MSc, Imperial College, 2005).

Lefevere, A., *Translation, rewriting and the manipulation of the literary frame* (London, 1992).

Lefevere, André, *Translation/History/Culture* (London, 1992).

Leighton, Lauren G., 'Translation and plagiarism: Pushkin and D.M. Thomas', *The Slavic and East European Journal*, 38:1 (1994), 69–83.

Leonard, Sean, 'Progress against the law: anime and fandom, with the key to the globalization of culture', *International Journal of Cultural Studies*, 8:3 (2005), 281–305.

Leppihalme, Ritva, *Culture bumps: on the translation of allusions* (Helsinki, 1994).

Levi, Antonia, 'The Americanization of anime and manga: negotiating popular culture' in Steven T Brown (ed.), *Cinema anime* (New York, 2006), pp 43–63.

Lewis, E. Philip, 'The measure of translation effects' in Venuti (ed.), *The translation studies reader*

Losse, Kate, *Achieving quality in a crowd-sourced translation environment*, Keynote presentation at the 13th Localisation research conference Localisation4All (Marino Institute of Education, Dublin, 2–3 October 2008.

Lucente, Gregory L., *Beautiful fables: self-consciousness in Italian narrative from Manzoni to Calvino* (Baltimore, 1986).

Luther, Martin, 'Ein Sendbrief D. M. Luthers. Von Dolmetzschen und Fürbit der Heiligenn' in *Dr Martin Luthers Werke*, vol. Band 30, Teil II (Weimar, 1909), pp 632–46.

Lyne, Raphael, 'Love and exile after Ovid' in Hardie (ed.), *Cambridge companion to Ovid*, pp 288–399.

Mangiron, Carme, 'El tractament dels referents culturals a les traduccions de la novella Botxan: la interacció entre els elements textuals i extratextuals' (PhD, Universitat autònoma de Barcelona, 2006).

Martial, L., & P. Watson (ed.), *Select epigrams* (Cambridge, 2003).

Marzal, Manuel M., 'The religion of the Andean Quechua in southern Peru' in Marzal et al. (eds), *The Indian face of God*, pp 67–118.

Marzal, Manuel M., Eugenio Maurer, Xavier Albó & Bartomeu Melià (eds), *The Indian face of God in Latin America*, trans. Penelope R. Hall (Maryknoll, NY, 1996).

Matamala, A., 'Main challenges in the translation of documentaries' in J. Díaz Cintas (ed.), *New trends in audiovisual translation* (London, 2009), pp 112–16.

Mateo, J., & F. Yus, 'Insults: a relevance-theoretic approach to their translation', *International Journal of Translation*, 12:1–2 (2000), 97–130.

Mayoral Asensio, Roberto, 'Nuevas perspectivas para la traducción audiovisual', *Sendebar*, 13 (2002), 123–40.

——, 'Procedimientos que persiguen la reducción o expansión del texto en la traducción', *Sendebar*, 14 (2003), 107–25

McCarthy, John, 'Why two translations?', *Donaire*, 14 (2000), 18–24.

McDonough, Julie, 'How do professionals organize themselves? An overview of translation networks', *Meta*, 52:4 (2007), 793–815.

Merino, R., 'La traducción del teatro inglés en España: cuarenta años de plagios', *Perspectivas de la traducción inglés/español*, 3 (1995), 75–88

Miller, J. Hillis, 'Border crossings, translating theory: Ruth' in Sanford Budick & Wolfgang Iser (eds), *The translatability of cultures. Figurations of the space between* (Stanford, 1996).

Mills, Kenneth, 'The naturalization of Andean Christianities' in R. Po-Chia Hsia (ed.), *The Cambridge history of Christianity* vi: *Reform and expansion, 1500–1660* (Cambridge, 2007), pp 504–35.

Montagu, Ashley, *The anatomy of swearing* (London, 1968).

Moya, Virgílio, *La traducción de los nombres propios* (Madrid, 2000).

Muir, Edwin, & Willa Muir, 'Translating from the German' in Reuben Brower (ed.), *On translation* (New York, 1996), pp 93–6.

Mullan, John, 'Review of *The forger's shadow: how forgery changed the course of literature* by Nick Groom', *The Guardian*, 13 Apr. 2002.

Mullen, Anne, & Emer O'Beirne (eds), *Crime scenes: detective narratives in European culture since 1945* (Amsterdam, 2000).

Munday, J., 'Advertising: some challenges to translation theory', *The Translator*, 10:2 (2004), 179–220.

Munday, Jeremy, *Introducing translation studies: theories and applications*, 2nd ed. (London, 2008).

Nakamura, Ichiya, & Megumi Onouchi (eds), 日本のポップパワー *[Japan's pop power]* (Tokyo, 2006).

Napier, Susan J., *Anime from* Akira *to* Princess Mononoke*: experiencing contemporary Japanese animation* (New York, 2000).

——, *From impressionism to anime* (New York, 2007).

Newman, Andrew Adam, 'Translators wanted at LinkedIn. The pay? $0 an hour', *New York Times*, 28 June 2009.

Newman, James, *Playing with videogames* (New York, 2008).

Newmark, Peter, *Approaches to translation* (Oxford, 1981).

——, *About translation* (Clevedon, 1991).

Nikolowski-Bogomoloff, Angelika, 'More than a childhood revisited? Ideological dimensions in the American and British translations of Astrid Lindgren's *Madicken*' in E. Ní Chuilleanáin, C. Ó Cuilleanáin & D. Parris (eds), *Translation and censorship* (Dublin, 2009), pp 173–83.

Nornes, Abe Markus, 'For an abusive subtitling', *Film Quarterly*, 52:3 (1999), 17–34; also in Venuti (ed.), *Translation Studies Reader*, pp 447–69.

Nortwick, T. Van, 'Who do I think I am?' in Hallett & Van Nortwick (eds), *Compromising traditions*, pp 16–24.

Nunberg, Jeffrey, 'Languages in the wired world' in Judt & Lacorne (eds), *Language, nation, and state*, pp 231–4

Nunnally, Tiina, *Runemaker: a Margit Andersson mystery* (Seattle, 1996).

——, *Fate of ravens* (Seattle, 1998).

O'Connell, Eithne M.T., *Minority language dubbing for children: screen translation from German to Irish* (Oxford, 2003).

O'Hagan, Minako, *The coming industry of teletranslation* (Clevedon, 1996).

——, 'Evolution of user-generated translation: fansubs, translation hacking and crowdsourcing', *The Journal of Internationalization and Localization*, 1:1 (2009), 94–121.

——, 'Fan-translation networks: an accidental translator training environment?' in John Kearns (ed.), *Translator and interpreter training: methods and debates* (London, 2008), pp 158–83.

O'Sullivan, Emer, 'Narratology meets translation studies, or, the voice of the translator in children's literature', *Meta*, 48/1–2 (2003), 197–207.

Offord, Malcolm, 'The Role of private associations' in Landick (ed.), *La Langue française*, pp 95–109.

Oittinen, Riitta, 'No innocent act: on the ethics of translating for children', in Van Coillie & Verschueren (eds), *Children's literature in translation*, pp 35–45.
——, *I am me – I am other: on the dialogics of translating for children* (Tampere, 1993).
——, *Translating for children* (New York, 2000).
Ordóñez López, Pilar, 'Revisión del pensamiento de Ortega sobre la traducción a la luz de la tradición hermenéutica', *Sendebar*, 17 (2006), 49–60
——, 'Ugly translations: Ortega y Gasset's ideas on translation within contemporary translation theories', *Cadernos de Tradução*, 21 (2008), 41–66.
——, *Miseria y esplendor de la traducción: La influencia de Ortega en la traductología* (Castellón de la Plana, 2009).
——, 'The misery and splendour of translation: a classic in translation studies', *Skase Journal of Translation and Interpretation*, 4:1 (2009), 53–78.
Ortega y Gasset, José, *Obras completas*, 12 vols, vol. viii (Madrid, 1983).
——, 'The misery and the splendor of translation' in R. Schulte & J. Biguenet (eds), *Theories of translation: an anthology of essays from Dryden to Derrida* (Chicago, 1992), pp 93–112.
Ovid, *The poems of exile*, trans. Peter Green (London, 1994).
Ovid, ed. J.A. Harrison, *Ovid on himself; selections from the works of Ovid illustrating his life and development as a writer*, The Alpha classics (London, 1965).
Padoan, Gianni, *I miei animali da I libri della giungla* (Verona, 1987).
Paratesi, N. Galli de', *Le brutte parole: semantica dell'eufemismo* (Turin, 1964).
Parini, Ilaria, 'Pulp dubbing: doppiaggio da rapina?' in Bollettieri Bosinelli et al. (eds), *La traduzione multimediale*, pp 243–59.
——, 'Quentin Tarantino in italiano' in T.G. Giordano, L.Leporati & I. Parini (eds), *Quaderni di doppiaggio* (Finale Ligure, 1998), pp 160–222.
Patou-Patucchi, S. (ed.), *L'italiano del doppiaggio: I convegno per la ricerca 'l'influenza del linguaggio cinematografico sulla lingua italiana parlata'* (Rome, 1999).
Pavesi, M., *La traduzione filmica: aspetti del parlato doppiato dall'inglese all'italiano* (Rome, 2005).
Pavesi, M., & A.L. Malinverno, 'Usi del turpiloquio nella traduzione filmica' in Taylor (ed.), *Tradurre il cinema*, pp 75–89.
Pearse, Patrick, 'Irish literature', *An Claidheamh Solais*, 13 Apr. 1907.
——, 'Recent booklets', *An Claidheamh Solais*, 7 Oct. 1905.
——, *The Mother and other tales*, trans. Thomas A. Fitzgerald (Dundalk, 1916).
——, *Gearrscéalta an Phiarsaigh* ed. Cathal Ó Háiinle (Dublin, 1999).
——, *Short stories*, trans. Joseph Campbell, ed. A. Markey (Dublin, 2008).
Pérez González, Lewis, 'Fansubbing anime: Insights into the "butterfly effect" of globalisation on audiovisual translation', *Perspectives*, 14:4 (2006), 260–77.
Pieri, Giuliana (ed.), *Crime fiction in Italian: an introduction* (Cardiff, 2011).
Pillsbury, Joanne (ed.), *Guide to documentary sources for Andean studies, 1530–1900*, vol. 1 (Norman, OK, 2008).
Pinker, Steven, *The seven words you can't say on television* (London, 2008).
Pistelli, Maurizio, *Un secolo in giallo: Storia del poliziesco italiano (1860–1960)* (Rome, 2006).
Porter, Dennis, *The pursuit of crime: art and ideology in detective fiction* (New Haven, 1981).
Pratchett, Terry, & Neil Gaiman, *Good omens* (London, 1990).
Preece, Julian, 'The letters and diaries' in Preece (ed.), *The Cambridge companion to Kafka* pp 111–30.

—— (ed.), *The Cambridge companion to Kafka* (Cambridge, 2002).

Priestman, Martin (ed.), *Crime fiction: from Poe to the present* (Plymouth, 1998).

Pym, A., 'What technology does to translating', *The International Journal of Translation & Interpreting Research*, 3:1 (2011).

Rabadán, Rosa, 'The applicability of description: empirical research and translation tools', *Revista Canaria de Estudios Ingleses*, 51 (2005), 51–7.

——, 'Divisions, descriptions and applications: the interface between DTS, corpus-based research and contrastive analysis' in M. Shlesinger & R. Stolze (eds), *Translation studies: doubts and directions* (Amsterdam, 2007), pp 237–52.

——, 'Refining the idea of applied extensions' in M. Shlesinger, D. Simeón & A. Pym (eds), *Beyond descriptive translation studies. In homage to Gideon Toury* (Amsterdam, 2008), pp 103–18.

Rabassa, Gregory, *If this be treason: translation and its dyscontents: a memoir* (New York, 2005).

Radtke, E., 'Eufemismo e norma sociale', *Atti dei convegni della società linguistica italiana* no. 21 (1983), 387–395.

Rambelli, Loris, *Storia del 'giallo' italiano* (Milan, 1979).

Ramón, N., & B. Labrador, 'Translations of "-ly" adverbs of degree in an English-Spanish parallel corpus', *Target*, 20:2 (2008), 275–96.

Reid, Helen, 'Subtitling: the intelligent solution' in P. Hoguelin (ed.), *Translating, a profession; proceedings of the VIII world congress, international federation of translators* (Montreal, 1977), pp 420–28.

Reiß, Katharina, 'Der text und der übersetzer' in R. Arntz (ed.), *Textlinguistik und frachsprache: AILA symposium* (Zurich, 1988).

Remael, A., 'Whose language, whose voice, whose message? Different AVT modes for documentaries on VRT-Canvas Television, Flanders', *TradTerm*, 13 (2007), 31–50.

Reyes, Alina, *Nus devant les fantômes: Franz Kafka et Milena Jesenská* (Paris, 2000).

Richlin, Amy, *The garden of Priapus: sexuality and aggression in Roman humor* (New Haven, 1983).

Rilke, Rainer Maria, *Orpheus: a version of Rilke's* Die Sonette an Orpheus, trans. Don Paterson (London, 2006).

Rimer, J. Thomas, & Van C. Gessel, *The Columbia anthology of modern Japanese literature* (New York, 2005).

Risch, B., 'Women's derogatory terms for men: that's right, "dirty" words', *Language in Society*, 16 (1987), 353–8.

Rodríguez Tapia, J.M., 'Traduttore, traditore: plagio y originalidad de una traducción. Comentario a la sentencia del tribunal supremo (sala 1ª) de 29 de diciembre de 1993', *Revista General de Derecho*, no. 604–5 (1995), 771–9.

Rose, Jacqueline, *The case of Peter Pan, or, The impossibility of children's ficton* (London, 1984).

Rosenfeld, Alvin H., 'Popularization and memory: The case of Anne Frank' in Peter Hayes, Jeffry M. Diefendorf & Dagmar Herzog (eds), *Lessons and legacies* (Evanston, IL, 1991), pp 243–78.

Ross, Maggie, *Milena* (London, 1983).

Rostworowski de Diez Canseco, María, & Craig Morris, 'The fourfold domain: Inka power and its social functions' in Frank Salomon & Stuart B. Schwartz (eds), *The*

Cambridge history of the native peoples of the Americas, iii, South America, Part I (Cambridge, 1999), pp 769–863.
Rowan, David, *Glossary for the 90s* (London, 1998).
Rowling, J.K., *Harry Potter and the prisoner of Azkaban* (London, 1999).
——, *Harry Potter and the goblet of fire* (London, 2000).
——, *Harry Potter and the deathly hallows* (London, 2007).
——, *Harry Potter et les reliques de la mort*, trans. Jean-François Ménard (Paris, 2007).
——, *Harry Potter und die Heiligtümer des Todes*, trans. Klaus Fritz (Hamburg, 2007).
——, *Harry Potter e i doni della morte*, trans. Beatrice Masini (Milan, 2008).
——, *Harry Potter i insygnia śmierci* trans. Andrzej Polkowski (Poznań, 2008).
——, *Harry Potter y las reliquias de la muerte*, trans. Gemma Rovira Ortega (Barcelona, 2008).
Rudvin, Mette, *Colonialism, children's literature and translation. The colonial gaze: A reading of the text and illustrations in Italian versions of The Jungle books*, Quaderni del CeSLiC (Bologna, 2011).
Rudvin, Mette, & Francesca Orlati, 'Dual readership and hidden subtexts in children's literature: The case of Salman Rushdie's *Haroun and the sea of stories*' in Van Coillie & Verschueren (eds), *Children's literature in translation* (Manchester, 2006), pp 157–84.
Ryan, Desmond, *Remembering Sion. A chronicle of storm and quiet. [On Irish politics in the twentieth century.]* (London, 1934).
Salomon, Frank, 'Introductory essay: the Huarochirí manuscript' in George L. Urioste (ed.), *The Huarochirí manuscript. A testament of ancient and colonial Andean religion* (Austin, 1991), pp 1–38.
——, *La textualización de la memoria en la América andina: Una perspectiva etnográfica comparada*, ed. Sabine Dedenbach-Salazar Sáenz & Iris Gareis, vol. 54:4, 48° Congreso Internacional de Americanistas: América Indígena (Etnohistoria latinoamericana: Aportes metodológicos) (Stockholm-Upsala, 1994).
Sanderson, John D. (ed.), *Research on translation for subtitling in Spain and Italy* (Alicante, 2005).
Santiago Araújo, Vera Lúcia, 'Closed subtitling in Brazil' in P. Orero (ed.), *Topics in audiovisual translation* (Amsterdam, 2004), pp 199–212.
Santoyo, Julio César, 'El plagio en las traducciones inglés-español', *Atlantis*, 2:1 (1981), 60–4.
——, 'En torno a Ortega y Gasset: miseria y esplendor de la reflexión traductora' in J.C. Santoyo (ed.), *Historia de la traducción: quince apuntes* (León, 1999), pp 237–50.
Schlink, Bernhard, *Die gordische Schleife* (Zürich, 1988).
Schmitt, Christian, 'Traduction et linguistique', *Babel*, 27:33 (1991), 150–65.
Schneider, Jessica, 'Botchan (Tuttle Classics) by Soseki Natsume', *Seattle PI*, 26 Apr. 2011.
Schroth, Simone, *Das Tagebuch/ The diary/ Le journal: Anne Franks "Het achterhuis" als Gegenstand eines kritischen Übersetzungsvergleichs* (Münster, 2006).
Scott, C., 'Our engagement with literary translation' in *Other Words*, 32 (2008), 16–29.
Selfe, R.E., *How Dante climbed the mountain: Sunday readings with the children from the 'Purgatorio'* (London, 1887).
——, *Selections from the first nine books of the Chroniche Fiorentine of Giovanni Villani translated for the use of students of Dante and others* (London, 1896).

Shandley, Robert R., *Unwilling Germans? the Goldhagen debate* (Minneapolis, 1998).

Shavit, Zohar, 'The ambivalent status of texts: the case of children's literature', *Poetics Today*, 1–3 (1980), 75–86.

——, '"The ambivalent status of texts": a rejoinder', *Poetics Today*, 2–1b (1980/1), 199–201.

——, 'Translation of children's literature as a function of its position in the literary polysystem', *Poetics Today*, 2:4 (1981), 171–9

——, *Poetics of children's literature* (London, 1986).

Simon, Sherry, *Gender in translation: cultural identity and the politics of transmission* (New York, 1996).

Simons, Margaret A., 'The silencing of Simone de Beauvoir: guess what's missing from the second sex', *Women's Studies International Forum*, 6:5 (1983), 559–63.

Singleton, David, 'Unspeakable words: the taboo fringe of the lexicon' in M. Dynel (ed.), *Advances in discourse approaches* (Newcastle upon Tyne, 2009), pp 130–46

Skinner, Marilyn B. (ed.), *A companion to Catullus* (London, 2007).

Smith, S., 'Accessibility: a Catullus for now?', *Poetry Review*, 95:1 (2005), 98–100.

Somoza, José Carlos, *The Athenian murders* (London, 2002).

Sōseki, Natsume, *Botchan* (Tokyo, 1906, 1992).

——, *Botchan*, trans. Yasotaro Morri (Tokyo, 1919).

——, *Botchan*, trans. Umeji Sasaki (Tokyo, 1922, 1968).

——, *Botchan*, trans. Alan Turney (Tokyo, 1972).

——, *Botchan*, trans. Joel Cohn (Tokyo, 2005).

——, *Botchan*, trans. Matt Treyvaud (Tokyo, 2005).

Spadafora, Alessandra, *InterMedia: la mediazione linguistica negli audiovisivi* (Viterbo, 2007).

Steig, Michael, '"The ambivalent status of texts". Some comments', *Poetics Today*, 2–1b (1980/81), 193–197.

Stewart, Ralph, 'William Brown's world', *Children's Literature Association Quarterly*, 13:4 (1988), 181–5.

Stolt, Birgit, 'How Emil becomes Michel: on the translation of children's books' in Göte Klingberg, Mary Ørvig & Stuart Amor (eds), *Children's books in translation* (Stockholm, 1978), pp 130–46.

Strümper-Krobb, Sabine, *Zwischen den Welten: die Sichtbarkeit des Übersetzers in der Literatur* (Berlin, 2009).

Sugiyama, Tomoyuki, *Cool Japan: 世界が買いたがる日本 [Japan – the world keen to buy]* (Tokyo, 2006).

Sullivan, J.P., *Ezra Pound and Sextus Propertius: a study in creative translation* (London, 1964).

Sullivan, Zohreh T., *Narratives of empire: the fictions of Rudyard Kipling* (Cambridge, 1993).

Supiot, Alain, 'The condition of France', *London Review of Books*, 8 June 2006.

Surowiecki, James, *The wisdom of crowds: why the many are smarter than the few and how collective wisdom shapes business, economies, societies, and nations* (New York, 2004).

Susam-Sarajeva, Sebnem, & Luis Pérez-González (eds), *Non-professionals translating and interpreting: participatory and engaged perspectives: The Translator*, 18:2 (special issue: 2012).

Tabbert, Reinbert, 'Approaches to the translation of children's literature', *Target*, 14:2 (2002), 303–35.

Tang, Jun, 'A cross-cultural perspective on production and reception of Disney's *Mulan* through its Chinese subtitles', *Journal of English Studies*, 12 (2008), 149–62.

Tani, Stefano, *The doomed detective: the contribution of the detective novel to postmodern American and Italian fiction* (Carbondale, 1984).

Tapscott, Don, & Anthony D. Williams, *Wikinomics: how mass collaboration changes everything* (New York, 2006).

Taylor, C. (ed.), *Atti del convengo 'Tradurre il cinema'* (Trieste, 2000).

——, 'Multimodal transcription in the analysis, translation and subtitling of Italian films', *The Translator*, 9:2 (2003), 191–204.

Taylor, Gerald, 'Supay', *Amerindia*, 5 (1980), 47–64.

Timberlake, Marie, 'Provincial councils of Lima' in Pillsbury (ed.), *Documentary sources*, pp 197–208.

Titford, Christopher, 'Subtitling: constrained translation', *Lebende Sprachen*, 27:3 (1982), 113–16.

Tomlinson, Charles, *Metamorphoses: poetry and translation* (Manchester, 2003).

Torresi, Ira, *Translating promotional and advertising texts* (Manchester, 2010).

Toury, Gideon, *In search of a theory of translation* (Tel Aviv, 1980).

——, *Descriptive translation studies and beyond* (Amsterdam, 1995).

Truchot, Claude, *L'anglais langue étrangère: formes et fonctions; introduction déscriptive à l'étude de nouvelles variétés d'anglais* (Lille, 1989).

——, *L'anglais dans le monde contemporain* (Paris, 1990).

——, 'The spread of English: from France to a more general perspective', *World Englishes*, 16:1 (1997), 65–76.

——, *L'Anglais en Europe: Repères* (Strasbourg, 2002).

Trudgill, Peter, *Sociolinguistics: an introduction to language and society* (London, 2000).

Trykowska, Natalia, 'Manga scanlation in Poland', *Translation Ireland*, 18:1 (2009), 5–24.

Turell, M.T., 'Textual kidnapping revisited: the case of plagiarism in literary translation', *The International Journal of Speech, Language, and the Law*, 11:1 (2004), 1–26.

——, 'El plagio en la traducción literaria' in M.T. Turell (ed.), *Lingüística forense, lengua y derecho: conceptos, métodos y aplicaciones* (Barcelona, 2005), pp 275–97.

Tveit, Jan Emil, *Translating for television: a handbook in screen translation* (Bergen, 2004).

Tymoczko, Maria, 'Trajectories of research in translation studies', *Meta*, 50:4 (2005), 1082–97.

Valdés Rodríguez, Cristina, *La traducción publicitaria: comunicación y cultura* (Barcelona, 2004).

Van Coillie, Jan, & W.P. Verschueren (eds), *Children's literature in translation: challenges and strategies* (Manchester, 2006).

Van der Stroom, Gerrold, 'The diaries, Het achterhuis and the translations' in G. Van der Stroom et al. (eds), *The diary of Anne Frank* (New York, 2003), pp 59–77.

Varney, Jennifer, *Taboo and the translator: a survey of translators' notes in Italian translations of Anglo-American fiction, 1945–2005* (Tarragona, 2005).

Venuti, Lawrence (ed.), *Rethinking translation: discourse, subjectivity, ideology* (New York, 1992).

——, *The translator's invisibility: a history of translation* (London, 1995).

——, *The scandals of translation: towards an ethics of difference* (London, 1998).

—— (ed.), *The translation studies reader*, 2nd ed. (London, 2004).

Vernon, William Warren, *Readings on the Paradiso of Dante: chiefly based on the commentary of Benvenuto da Imola*, introduction by the bishop of Ripon (London, 1900).

Wagnerová, Alena *Milena Jesenská* (Prague, 1996).

Waisman, Sergio Gabriel, *Borges and translation: the irreverence of the periphery* (Cranbury NJ, 2005).

Wall, Barbara, *The narrator's voice: the dilemma of children's fiction* (New York, 1991).

Walter, Henriette, *Le Français dans tous les sens* (Paris, 1988).

Waquet, Françoise, *Latin, or, The empire of the sign: from the sixteenth to the twentieth century* (London, 2001).

Wheeler, Arthur Leslie, *Catullus and the traditions of ancient poetry*, Sather classical lectures (Berkeley, CA, 1934).

White, P., 'Dialogue and inter-subjectivity: reinterpreting the semantics of modality and hedging' in M. Coulthard, J. Cotterill & F. Rock (eds), *Working with dialogue* (Tübingen, 2000), pp 67–80.

Widłak, S., *Alcuni aspetti strutturali del funzionamento dell'eufemismo. Antonimia, sinonimia, omonimia e polisemia* (Wroclaw, 1972).

Wierzbicka, Anna, *English: Meaning and Culture* (Oxford, 2006).

Williams, Gareth, 'Ovid's exile poetry' in Hardie (ed.), *The Cambridge Companion to Ovid*, pp 233–48.

Williams, Jenny, & Andrew Chesterman, *The Map: a beginner's guide to doing research in translation studies* (Manchester, 2002).

Williams, Kay, *Just – Richmal: the life and work of Richmal Crompton Lamburn* (Guildford, 1986).

Wilson, Barbara, 'An Expatriate Death' in *The death of a much-travelled woman.*

——, 'Mi novelista' in *The death of a much-travelled woman.*

——, *Gaudi afternoon* (London, 1994).

——, *The death of a much-travelled woman and other adventures with Cassandra Reilly* (Chicago, 1998).

Wiseman, T.P., *Catullus and his world: a reappraisal* (Cambridge, 1985).

Woodmansee, Martha, & Peter Jaszi (eds), *The construction of authorship: textual appropriation in law and literature* (Durham, 1994).

Woods, Michelle, *Translating Milan Kundera* (Clevedon, 2006).

Yavuz, S., 'Turkish translators seek to be protected by law', *Hürriyet Daily News*, 29 Sept. 2010.

Yeats, W.B., *Poems* (London, 1989).

MANUSCRIPTS

Tradiciones de Huarochirí: Runa yndio ñiscap machoncuna ñaupa pacha, MS 3169 vols (*c.* 1608). Madrid: Biblioteca Nacional.

Campbell, Joseph, MS 10185/3-9, TCD.

FILMS AND TV

Cameron, James, *Aliens* (Film, 1986).

Davies, John, *Just William* (London Weekend Television, 1977–8).

Parker, Alan, *The Commitments* (Film, 1991).

Smith, Richard, *Crude* (Australian Broadcasting Corporation 2007).

Tarantino, Quentin, *Reservoir dogs* (Film, 1992).

——, *Pulp fiction* (Film, 1994).

——, *True romance* (Film, 1993. Written by Quentin Tarantino, directed by Tony Scott).

Index